The Last Blitz

Operation Steinbock

Luftwaffe operations over Britain

January to June 1944

First published 2011 by
Red Kite
PO Box 223,
Walton on Thames
Surrey, KT12 3YQ

Printed in Poland
by Dimograf Sp. z o. o.

ISBN 978-0-95554735-8-6

The Last Blitz

Operation Steinbock

Luftwaffe operations over Britain
January to June 1944

Text by Ron Mackay

Edited by Simon W Parry

Luftwaffe losses team:
Simon W Parry, Brian Bines,
Nigel Parker, Julian Evan-Hart.

Editor's Note

The story of this book can be traced back more than 30 years, to the time that I began to compile details of the aircraft and crew losses sustained by the Luftwaffe during its operations over Britain. In the 1980s the only period of such operations that had received attention was that of the Battle of Britain; operations and losses beyond October 1940 had not been compiled or published.

My first listing of losses outside of the period of the Battle of Britain appeared in the seminal work, 'The Blitz – Then and Now', yet space precluded many of the details from being included. Another restriction on the comprehensiveness was the paucity of information available. German records for Luftwaffe losses (LQMG) for the entire year of 1944 have not survived, and had to be pieced together from other sources. Also in the early 80s details of the interrogation of Luftwaffe aircrew and intelligence gathered by the RAF's Air Intelligence department AI2(k) were 'Closed' to public scrutiny and therefore were not available as a source. Fortunately in recent years the files of AI2(k) have been released and are now freely available in the National Archives. The knowledge of Luftwaffe operations and losses has also advanced thanks to the continued work of several researchers.

The considerable task of distilling the many hundreds of documents relating to Operation Steinbock into a concise and readable account was ably taken on by author Ron Mackay who was able to bring his knowledge to bear on the subject. Researcher Brian Bines was invaluable in contributing to and checking the Luftwaffe losses, as well as supplying many reports of bomb damage and RAF reports. Further details of Luftwaffe losses have been provided by Nigel Parker, who has identified the graves of many of the crewmen killed in Britain. Thus a typical crew will be shown as:

Oblt Karl Waterbeck (F) (Killed CC 1/235), Ogefr Jann Bikker (B) (PoW), Ofw Erwin Mirbach (Bf) (PoW), Ofw Georg Six (Bm) (PoW), Ogefr Werner Doge (Bs) (PoW) landed with aircraft – injured. Gefr Johannes Conrad (Bs) (Killed CC 1/234).

Here the ranks are shown:

Major - Major

Oblt - Oberleutnant

Lt - Leutnant

Ogefr - Obergefreiter

St Fw - Stabs Feldwebel
Ofw - Oberfeldwebel
Fw - Feldwebel
Gefr - Gefreiter
Uffz - Unteroffizier

The crew positions:
F - Flugzeugführer (pilot)
B - Beobachter (observer).*
TB - Truhe Beobachter (radio specialist carried by 2/KG66 to operate the Truhe Gerät).
Bf - Bordfunker (radio operator).
Bm - Bordmechanicer (flight engineer).
Bs - Bordschütze (gunner).

* *Early in WW2 this crewman received pilot training up to 'C' school standard and was the aircraft captain, getting the combined pilot/observer badge i.e. gold wreath and outstretched eagle wings. As the war progressed the pilot training was dropped the wings were all silver with an eagle with folded wings and the Beobachter was no longer the aircraft captain. As well as being the navigator the Beobachter was also the bomb aimer and would also man a gun when required.*

Where a place is shown e.g. (Killed Folkestone) this indicates where the man is now buried. Where (Killed CC 1/234) appears the man now lies buried at the Deutscher Soldatenfriedhof, Cannock Chase, having been exhumed from his original burial location and moved there in the 1960s. The row and plot number are also shown.

It has been decided to include many verbatim transcripts of the official records used in compiling this work. Whilst at first sight this might seem to result in some duplication, or even contradiction, their use as 'raw' primary sources add considerably to our understanding and appreciation of the events in context. On occasion several contemporary accounts of the same incident have been featured where it is possible to see the inner workings of the RAF intelligence gathering organisation. When RAF knowledge gathered from captured men and machines is compared directly to records of the Luftwaffe it is clear to see how advanced AI2(k) had become, but they were certainly not infallible. The un-edited use of several sources brings to light many inconsistencies. British sources used Double British

Summer Time, with the clocks one hour ahead of Greenwich Mean Time in winter and two hours ahead in summer, in their reports; whereas the Luftwaffe quoted the time based on the system prevailing in occupied Europe. This can play havoc then calculating flight times and interpreting Fighter Command claims against Luftwaffe losses. Units of measurement are a more obvious source of confusion. The metric Luftwaffe flew at kilometres per hour and metres height, but RAF Air Intelligence did a rough conversion to imperial units for their reports – but not always! Both systems are used here – without apology.

When Fighter Command combat reports have been used they have been quoted verbatim, with all the idiosyncratic punctuation, abbreviations and code words. Similarly, reports of bomb damage and diary extracts appear un-edited.

Acknowledgements:

Theo Boiten, Alan Brown, Melvin Brownless, Frank Philipson, Julian Evan-Hart, Peter Foote, John Foreman, Chris Goss, Steve Hall, Ian Hodgkiss, Ian Maclachlan, Nigel Parker, Brian Sadler, Andy Saunders, Marcel van Heijkop, Steve Vizard, Philippa Wheeler.

CHAPTER ONE

Preamble

Chapter One

Preamble

29 December 1940 - London

The Luftwaffe's 'Blitz' Offensive was heading towards its fourth month and the He111, Ju88 and Do17 crews were largely having the air over the southern half of the British Isles to themselves. RAF Fighter Command's night fighter strength was minimal in numbers and ineffective in making any material, let alone lethal, inroads into the enemy force's ranks. General Pile's Anti Aircraft Command was inhibited to a lesser extent due to a shortage of guns and radar-support equipment for searchlight and gun-laying with which to effectively track down the aerial intruders.

Towards late afternoon came the initial indication of the latest planned assault upon Britain's already sorely-battered capital; the radar site operators picked up traces heading in across the Channel. An hour later the first bomb and incendiary loads carried by 136 bombers began to cascade into the City of London. By 2130 hours approximately 150 tons of ordnance had been sewn to leave swathes of destruction with St. Paul's Cathedral as the (amazingly almost unscathed) epicentre. Even more damage would have ensued had not adverse weather over France, Belgium and Holland forced the cancellation of a follow-up wave of bombers. The presence of KGr100 with its specialist *X-Verfahren* equipped He111s had ensured the precision of the bombing. As regards losses, not a single bomber was been brought down over British territory, although one Ju88 crashed during its landing approach.

RAF Bomber Command, in contrast, possessed an overall strength that was away below its Luftwaffe contemporary. The Whitleys, Hampdens and Wellingtons were ranging into Nazi-occupied Europe, but in numbers that were totally inadequate for the duty of hammering German industry. Not only was the selection of bombs almost laughably small, and therefore incapable of seriously damaging their targets, the navigational means with which to locate targets were tragically deficient and would not be corrected and improved upon for another year or two. In December for example, although night raids had been launched on 25 nights, only two involved forces totaling three figures, with a further twelve involving between 50 and 100 aircraft. In addition, the one operation where an attempt had been made to start fires in the heart of Mannheim (16/17 December 1940) using selected Wellington crews was an abysmal failure, with bombing very scattered despite a full moon, an almost cloudless sky and weak ground defenses. The art of Path Finding, which the Luftwaffe had already perfected, was a further aspect of bomber operations where the RAF was lagging well behind....

20 January 1944 - Berlin

Barely three years had elapsed since the Luftwaffe reigned supreme over Britain in stark contrast to RAF Bomber Command's lack of performance. Now, by 1944, the tables had been steadily, sometimes painfully, but ultimately inexorably turned. RAF Bomber Command possessed well over 1,100 four-engine aircraft with the mighty Lancaster and its Halifax and Stirling contemporaries striding almost nightly across the deadly night skies of the Nazi Empire's western territories. The 1943/44 winter offensive, the so called 'Battle of Berlin', had been in progress for over two months and on 20th January nearly 800 of the Avro and Handley-Page machines headed again towards the 'Big City'. The Nachtjagd fighter defenses were well marshalled and continued to cause serious losses to their opponents. On this, the eleventh assault in the series of operations launched against Berlin, a solid under-cast prevented immediate confirmation of bombing accuracy although the pathfinder crews were satisfied that their *H²S* screens confirmed the marker flare patterns were above the eastern suburbs. Thirty-five crews were declared missing on the operation's completion, a figure of 4.6%, just within the 5% tolerance for sustaining the campaign.

The once strong and dominant Luftwaffe bomber force was a very pale shadow compared to its 1940/41 situation. Unlike the RAF whose three elderly 'twins' had been effectively retired from Main Force operations, the Luftwaffe was still soldiering on with a polyglot mix - a 'first generation' design (the Ju88) and an up-dated successor (Ju188), the Do17's up-dated successor (Do217) and finally the He177. The latter was the sole four-engine bomber among the collection, but its potential to match the RAF and USAAF 'Heavies' had been badly compromised, not least by technical problems with the novel pairing of engines that provided four-engine performance, but with just two engine mounts and propellers.

The steadily mounting Allied bomber operations had led to a 'Führer Befehl' from Hitler to Göring that immediate counter-measures must be carried out against Britain with London as the central focus. With the Allied armies already pressing the Wehrmacht in Italy and Russia there had been little or no opportunity to maintain a sizeable home-based bomber force matching those based in Britain; in fact by late 1941 the number of Gruppen on hand for operations over Britain had reduced to a seventh of its peak strength in 1940/41 with KG2 and KG40 the last units on the Western Front. In order to bolster this weak position a number of Gruppen, mainly operating in the Mediterranean, had returned home. However, impending operations under the *'Steinbock'* code-name displayed an interesting variation. Instead of conducting operations from one airfield, the units would sometimes move between their assigned bases in Germany and airfields in France and the Low Countries.

The foregoing pair of accounts provides a general insight into the gradual, but ultimately decisive, change of fortunes for the respective bomber fleets of the Luftwaffe and RAF Bomber Command between the height of the *'Blitz'* and the mid-point of the *'Battle of Berlin'* by which latter date the main subject of this book Operation *'Steinbock'* was on the point of launch.

Luftwaffe Operations - 1941 into 1942

The wholesale transfer of the Luftwaffe's Kampfgeschwadern from the western zone of the Nazi Empire to support the German onrush into Russia provided the British Isles with a very welcome respite from the *'Blitz'* Offensive. Naturally, there was no way that the Government or population could realize that the high tide of assault from this direction had passed and would never be more than marginally indulged in again. The possibility of a renewed bombing offensive on a similar scale and duration in 1942 could not be excluded, even if Germany was now engaged in a two-front war. The initial pace and success of Operation '*Barbarossa*' did not bode well for the long-term future of the Soviet armies in even holding out against their opponents.

All of Luftflotte 2 and two bomber-equipped Fliegerkorps from Luftflotte 3 were on hand for the opening of operation *'Barbarossa'* on 22 June 1941. By the following August the resources available for attacking either the British mainland and/or interdicting its mercantile fleet at sea were greatly reduced, from the nearly 50 Gruppen operating during the '*Blitz*' to less than ten. Over two-thirds of the force was allotted to maritime duties, although these were capable of being switched to operations over land whenever deemed necessary. So it was that any prospect of resurrecting heavy attacks over Britain in the foreseeable future was, basically, nil. Worse for the bomber crews tasked with carrying out raids was the rapidly burgeoning strength in RAF night fighter numbers. The Beaufighter, bearing the first airborne-interception (AI) sets and a fearsome mixed armament of four cannon and six machinegun-calibre weapons, was on hand in sizeable numbers. They were backed by nearly 30 Ground Control Interception (GCI) stations. AA provision was equally improved in quantity and quality as was the number of searchlight batteries. The searchlights were arranged in huge 'boxes' many miles in length and breadth and operated in liaison with the night fighters; the latter held station at one searchlight point within the box and whenever an enemy bomber was picked up by the beams it would visually home-in on its prey while also holding radar contact in the event of the visual contact being lost. The system was similar to the original German technique known as *'Helle Nachtjagd'* (searchlight-assisted night fighting) although the Luftwaffe night fighters had been totally dependent upon visual contact since both GCI assistance, through the use of *'Freya'* and *'Würzburg'* ground sets, as well as airborne radar sets were not on hand in numbers until 1941/42.

The Tools on Hand

The bomber designs in use by Luftflotte 3 in 1941/42 which would now be matched against Britain's defences were the Do217E and the Ju88A-4, although the He111 and even the odd Do17 would also feature on operations. The Dornier Do217 was a replacement for the obsolescent Do17Z 'Flying Pencil' and the first examples had been assigned in March 1941 to II/KG2, followed in August by II and III/KG40, the latter Gruppe then serving in Russia. Although able to carry a much larger bomb load than its predecessor thanks to its deepened fuselage, the overall performance was not much better, while the single-engine flight characteristics were distinctly unpleasant. The Ju88A-4, by contrast, was generally more pleasant to fly although more limited in its maximum internal bomb load. In keeping with Luftwaffe practice both had provision for external bomb racks. In the case of the Do217 nearly 40% of the overall 4,000 kg maximum load was carried externally and two-thirds for the Junkers machine.

The defensive armament with which to take on the RAF night fighters was theoretically adequate. The Do217E-1 mounted seven MG15 (7.9mm) machine guns and a single MG151/15 cannon; its Junkers contemporary mounted between four and six MG15s along with one MG131 (13mm) weapon. However, these were generally mounted singly and were manually operated; in addition the MG15s were fed from pannier-type ammunition containers with a maximum content of seventy-five rounds. This factor, along with the cramped cockpits, made it very difficult for a sustained concentration of fire to be brought to bear against a marauding night fighter. Another limitation in defensive capability lay in the fact that carrying two, and sometimes three, different calibre weapons meant that ammunition interchangeability was restricted. This contrasted negatively with the RAF bombers whose current weapons were virtually all .303 calibre, or the American equivalents that were mainly equipped throughout with .5 machine guns.

The close proximity of the crews positioned within all of the Luftwaffe's twin-engine bomber designs imposed another potential penalty, this time personal. Should a night fighter land its fire around or into this section of the aircraft there was a strong possibility of most, if not all, of the four or five crewmembers being killed or injured. This was another contrast with the Anglo-American bombers where the crew positions were generally better spaced out; should the pilot or pilots be incapacitated in any way there was some prospect of the other crewmembers being able to either hold the aircraft steady long enough for all still

The Junkers 88 (above) and the Dornier 217 (opposite) were the main Luftwaffe types employed over England during 1941/42.

capable of doing so to bale out; and there were to be a number of occasions where the substitute 'pilots' were even able to bring their charge back home.

Luftwaffe Operations – May/December 1941.

The Luftwaffe's brief over Western Europe was now two-fold. One was to interdict merchant ship convoys plying the North Atlantic and Gibraltar sea-lanes. The other was to apply some form of pressure, however limited, that might adversely affect Britain's industrial output as well as assist in limiting RAF night fighter squadrons from being deployed outside the British Isles.

The final London *'Blitz'* on May 10th/11th 1941 involving the bulk of Luftflotte 2 and 3's strength was reputedly laid on to create the illusion that the Luftwaffe was going to continue such large-scale assaults indefinitely as well as to cover the fact that its units were already commencing an eastward deployment. In fact two further attacks on Manchester and Birmingham by the beginning of June were launched with bomber numbers approaching or just exceeding three figures, followed by a 60-strong force striking at London at the end of July. Thereafter, the numbers of bombers attacking on any one night were extremely small up to the end of 1941. British intelligence was aware of the transfers occurring in May and June and the likely reason for this action; at the same time, there could be no guarantee that a switch back to west Europe, by at least some of the units, would not be made.

As the UK air defences improved, the bombers were forced to blacken all their national markings in an effort to hide their presence from roaming RAF night fighters.

Losses borne by the Gruppen held back in the west were generally suffered in an accordingly piecemeal fashion although there were one or two surprising variations. Two of the three afore-mentioned raids that entailed lengthy penetration flights by the crews concerned cost just six crews in all. On the other hand the same number of crews, representing some 10% of the attacking force, failed to return from bombing Chatham on $13^{th}/14^{th}$ June. One of this number involved a Ju88C-2 'intruder' belonging to 4/NJG2 that dug a wing into the sea while circling a 'ditched' He111 from KG54! Beaufighter equipped squadrons were responsible for at least two-thirds of the overall casualty figure.

From August 1941 onwards, the following pattern of Luftwaffe activities around and over the British Isles could be perceived.

1) Four Gruppen would primarily operate in an overland bombing role;

Unit	Aircraft assigned
II/KG2	Do217E
Epro/KG30	Ju88A-5
III/KG30	Ju88A-4
II/KG40	Do217E (also Do17Z)

2) Anti-shipping duties including mine-laying around British shores fell to;

Unit	Aircraft assigned
III/KG40	He111
I/Küstenfliegergruppe 106	Ju88A-4, A-5 and D-1
I/Küstenfliegergruppe 506	Ju88A-1
I/Küstenfliegergruppe 606	Ju88A-5
I/Küstenfligergruppe 906	Ju88

3) The third strand of Luftwaffe operations involved armed-reconnaissance with the following;

Unit	Aircraft assigned
1(F)/120	Ju88D-2
1(F)/122	Ju88A-5 and D-1
1(F)/123	Ju88A-5 and D-2

4) Finally there was the single unit that had been tasked with 'intruder' duties since late 1940;

Unit	Aircraft assigned
I/NGJ2	Ju88C-2 and C-4

Blockade

The possibility of blockading Britain to a point where a capitulation might be achieved was ever on the cards until well into 1943. The U-Boat offensive was the central pillar of this action, but the Luftwaffe was also to play a part. During the second stage of the *'Blitz'* the bomber crews' attention had been switched to attacking Britain's major seaports, but shipping was also attacked while at sea. Loss of port facilities with which to unload and store imported goods was undoubtedly a key factor in applying pressure to its enemy's economy. Better still was the non-arrival of material on vessels destroyed while in transit, particularly if those in question had managed to escape the U-Boats' attention out in the open reaches of the Atlantic or were too close to friendly shores for the underwater raiders to risk the attentions of the Royal Navy and Coastal Command escorts.

The emphasis on anti-shipping duties was destined to affect many of Britain's towns, particularly those situated along its coastline. Convoys sailing up and down the North Sea were natural targets to be sought out, but should these not come to hand then a regular number of attacks were to be delivered against any available port facility – or indeed any location possessing what appeared to be industry of any material interest. Lowestoft and Great Yarmouth appeared to be the particular focus of attention from the very beginning of this phase since they were closest in flight duration to the Continent as well as possessing harbour facilities that were technically legitimate targets. Sadly, many of the buildings struck were civilian dwellings with attendant numbers of fatalities and serious injuries – one more indication of the 'Total War' scenario emerging during WWII.

The fact that the Luftwaffe crews were operating mainly in a solo role, or at best in limited numbers, meant an increased vulnerability to being intercepted and shot down.

The obvious cause of the losses was RAF night fighters, while the AA batteries were also beginning to make their presence felt, albeit on a much smaller scale. A third risk-factor was the weapons mounted on both Royal Navy warships and now in steadily increasing numbers on their Merchant Navy charges. This latter provision had been extended down to Britain's fishing fleet as some Luftwaffe crews discovered to their cost. Attacks on fishing boats could be regarded as falling within the Rules of War since their cargoes in turn could be construed as indirectly supporting the war effort. On 9th August 1941 an He111H-5 of 9/KG40 swooped in to machine-gun several trawlers off Grimsby. The 'biter' was fatally 'bitten' by a return machine-gun fusillade that sent the Heinkel bomber into the North Sea along with all but one of Staffelkapitän Hauptman Meyer's five-man crew!

By the year-end well over 100 crews had failed to return from operations - a figure representing more than a 100% loss-rate from available bomber strength in this period. Every one of the previously-listed units contributed to this negative aspect of operations. The 'intruder' Ju88Cs of I/NJG2 tasked with disrupting Bomber Command operations were not exempted either. The final unit loss was ironically incurred shortly before Hitler ordered cessation of its activities over Britain. Even more ironic was that Leutnant Hahn was the Gruppe's leading *Experte* (Ace) in terms of 'kills'. Late on 11th October he was ranging over Lincolnshire in his Ju88C-4, coded R4+NL when his path crossed with an Oxford from No. 12 FTS; the resulting collision left no survivors among the three-man Luftwaffe crew.

At least two crews were lost thanks to a passive form of defence that was none the less effective. The British scientists had developed a way of adversely affecting the German homing beacons by 'masking' the signals with their own false bearings, thereby creating uncertainly as to the precise course they were following and indeed whether or not the crews so affected were even over their own side of the Channel. On 11th/12th October 1941 a 5/KG2 Do217E flown by Oberleutnant Dolenga picked up the false bearings, wandered back and forth in hopeless confusion and finally, with fuel running out, ended up crash-landing on the Sussex coast - in a dyke. In late November the four-man crew of a Ju88A-5 from 1/KuFlGr.106 stepped out of their aircraft parked in its dispersal – only to find they were in 'Indian territory' at RAF Chivenor, their radio system having been similarly compromised by the *'Meacon'* procedure!

Civil Defence Advances

Crucially important lessons had been learned from the *'Blitz'* experience that were to be reflected not only in military terms but also as regards Civil Defence. Prior to the onset of the Luftwaffe's

Opposite page and above: Oblt. Dolenga's Do217 being salvaged after crash landing in a Sussex dyke on 12th October 1941.

campaign, Britain's firemen had operated as a regional rather than a national force; the Auxiliary Fire Service. Furthermore there were fundamental variations in equipment used by the 2600 individual fire brigades as well as operational procedures. One basic problem lay in the fact that there were different sizes of hose connections, as well as variations in fire hydrant outlets, even within the boundaries of major cities. Adaptors were on hand, but not in sufficient quantity to accommodate every eventuality. In addition when experienced fire fighters who had dealt with severe bombing were sent to assist a town or city experiencing its baptism of bombing there could be friction, as the resident Chief Fire Officer was in unconditional charge.

The AFS personnel (those sceptics who saw them joining in order to dodge military service said the initials stood for 'Afraid of Foreign Service') certainly did their level best against the challenge posed by bombing, but were often placed on the back foot, and not only in respect of their equipment. A major requirement was a sufficient and un-hindered flow of water, but during 1940/41 there were two critical limitations upon this necessity. Most city mains supplies were via underground cast-iron pipes. All too often bomb strikes fractured the pipes, whose subterranean location meant that they could not be easily repaired and/or replaced. The answer lay in steel piping laid in continuous sections above ground. Although these were liable to similar disruption, they were generally more secure from fracturing while their above-ground location permitted swift replacement in the event of damage.

The other problem lay in the very provision of sufficient water supplies. In London's case - and indeed in the majority of the other large built-up areas throughout Britain - there was initially very limited provision for custom-built reservoirs. It would transpire that the reservoirs that did exist had totally inadequate water capacity to cope with fires in closely-packed boroughs. The normal subterranean-channelled mains were also totally unable to supply enough water for the degree of fire-raising created by the bombers' high explosives and even more lethal incendiary loads. Drawing water from the River Thames provided a notable back-up source, but only if the tide was high enough. The Luftwaffe struck on at least two occasions when water levels were minimal and the firemen had to wade across the mud to get to the water. Even then the water quality from the thoroughly polluted commercial waterway tended to clog-up the fire-pump's filters quickly. Ironically, it was only when bombed and subsequently levelled areas had become available on which to site metal or brick-built Emergency Water Supply (EWS) reservoirs that this problem was eased. Then, when the steel piping chain was linked to the Emergency Water Supply reservoirs a comprehensive and efficient answer to the problem raised during the *'Blitz'* was fully in hand – even if Britain's cities would never face anything like the same crisis again!

By August 1941 the National Fire Service had been created under an Act of Parliament and would continue to operate under Home Office supervision until the end of WWII. Each of the twelve Civil Defence regions took charge of several Fire Forces from among the national total of 39 such units. A fire-fighting college was also established.

Another basic omission affected the Air Raid Precaution facilities in respect of fire-watching personnel. All too many commercial properties, many of key importance to the war effort, had been needlessly burnt down by incendiaries thanks to the absence of personnel whose presence could have resulted in fires either being promptly extinguished, or better still prevented from arising. Unlike the situation with the AFS that was not corrected until August 1941, new fire-watching measures were put in force during the course of the *'Blitz'*.

1942 – A Year of Transition

The third full year of the now global conflict witnessed an initial operational stagnation in the west for the Luftwaffe and a similar situation for RAF Bomber Command, especially following the Butt Report. The civil servant whose name was appended to this resume of the Command's activities up to the latter part of 1941 had confirmed the very unpalatable fact that the vast bulk of bombing effort was not only not encroaching upon the briefed targets, but was descending at least 5 to 10 miles distant. In essence the crews' gallant efforts were only ensuring that so many tons of bombs and incendiaries were being 'exported' to Western Europe and creating virtually no impact upon the enemy's industrial or military capacity! As it transpired, the arrival of a new Commander-in-Chief in February 1942 would see new measures start to stabilize, and then gradually improve, the Command's performance.

An even greater degree of stagnation affected Luftwaffe operations between January and mid-April – hardly surprising since III/KG2 and JG26's Jabo Staffeln were the sole available units for direct attacks on Britain. III/KG2 was down to one quarter of its overall strength in terms of operational aircraft. The fighter-bombers of JG26 carried out 'tip-and-run' raids on targets along England's Channel coastline that caused material damage to industrial and public facilities with factories, harbours, railway stations and gasworks struck with varying degrees of severity.

In spite of this huge logistical shortfall, operations to inland targets in this period were flown occasionally, not only by III/KG2 but also II/KG40 whose basic brief, along with two other Gruppen, was in the field of anti-shipping operations. A total of eight crews from these Gruppen were lost out of 21 downed from all Luftwaffe operations over British soil or in its coastal waters. Strangely, only six were accredited to RAF night or day fighters; the remaining 13 were either downed by AA fire, several of these falling to convoy escorts, hit barrage balloon cables or, in one case, flew into the ground. A second self-inflicted loss occurred on 30th January when a Ju88 from 2/KuFlGr506 was observed by a Royal Naval ship to pull sharply up before side-slipping into the North Sea!

Baedeker 'Revenge'

Arthur Harris implemented the first stage in bringing about permanent improvements of his Command's operational performance during late March and into April 1942. This consisted of a series of assaults upon the ancient Hanseatic trading ports of Lübeck and Rostock on the Baltic. Both locations, apart from being somewhat easier to pin-point compared inland cities, were natural 'fire-traps' since most of their buildings were of wood construction. So it was that the incendiary loads borne by the RAF bombers left both targets ablaze. The presence adjacent to Rostock of the Heinkel plant at Marienehe and the fact that both towns possessed port facilities was naturally lost upon Dr. Goebbels and his Führer, who lost no time in branding the attacks as 'terror' in nature and worthy of reprisals upon Britain's civilian population.

A directive from Hitler's HQ (Führerhauptquartier) to Göring, dated 14th April 1942, was issued; *"The Führer has ordered that air warfare against England is to be given a more aggressive stamp. Accordingly, when targets are being selected, preference is to be given to those where attacks are likely to have the greatest possible effect on civilian life. Besides raids on industry and ports, terror attacks of a retaliatory nature are to be carried out against towns other than London"*. Then, in a bid to give as great a concentration of aircraft as possible, the directive concluded; *"Mine-laying is to be scaled down in favour of these attacks"*. This latter stipulation displayed Hitler's irrational nature; any measure to hinder merchant shipping was of much greater benefit to the Nazi cause, especially with the key 'Battle of the Atlantic' still tilted in its favour.

Orders were accordingly dispatched to Luftflotte 3 to lay on operations, a duty that encompassed II and III/ KG2, II/KG40 and KGr106 as well as the recently-arrived ErprKdo 100 that was specifically trained in the use of both *X and Y-Verfahren*. Also destined to be utilised during the campaign were crews from IV/KG2, KG3, KG4, KG27, KG40 and KG55. The first operation, to Exeter (23rd/24th April), was foiled by the weather although the respite for its citizens was brief. Next night a full moon and cloudless sky promised a high level of destruction and death. Much of the bombing effort went astray, although this was of no consolation to those who were killed or injured. On the other hand the night fighter opposition appears to have been surprisingly sparse, or alternatively was not deployed in time to counter the attacking force's incursions. The Beaufighters of No. 307 (Polish) Squadron were based at Exeter at this time and were fully operational, so the latter explanation is the more likely. Just one successful interception was recorded when a No. 604 Squadron crew homed in upon and dispatched a 5/KG2 Do217E-2, all four of Oberleutnant Gumbart's crew baled out.

The cathedral city of Bath was the next to be targeted over the ensuing two nights. This time the bombing was more concentrated. Although only half the 150 tons of bombs and incendiaries released in the twin-wave assault was adjudged to have landed within the city, this was sufficient to set much of the inner zone ablaze. Many Georgian-period buildings were lost while material damage was also inflicted upon a railway goods yard.

Frank Hancock, an engine driver based at Bath, had been carrying out shunting duties at the town station after delivering the day's final passenger service. The severity of the initial attack caused him and his engine to be stranded on the bridge just outside the station where he was a helpless witness to the assault. He later recalled; *"The German planes were so low I could have*

Airmen load bombs onto the external racks of a Ju88. The Luftwaffe never had a chance of matching the destructive power of RAF Bomber Command as its medium bombers could only carry half the bomb load of the RAF's 'heavies'.

touched them with a bean stick!" Incendiaries set fire to the goods depot offices while a bomb scattered sheets of metal, girders and soil from an adjacent industrial site in sufficient quantity to block the main line. Two of Hancock's colleagues were killed when, having finished their duty and heading for home, the second wave of attackers appeared overhead; they decided to seek cover in a public shelter that was then struck squarely. The follow-up raid 24 hours later added to the destruction as well as raising the final fatality list to 401 citizens. The pressure on Britain's cathedral cities was maintained over York ($28^{th}/29^{th}$) and Norwich ($27^{th}/28^{th}$ and $29^{th}/30^{th}$). Although the forces dispatched were consistently well below treble-figures, the use of incendiaries, assisted by the unfortunate fracturing of the water mains in Norwich, worked in the Luftwaffe's favour.

Exeter came in for its third, and unquestionably most devastating, experience on $3^{rd}/4^{th}$ May. Much of the compact city's centre was burnt-out, and the fire-fighting services were overwhelmed. Casualties were much more severe, approaching 200 deaths. However, the Luftwaffe was by now experiencing a steady level of attrition; on $25^{th}/26^{th}$ April four crews were lost on the two Bath raids and another four on Exeter. Night fighters from Nos. 219, 255, 307 and 604 Squadrons took down five of this total. Two of those lost from the second Bath raid were IV Gruppe machines from KG2 and KG3, with two more from 10/KG30 downed on 3rd/4th May. Such losses would in turn hinder the future development of trainee crews, given the loss of expertise among what were instructor crews.

To date none of this effort, however painful the loss of lives and property might have been, could even dent let alone 'materially damage' Britain's war effort. In addition the

Some of the notable English towns and cities that were bombed during the Baedeker campaign. With the exception of Birmingham and York, all targets were reasonably close to the coast and therefore easier to find at night, a strategy that had served RAF Bomber Command well in the early part of the war.

natural reaction to 'Give it back to them' that had been first engendered among Britons by the *'Blitz'* was surely ratcheted-up a notch thanks to the nature of the attacks. This was clearly a 'Total War' with serviceman and civilian involved, a cold fact the Germans were to experience in the three years ahead as Bomber Command went about its awful, but legitimately-perceived function of 'de-housing' the population and laying the grounds for bringing about an irrevocable collapse in its morale.

The current offensive was continued in varied strength during May 1942 with further raids launched upon widely-spread locations ranging from Hull to Poole. During May, these two targets each had between 100 and 160 tons of bombs and incendiaries directed their way, although a good proportion landed outside their boundaries. Casualties were few in number on these occasions compared to Canterbury's ordeal at the month-end when over 100 citizens were killed. As it was, the *'Baedeker'* (historic towns) aspect of May operations was restricted to Norwich ($8^{th}/9^{th}$) albeit with little success by the 40-strong force. June operations witnessed the same wide spread of targets, most attacked in penny-packet numbers. Luftwaffe losses remained almost constant in May with thirteen machines downed. Once again targets falling within the *'Baedeker'* category were limited to Canterbury (June $2^{nd}/3^{rd}$ and $6^{th}/7^{th}$) and Norwich (June $26^{th}/27^{th}$). The West Country was focused on over most of the month with Weston-Super-Mare receiving two sharp assaults.

Prior to July the target-choice in the case of concentrated raids had involved towns or cities on or near the coast. Birmingham, on the other hand, was well inland and featured in three nocturnal sorties between July $27^{th}/28^{th}$ and $30^{th}/31^{st}$. In an effort to evade the worst attention of night fighter activity the bombers were routed up over the Irish Sea at low level before swinging east across central Wales and out over East Anglia. A second feature of such raids was that the bombers climbed to altitude upon altering course towards the target and then, having bombed, the pilots accelerated in a gentle decent to finally clear the English coast at a low altitude.

August and September witnessed a gradual end to the campaign, with nine small-scale and largely ineffective raids. Losses had amounted to an apparently sustainable level (sixteen) but bombing results were very poor, especially given the availability of the *X and Y-Verfahren* systems. Instead, the use of flare-dropping aircraft to mark targets had probably contributed to the poor results by misjudged release of the markers.

The inevitable autumnal deterioration in the weather permitted the Luftwaffe to indulge in daylight sorties by single aircraft with a view to disturbing the population as much as wreaking destruction upon industrial facilities. On several occasions social buildings such as public houses or hotels were struck with notable casualties

The Winner –Sir Issac Newton

Hauptmann Siegfried Langar was a combat-experienced officer, having served with 2/KGr.100 as its Staffelkapitän during the 'Blitz' period and therefore was well-versed in the operational use of the X and Y-Verfahren systems. In April 1942 he returned to Chartres in France at the head of ErprKdo 100, the unit being tasked with the continued testing of both systems. On 23rd May he took off on a daylight raid against Avonmouth, his He111H-5 6N+FR being under the control of the Y-station at St. Valery. The heavy cloud cover promised a trouble-free sortie for the attack planned for the late afternoon, but Nemesis in an unusual form was waiting in the wings....

At 'readiness' status on RAF Middle Wallop was No. 604 Squadron's Flight Lieutenant John Cunningham along with his radar-operator Flying Officer 'Jimmy' Rawnsley. This dedicated night fighter team had already racked up twelve of Cunningham's fifteen confirmed night fighter 'kills' with several 'probables' added in since linking up in early 1941. Now they were ordered to take off and duly did so at 16.00 hours; no sooner had the undercarriage been retracted than the Beaufighter was swallowed up in the low-lying cloud. 'Starlight' GCI Station was contacted, whereupon Cunningham was informed of the progress of an in-coming 'bandit' that soon evolved into Langar's He111. As the night fighter caught sight of its prey and began to close in from around 1,000 yards the bomber crew caught sight of it, whereupon Langar threw his bomber into a tight left-hand bank and flashed past his adversary with all guns blazing before disappearing into the murk.

Rawnsley had lost radar 'contact' but the GCI controller managed to vector the Beaufighter onto the He111's trail. There then ensued an ever tighter series of turning, diving and climbing manoeuvres as Cunningham sought to get inside the track of Langar's aircraft in order to deliver a burst of gunfire. In a final bid to elude his tormentor Langar almost stood the He111 on its nose and faded from both visual sight and the radar screen that was by now full of ground 'traces'. Both aircraft were dangerously close to the high ground in the region. Cunningham returned to Middle Wallop at the end of what was a prolonged physical and mental battle with both the Luftwaffe and Mother Nature. By then Langar and his crew were also on the ground – but not alive. East of Shaftsbury, their He111 had just failed to pull out of its dive and was smashed to pieces. Bomber and crew had become the latest victim of Sir Issac Newton, or as he was known by the No. 604 Squadron crews, the 'Black Knight'.

CHAPTER TWO

1943 and ever-diminishing returns

Chapter Two

1943 and ever-diminishing returns

During 1942 the use of at least six IV Gruppen units on operations had added an artificial dimension to Luftflotte 3's overall regular strength. The primary function of the IV Gruppen were as *Ergänzungs* or training/reserve sources of aircraft and crews for their respective Geschwader. The flying personnel were not on hand to carry out regular operations, but the more experienced instructors were utilised for this duty. Ironically, since these sub-units were not listed on the Luftflotte's order of battle, any sortie flown by the crew or crews in question was not credited to them in assessing their eligibility for decoration awards – clearly a matter of 'all risk and no reward'!

At the beginning of 1943 the following units featured on the Order of Battle;

Unit	Aircraft Type	A/C on hand	(Operational)
10 (Jabo)/JG2	FW190	10	(1)
10 (Jabo)/JG26	FW190	13	(10)
Stab/KG2	Do217E	1	(1)
I/KG2	Do217E-4	42	(23)
III/KG2	Do217E	29	(17)
Stab/KG6	Ju88A-4	2	(2)
I/KG6	Ju88A-4	29	(17)
		126	**71**

The involvement of 10(Jabo)/JG2 and 10(Jabo)/JG26 was just a continuation of similar operations conducted by fighters converted to a bombing role, a function that went back to the latter stages of the Battle of Britain. 10(Jabo)/JG26 had been functioning in the revised role ever since its creation on 10 March 1942 along with its JG2 contemporary; both had been part of the force raiding Canterbury the previous October.

The British defenses were now even more formidable. Twelve Beaufighter-equipped squadrons were backed by six squadrons operating the even more deadly Mosquito Mk. II. Just over 2,000 heavy AA guns provided with radar-control were similarly supported by around 1,400 Bofors light AA weapons and numerous smaller-calibre weapons. A comprehensive high and low level radar system completed the network by generally ensuring early warning of approaching aircraft, other than at minimum altitude.

Challenging this military barrier with the small numbers of aircraft and crews available appeared suicidal at normal bombing altitudes. Nevertheless, London appeared on the briefing maps on 17th January 1943 when 90 crews attacked in two waves, a number flying double sorties. The London Dockland was the specific target, but bombing was largely scattered outside the city boundaries. A measure of damage was inflicted by approximately one-third of the 115 tons of bombs carried by the attacking force of 118 aircraft.

A twin-wave low-level strike on London involving 10(Jabo)JG2, 10(Jabo)JG26 and other elements of JG2 and JG26 was laid on three days later. A diversionary manoeuvre by a sub-force confused the British defences to the extent that the main wave not only traced an un-interrupted path in across Kent, passing close to Biggin Hill and alerting the RAF duty flight to 'scramble' in the process, but also caught the London balloon barrage force un-deployed. The overall effect of the bombs released proved sketchy, although a major fire was started in Surrey Docks. A school in Catford was hit resulting in the deaths of six teachers and 38 children – almost certainly an error rather than a deliberate act on the part of the pilot concerned – while more fatalities were recorded in several City boroughs.

The raiders' success in gaining London with impunity was not matched on the return leg. The force was assailed as the FW190s crossed out near Dover by several RAF fighter squadrons previously 'scrambled' to intercept. In the resulting air battle the Luftwaffe lost at least five aircraft. Two were lost as a result of colliding, thanks to a failed cross-over manoeuvre during an interception by a pair of Manston-based Typhoons. Losses this day were eight according to Luftwaffe records.

Casablanca's psychological blunder?

Around the same time as the Luftwaffe fighter-bombers were delivering their strike on London, Winston Churchill and President Roosevelt were in conference at Casablanca. Among other key issues discussed were the likely terms under which surrender would probably be accepted. In the past, such terms had granted the defeated adversary some degree of latitude in the course of negotiating a mutually satisfactory surrender. All such considerations were summarily rejected (at least by Roosevelt) in favour of an unconditional cessation of hostilities. The appalling conduct of elements of the Nazi Party-led Germans during their advances throughout Europe and particularly within Soviet Russia had undoubtedly fostered this attitude. The even more barbaric activities of the Japanese armed forces, initially in pre-WWII China and now against the Allies in the Far East, had further added to this 'no negotiation' stance.

In retrospect, the decision to proceed in this manner can now be regarded as a political example (however understandable in the context of WWII) of 'Heart ruling the Head'. However long the anti-Nazi groups within Germany prevaricated before taking action against their Führer, they did exist and were known to be so in Allied circles. In forcing all Germans into the same 'no leeway' situation, regardless of any pro or anti-Nazi stance, the result would be to produce a mood of 'sticking it out' against the worst depredations of bombing and ultimate physical occupation by the Allied armies – hence the likely reason why resistance on a steadily diminishing, but never absent, scale was encountered right up to VE-Day.

Goebbel's Riposte to Casablanca?

By grim coincidence, a speech by Dr. Goebbels delivered shortly after the Casablanca Conference on 18th February 1943 appeared to justify the unconditional surrender decision at Casablanca. He addressed a picked audience of Gauleiters and other Nazi Party satraps in Berlin. The atmosphere should have been depressing since it was only some two weeks since the cataclysmic defeat and final surrender of Von Paulus's 6th Army had occurred at Stalingrad. A fiendishly skilful orator, the Doctor still managed to build up his audience step-by-step to a feverish pitch. Then he said; *"The English say that Germany is nearly finished. Are we? Shall we fight to the end?"* At which point he bawled out; *"Wollen Sie Totalen Krieg?" (Do you want Total War?).* He gained the audience's full support as they leapt to their feet, yelling back, vigorously, applauding, and throwing Nazi salutes. Afterwards, Goebbels cynically observed; *"If I had asked them to jump out of the window, they would have obeyed!"*

Once again, one cannot be dismissive of this apparently hard-headed reaction by what were, after all, loyal and often fanatical Nazi supporters. Many WWII Germans, however misguided their reasoning was in retrospect, fought on in loyal fashion not just for their Führer but for their country. This was especially so as the Allied advances, particularly those by the perceived Soviet 'barbarians', closed in upon their territory.

It is not unreasonable to ponder the scenario where a negotiated surrender, especially after the Western Allies were firmly ashore in Europe, could have culminated in the Soviet onrush being contained much further to the east. This by extension would have limited the post-war pressures created by the Cold War. On the other hand, even an inveterate anti-communist like Churchill felt more 'loyalty' to maintaining the Triple Alliance with a view to utterly wiping out the Nazi scourge, than to betraying that laudable cause purportedly fighting for the democratic principal – all the more ironic in the light of Stalin's arbitrary intentions towards any form of post-war democracy anywhere within Soviet-'liberated' – or rather occupied – Europe.

'Pin-prick' Offensive

The fighter-bomber incursions, whose daytime efforts were sometimes supported by their twin-engine bomber contemporaries, continued into 1943 with England's south coast absorbing much of this effort. A succession of what had been termed 'tip and run' raids left a trail of damage and human casualties in a number of coastal locations as well as the occasional inland region when several towns scattered across three Home Counties were targeted. A particularly high toll of civilian deaths (50) was recorded in Ashford when just one 10 (Jabo)/JG54 fighter went down. The attackers did not always escape so lightly, especially when their formations were confronted by the Hawker Typhoons, of which No. 609 Squadron was a leading exponent. The cannon-armed fighter was more than a match for its Focke-Wulf adversary as a steady number of the Luftwaffe pilots were discovering. In addition the various AA batteries, operating both light and heavy-calibre weapons, were adding to their tally. On 10th February 1943, for example, two Do217s of 5/KG40 were shot out of the sky as they headed home at minimum altitude over Sussex; one of these made the cardinal error of setting a course that took it directly over RAF Tangmere, whose Bofors gunners gave it short shrift!

The extremely restricted number of KG2 and KG6 bombers and crews, barely amounting to treble figures at any one time, naturally meant that any effort at striking more than one target within Britain would involve a scattering of the force dispatched. A strike by the two Gruppen directed at the Anglo/Scottish borders region on 24th/25th March 1943 was an extreme example in terms of the distance flown. The nature of the locations to be attacked was never clear since no incidents of any kind were recorded. Worse still for the attackers was the loss of no less than eight crews, with six downed either over the Scottish Borders or Northumberland. An added twist to these losses was the fact that only one was credited to AA batteries, the others having apparently taken the low route home – and flown into the ground in the process!

A Needless Tragedy

3rd March 1943 witnessed a largely unsuccessful attempt at a nocturnal raid upon London when the force of 117 bombers dropped most of their loads well outside the capital and departed less six of their number. A measure of human loss was exacted, but only in a cruelly indirect manner. A stream of civilians going down the handrail-less stairway to the Bethnal Green tube shelter were seemingly panicked by the unfamiliar noise of a 'Z' rocket battery fired off in the immediate vicinity. The resultant mass collapse, caused initially by one or two people losing their footing, ended in seconds with a veritable heap of bodies

Dr Goebbels was never far from Hitler's side as the war slipped from their grasp.

accumulating at the bottom of the stairs. The fatalities, caused primarily through suffocation, added up to 173. Similar assaults upon several other cities within the month met with even less success and more losses. March sorties by the fighter-bombers, in contrast, were still inflicting damage of some proportions at a minimal cost, but once again the 'pin-prick' nature of the assaults hardly affected Britain's industrial capacity overall. The two Jabo Staffeln would soon be absorbed into IV/SKG10 (SKG = *Schnellkampfgeschwader* or Fast Bomber Wing) whose full strength would soon after be directed at Britain.

Propaganda Pointer for *'Steinbock'*?

On March 20th 1943 an indication appeared of what the attacks upon Britain should concentrate on. It emanated from that master of propaganda Dr. Goebbels, and its content stressed the possible psychological, as opposed to the physical effects, of bombing Britain. His diary entry for this date reads as follows;

> "I proposed to the Führer that we should bomb not slums but the residential sections of the plutocracy when making air raids on Britain. According to my experience this makes the deepest impression. The Führer agrees that it doesn't pay to attack harbours or industrial cities. At present we haven't sufficient means for such attacks. The Führer agrees that air warfare against England must now be conducted according to psychological rather than military principles. It is of course very difficult to make this clear to the Luftwaffe since it has remained completely in its own rut. Our air reprisals cannot begin for another five or six weeks; then, however, they can be carried out on a pretty large scale. The Luftwaffe has accepted this new policy for air warfare, but only slowly and grudgingly. The Führer remains deeply dissatisfied with the Luftwaffe generals".

Goebbels was probably pandering to Hitler's jaundiced attitude towards the Göring-commanded Luftwaffe and its manifest overall inefficiency stretching back to the Battle of Britain. In this case, just how 'the Luftwaffe Generals' could effectively manage matters in order to satisfy the Hitler/Goebbels accord on the subject was left conveniently unclear by Nazi propaganda. Just how were the Luftwaffe airmen going to meet Goebbel's main contention by searching out the specific regions where the British plutocracy skulked in the view of the Nazi hierarchy? Many of this august body dwelled other than in the obvious place – London – although the capital would end up as the cynosure for the bulk of *'Steinbock'* operations. Even this aspect of operations was to stray somewhat from Goebbels' comments, in that a number of the target locations were centered on boroughs whose citizens were the very slum-dwellers he wished to divert Luftwaffe attention away from – very few 'plutocrats' lived in East Ham and Bermondsey!

Oberst Dietrich Peltz

Peltz Appointed

The airman whose name would be directly linked to future bomber operations over Britain was appointed during April 1943 in accordance with Hitler's orders. Hitler had, unsurprisingly, become totally disenchanted with the scale and returns from the offensive to date. The rather grandiose title of *Angriffsführer England* was bestowed upon 29-year-old Oberst Dietrich Peltz. This combat-experienced airman had risen from the command of several bomber units between 1939 and 1941, thence to a Staff position linked to bomber operations. His current rank had only just been granted, and would be further raised to Generalmajor (Major General) in July 1943.

The prospects for an increased, and hopefully much more successful, campaign against Britain lay many months ahead. Certainly, the numbers of aircraft available shortly after his appointment (135 Ju88s and Do217s along with around the same number of FW190s) provided no hope for the intended mass assault. The need to accurately mark targets had, ironically, placed the Luftwaffe way ahead of the RAF from the beginning. The electronic systems *'Knickebein', X-Verfahren and Y-Verfahren* had provided the potential for knocking out Britain's industrial cities and even specific locations within their boundaries. *'Knickebein'* had subsequently come to be treated with suspicion by the bomber crews, as many were convinced that British counter-measures had compromised its operation. *X-Verfahren* had latterly functioned on an enhanced mega-cycle band similar to its *Y-Verfahren* contemporary, but was withdrawn from service in mid-1942. Now, Peltz selected a Staffel from KG6 whose Do217-equipped crews were to specialize in the pathfinder role, using the latest radio and radar equipment for this function. In time a full Gruppe would be assembled to become I/KG6.

'Reaping the Whirlwind'

By grim contrast the hitherto very mixed fortunes of RAF Bomber Command – at least up to mid 1942 - were taking an upward trend that would suffer the occasional set-back, but would never be totally reversed. On 5th/6th March 1943 the first of a trilogy of campaigns was launched. The first target was the Rühr, Germany's key industrial zone, with the massive and hitherto unscathed Krupp armament plant in Essen as the main focus. The advent of the precise blind-bombing equipment known as *'Oboe'* permitted an initial and extremely accurate marking of this key complex by Pathfinder Force Mosquitos. The Main Force of Lancasters, Halifaxes, Stirlings and Wellingtons accordingly laid their bomb loads in a highly destructive pattern that would be repeated on several occasions over the ensuing four months before what was termed the *'Battle of the Rühr'* was terminated.

The *'Oboe'* system in which the flare-dropping aircraft was tracked by two radio stations in England was limited to targets extending along a line that intersected the Rühr, because the signals were restricted by the curvature of the earth. After D-Day, mobile tracking stations would extend the operational range of *'Oboe'* well into Germany.

Costly 'own-goal' for SKG10

On 16th/17th April 1943 SKG10 was deprived of three pilots in yet another self-inflicted incident. RAF West Malling lay in the centre of Kent and at the time was the home for No. 29 Squadron's Beaufighters, tasked with the nocturnal guarding the south-eastern approaches to London. Weather conditions were clear and a single 'Beau' was up on patrol just after midnight when a single-engine aircraft was heard over the airfield. The controller naturally assumed this to be an RAF machine, for which the flare path was duly lit-up. The aircraft's pilot responded by entering the landing circuit, and finally taxiing up to the control tower: Feldwebel Bechtold became the latest Luftwaffe PoW to arrive in Britain!

However, the navigational farce continued. Scant minutes later, Leutnant Setzer arrived overhead and followed exactly the same course of action. He nearly got away after realising his error; he opened the throttle after swinging back onto the runway, but two bursts of fire from a vehicle-mounted Vickers machine gun set his fuel tanks ablaze. After coming to a halt the pilot clambered out of the cockpit, badly burnt, but destined to survive. But the night's macabre events were still not over as a third SKG10 FW190 appeared overhead. Whether the pilot was intending to land before the airfield's AA gunners opened fire was never established, but the aircraft struck the ground close to the runway-end; Oberfeldwebel Schultz survived. A fourth pilot, Oberleutnant Klahn, abandoned his FW190 near West Malling, but was too low for his parachute to properly deploy and was killed.

SKG10 was based at Amiens-Glisy, which lay in a direct line south-east of London and West Malling. It may be that the West Malling trio along with their fellow-pilots - most of whom had scattered their bombs across southern Essex – had flown over the Thames estuary at its widest point and mistaken it for the Channel between Dover and Calais. The guidance searchlight displayed for the patrolling Beaufighter was directed towards West Malling at the time the first two FW190s appeared in the area and may have further deluded each pilot into thinking he was over France.

Fw Bechtold's FW190 parked at West Malling after SKG10's disastrous night over London.

The wreckage of another SKG10 FW190 brought down near West Malling.

SKG10 Signs off - temporarily

SKG10 continued its ever-threatening sorties into May 1943, with two particular raids upon Lowestoft and Great Yarmouth. These raids fully demonstrated the deadly efficiency of the four-plane formations flying line abreast in successive waves, as well the inherent weakness in the coastal defences when approached by low-flying aircraft. Further destruction to commercial and civilian property was visited upon the already martyred seaside locations. 24 ATS personnel were killed when their requisitioned hotel in Great Yarmouth was squarely struck - a total of 81 people were killed in the two raids. Four days later the raiders closed in upon Lowestoft again, but this time found their path barred by a forest of barrage balloons. General Pile (C-in-C, AA Command) had ordered their dispatch to both towns following his visit to the region. Before long SKG10 operations reduced as elements were detached to the Mediterranean Theatre in response to the final expulsion of Axis forces from North Africa and the distinct possibility of an imminent Allied invasion of Sicily.

Although this unit had landed a number of hard blows upon their targets the cost had been high. In May and June a total of 26 pilots along with their aircraft were struck off the Luftwaffe's strength.

Panacea target-choice

The possibility during WWII of literally grinding a nation's industrial effort to a halt found common cause with both the German and American authorities. The source of this potential disruption was deemed to be the humble ball bearing; whose specialist manufacture limited production to a very few locations. Knock these factories out, so logic dictated, and the war machine would, literally, stop rolling. The American VIII Bomber Command would attempt to carry out their intentions over Schweinfurt in August and October 1943, with only marginal success coupled to a horrendous casualty-list in bombers and crews. British production plants at Newark, and particularly Chelmsford, had been targeted several times from mid-1942. On 13th/14th May 1943 Newark faced its latest battering during which the ball-bearing factory suffered damage to add to that caused in mid-April. Even less industrial disruption was created by these Luftwaffe raids than by the Americans over Germany.

Battle of the Insects

Aircraft recognition was a subject that was often vital to survival in air combat. There was, however, an art to perfecting one's knowledge; apart from which the level of enthusiasm in studying the matter varied from person to person. An added difficulty, not to say mortal danger, lay in the existence of Allied and German aircraft designs that were similar in overall outline. For instance the rear view of a C-47 and an He111 present the same low-wing, close-packed engine mounts and sharp outer-wing dihedral. Other dangerously similar 'twins' were the Bf109 and the P-51B, the P-47 and FW190, the Blenheim and the Ju88 and the Hampden and Do215/217.

In June 1943 the first examples of the Me410 '*Hornisse*' (Hornet) appeared in the west, having been assigned to V/KG2 and based in northern France. The latest of Willi Messerschmitt's designs to enter combat, the Me410 mounted two DB603 in-line engines on a low-wing; along with an overall plan-form similar in proportions to the RAF's own 'insect' the Mosquito as well as a general performance at least approaching that of its de Havilland opponent, there was clearly every chance of confusing one with the other, especially at night.

The first opportunity to test the RAF crews' recognition skills occurred on 13th/14th July 1943. Flight Lieutenant Bunting and his navigator/AI operator Pilot Officer French of No. 85 Squadron were up on patrol near Dover when they were warned of a north-bound 'bandit'. Scarcely had this been closed in upon when a second aircraft was picked out, to which Bunting diverted his attention. Although initially overhauling the 'bogey' that had now adopted a slight climbing attitude, problems with the Merlin engines overheating and the resultant drag caused by the need to open the engine radiators saw the gap again widen.

The Messerschmitt 410 'Hornisse' started to appear in the skies over England in June 1943 and initially caused some confusion due to its similarity to the Mosquito.

All too slowly the 'Mozzie' was brought into visual contact, with the lighter northern horizon providing an enhanced degree of sighting. The low-wing position compared to the RAF design's mid-wing setting, as well as its under-slung Merlin engine mounts contrasting with the centrally positioned DB603s was enough to satisfy the 'stalkers' that the 'bogey' was definitely in the hostile category. Turbulence caused by the Me410 threw Bunting's aim off on his first pass, but the second attack upon the still-unwary two-man crew sealed their fate along with their charge. U5+KG burst into flames, was propelled onto its back and descended inexorably into the North Sea. One technical insect's sting had proved lethal to the other!

Anti-personnel threat

The offensive armoury of the Luftwaffe bore a similarity to that of the RAF. A range of high explosive bombs, some categorised as SC (*Sprengbombe-cylindrisch*) that were general purpose weapons, thin-cased to cause maximum surface damage; SD (*Sprengbombe-Dickwandig*), demonstrating a semi-armour piercing capacity; and PC (*Panzerbombe-Cylindrisch*), a fully armour-piercing contemporary. Added to these were variations on incendiary bombs, some fitted with explosive devices as well as two types of sea-mines that were also adapted for dropping by parachute - the infamously inaccurate, and therefore casually dreadful, form of German ordnance.

Up to 1943, at least over Britain, the most prevalent anti-personnel threat to either the military services or civilian population came from delayed-action fuses fitted to some bombs. These were dropped with a view to hindering the fire and rescue services in the course of clear-up work conducted in the aftermath of a raid. Now this extremely impersonal (and for Allied propaganda purposes 'indiscriminate') aspect of bombing practice was to be intensified in the run-up to, as well as in the course of, Operation *'Steinbock'*.

The SD2 (*Splitterbombe*) 'Butterfly Bomb' was just one of four types of anti-personnel weapons employed in WWII by the Luftwaffe, but was destined to be the variant by far the most used over Britain. It looked like a large tin can with a thin handle extending out of one end. When released from its AB (*Abwurfbehalter*) aimable container, the outer casing opened out to form a crude parachute, while the ends also deployed - the latter acting as wind-vanes that rotated in the airflow to provide the arming mechanism. The fuses could be of the air-burst, impact or delayed-action type. In the case of the latter being fitted, there was no known way of de-fusing this innocuous-looking device, while the slightest disturbance could set it off. And so it was that the SD2 was destined to present one of the most intractable challenges to the authorities as well as proving a particularly lethal threat to any individual unaware of its true function. Children, whose natural curiosity made them particularly vulnerable, all too often fell victim of its inevitable detonation when handled.

Still in the doldrums...

The second half of 1943 was to prove little more productive for Peltz's still meagre bomber force, especially when compared to his RAF contemporary Arthur Harris. In late July Germany's second-largest and most important industrial and commercial city was devastated when Hamburg suffered a series of massive raids under the title *'Gommorah'*. Harris's intentions to deal with the Hanseatic port in the same manner as the operation's biblical location came brutally true; not only was the city's industrial base badly, if not terminally, struck but thousands of its citizens were literally consumed by a massive 'firestorm'. This frightful phenomenon emanated primarily from the concentrations of explosives and incendiaries dropped, but was further aggravated by a combination of very humid weather, the storage of coal and other heating supplies in houses and the close-packed nature of structures. A British critic of Harris recently asserted that he deliberately planned 'firestorms'; certainly he was determined to destroy Germany's cities, but there was no sure way in which such a deliberate action could have been initiated.

By the end of September, Peltz's Luftflotte 3 possessed seven full and one partial Gruppen of multi-engine aircraft along with I/SKG10. The partially-complete unit comprised 7 and 9/KG40 with its FW200s, whose function was still wholly involved with anti-shipping sorties.

Consequently, the declared total of aircraft on the order of battle for bombing operations was just 146 in all! The one thread of hope for a future improvement in operational quality was the presence of the Ju188 and He177 designs, albeit in very limited numbers.

Pathfinder Developments

The return to Belgian airfields of I and III/KG6 following service in the Mediterranean occurred in August/September 1943. Although British intelligence was not aware of this fact at the time, PoWs from III/KG6's 8 Staffel interrogated in early 1944 threw light upon specialist operations relating to pathfinder techniques. It appears that a number of Ju88S variants were on hand whose crews practiced pathfinder trials over Britain between October and December 1943. One PoW flew some fifteen sorties during which his bomber carried a mix of bombs and flares. He asserted that the *'Knickebein'* system was used and when in the target area a direction finding signal based on repetition of the aircraft's individual letter was sent on the FuG 10 set. During the subsequent de-briefing the airmen were informed of whether the bombs had landed in the target area based on the D/F plots. In addition the pilot and observer submitted written reports. He was unable to clearly explain why flares were also released, other than that his bomber was the first in the group of Staffel machines to bomb, and therefore the flares were a follow-up indicator; he did assert that it was only the leading bomber that carried flares among its load. These duties ceased in December 1943 and the Ju88Ss were transferred-out, presumably to I/KG66 that was specifically tasked with pathfinder duties under *'Steinbock',* after which III/KG6 reverted wholly to bombing operations. The expanding use of flares to illuminate targets had reportedly been used by KG6 during its Mediterranean sojourn, which added strength to the PoW's statements.

The sleek Junkers Ju88S which was to undertake Pathfinding duties during Steinbock.

Catalyst for '*Steinbock's*' Initiation

What was to be regarded as the second of three 'Battles' in Air Chief-Marshal Harris's prolonged 1943/44 bomber offensive was quickly mounted, with Berlin as its epicentre. The run of three August operations over the German Capital was but a foretaste of what would, in varying degrees of destructive effectiveness, befall the city up to the following March. History now records the official commencement of the 'Battle of Berlin' as the operation dispatched on 18th/19th November 1943, which ended in general failure thanks to indifferent pathfinder marking that saw bomb loads released all over the cloud-covered city with no real concentration. Four nights later 469 crews were dispatched and landed back less 26 aircraft missing and six involved in accidents over Britain. This time round 'The Big City' as Berlin became known to Bomber Command, mourned the loss of over 2,000 citizens as well as suffering much material destruction. This was due to first-class 'blind' marking efforts despite a solid undercast.

Perhaps fearing another outburst from Hitler over the Luftwaffe's current performance, Göring called for a conference on November 28th with Peltz among the senior personnel. The gathering was informed that Göring had assured the Führer that Operation *'Steinbock'* would be launched within no more than fourteen days. He further expressed the hope that around 300 aircraft would be operationally ready for the first attack and added; "*If I can have about 100 in the second attack and early in the morning another 150; that will come to between 550 and 600 sorties – that is what we must aim at*".

Göring later issued a more fulsome written directive on 3rd December 1943 that was forwarded to the Chiefs of Staff for Bombers, Luftflotten 2 and 3 as well as General Erhard Milch who was in charge of equipment:

Key points of note contained within the document were;

1) Additional units were to be assigned to Luftflotte 3 as follows;

a) from Luftflotte 2 – Two Gruppen of KG30 and KG54 and one of KG76.

b) from re-equipped units – II/KG6, I/KG100, I/KG51.

2) Operational readiness was to be speeded up by all means in order to commence operations by the end of December's full moon period.

3) Operational strength was expected to be maintained at peak levels at all times, not only in order to exert maximum pressure on Britain, but conversely (in the Reichsmarschal's words) "to maintain a permanent defensive capability against the ever-present threat of an Allied Invasion in the west".

4) The attacks would be launched from advanced airfields only, with each unit's main and reserve staffs held back on German airfields. Aircraft were to be well dispersed and parked well away from the runways as well as being located in revetments – the worthy Göring was only too well aware of the risk posed by Allied bombing and 'intruder' activities. He insisted on 'dummy' airfields being set up in those regions containing the operational advanced airfields.

5) Bomb loads were to represent a 70% - 30% mix of incendiaries/bombs. In the latter instance no weapon of less than of 500kg capacity was to be used, other than to complete a bomber's full load.

6) Fliegerkorps IX was to inform Luftflotte 3 of :

a) its planned operations for the current and following month and

b) how these would be carried out.

The references in points 3 and 4 to possible Allied tactical and strategic counter-actions surely indicates how the Luftwaffe High Command at least was becoming aware of the burgeoning threat to their nation's military existence. In this context *'Steinbock'* could only be regarded as a holding action rather than one that could conceivably reverse the overall aerial conflict in Germany's favour.

CHAPTER THREE

Battle is Joined

Chapter Three
Battle is Joined

The Morale Issue

As 1943 gave way to 1944 the British population was facing up to the fifth full year of conflict. The worst effects of both the Luftwaffe *'Blitz'* and the U-Boat offensive – the latter threat having raised the distinct possibility of food and supplies running down to unsustainable levels – were fading into the background. The drab reality of food and clothes rationing, extended working hours and restrictions on travel were among the pressures being faced. A proportion of the population had suffered the additional trauma of being bombed out of their homes with little or no hope of moving back within the near future, or of finding an alternative property. Salvation from this ongoing atmosphere of drudgery could only come with the utter defeat of Nazism and its Italian and Japanese political contemporaries. "But when?" was the persistent question on every Briton's mind. The national spirit was still in a basically sound, if weary, condition but the onset of any German attack, especially if directed from the skies, could upset this delicate psychological balance.

Quantity versus Quality?

By 20th January 1944 the force available to General Peltz with which to launch *'Steinbock'* was not only well established, but possessed a very high percentage of serviceable bombers – 431 out of 491. However, this very positive aspect of operations had to be balanced against the manifold design-types on hand, and more importantly their ability to survive the impending offensive when pitted against the British defences. At the upper end of the performance-efficiency scale were the Me410 and FW190, but only the Messerschmitt 'twin' was capable of bearing an significant bomb load. The Ju188 and Do217 could carry greater bomb loads, but were generally the losers when intercepted by Mosquitos or Beaufighters. This left the Ju88 in the A-4, A-14 and S variants to make up the numbers. The Junkers 'schnellbomber' was a well-proven machine, but only the S possessed a performance even approaching that of the 'Mozzie' or even the venerable Beaufighter. The Ju88S was equipped with GM1 units to boost engine performance so that a top speed of around 380 mph could be achieved, albeit only for a short period. Finally, the sole 'heavy' on hand was the He177 *'Greif'* but less than fifty were assigned to Peltz.

The stark truth was that the Luftwaffe force available could not carry anything like the tonnage total currently enjoyed by Bomber Command. The single-cell bomb bay on a Lancaster could easily take five to six tons of high explosives and incendiaries, while the Halifax had a

Luftflotte 3 - Order of Battle - 20 January 1944

Unit	Type	Strength	Serviceable
Stab/KG2	Do217	3	3
I/KG2	Do217	35	35
II/KG2	Ju188	35	31
III/KG2	Do217	38	36
V/KG2	Me410	27	25
Stab/KG6	Ju88	3	3
I/KG6	Ju88	41	41
II/KG6	Ju88	39	39
III/KG6	Ju88	41	37
II/KG30	Ju88	36	31
I/KG40	He177	15	15 (1 Staffel)
Stab/KG54	Ju88	3	3
I/KG54	Ju88	36	25
II/KG54	Ju88	33	33
I/KG66	Do217	45	23
Stab/KG76	Ju88	5	4
I/KG100	He177	31	27 (2 Staffeln)
1/SKG10	FW190	25	20
		491	431

similar capacity. The Stirling's bomb bay was divided into three parallel longitudinal cells that limited it to carrying 500 pound bombs, but its overall lifting capability was still well above that of the majority of Peltz's bombers - and equal to that of the He177.

Tactics for *'Steinbock'*

A distinctive and necessary sea-change in Luftwaffe tactics compared to those of 1940/41 was now being applied in regard to *'Steinbock'*. During the *'Blitz'* the bombers had been dispatched individually; alternately, each Gruppe had been briefed to take-off and bomb over a period extending anywhere up to ten hours during the darkest period of the 1940/41 winter. The intention behind this act was to keep the British AA gunners and Civil Defence Authorities under maximum physical pressure for as long as possible, while an added 'bonus' was the perceived psychological pressure placed upon the citizens in each target location. In 1940/41 this method of operation could be indulged in with the crews secure in the knowledge that they faced little or no threat from RAF night fighters or heavy AA guns.

Now in 1944, just as the Bf110s and Ju88 night fighters backed by their ground-support organisation had forced RAF Bomber Command to adopt the 'bomber stream' principle as a means of (hopefully) swamping the German defensive system, so Peltz's crews were about to try the same tactic. There were material differences in the tactics employed. Ever since the 'stream' principle had been initiated during early 1942, the RAF crews had climbed to operational altitude either over Britain or out over the North Sea, and then maintained this height until well out of perceived Luftwaffe attention on the way home. This pattern contrasted with the '*Steinbock*' crews, who were briefed to take-off and proceed at low altitude to designated coastal crossing-out points before climbing to altitude prior to reaching the English coast. Then, a shallow diving course would be maintained to and beyond the target with a briefed minimum altitude achieved prior to regaining the continental coastline.

Bombing/Navigation aids

The first German radio navigation system was *'Knickebein'* - a twin-beam guidance system; the bombers flew along one beam using its Morse-code signal-guidance and released their loads at the point where the beams inter-locked. This was closely followed by '*X-Verfahren'* that was also a multi-beam system; it provided information to the pilot and observer as to the distance to the target which culminated with an automatic release of the bombs or markers. Finally, *'Y-Verfahren'* operated on a single-beam basis, with a ground controller monitoring the aircraft's progress and transmitting the relevant information as to how far the aircraft had progressed and the point at which bomb-release was to be initiated. The latter two systems were limited in range by the curvature of the earth, but were nevertheless a serious threat to Britain's industrial capacity.

By stark contrast the early RAF crews were clearly not in the same league, since they had to rely on 'deduced' reckoning and astro-navigation by their navigators in order to (hopefully) wend their way to their targets, let alone find them – methods that were 'stone-age' in terms of efficiency and reliability! Between mid-1941 and early 1943 radio systems became operational when '*Gee', 'H2S'* and *'Oboe'* would bring Bomber Command back into contention as an effective attacking force.

As 1944 commenced the Luftwaffe bomber force still had recourse to *'Knickebein'* and 'Y-*Verfahren'*. However, the Germans had developed a similar system to *'Oboe'* that was code-named '*Egon'*. Additionally the RAF's *'Gee'* navigation system would be utilised to their perceived advantage.

The *'Gee'* Factor

The first electronic navigation aid introduced by RAF Bomber Command appeared in late 1941. This was code-named *'Gee'* and the apparatus provided an accurate wireless 'grid-map' for the navigators. The signal reception was limited by the earth's curvature and was undermined by jamming following capture and examination of sets. The German interest in the captured Gee sets was not limited to disrupting the RAF's use of the system – it was realised the Luftwaffe could also use it for navigation. On January 2nd the first of several aircraft from the specialist unit 2/KG66 was fitted with a captured Gee set – the first of at least five aircraft. The Luftwaffe named the equipment 'Hyperbel Gerät', but the equipment was marked 'Truhe - Gerät' or 'T - Gerät'. Training took place at Montdidier, both in the air and with simulators on the ground.

Target and route marking

It could be construed as somewhat of an irony that, although the Luftwaffe still possessed in *'Knickebein'* and *'Y-Verfahren'* the ability to pin-point targets, it would substitute these methods for one already in wholesale use by the RAF, namely marker flares; although the Luftwaffe would also use incendiaries as ground markers.

Two basic variations would be employed, confirmed by lecture notes found on a captured airman, a prime example of poor security.

1) The 'Ablauflinie' method

The first method was to be used when the target area was fully visual. First, a group of incendiary bombs would be released in a line that was at right angles to the briefed target approach. In addition the line was to be placed six kilometres from the edge of the planned target area. Then, when level with this visual line that was known as the '*Ablauflinie'* (final approach line), the bomber crews were to make a timed bomb-run. In addition, selected crews in the initial attack-wave would supplement the incendiary pattern laid by the pathfinder unit by laying lanes of incendiary bombs on both lateral fringes of the illuminated target area.

2) The 'leuchtpfad' method

The alternative marking system was employed in semi-overcast conditions when cloud cover was no greater than 6/10th in concentration. A line of seven alternate white and

A painting by Mark Postlethwaite depicting a Ju88S of KG66 laying a 'leuchtpfad' over England during Operation Steinbock.

coloured flares would be released along the briefed target approach; this was known as the *'leuchtpfad'* (path of light). Once again the distance of the line's start-point was to be six kilometres from the target area. Each crew selected one of the target markers as their aiming point; bombing was to be made using a glide approach and the bombs' release timed by stop-watch, the time having been stated at the briefing session. The target approach could be briefed to occur directly up, or down, wind.

Variations

The *'Ablauflinie'* and the six kilometre run-up to the target area would still apply. However, the groups of coloured and white incendiary bombs released as ground markers were to be supplemented by a combination of four coloured sky marker flares and white flares, the latter released in a pattern surrounding the marker flares and intended to further illuminate the area at an altitude of 2,000 metres. One interesting variation was that the target-approach was only to be made in a down-wind direction.

The variation to the *'Leuchtpfad'* sky marker process involved the crews adopting the same target-approach method. However, when the final white flare was reached they would expect to see a line of seven alternate white and coloured flares laid at right angles in between the end of the *'Leuchtpfad'* and the first target-marker flare; the central flare of this secondary line would (ideally) be coloured, be in line with the target-marker flares laid over the target area and therefore provide an accurate final bombing run-up for the crews.

The short life-span of sky-marker flares meant that the initial layout over the target had to be renewed in concert with the briefed arrival of succeeding attack-waves, with a differing pattern for each wave. In any instance where the attackers fell behind schedule or the flare pattern began to fade away, the pathfinder crews were briefed to lay a line of red or coloured flares along the area's windward side at a 90 degree angle to the wind direction, after which target re-illumination would be made in the same pattern and colours. In the event of a marking pattern being incorrectly positioned, the pathfinder crews were then expected to release a flare beside each of the incorrectly laid items. This was surely none too easy to achieve, as well as prolonging the aircraft's orbit-time over the target - and furthermore adding to the already severe psychological pressure bearing upon the crews concerned.

An alternative procedure was be suggested by German PoWs under interrogation. This was that no corrective action would be taken in regard to the marking procedure; rather the attacking force would be informed by radio of the fact and extent of the error, so that the necessary corrections in bearing and distance could be made. Other PoWs would assert that as a second alternative, a greater density of flares would be released over the aiming point.

To indicate the route to and from the target, marker flares would be released at designated points on the way over, in a manner paralleling the 'Route Markers' dropped by Bomber Command pathfinder crews as a guide to the Main Force. Where these were to be laid over the sea, *'Lux'* buoys would serve in this role. Further assistance would be provided by radio beacons *('Funkfeuer')* positioned at fixed points on land, in addition to which rotating columns of searchlights *('Drehscheinwerfer')* also positioned at fixed points, would provide more visual guidance for the crews. In a further measure to confuse the defences, the crews would release *'Düppel'* aluminium strips intended to jam the radar network from the point of approach to crossing out over the British coast.

Odds against survival....

Peltz's crews were ready to do their duty in the full, and generally honourable, tradition of their service. Whether their enthusiasm, allied to at least an adequate grounding in operational techniques, would be enough to guarantee landing effective punishment upon their adversaries was naturally open to question. Certainly, Peltz among other *'Steinbock's'* commanders, was of the opinion that 'terror for terror's sake' would not bring about any lasting benefit to Germany's already fraught situation. Concentration upon a specific type of industrial source, such as power stations, could bring about much more disruption to the economy.

Immeasurably more certain were the potential hazards facing the crews as they sought to penetrate the defensive screen around and over Britain. The majority of the night-fighter squadrons were equipped with the Mosquito Mk. XIII or the Beaufighter Mk. VIf. Of equal importance in terms of overall efficiency was the availability of Airborne Interception (Radar) equipment.

Four squadrons out of the sixteen Mosquito and Beaufighter-equipped units were still operating the A.I. Mk V sets that provided the pilot with a separate screen presentation – all fine in theory, but a method forcing the pilots to divert their attention from the screen in order to scan the sky for their target. In practice the Mk. V system depended primarily on operator advising his pilot via his main radar screen in the normal manner when within visual range.

AI Mk. VIII was in regular use by ten night fighter squadrons and provided the crews with the ability to latch onto targets low down without fear of ground traces (known as 'grass' from their spidery appearance on the radar screens) blotting out the 'blips'.

The best set was the AI Mk. X. Adapted from the American SCR720B set that operated on a 3cm wave-band, it was vastly superior to the original 150-cm wave-band, and even the 10-cm equivalent of the AI Mk. VII. The original range of AI Mk. I to Mk VI sets had provided an often contradictory image to the radar operator as regards distance from and angle of approach to the target. In addition to that it was all too easy for the 'blip' indicating the target's presence to slip off the screen and not be picked up again. The AI Mk. X provided an enhanced degree of electro-magnetic energy and produced a more reliable screen display, although at the beginning of 1944 it was only available to two squadrons.

A now comprehensive range of Ground Control Interception (GCI) stations provided a network that ensured the RAF night fighter crews would be promptly directed or re-directed onto any 'bogey'. The searchlight batteries on hand were similarly spread out across the country. Finally, AA Command was well stocked with 3.7 and 4.5-inch weapons with gun-laying radar sets located on the various battery sites. The guns that now posed a real threat to the Luftwaffe's incursions.

2nd-3rd January 1944

The first Luftwaffe attacks of the New Year on Britain came on the night of 2nd-3rd January. The Observer Corps plotted the fast-moving Me410s of KG2 and the FW190s of SKG10 as they swept over Kent, Sussex, Surrey, London, Berkshire and Hertfordshire. One person on the ground was unfortunate enough to be killed by the scattered bombs, but the Luftwaffe paid heavily.

The War-time Diary of Miss J. M. Oakman - Chelsea*, Sunday 2 Jan 1944

23.50 Sirens. A perfect night bright bit of moon: flares almost at once of all colours of the rainbow (reminded me of my Christmas tree which never was). All gunfire seemed to lie S. direction – could not hear anything but only see shell bursts.

Luftwaffe Losses 2nd-3rd January 1944

Ju188 E-1 2/KG66 Z6+CK Wnr 260309

Crashed whilst on a training flight near Gratibus, Montdidier. 15.15 hrs.

Uffz Gustav Peters (F) (Inj), Uffz Friedrich Meichentsch (B) (Inj), Uffz Otto Gross* (B) (Inj), Obgfr Karl Tullius (Bf) (Killed), and Uffz Ernst Fabig (Bw) (Killed). **Extra crewman 'Truhe - Gerät' operator.*

FW190 A-5 I/SKG 10

Camber Sands, Rye, Sussex. 23.55 hrs.

Shot down by F/Lt N S Head of 96 Sqn in a Mosquito at 25,000 ft. The Mosquito fired a long burst from 150 yards and this aircraft immediately burst into flames. It is probable that the pilot tried to make a belly landing but the aircraft turned over onto its back on the shore at low tide a quarter of a mile below high water mark and was burned completely. A UXB was found some 300 yards away.

The body of the pilot, a Leutnant, was found but his remains defied identification.

FW190 A-5 I/SKG 10

Oxney Court, St Margaret's at Cliffe, Dover, Kent. 00.15 hrs.

This aircraft was brought down by AA fire at 16,000 ft. the pilot taking violent evasive action, diving to 7,000 ft. The aircraft then burst into flames and dived into the ground at an angle of 45° and exploded on impact, scattering wreckage over a wide area. The pilot baled out, but fell in the sea and his body was not located.

**A remarkable diary was kept by Miss J M Oakman during this period, her comments will appear throughout the days set out beyond this point*

The hole in the ground left by one of the SKG10 FW190s on the night of 3 January.

2/SKG10 lost two FW190s.

FW190A-5 Wnr 51403 BK+UW Lt Karl Krakhofer (Missing).

FW190A-5 Wnr 52528 TF+LR Lt Gerhard Stein (Missing).

These were the aircraft mentioned previously, but as both were Leutnants, it is not possible to say which crashed where.

Me410 14/KG2 U5+FE WNr 017

Crashed at Marquise near Boulogne, France, returning from London.

Oblt Helmut Schültze (F) (Killed), Gefr Heinz Beger (Bf) (Killed).

A claim for an Me410 destroyed off Le Touquet at 23.59 hrs was made by W/Cdr J Cunningham in a Mosquito of 85 Sqn.

Me410 16/KG2 U5+AJ WNr 420005

Failed to return from a sortie to London.

Fw Friedrich Hess (F) (Missing), Uffz Maximilian Von Poblotzki (Bf) (Missing).

A claim for an Me 410 destroyed 15 miles south of Dover at 23.59 hrs was made by F/O R D Bergemann in a Mosquito of 488 Sqn.

Fw. Friedrich Hess who failed to return after his Me410 was shot down off Dover.

4th-5th January 1944

A small raiding force was plotted over southern England again. Six children and three adults were killed when a bomb fell on houses in the picturesque Surrey village of Westcott. The raiders suffered at the hands of the RAF night fighters.

Luftwaffe Losses 4th-5th January

Do217E-4 7/KG2 U5+GR WNr 5377

Shot down by a fighter whilst on a training flight at Gilze-Rijen. 15.07 hrs.

Oblt Otto Schafer (F) (Killed), Uffz Wolfgang Bottcher (B) (Killed), Uffz Werner Zange (Bf) (Killed), Uffz Willi Strenzke (Killed). All buried at Tilburg.

Do217M-1 1/KG2 U5+BH WNr 6123

Eindhoven.

'Bomb Exploded' Uffz Helmut Grosser (B) (Inj), Uffz Walter Klie (Bf) (Inj), Uffz Josef Slabon (Bs) (Inj).

FW190G-3 3/SKG10 WNr 160820

Failed to return from a sortie to England. Fw Hermann Heinrich Greeve (Missing).

Ju88S-1 1/KG66 Z6+KH WNr 140609

Shot down by a night fighter during a sortie to London and crashed 5 km south of Hastings. 02.04 hrs.

Uffz Kurt Windelband (F) (Missing), Ogefr Heinrich Schwarz (Bm) (Missing), Uffz Gerhard Jarolim (Bf) (Missing).

Ju88S-1 1/KG66 Z6+FH WNr 140602

Gamaches, south-west of Abbeville, France. 03.10 hrs.

Shot down by F/O E R Hedgecoe in a Mosquito of 85 Squadron returning from London.

Hpmn Paul Grunau (F) (Killed), Ofw Josef Schmidt (B) (Killed), Fw Erich Heinze (Bf) (Killed).

Fighter Command Claims, not attributable to a particular loss

Two claims were made for Me410s destroyed by W/Cdr E D Crew in a Mosquito of 96 Sqn; off Beachy Head and off Hastings at 02.00 and 02.04 hrs.

Combat Report of Flying Officer E. R. Hedgecoe
4/5 January 1944
Ju88 destroyed 'Off Dieppe'

One Mosquito XIII A.I. Mark VIIIA No. 85 Squadron, F/O E. R. Hedgecoe (Pilot) and P/O N. L. Bamford (Operator) took off West Malling 0040 hours and landed Ford 0400 hours 5th January 1944. Pilot was on patrol under G.C.I. Wartling (Controller F/O Powell) at about 0150 hours. At 0205 hours contact was obtained on a bandit flying at 29,000 feet, Mosquito being at 23,000 feet, and a chase ensued involving violent evasive action and lasting about 25 minutes. The chase was abandoned close to the French coast at height 8,000 feet. Pilot was turned on to a northerly vector and he climbed again to 23,000 feet to resume patrol under G.C.I Wartling. At 0250 hours, he was given vector 270 degrees on to a bandit flying 140 degrees, height being given as 15,000 feet. At 0253 hours, contact was obtained at 4 o'clock, 20 degrees, range 3 1/2 miles, Fighter's height now being 21,000 feet. Pilot dived at full speed and range began to close. Apart from diving, bandit appeared to take little or no evasive action. Pilot dived still harder to gain more speed (I.A.S. at one time 370 m.p.h.) and at 0258 hours he obtained a visual at 1,800 - feet range, dead ahead and 20 to 30 degrees above. Pilot moved over to port and closed in to recognise e/a as Ju. 88. He fired a short burst at 300 yards range, about 10 degrees off, ½ ring deflection, e/a doing about 260 m.p.h. I.A.S., and, although no strikes were observed, e/a appeared to slow down sharply. Pilot fired a second burst from dead-astern, range 150 yards closing to 75 yards, making many strikes and causing a violent explosion in the fuselage, pieces of which flew off. The e/a fell away below Pilot and visual was lost. He orbited to port and saw the e/a glowing on the sea. Wing Commander E. D. Crew (O.C. 96 Squadron), on patrol off the English Coast after his own combats, reports having seen this e/a going down in flames well to the South of his position at the time of F/O Hedgecoe's combat.

Weather: Half moon, clear, starlight, haze over Channel, very thin cloud over French coast.

Armament Report: Rounds fired : 20 mm SAPI 80
20 mm HEI 80
Total 160
Stoppages : Nil. Length of bursts : 3.33 secs.

**(Hedgecoe's victim did not fall in the sea as he believed, but just in land at Gamaches; the Ju88S-1 Z6+FH of 1/KG66.)*

WEEKLY APPRECIATION OF DAMAGE TO KEY POINTS AND PROGRESS OF REPAIRS.

Period from 09.00 hours Wednesday 29th December 1943
To 09.00 hours Wednesday 5th January 1944.

GENERAL

Enemy air-activity during the past week has been slight. Sorties have been flown against land-targets on three nights; in addition a single reconnaissance was flown over Deal on Wednesday (29th December) without incident.

On Thursday / Friday (30th / 31st December) 3 long-range bombers crossed the Sussex coast and made penetrations of up to 30 miles; on Sunday / Monday (2nd / 3rd January) 10 long-range bombers and 10 fighter-bombers flew over parts of South Eastern England, London and the Home Counties; on Tuesday / Wednesday night (4th/5th January) a mixed force totalling 16 aircraft flew in over Kent and Sussex, four of them penetrating to the Greater London area.

Total civilian casualties for the week due to enemy action are 4* fatal and 24 serious. There was no damage of a major character. Six aircraft (15%) are known to have been destroyed.

One Key-point was affected and there was also one railway incident.

Thurs / Fri 30/31st Dec Night

S.P. Lenham, Kent

It was suspected that an UXB had fallen near the railway line and the up and down lines between Harrietsham and Charing were closed. Later the bomb was discredited and normal traffic was resumed.

On the same night bombs fell at 4 places in Sussex and at 1 place in Kent.

Sun / Mon 2nd/3rd Jan Night

NO KEY POINTS WERE AFFECTED but bombing incidents occurred at 3 points in the London area, 10 places in Kent and 2 places in Sussex- a total of 15 incidents.

Tues/ Wed 4/5th Jan Night

GENERAL AIRCRAFT LTD. London Air Park, Feltham, Middlesex.

Sub-assembly of gliders.

Ministry interested: Ministry of Aircraft Production.

At 02.36 hours on 5th January slight damage was caused by H.E. blast to a wooden building and the hangar roof. The night shift had to cease work owing to lack of blackout facilities. At about the same time as the above incident bombs fell at 3 other points in

**This seems not to take account of the incident at Westcott.*

the London area, 3 places in Surrey 2 places in Kent and 1 place in Sussex, a total of 10 incidents.

NOT ENEMY ACTION

KEY POINTS AFFECTED

BRIGGS MOTOR BODIES LTD, Carr Hill, Dalby, Doncaster, Yorkshire

Production: Airframe components.

Ministry interested; Ministry of Aircraft Production.

Electricity breakdown, 16.45 hours Thursday 30th December.

The electric plant which supplies power for lighting and for driving machinery broke down and all work was stopped. Repairs were completed and normal working was resumed on the following morning.

WEEKLY APPRECIATION OF DAMAGE TO KEY POINTS AND PROGRESS OF REPAIRS.

Period from: 09.00 hours Wednesday 5th January 1944.

To: 09.00 hours Wednesday 12th January 1944.

GENERAL

For the first time for fourteen months, the week has been entirely uneventful, so far as enemy activity is concerned. No aircraft has crossed our coast and there has been no shelling.

NOT ENEMY ACTION

KEY POINTS AFFECTED

Fire 03.00 hours Thursday 6th January.

PREMIER OIL EXTRACTING MILLS, Stoneferry, Hull, Yorkshire

Production: Edible Oils.

Ministry interested: Ministry of Food.

In the Castor seed crushing building a heavy pulley wheel of the machinery became loose and threw off a heavy belt which contacted the metal girders overhead. The sparks as a result caused a small fire in the fluffy material which invariably lies around girders in all oil mills. The fire spread but little damage was done, due to the prompt action of the works fire squad. No damage was caused to the plant and the production was only affected to the extent of 12 hours work. The total material loss was about 6 tons of castor oil.

Luftwaffe non-operational losses 8th to 10th January 1944

He 177A-3 2/KG100 5J+NK WNr 2212

8/1/44 11.36 hrs 3 km east of Chemsee.

Aircraft involved in a non operational flight and crashed on overshoot due to engine failure.

Lt Josef Lehl (B) (Killed), Fw Hans-Joachim Kölpin (F) (Killed), Uffz Willi Höfer (Bf)(Killed), Uffz Johann Kiesler (Bw) (Killed), Fw Karl Grützne (Bs) (Inj), Uffz Walter Böhmer (Bs) (Inj).

The tail of He177 5J+NK after it crashed due to engine failure on 8 January 1944.

Ju88 8/KG6

8/1/44 Melsbroeck. Involved in a collision on airfield – non operational.

Uffz Günther Eckhardt (F) (Killed), Gefr Helmut Meyer (Bf) (Inj), Ogefr Friedrich Uhrig (Bs) (Killed).

Ju88 8/KG6

8/1/44 Melsbroeck. Involved in a collision on airfield – non operational.

Lt Walter Dorn (F) (Killed), Ogefr Martin Sauer (B) (Killed), Gefr Hans Melerski (Bs) (Killed), Uffz Hermann Klöckner (Groundstaff) (Killed).

Ju88 6/KG54 B3+VP WNr 888759

10/1/44 Jaderberg Varel / Oldenburg Crashed whilst on non-operational flight.

Fw Theodor Möltgen (F) (Killed), Uffz Ernst Eussner (B) (Killed), Ogefr Walter Knauth (Bf) (Killed), Uffz Josef Weiss (Bs) (Killed).

13th-14th January 1944

WEEKLY APPRECIATION OF DAMAGE TO KEY POINTS AND PROGRESS OF REPAIRS.

Period from: 09.00 hours Wednesday 12th January 1944.

To: 09.00 hours Wednesday 19th January 1944.

GENERAL:

Enemy air activity during the past week has occurred on three nights. On Thursday / Friday (13th/14th January) seven long-range bombers were plotted over Kent, Essex, and Suffolk, one of them reaching London. On the following night (14th/15th January) two long-range bombers, which at the time were not identified as hostile, dropped bombs at Croydon and Dartford. On Saturday / Sunday (15th/16th January) ten fighter-bombers made penetrations over parts of South Eastern England, East Anglia, Hertfordshire and Bedfordshire, five reaching London.

At Croydon 5 fatal and 33 civilian casualties occurred, the only ones during the week. Two enemy aircraft are known to have been destroyed.

No incidents involving key-points or railways have been reported.

The War-time Diary of Miss J. M. Oakman - Chelsea   Friday 14 Jan 1944

Some bombs fell at Croydon during early night "with no sirens". One pierced a big cinema in Davis Road, Croydon – killed 7 and injured 25. A big drapery store was burnt out.*

**Some sources quote five killed.*

Luftwaffe Losses 13th to 15th January 1944

Me410   15/KG2   U5+HF   WNr 402

13-14/1/44 Failed to return from a sortie to London.

Lt Mathias Emberger (F) (Missing) Gefr Hans-Helmut Becker (Bf) (Missing).

Me410   16/KG2   U5+CG   WNr 420464

13-14/1/44 Failed to return from a sortie to London.

Lt Hans-Heinrich Uecker (F) (Missing) Uffz Emil Loppe (Bf) (Missing).

An Me410 was observed to crash at 19.44 hrs 5,000 yards off Landguard Point, Essex, near to the Cork Light Vessel, after being shot down by 3.7 inch anti-aircraft guns. This must relate to one the two losses above.

Ju188E-1 6/KG2 U5+CP WNr 260330

13/1/44 Werther / Bielefeld. Flew into ground whilst on an instrument checking flight.

Uffz Ludwig Wagner (F) (Killed), Uffz Josek Kastelik (B) (Killed), Ogefr Walter Krane (Bf) (Killed), and Ogefr Heinz Dietrich (Bs) (Killed).

Caudron 445 16/KG2 TN+QN

13/1/44 20Km south of Poix. Shot down by a fighter whilst on a local flight.

Fw Alfred Kunschke (Killed), Fw Erich Gumnor (Killed), Uffz Wilhelm Kamin (Killed), Ogefr Philipp Bodewig (Killed). All were ground crew.

Ju88A-4 6/KG30 4D+AP WNr 550481

14-15/1/44 Nordholz. Crashed whilst on a non-operational night flight.

Uffz Georg Börner (F) (Killed), Gefr Rudolf Schürer (B) (Killed), Uffz Emil Rolli (Bf) (Killed), Ogefr Heinz Wedwart (Bs) (Killed).

FW190G-3 2/SKG10 WNr 160413

15-16/1/44 Failed to return from sortie to England. Fw Georg Sprint (Missing).

FW190G-3 2/SKG10 WNr 160396

15-16/1/44 Failed to return from sortie to England. Ofw Rudolf Berghäuser (Missing).

A claim for an FW190 shot down off Dungeness at 20.10 hrs was made by S/Ldr Parker-Rees in a 96 Sqn Mosquito and probably relates to one of the above aircraft.

Ju88A-4 9/KG30 4D+DR WNr 801356

15/1/44 Kühsen 9Km NW Mölln 27Km South of Lübeck.

Crashed whilst on a non-operational flight due to an engine fire.

Oblt Martin Frohberg (F) (Killed), Fw Ernst-Friedrich Deppe (Bf) (Killed), Fw Werner Ortseifen (Bs)(Killed), Ofw Fritz Krüger (1 wart) (Killed), Uffz Josef Mirbeth (2 wart) (killed).

Fighter Command Claims, not attributable to a particular loss

16-17/1/44 F/Lt Hickin in a 68 Sqn Beaufighter claimed a Ju88 shot down at 05.18 hrs 56 miles NE of Kinnards Head, Aberdeen. The enemy aircraft broke up and parts hit the Beaufighter before it fell into the sea and burnt.

Major Bomber Command Operations 1st to 21st January 1944

1-2 January	**Berlin**	**79 killed**	**421 aircraft-28 lost**
2-3 January	**Berlin**	**36 killed**	**383 aircraft-27 lost**
5-6 January	**Stettin**	**244 killed**	**358 aircraft-16 lost**
14-15 January	**Brunswick**	**14 killed**	**498 aircraft-38 lost**
20-21 January	**Berlin**		**769 aircraft-35 lost**
	Most bombs fell on the outskirts of Berlin.		
21-22 January	**Magdeburg**		**648 aircraft-57 lost**
	Most bombs fell away from the target.		

21st-22nd January 1944

Let Battle Commence!

The opening *'Steinbock'* gambit by Peltz's crews was planned for Friday 21st January. The airmen assembling for briefing were probably unaware of the fact that just 24 hours before their RAF contemporaries had taken to the air in numbers approaching 800 Lancasters and Halifaxes for the latest strike against Berlin. Adverse weather conditions over the Nazi capital caused a well-scattered bomb pattern with a fair proportion of the bombs descending well outside the city boundaries; this poor result was achieved at a cost of 35 aircraft and crews. Now, with a much shorter distance to fly and a geographically easier target to navigate to, the Luftwaffe attackers would appear to have a distinct edge in delivering an accurate and punishing strike against London.

On fourteen airfields well spaced out in a rough arc between Soesterburg in central Holland, St. Trond - due east of Brussels, and Montdidier - north of Paris, the crews were informed that the strike would be conducted in two waves. Peltz was at Chateaudun, the forward operational base for I/KG40 and I/KG100 equipped with He177s. These bombers, in common with some of the other participating units' machines, had been dispersed elsewhere in a bid to escape Allied fighters or 'intruders' before assembling at their selected forward airfields within the last 24 hours. A good example of this was provided by II/KG54 who transferred from Marx near Wilhelmshaven in northern Germany to Laon/Athies, northeast of Paris. II/KG54's crews were to return to Laon/Athies after the first sortie, but go directly back to Marx after the second.

Operation Steinbock
21st-22nd January 1944

Order of Battle

Unit	Location	Type	Strength
I/KG2	Melun	Do217	25
III/KG2	Gilze-Rijen	Do217	10
V/KG2	Vitry-en-Artois	Me410	20
I/KG6	Chievres	Ju188	25
II/KG6	Le Culot	Ju88	15
III/KG6	Melsbroek	Ju88/188	30
II/KG30	Eindhoven	Ju88	15
III/KG30	St. Trond	Ju88	15
I/KG40	Chateaudun	He177	15
I/KG54	Juvincourt	Ju88	20
II/KG54	Laon/Athies	Ju88	20
I/KG66	Montdidier	Ju88/188	15
I/KG76	Laon/Couvron	Ju88	15
I/KG100	Chateaudun	He177	15
I/SKG10		FW190	20

Nearly 20 crews of I/KG76 were alerted just after noon and took off from Varrelbusch, still in ignorance as to the reason for this sudden transfer to Laon/Couvron. The Gruppe's troubles began even before the crews reached their forward base. The Ju88 flown by Leutnant Ernst Rethfeldt was shot down by a prowling fighter thirty miles from his destination; only one of the five man aboard survived. At their destination crews of I/KG76 were briefed for their part in the revenge attack (Vergeltungsangriff) on London, but did not take part in the first attack. On the second attack I/KG76 left Couvron, but those that survived were to return directly to Varrelbusch from London.

This nomadic existence was to be a recurring feature of *'Steinbock'* operations and was another indication that the air war was not going well for the Luftwaffe. It caused a great

The crew of a Dornier 217M of 1/KG2 prepare for a Steinbock mission.

deal of difficulty, such as when only a single Ju188 crew of II/KG2 was able to take part in the night's first attack from the forward base of Coulommiers, due to a lack of preparation on the part of the airfield's staff.

The first wave was briefed to attack a four square-kilometre zone around Waterloo. The target-marking method was to be based on the *'Leuchtpfad'* principle, that is, with the target area marked by incendiary bombs alone. The pathfinder crews were expected to have little difficulty in carrying out their key duty since the weather forecast predicted the necessary level of visibility. The electronic services of *'Egon'* and *'Y-Verfahren'* were also available to the pathfinder crews to pinpoint the target – at least in theory. From Montdidier, Hauptmann Schmidt, Staffelkapitän of 2/KG66 took off with a captured Gee system aboard his Ju188 and a second observer/navigator (Truhe-Beobachter) whose job was to accurately mark the target with flares.

An estimated force of 230 aircraft, carrying around 500 tons of bombs and incendiaries, opened up their engines and lifted off into the January night sky between 19.30 and 20.00 hours. In the case of II/KG54 the crews had been briefed to cross the English coast near Rye at an altitude of around 16,000 feet and to complete their bombing run by 21.15 hours at a reduced altitude of 13,000 feet. Navigation was down to deduced (also known as 'Dead') reckoning. The approach to London, given the disposition of the Continental airfields would see the bombers funnelling in and out along a cone-shaped flight-path whose limits were roughly between the Sussex and Essex coastlines.

By 20.30 hours the first 'blips' appeared on British radar screens. The final count of around 100 such 'signatures' recorded between 20.30 and 22.00 hours on stations located between Hastings and Dungeness was the first indication that plans for the mass assault were going badly wrong. Even worse was the paltry number of crews (15) recorded as over-flying London. As if this abysmal operational return was not bad enough, eighteen bombers were lost; three came down on British soil, seven were lost at sea and eight over Europe.

Fatal Operational 'Blooding'

The trouble-ridden Heinkel He177s of I/KG40 had taken off from Chateaudun at 20.00 hours, each loaded with two 2,500 kg bombs. Even before the French coast was crossed the Heinkels were struck by engine failures. The crew of WNr 535743 CJ+FO successfully baled out when an engine caught fire, and WNr 535560 NN+QZ was destroyed after it was forced to land, again after an engine fire.

Over England Oberleutnant Waterbeck's WNr 5747 was intercepted and shot down by a Mosquito. Oberleutnant Botterbrodt's WNr 5741 went down in the sea and disappeared along with its crew.

The formidable Heinkel 177 was plagued by engine problems throughout its service life.

On the return leg over France Oberfeldwebel Fleischer's WNr 5745 crashed near Rouen killing five of the six men aboard. Leutnant Melcher's WNr 2225 5J+VL crashed at Amy, killing four of its crew.

Of the few aircraft still serviceable for the second raid Oberfeldwebel Billing's WNr 2231 5J+ZL was shot down into the sea by a Mosquito.

Britain's First He177

One of the bombers that fell in Britain was He177A-3, marked F8+HH from 1/KG40 flown by Oberleutnant Waterbeck. All six airmen were making their first operational sortie in the Heinkel bomber. Up this evening from Colerne, Wiltshire, was a Mosquito Mk. XII from No. 151 Squadron in the hands of Warrant Officer Kemp along with Flight Sergeant Maidment. The crew had originally been dispatched at 20.15 hours on a *'Bullseye'* (navigation) exercise fifteen minutes ahead of the first indications that a raid was developing. Middle Wallop sector then ordered Kemp to orbit over Beacon 'F' at 16,000 feet, but after thirty minutes with no 'contacts' Sopley CGI took over and vectored the night-fighter several times over the next half hour. Finally a head-on 'contact' was established at 14,000 feet and two miles range. A swift orbit was made and the 'contact' was again picked up, this time visually after the original 1½ mile range was closed to 3,000 feet and the searchlight batteries that the Mosquito had previously dived into were requested to douse their beams.

When the range was closed almost to touching distance (100 feet according to the official intelligence report) what was tentatively identified from its cockpit shape as a 'Ju88' peeled violently off and down, and was soon lost both visually and on AI. Unfortunately for the Luftwaffe crew contact was soon re-established, even though Waterbeck continued to take sharp evasive action before finally levelling off at around 11,000 feet while maintaining a north-easterly course. The second time around, Kemp and Maidment studied the 'bogey's general outline from close behind and below. They noted how the wings tapered considerably and had square tips, the engines were close to the fuselage and the tail-plane was square-cut. This time the two men decided that it was a 'Ju188'. Kemp dropped back before opening fire with a two-second burst of cannon fire.

The result was dramatic. A violent explosion that took the form of a white flash with orange edges erupted from the port wing. The garish light permitted a fleeting sight of the vertical fin on which was applied a white Swastika. The bomber skidded violently to port and fell away in an ever increasing spiral that its attacker could not follow. The last sight Kemp had was of a trail of fire from the stricken machine, which shortly after hit the ground near Hindhead, Surrey. By then only the pilot and two gunners remained on board. Perhaps this was because the gunners did not hear the call to bale out, or Waterbeck may have stayed at the controls because he knew the two were still aboard. Two of the three men lost their lives in what was described as a failed attempt to make a force-landing. The He177 struck rising ground at a very shallow angle and broke up. The fuselage split in two just forward of the horizontal stabiliser and fire consumed all but the port-outer wing panel.

Obergefreiter Doge*, in the tail turret, managed to escape relatively unscathed and scrambled clear. The other three men, who baled out, joined him in captivity.

The He177 had been fatally 'blooded' in action over Britain on its initial sortie.

** 22 year-old Werner Doge had been in the Luftwaffe for two-and-a-half years and had been a batman in the officers' mess in Trondheim, but to augment his pay volunteered for flying duties. He had a short period of training at Trondheim and was assigned to a FW200 crew in June 1943. He then joined Waterbeck's crew at Fassberg in September1943, having never attended formal gunnery school. RAF intelligence noted the lack of attention paid to gunnery training in the Luftwaffe, but those who got formal training wore a different badge to those locally trained.*

A single I/KG2 crew went down during this stage of operations, but this was far from the final tally for the Geschwader. The Do217M in question was U5+IH which, despite its Gruppe's presence at Melun, was recorded as taking off from Eindhoven at 20.15 hours.

Leutnant Anders must have got through to release the load of AB 1000 incendiaries since his interception by Flight Lieutenant Hall's Mosquito from No. 488 Squadron only occurred as the bomber was crossing-out over the Kent coast near Dungeness. Flames took hold as a result of the night fighter's short burst of cannon fire, whereupon the pilot gave the bale out order. Only two of the four crew members survived in amazing circumstances, since they were fished out un-injured from the Channel by a launch.

Arrival in Dover

Gunner Heinz Grün was flying on his very first operation. His pilot, Karl Dorschner, had successfully got his Ju88 over England and released his bombs, but on the way back ran into Dover's anti aircraft defences. The bomber immediately went into a steep dive, giving only one man a chance to escape before it crashed into barracks at Dover.

Heinz Grün made the national and local papers!

The Standard reported:

Captured Pilot Got Brandy

A farmer and Home Guard private shared the capture of a German pilot who baled out after his bomber had been hit over the South-East Coast last night.

The farmer said to-day:

" I was looking out of the door at the A.A. bursts when I thought I heard something falling. I went into the field and there saw a parachute on one side of the hedge and a man on the other.

"I spoke to him and he said something, but I couldn't understand him. He then groaned and said 'Doctor' and I found that he was injured. I called to the Home Guard.'"

Private Percy Atkins, the Home Guard, who is a bricklayer, gave the farmer his rifle and went to call out the other H.G.s, who took the pilot into the farmhouse.

The farmer's wife made him a cup of tea.

"He was only a young fellow, about 22 years old," she said. "He was in pain, so although I knew he was an enemy, I put a little brandy in the tea."

The German pilot was laid on a sofa until the police arrived with a stretcher and took him to hospital.

The Dover Express followed up the story of the aircraft:

Lieut. John White, plotting officer on a Dover gun site, said last night: "It was the biggest concentration of flak we have seen for some time – just like the Battle of Britain, except that this was night time. There was enemy traffic in the sky all the time, and one raider came screaming down over our heads and crashed on a gun site."

An officer, two sergeants and six men fought the flames, despite the exploding petrol tanks and bursting small arms ammunition and grenades. And the A.A. gunners kept their guns in action. "The battery thought they were being dive-bombed," said Lieut. J. D. MacMillan, "but they are old hands, and stood by their guns. When our boys went down in the town during the week-end, people were slapping them on the back for the show they put up."

RAF Intelligence A.D.I.(K) interrogated Grün and issued their Report No. 40/1944 on 24 January and reported, amongst other things:

"In spite of his injuries the survivor refuses all information, and it was only under pressure that he revealed even the names of the other remaining members of the crew."

"Morale: Very High. P/W was an inexperienced youth on his first war-flight, but he was a strongly indoctrinated type of Nazi, convinced of his cause. He spoke of retribution coming to this country 'not from the air alone'.

Soldiers examine the wreckage of the Dover barracks Ju88.

KG54 crew Jehle, Kuhnert, Hellwig and Flossmann who were shot down over Rye.

Fully twenty-seven II/KG54 crews had been dispatched on this occasion. Take off commenced at 19.30 hours for a briefed time over target of 21.15 hours with bomb release at 4,000 metres. The last Ju88 (an A-14 variant) only got as far as the coast at Rye before it was 'coned' by searchlights despite the wholesale release of *'Düppel'* having been commenced shortly before. Then a Mosquito of No. 488 Squadron caught up with the exposed bomber and dealt summarily with its victim, setting its left engine on fire. Oberleutnant Hellwig jettisoned his load of two AB 1000 wing-mounted incendiary containers and fought vainly to extinguish the flames as his charge descended to around 7,000 feet. At this point Hellwig gave the order to jump and the cabin roof was jettisoned. Only Unteroffizier Flossmann took the opportunity to exit upwards, although in his recollection he was given no choice since he was immediately sucked out by the slipstream. His two companions went out through the belly hatch. Hellwig was the sole fatality and it was Flossmann's opinion that this was due to the Ju88 entering into a spin with centrifugal forces exerting a lethal barrier to any effort by Hellwig to bale out.

Luftwaffe Losses – First Raid - 21st-22nd January 1944

Do217M-1 U5+LH 1/KG2 WNr 722752

13 miles south of Dungeness. 21.30 hrs. Shot down by F/Lt J. A. S. Hall in a 488 Sqn Mosquito.

This aircraft came in over the Essex coast at about 10,000 ft and went out near Dungeness. Over the Channel it was attacked by a night-fighter and the pilot gave the order to bale out. The wireless operator and bordmechaniker were picked up by a launch and landed at Dover.

Bomb load; two AB 1,000 containers of incendiaries.

Lt Horst. Anders (F) (Missing), Uffz Erich. Kleine (B) (Missing), Uffz Willi Engelhardt EK1(Bf) (PoW), Uffz Wilhelm Kühne EK1 (Bs) (PoW) both the latter were picked up by a launch and landed at Dover.

Do217M-1 1/KG2

Abandoned by its crew on return from London after engine failure.

The observer, Oblt Kurt Schulze, later trained as a fighter pilot and ended the war commanding 13/JG5.

Ju188 Stab I/KG6 3E+BB WNr 260228

St Trond

Uffz Wilhelm Ferdinand (Bs) (Killed). Baled out of aircraft, but later found dead.

Ju188 3/KG6 3E+DL WNr 260334

Uff Karl Patzer (Bs) (Killed). Baled out of aircraft, but later found dead.

Ju88 A-4 4/KG6 3E+LM

Physical Training Barracks, Western Heights, Dover, Kent. 21.10 hrs.

Whilst on its way back from the target, this aircraft was caught by searchlights and despite evasive action it was held for considerable time. It then suddenly went into a steep dive and the order was given to bale out. The gunner, the sole survivor, baled out and landed with serious injuries. The aircraft crashed into a gym which collapsed on top of it, the wreckage was burnt and buried under masonry.

Uffz Karl Dorschner (F) (Missing), Ogefr Helmut Neumann (B) (Killed CC 5/104), Ogefr Heinz Waterkamp (Bf) (Missing), Ogefr Heinz Grün (Bs) baled out seriously injured.

Ju88A-4 4/KG6

Le Culot airfield. Collided with another aircraft when taking off.

Uffz Hermann Weisserth (F) (safe), Fw Siegfried Henze (B)(Inj), Ogefr Franz Wagner (Bf) (Inj).

(Uffz Weisserth was lost on the night of 13/14 February).

Ju88A-4 4/KG6 3E+?M

Bonlec (Belgium). Collided with the aircraft flown by Uffz Weisserth just after taking off for a raid on London.

Uffz Berthold Weis (F) (Killed), Uffz Werner Jung (B) (Killed), Ogefr Helmut Loew (Bf) (Killed), Gefr Kurt Höft (Bs) (Killed).

Ju88 5/KG6

Failed to return from a sortie to London.

Uffz Josef Marx (F) (Missing), Uffz Hans Heidrich (B) (Missing), Uffz Rudolf Roos (Bf) (Missing), Uffz Alfred Trechsler (Bs) (Missing).

Ju88 7/KG6

Failed to return from a sortie to London.

Uffz Theodor Conradt (F) (Missing), Ogefr Franz Von Bank (B) (Missing), Ogefr Reiner Hermanns (Bf) (Missing), Ogefr Alfred Hee (Bs) (Missing).

Ju 88 KG6

Failed to return from a sortie to London.

Ofw Helmut Vihrog (F) (Missing), Fw Georg Schorr (B) (Missing), Uffz Gunther Lippe (Bf) (Missing), Ogefr Heinz Neumann (Bs) (Missing).

He177 A-3 1/KG40 F8+HH Wnr 5747

Whitmore Vale, nr Hindhead, Surrey. 21.18 hrs. Shot down by F/O H Kemp in a 151 Sqn Mosquito

Took off from Chateaudun at 20.00 hrs. The aircraft was held by searchlights and then attacked by a night fighter whilst at 15,000 ft. on the way to the target. The bomb load was jettisoned and three members of the crew baled out. The pilot tried to make a belly landing, but the aircraft crashed and the rear gunner crawled out of the wreckage without serious injuries. The rest of the aircraft was completely burnt out.

This was the first operational flight of the crew with the He 177.

Oblt Karl Waterbeck (F) (Killed CC 1/235), Ogefr Jann Bikker (B) (PoW), Ofw Erwin Mirbach (Bf) (PoW), Ofw Georg Six (Bm) (PoW), Ogefr Werner Doge (Bs) (PoW) landed with aircraft – injured. Gefr Johannes Conrad (Bs) (Killed CC 1/234).

He177A-3 1/KG40 CJ+FS WNr 5745

Crashed near Rouen, France, on return from London.

Ofw Hugo Fleischer (F) (Killed), Uffz Karl-Heinz Altpeter (B) (Killed), Fw Walter Polaczy (Bf) (Killed), Gefr Hans Gnodtke (Bs) (Killed), Ogefr Willi Schmitt (Bs) (Killed).

He177A-3 1/KG40 CJ+FO WNr 5741

Failed to return from London.

Oblt Helmut Botterbrodt (F) (Missing), StFw Otto Schnelldorfer (B) (Missing), Fw Wilhelm von Trott zu Solz (Bf) (Missing), Fw Hans Streller (Bm) (Missing), Uffz Herbert Schulze (Bs) (Missing), Uffz Jacob Koch (Bs) (Missing).

He177A-3 2/KG40 5J+VL WNr 2225

Crashed at Amy, France, on return from London.

Lt Rolf-Heinrich Melcher (F) (Killed), Uffz Walter Oppermann (B) (Killed), Fw Theodor Schlagkamp (Bm) (Killed), Ogefr Horst Klippel (Bs) (Killed), Ogefr Hans Hoffmann (Bs) (safe), Uffz Georg Buder (Bf) (injured).

He177A-3 KG40 CJ+FQ WNr 535743

Crashed in France after an engine fire on the way London.

All crew baled out safely.

He177A-3 KG40 NN+QZ WNr 535560

Destroyed in an emergency landing after an engine fire on the way London.

All crew safe.

Ju88 2/KG54 B3+GK WNr 800924

Failed to return from a sortie to London

Uffz Wilhelm Bölstler (F) (Missing), Ogefr Erich Foche (B) (Missing), Gefr Karl Schäfer (Bf) (Missing), Ogefr Werner Walder Singer (Bs) (Missing).

Ju88 A-14 6/KG 54 B3+AP WNr 550296

Horton Priory, Sellindge, Kent. 21.50 hrs.

Shot down by F/Lt J A S Hall in a 488 Sqn Mosquito.

Started from Marx at about midday and after an intermediate landing at Laon/Athies took off from that aerodrome at about 20.30 hrs to attack London. Twenty-seven aircraft of II/KG 54 took part in this operation. This aircraft crossed the French coast at 15,000 ft. and made landfall at Rye. Shortly afterwards it was caught in a searchlight cone and despite violent evasive action, during which the bomb load was jettisoned, it was held continuously for about 10 minutes. During this time heavy AA was encountered and it was also attacked by a Mosquito night fighter and after two bursts one engine burst into flames; the aircraft lost height to 6,000 ft. and the pilot gave the order to bale out. The aircraft crashed and was completely burnt out, the pilot being found dead in the wreckage. The other members of the crew baled out successfully.

Oblt Helmut Botterbrodt pilot of He177 CJ+FO

Uffz Wilhelm Bölstler, pilot of Ju88 B3+GK

The observer had the Bronze (20) War Flights Badge and the gunner the Silver (60) War Flights Badge.

Oblt Karl Egon Hellwig (F) (Killed Folkestone), Uffz Hans Jehle (B) (PoW), Uffz Walter Flossmann (Bf) (PoW), Fw Roland Kuhnert (Bs) (PoW).

Ju188 E-1 2/KG66 Z6+EK WNr 260310

Landed at Montdidier airfield.

Uffz Kurt Langer (Bf) (died of oxygen failure at 20.50 hrs on the outward flight).

Ju88A-4 3/KG76 F1+KL WNr 801319

Shot down on a transfer flight from Varrelbusch and crashed 30 miles north-east of Couvron, France.

Lt Ernst Rethfeldt (F) (Killed), Uffz Erich Haller (B) (Injured), Uffz Erich Feustel (Bf) (Killed), Ogefr Justus Eidam (Bs) (Killed), Fw Karl Hettwer (1 wart) (Killed).

FW190A-5 1/SKG10 WNr 1465

20 miles south-east of Beachy Head. 20.45 hrs

Claim made by F/O B C Jarvis and F/O G J Smith in a 29 Sqn Mosquito. Pursued a/c to 25,000 feet and closed to within 2,000 feet. Aircraft appeared to have three exhaust flames, two at the side and one beneath, characteristic of the FW190. Closing the distance to 200 feet they opened fire, whereupon enemy aircraft immediately exploded and a burning mass flashed past the attacker's starboard wing.

Ofw Kaspar Flossdorf (Missing).

Fighter Command Claims, not attributable to a particular loss

A claim for a Ju88 destroyed at 22.10 hrs was submitted by F/Lt D M Dixon in an 85 Sqn Mosquito 15 miles south of Dungeness.

A claim for a FW190 damaged at 21.45 hrs was submitted by F/Lt A C Musgrove in a 29 Sqn Mosquito over the Channel south of Ford.

Second Raid

The second wave of attackers on 21st/22nd January was dispatched in the early hours in the face of deteriorating weather conditions that included a continued build-up of cloud that had been encountered in part by the preceding *'Steinbock'* force. The need to use electronic means to mark the target area meant that the pathfinder crews had to have recourse to the *'Y-Verfahren'* system. By this stage of WWII counter-measures were in force that could, and often did, hamper its proper function. Whether or not this was the case, the fact remains that no better rate of success was achieved on this occasion. Barely half of the estimated force of 200 bombers even crossed into southern England, while only 25 aircraft were judged to have got through to London to release their loads.

At Laon/Couvron the briefed route for I/KG76 was initially 232 degrees true to a radio beacon (*Funkfeuer*) VIII 4 at Luzarches. The route then went roughly north-west to 'Zange 11 and 12' directional searchlights at St. Valery-en-Caux and continued out across the Channel. Finally a third course alteration took them due north from Eastbourne to London. Take off was scheduled to commence at 02.30 hours. Release of the loads of two AB 500 container-held, and twelve 50 kg, incendiaries was to commence at 05.00 hours from 14,500 feet. All aircraft would be clear of the target by 05.30 hours at the latest. The return route would be via Zandvoort and Hardenburg to Varrelbusch. Briefed weather conditions were for a north-west wind at 40 kph at 1,500 metres and 80 kph at 4,000 metres. This contrasted noticeably with the equivalent figure of 100 kph westerly briefed to I/KG40, and could have been a material factor in the ensuing dispersal of the bomber stream. It would not, however, account for why so many crews failed to even cross the British coast!

Sixteen aircraft and crews were lost in the second wave; three by night fighters and two by anti aircraft fell in England. Seven aircraft and crews disappeared completely, presumably having fallen into the sea, and four more were lost in occupied Europe.

The second I/KG2 loss of the night was Do217M U5+CK, which was struck by radar-predicted fire from AA batteries stationed at Chelmsford. The bomber plunged to its destruction into a mental hospital at Wickford along with all four of Unteroffizier Kablitz's crew. Three crews from III/KG2 failed to return to Gilze-Rijen.

Anti aircraft fire brought down Ju88A-4 of 3/KG76; F1+BL near Canterbury. Its crew had suffered partial compass failure, but believed they were over London around ten minutes ahead of the briefed bomb-release time. Earlier they had failed to pick out the St. Valery searchlight guide and in fact were over Kent when attacked and therefore well adrift from the target. The AA fire struck home to fatally disable the controls, whereupon the bale-out order was promptly given. Although Unteroffizier Marliot seemingly managed to get clear, along with three companions, his headless body was later discovered hanging from a building.

The wreckage of Ju88A-4 F1+BL which fell to earth near Canterbury.

A 1/KG76 Ju88 was temporarily thrown out of control by damage caused by AA guns, whereupon the pilot ordered a bale-out. A quick response by two crew members saw them parachute into the pitiless Channel waters. Subsequently their bodies were washed-up near Worthing – all the more tragic since control was recovered and the aircraft brought back home.

II and III/KG30 based at Eindhoven and St. Trond were participating in what would be their only *'Steinbock'* operation up to mid-March. The II/KG30 crews would face one of the most protracted flights to the target, as evidenced by 4D+EP from 6 Staffel flown by Leutnant Petzinna. The Ju88A-4 took off at 02.30 hours and headed for Beauvais, just north of Paris, from where, having picked up the signal from H/F Beacon VIII/2, it would head up to St. Valery's visual beacon, scheduled to be flown over at 04.29 hours. The remainder of the course to London would be the same as for the main bomber stream. The Beobachter's (observer / navigator) notes referred to a bombing time of 05.00 hours. Twenty minutes after passing over Tonbridge the bomber was ten minutes ahead of its flight-plan as it prepared to go in on the target. Suddenly what Feldwebel Scherrer described as an AA shell struck the starboard engine, and almost immediately he baled out.

In fact the 'shell' damage was caused by 20mm cannon shells fired from Sub Lieutenant Wakelin's Mk. XIII Mosquito. The 96 Squadron night fighter had lifted off from West Malling at 03.44 hours and was handed over by Sector Control to Wartling GCI, who instructed Wakelin to climb to 20,000 feet on a southerly course. Around 04.25 hours 4D+EP made a 'trace' on Williams's Mk. VIII radar scope, indicating a north-westerly course at 19,000 feet. It was closed in upon and visually identified, as Leutnant Petzinna described an easy weaving manoeuvre conducted both in azimuth and elevation. Wakelin's initial dive to firing range was too swift and he pulled off to one side before easing into position. His fire from 700 feet was observed to strike the starboard engine, which blew up. The wing was seen to crumple, and the now flaming mass heeled over to crash close to Paddock Wood railway station.

A second He177, this belonging to 2/KG40, went down in the Channel in the early hours of the 22nd, having participated in the second wave. This time the night-fighter was a Mk. XII Mosquito from No. 85 Squadron flown by Flying Officer Nowell along with Flight Sergeant Randall. The West Malling based aircraft had already tackled a Ju88 that, although struck by gunfire, managed to evade destruction in the solid cloud cover at around 13,000 feet. Almost immediately a second 'contact' developed into what was also described as a 'Ju88'. This time the cannon shells caused a large explosion that appeared to throw the bomber out of control, with objects cast out that were believed to be two crew members baling out. This was probably correct since two airmen did reach the ground alive.

Oberfeldwebel Billing of I/KG40 had previously served with 9/KG40 and his crew were experienced operationally on the FW200. The Beobachter, Feldwebel Andrae, had been with 8/KG40 (later 2/KG40) up to August 1942 when the Staffel transferred to Fassberg. He returned briefly to 9/KG40 before moving back to Fassberg. He also briefly attended an Hs293 course at Garz, before being posted back again to Fassberg. The Bordmechaniker, Feldwebel Beitter, had served with III/KG40 up to August 1943 before joining this crew and had completed 23 sorties in FW200s.

According to either Beitter or Oberfeldwebel Andrae one engine failed as the He177 was approaching the English coast at 20,000 feet and the pilot called for a bale out, to which both airmen responded. They were fortunate to survive since the wind direction caused their parachutes to drift sufficiently northwards for both to descend safely near Hastings. Later the same day two more of the crew were washed ashore between Dover and Lydd. The remaining two men almost certainly went down inside the bomber that was adjudged to have gone in several miles south of Hastings.

Once again the 'executioner' appears to have been a night-fighter from West Malling, this time a Mk. XII Mosquito from No. 85 Squadron. Take-off time and initial GCI directions for Flying Officer Nowell were almost identical to Sub Lieutnant Wakelin's. Around 50 minutes into his sortie Nowell engaged a Ju88, which was claimed as 'damaged' since it disappeared into the solid undercast. Nowell was then informed of a second 'bandit'. This aircraft was on a north-bound course and was duly picked up on radar four miles east of the Mosquito's heading. The 'Ju88' as identified by Nowell was maintaining a level flight-path at 19,000 feet and presented no aiming problem for its attacker. Just forty 20mm shells were fired, but these induced a huge explosion that sent the bomber immediately diving out of control. In addition, Nowell and Flight Sergeant Randall noticed two objects falling out, which ties in neatly with Beitter's and Andrae's bale out.

Face-to-Face Encounter (1)

As Beitter and Andrae were floating down towards captivity, a Mr. R Wise was proceeding to his place of work at an NFS Station on the coast near Hastings; the subsequent newspaper article in the 29th January edition of the Hastings and St. Leonard's Observer naturally did not disclose any specific details.

This witness stated that he had heard bombs falling and was making his way to his place of work to report for possible duty when he saw an aircraft descending in flames. It skimmed along just above the Channel surface before diving and violently exploding. Mr. Wise then encountered a woman on fire-guard duty with her daughter

Opposite page: 96 Squadron Mosquitos wait for the night at West Malling.

who called his attention to 'something white' dangling and flapping from a telegraph pole. His initial impression was that it had supported a parachute flare and in fact he did not immediately spot Oberfeldwebel Beitter, who was positioned in between the pole and the wall of an adjoining garden. Only when he heard something rattling and glanced backward did he make out the German airman's outline.

Wise said "Come on" to which Beitter responded "Yes, yes" before standing up from his seated location on the low wall. He reached down to a pocket, an action which startled the fireman since he thought his involuntary 'guest' was about to produce a pistol. Instead, Beitter raised his hands and when Wise placed his hands on the airman's tunic Beitter responded by saying, "No gun".

He was apparently unhurt, but was bereft of his flying boots that had either been pulled off by the shock of his opening parachute or deliberately removed in anticipation of his landing in the sea. He requested and was granted a cigarette before being escorted to the fire station, where he received a second cigarette to accompany the universal British 'welcome' – a cup of tea! The presence of a fire in front of which he could warm up his feet must have raised his spirits somewhat. To the question of how many had baled out, he replied 'six' in French, a sadly optimistic figure in the light of events.

A very human reaction to the incident was raised by Mrs. Sutton the female fire-guard. She had thought while sheltering in a doorway close to where Beitter landed that the swishing sound had been created by a parachute, but the darkness was too intense for visual confirmation. She then met Mr. Wise and informed him of her impressions, after which he took over.

On being interviewed for the newspaper article she commented that, perhaps it was just as well she did not know there was a German there all the time she and her daughter were standing outside their door as they might not have known what to do. Then she added;

> *"I expect though that we would have brought him in and given him a cup of tea because you can't stifle feelings of humanity - even towards an enemy".*

These final words echo the supreme irony attending any conflict, namely how latent or open feelings of hostility towards an adversary can switch abruptly to a sense of sympathy towards what has become just another individual caught up in what is generally a universal web of tragedy.

Face-to-face Encounter (2)

Feldwebel Beitter's fellow airman, Oberfeldwebel Andrae, after landing and divesting himself of his parachute, was stumbling along a road when he ran into a Mr. Frederick R Smith, who was a quarryman. The latter recalled;

> *"I was on my way to work when I saw a uniformed figure approaching and very surprised to discover he was German. I had a little knowledge of German and said; "Arbeit kaput" (work finished). With this, the German put up his hands and said 'Kamerad'. I took him along and handed him over to my acting foreman, Mr. Sendall".*

Smith also informed the 'Observer' reporter that the German was a big fellow and powerfully built. Having taken his revolver, Mr. Sendall escorted him to the quarry office where a Mrs. Pocock was working. On entering the room, Sendall said to her;

> *"Look what I have brought you". She expressed surprise as the airman staggered in along with his revolver wielding 'escort'. She added; "His eye was swollen up like a big black egg, there were scratches over the left side of his face and his ear was bleeding. On his uniform 'which was of very shoddy material' he bore an Iron Cross with two other golden decorations. Stars were borne on both shoulders which we believed denoted a Lieutenant. There were five small wings on yellow tabs on his collar. He started to talk in French and asked for coffee before being helped into another room where an electric fire afforded him warmth".*

Mr. Sendall administered First Aid and Mrs. Pocock gave him, not coffee – but tea! Using sign language the airman asked for some shoes as his flying boots having been lost; he was in a very dazed state and wanted to know if he was in England. Later on a police car arrived and took him away to start an indeterminate period as a 'Kriegsgefangener'.

Elements of no less than eight of the participating Gruppen had suffered losses amounting to 34 aircraft and most of the crews for what was a truly abysmal result. A further irony regarding this operation is that British records indicate its night fighter force was confused as to what constituted friend or foe; this was allegedly due to RAF bombers or 'intruders' returning from operations over France being mixed in with the Luftwaffe force. On the same night Bomber Command sent 648 aircraft to Magdeburg and lost 57. The clear inference from this was that the German casualties may have been even higher had the airspace over southern England been free of 'friendly' aircraft!

Bullseye Casualty

Regular navigational exercises, known as 'Bullseyes' were flown to train new crews at Operational Training Units. As luck would have it, a 'Bullseye' was planned for the evening of January 21st - a large number of Wellingtons, Halifaxes and Lancasters assembled at 10,000 feet to make a mock attack on London! The force crossed the coast near Dungeness, flew over Canterbury and headed for London's Green Park causing a great deal of confusion.

One of the crews taking part was that of Flying Officer Brewer of 1667 HCU flying in Halifax EB152. They took off from their base at Faldingworth and were believed to have entered the London Defensive Zone – nothing further was heard. It was assumed that the aircraft had fallen into the sea as no wreckage or bodies were ever found. An enquiry concluded that the Halifax may have fallen foul of enemy fire from one of the attacking aircraft, or had been mistakenly shot down by an RAF night-fighter or AA guns. It was also considered possible that icing caused the altimeter to malfunction, leading to the pilot flying into the sea.

The German Viewpoint

German records on the progress of *Steinbock's* initial raid presented a rosier impression, at least as regards the first stage, compared to what had transpired. The first-wave attack involved 227 crews and was recorded as follows; *"The attack took place in the early hours of the evening and was apparently unexpected with moderate defence over the target area. The attack was carried out at heights of 700 and 1,700 metres. Numerous fires were observed in the centre of the city".*

A more sober assessment applied to the second-wave assault; *"The second attack came towards 05.00 hours and was met with strong defence, although good results were observed on the target involving 30-40 fires, amongst which some extensive examples were reported."* The final comment was even more sobering;

"Our losses were 38, of which 14 were over home territory".*

The number of crews gaining their goal and the scale of destruction had clearly been badly exaggerated, while the recorded bombing altitudes were pure fantasy, especially given those quoted at the briefing sessions.

The British Viewpoint

The Home Office Key Point Reports show that the Luftwaffe hit a factory in Ealing, Dagenham Docks, Tilbury Docks, Thames Board Mills Purfleet, Vickers Armstrongs Dartford, the BBC Transmitter at Folkstone, East India Docks, Barking Power Station, Westminster Bridge (IB's), the Royal Ordanance Factory Woolwich, RAF Gravesend, the Southern Railway at Barcombe, Bexhill, Chilham and Glydne. LNER at Enfield and West Ham and the LMS at Poplar.

* *This total is greater than identified in detail here, and may include some aircraft written off with no crew casualties.*

A brewery at Romford was hit (it was hit again on 18/19th April), Bexley Mental Hospital and a house at Hailsham, Sussex, killing several people including an RAF Group Captain on leave.

Many anti-aircraft shells fell to explode when they hit the ground. In the second raid at Eltham three shells exploded in adjacent streets, one of these blew Fire-Watcher Mr Charles Harcourt across the street. He was taken to Woolwich Memorial Hospital, but had to have a foot amputated. Also on the second raid, at Gravesend, a Voluntary Rescue Service worker who was leaving his house was killed by shrapnel when an exploding shell hit his house, his wife who remained inside was uninjured.

Incendiaries were littered around Westminster, Parliament Square and New Scotland Yard. Buildings along Parliament Square were on fire and lit-up the windows of the Houses of Parliament. More incendiaries started fires at Cannon Row police station and the council depot in Pimlico. The ancient wooden beams in the roof of Westminster Hall caught alight, but the fire service contained the fire and saved the hall.

There were reports of houses damaged around London and the Home Counties. The 'London' of 1944 was smaller in area because boroughs now in 'London' were considered to be in surrounding counties at the time. A hit on Romford, for example, was considered to be in Essex, while now it is a London Borough. On 22nd January Romford reported at 05.20 hours: Incendiaries – Albert Road / Victoria Road area (1 fatality) and in the High Street area a bottling department of a brewery was badly damaged. The '30-odd' bombers reported over London probably meant the central area, but many more crews bombed the surrounding area.

The War-time Diary of Miss J. M. Oakman – Chelsea Friday 21 Jan 1944

20.50 Sirens. Oh! Boy! Some noise! Flares (all colours) guns (some I've never heard before). Fires NE and SE and N. Quite like old times. Good supply of "bits" dropping about. Odd planes seemed dotted about and consequently all guns were going.

20.18 All clear.

Saturday 22 Jan 1944

Low cloud and good wind. 04.27 sirens. Guns after a little while – louder than previous alert. Heard a whiss over E of Post. (The whiz was "a supposed UXB" in Radnor Walk – I thought it might be a shell). Evacuation took place – and road was roped off. Sewer and water main have gone!)

5.50 All clear.

So, after so many months. Chelsea a BOMBA! A second bomb, suspected UX, fell in Royal Hospital Grounds near Laundry. TWO BOMBAS.

Wednesday 25 Jan 1944

BDS went down hole in Radnor Walk and found the bomb had gone off after piercing road and sewer – it was a 50 kg firepot 15. The same type was found with nose and HE fitting in hole in Royal Hospital grounds but 6 firepots were missing. As 6 firepots were found in Westminster minus the rest of the firepot, it was presumed they came from the same bomb. The raids seem to be incendiary – phosphorus IBs were dropped as well, and the 1 kg type of anti-personnel – 80 of which did not go off. Westminster Hall had a good fire.

WEEKLY APPRECIATION OF DAMAGE TO KEY POINTS AND PROGRESS OF REPAIRS.

Period from: 09.00 hours Wednesday 19th January 1944.

To: 09.00 hours Wednesday 26th January 1944.

GENERAL

After a long period of scattered or relatively small attacks, enemy air-activity flared up on Friday/Saturday night, when London was the primary target and 92 aircraft were plotted overland, the largest force to attack land-targets on any one night since 29th/30th July 1942, when 100 long-range bombers made penetrations and Birmingham was the main target.

The enemy used a mixed force of aircraft, eight were long-range bombers, including the He 177 which, so far as is known has not before operated against land-targets in this country; the remainder were fighter-bombers. Fourteen aircraft (15%) are reported to have been destroyed.

The attack was conducted in two phases, the first from 2040 to 2209 and the second from 0419 to 0545. In the first phase only 14 aircraft succeeded in reaching London and in the second thirteen. As a result, there was a considerable spill, mainly in South-Eastern England; in Kent alone over 100 minor incidents occurred. In London itself, the bulk of the incidents were South of the River. A considerable number of UXB`s and I.B`s were dropped. Considering the scale of the effort, the results were very poor and compare unfavourably with those of the attack on Birmingham on 29th/30th July 1942.

		Casualties		Key-Points
	Fires	**Fatal**	**Serious**	**Affected**
London	4	74	12	91
Birmingham (1942)	95	289	35	333

In addition to this activity, the Kent Coast was bombarded on Wednesday / Thursday and Thursday/Friday nights. Overland reconnaissances were flown over Falmouth/ Lizard Point on Thursday morning and over Dartmouth area on Friday afternoon.

During the week there were 18 incidents involving Key-points 10 railways and 1 airfield.

None of the damage has proved of serious consequence.

Total civilian casualties for the week are 41 fatal and 113 serious.

Wed/ Thurs 19th/20th January Night

S.R. Dover Area, Kent

All traffic was suspended between 0525 and 0845 hours on 20th January while the area was being shelled from the French Coast.

Shells fired from the French Coast fell at 6 other places in Kent.

Thurs / Friday 21/22nd Jan Night

NO KEY POINTS AFFECTED, but a shell fired from French Coast fell in Deal, Kent.

Fri/Sat 21st / 22nd Jan Night

AIR-ATTACK ON LONDON AND SOUTH-EAST ENGLAND

Ninety-two aircraft operated against land-targets in two phases, each lasting somewhat under an hour and a half. The areas attacked lay South-East of the line Sudbury (Suffolk) / Ely / Horton (Bucks) Wootton (I.O.W.). In London itself, the bulk of the incidents were South-East of the line Erith / Westminster Bridge / Beckenham / Orpington, and outside London South – East of the line Watford / Westerham / Newhaven. The Bexley Mental Hospital was hit, 13 people being killed, but otherwise most of the bombing was of a relatively minor nature. It is provisionally estimated that there were 245 incidents of which 44 occurred in London, of the remaining 201 (82%), 110 occurred in Kent, 53 in Sussex, 15 in Essex, 8 in Surrey, 3 each in Cambridgeshire, Berkshire, and Hampshire, 2 in Buckinghamshire and 1 each in Bedfordshire, Suffolk, Oxfordshire and the Isle of Wight.

On this night the following Key-points were affected: - 10 factories and 9 other key-points (including 1 airfield); in addition 9 incidents involving railways have been reported. From present reports none of this damage appears to be serious.

FACTORIES

1) ARROW ELECTRIC SWITCHES LTD, Hangar Lane, Ealing W.5

Production: Switch tumblers.

Ministry Interested: Admiralty.

Production was temporarily stopped pending the removal of an UXB, but was normal by 24th January.

2) BRIGGS MOTOR BODIES LTD, River Plant, Chequers Lane, Dagenham Dock, Essex.

Production: Aircraft components, motor bodies, carrier bodies, A.S apparatus.

Ministries Interested: Admiralty, Ministry of Aircraft Production.

The premises were evacuated at approximately 2115 hours on 21st January owing to the presence nearby of an UXB resulting in the loss of 156 manpower hours. Slight damage was caused by an A.A. shell.

3) HENRY BROWNE & SON LTD, Station Works, Wakering Road, Barking, Essex.

Production: Compasses.

Ministry Interested: Ministry of Aircraft Production.

Superficial damage caused by blast to the roof and windows. Production was not affected.

4) GLACIER METAL CO. LTD, Ealing Road, Alperton, Wembley, Middlesex.

Production: Plain bearings.

Ministries Interested: Ministry of Supply, Ministry of Aircraft Production and Admiralty.

A.P.B`s fell here causing slight damage to the roof and plant. Production was not affected.

5) D.P.S ELECTRICAL CO.LTD, Ealing Road, Alperton, Wembley, Middlesex.

Production: Drawn wire and cables.

Ministry Interested: Ministry of Aircraft Production.

Anti-personnel bombs fell here and caused damage to the roof. One of them was unexploded and production was suspended until its removal at 1200 hours on 22nd January when it was restarted at 50%. On completion of repairs normal working will be resumed.

6) LONDON GRAVING DOCK CO.LTD, Tilbury Docks, Tilbury, Essex.

Naval and merchant ship repairs.

Ministry Interested: Admiralty.

IB`s fell here at 2120 hours on 21st January causing slight damage. Production was not affected.

7) PRITCHETT & GOLD & E.P.S CO.LTD, (Inc Radford and Hart Accumulator Co Ltd.)

Dagenham Dock, Dagenham, Essex.

Production: Accumulators.

Ministries Interested: Ministry of Aircraft Production, Ministry of Supply.

The roof and windows were damaged by blast from a nearby H.E. Production was not affected.

8) THAMES BOARD MILLS LTD, Thames Mills, Purfleet, Essex.

Production: Boards for shell containers.

Ministry Interested: Ministry of Supply.

At 2120 hours on 21st January an H.E. fell in the river of this Key Point. Extensive blast damage was caused to the glass roof and the roof structure. Production was stopped for 4 hours.

9) VICKERS ARMSTRONG LTD, Powder Mill Lane, Dartford, Kent.

Production: Shell and fuse filling, ammunition.

Ministries Interested: - Ministry of Aircraft Production, Admiralty, Home Office (Explosives Branch).

3 H.E. fell at 2125 hours on 21st January, the first bomb burst in the area of the General Store which was demolished; the light fitting shop was damaged by a fire which is believed to have been caused by a short circuit. Various buildings in the vicinity were damaged by blast. The second bomb fell about 10 yards from the Magnesium store which was destroyed by the resulting fire. Blast damaged other buildings nearby. The third bomb, which fell about 50 yards from the Works boundary caused a certain amount of superficial damage. The gas and sewage mains outside the works were severed, and the telephone lines were put out of action, but all services were restored within 24 hours, with the exception of the gas supply which was only 50% of normal. A preliminary report estimates the loss of production to be 2 full days.

10) JOHN WRIGHT & SONS (VENEERS) LTD, Chequers Lane, Dagenham, Essex.

Production: Veneers, plywood.

Ministries Interested: Ministry of Aircraft Production, Admiralty, Ministry of Supply.

Production was affected by the presence of an UXB. Although the bomb was still there production resumed on the morning of 24th January.

KEY POINTS AFFECTED AND OTHER INCIDENTS

1) B.B.C. The Harvey Grammar School, Cherry Garden Avenue, Cheriton Road, Folkestone, Kent.

Authority Interested: British Broadcasting Company.

An enemy aircraft crashed on the grid line at 2150 hours on 21st January and the power supply to this Key Point was cut off until 2327 hours.

DOCKS

2) EAST INDIA DOCKS (Port of London Authority), Blackwall, London S.E.

Ministry Interested: Ministry of War Transport.

I.B`s which fell at this Key Point at 0515 hours on 22nd January caused slight damage to sheds and the roof of the hydraulic station and a fire in the canteen. Some fish meal stored in "A" shed basin was affected.

3) TILBURY DOCKS, Tilbury , Essex.

Ministry Interested: Ministry of War Transport.

At 2205 hours on 21st Jan. I.B`s fell at various points on the roof and in the yard of the hydraulic station causing a number of small fires which were soon under control. A.P.B`s fell in the dock at the same time. I.B`s caused slight damage to oil seeds on No 4 shed.

ELECTRICITY

4) BARKING POWER STATION, (County of London Electric Supply Co.), River Road, Creekmouth, Barking, Essex.

Authority Interested: Electricity Commission.

An UXB fell behind the C.E.B. Transformer East.

ROAD BRIDGE

5) WESTMINSTER BRIDGE, London S.W.1

Ministry Interested: Ministry of War Transport.

A number of IB`s fell on the bridge at 0525 hours on 22nd January.

ROYAL ORDNANCE FACTORY

6) ROYAL ORDNANCE FACTORY, Woolwich, London S.E.18

Production: Guns and mountings, naval armament stores, storage of cased vehicles.

Ministries Interested: Admiralty, Ministry of Supply, War Office.

IB`s fell here at 0500 hours on 22nd January, causing a number of fires.

MILITARY FOOD STORE

7) No. 25 AUXILIARY SUPPLY RESERVE DEPOT, Tilbury, Essex. (Food Store).

Ministry Interested: War Office.

The road to the depot was blocked by an UXB.

TELECOMMUNICATIONS

8) COOLING WIRELESS STATION, Cooling, Nr Gravesend, Kent.

Authority Interested: General Post Office.

2 UXB`s were discovered within 15 yards of the radio installations. An alternative network was available.

AIRFIELD

9) R.A.F. AIRFIELD Gravesend, Kent.

H.E`s fell on this airfield at 0512 hours on 22nd January. One hangar was burnt out and another damaged.

RAILWAYS

1) S.R. Barcombe, Sussex.

All traffic on the Tunbridge Wells - Lewes line was suspended between Isfield and Barcombe Mills stations owing to the presence of an UXAPB which fell at 2100 hours on 21st January. Normal working was resumed at 1545 hours on 23rd January.

2) S.R. Bexhill, Sussex.

At 2125 hours on 21st January an UXB fell on the down side of the railway line, between Bexhill and St Leonards. Single line traffic was introduced on the up line until 1815 hours on 24th January when working on both lines resumed with a speed restriction of 5 m.p.h.

3) S.R Chilham, Kent.

H.E. and IB`s fell on the line at 0515 hours on 22nd January. Single line traffic was put into operation between Chilham and Wye, until the afternoon of 23rd January, when normal working was resumed.

4) L.N.E.R. Enfield, Essex.

An UXB was discovered on the morning of 22nd January 100 yards from the L.N.E.R. tunnel at Hadley Wood. A restricted goods service was in operation until 1445 hours on 23rd January when normal working was resumed.

5) S.R. Glynde, Sussex.

At 2110 hours on 21st January an UXB fell close to the railway line. Between Berwick and Glynde stations, traffic on the down line was suspended and that on the up line was allowed to proceed subject to a speed restriction.

6)L.M.S. Railway, Poplar, E.14.

At 0850 hours on 22nd January, 2 UXB`s were found in Poplar Coal Wharf. Goods traffic on the lines from Poplar Central to East Quay was suspended for a short time. Later a screen of coal was formed and traffic was able to pass at 5m.p.h. over a loop line. Normal working was instituted from 26th January.

7) L.N.E.R Potters Bar, Middlesex.

At 0505 hours on 22nd January about 350 IB`s fell across the cutting at Stag Hill.

8) S.R. Shortlands, Kent.

On the morning of 22nd January, 2 UXB`s were discovered between Shortlands and Beckenham Junction and all traffic was stopped. At 2030 hours on the same day, it was reported that normal working had been restored.

9) L.N.E.R. West Ham, Essex.

At 2125 hours on 21st January H.E. caused slight damage to the permanent way and to telephone wires between Fernhill Street and Mary Rose Street.

KEY POINTS AFFECTED BY A.A. SHELLS

WILLIAM NASH LTD, Cray Valley Paper Mills, St Paul`s, Cray, Orpington, Kent.

Production: Photographs and tracing paper.

Ministry Interested: Ministry of Supply.

A.A. SHELLS, 2100 hours Friday 21st January.

A.A. Shells caused superficial damage. Production was not affected.

S.R, Greenwich, London.

A.A Shell, 2130 hours Friday 21st January.

The down line was damaged near Maze Hill Station. There was some interference with traffic.

BRIGGS MOTOR BODIES LTD, Main Plant,Chequers Lane, Dagenham Dock, Essex.

Production: Mines and sinkers, S.P. components, A.T. Carriages, motor bodies, carrier bodies.

Ministries Interested Admiralty, Ministry of Aircraft Production, Ministry of Supply.

A.A. SHELLS, Friday night 21st January

Slight damage was caused, but there was no loss of production.

S.R. Nine Elms Marshalling Yard, Battersea, London, S.W.

(Listed Railway Key Point) Ministry Interested: Ministry of War Transport.

A.A. Shell 0515hours Saturday 22nd January.

Slight damage was caused to trucks.

HARLAND & WOLFF LTD, London Works, Woolwich Manor Way, North Woolwich, London E.16.

Production: Naval and Merchant ship repairs, barge building.

Ministry Interested: Admiralty.

A.A. Shell Morning Saturday 22nd January.

A wooden shed was destroyed and 2 steel plates were damaged. Blast damage was caused to windows. Production was not affected.

NOT ENEMY ACTION...KEY POINTS AFFECTED

G.W & L.N.E.R., West Wycombe Station, Buckinghamshire.

Crashed aircraft 1040 hours Wednesday 19th January.

An aircraft crashed here buckling up the line and causing a fire at the signal box. Traffic was operated over a single line until 1730 hours on the same day when normal working was resumed.

L.M.S.R, Widnes, Cheshire

DERAILMENT 1550 hours Wednesday 19th January.

A brake van and two wagons were derailed damaging the up and down lines. Traffic was diverted through the goods yard until 0745 hours on the following day when normal working was resumed.

L.M.S, Dutton, Lancashire.

DERAILMENT 2200 hours Wednesday 19th January.

Six trucks were derailed. Single line working was in operation until 0940 hours on the following day, when normal working was resumed.

Luftwaffe Losses – Second Raid - 21st-22nd January 1944

Do217 M U5+CK 2/KG 2 WNr 86017

Runwell Mental Hospital, Wickford, Essex. 05.15 hrs.

Took off from Villa-Roche at 03.45 hrs for London. Apparently hit by AA fire, it flew low over the hospital travelling in a north-easterly direction with one engine on fire. Shortly afterwards it hit a line of trees at high speed, and crashed when either the tanks or a bomb exploded causing a crater 10 feet deep.

Lt Erich Reiser (F) (Killed CC 9/42), Uffz Erich Kanz (B) (Killed CC 9/42), Uffz Günter Kaplitz (Bf) (Killed CC 9/42), Uffz Georg Sauer (Bm) (Killed CC 9/42).

Ju188 E-1 4/KG2 U5+CM WNr 260316

Failed to return from a sortie to London. Took off from Coulommiers at 03.35 hrs and nothing further ever heard of it.

Ofw Karl Thiel (F) (Missing), Fw Adolf Ehm (B) (Missing), Uffz Franz Kämmerling (Bf) (Missing), Flg Herbert Herok (Bs) (Missing), Flg Herbert Scholz (Bs)(Missing).

Do217 K-1 7/KG2 U5+KR WNr 4442

Took off for London at 03.38 hrs and failed to return.

Uffz Alfred Dümlein (F) (Missing), Uffz Georg Schober (B)(Missing), Uffz Heinrich Onkels (Bf)(Missing), Uffz Werner Thews (Bs) (Missing).

Do217K-1 7/KG2 U5+IR WNr 4492

Took off for London at 03.38 hrs and failed to return.

Uffz Hans Oberländer (F) (Missing), Uffz Herbert Grössl (B)(Missing), Gefr Willi Leberbrecht (Bf) (Missing), Ogefr Hans Mathies (Bs) (Missing).

Do217 K-1 9/KG2 U5+CR WNr 4598

Took off for London at 03.53 hrs and failed to return.

Lt Hans Eggert (F) (Missing), Uffz Johann Rauch (B) (Missing), Ogefr Günther Platsch (Bf) (Missing), Ogefr Max Lindinger (Bs) (Missing).

Me410 A-1 Stab V/KG2 U5+WJ WNr 2338.

Lydd Ranges, Kent. 05.15 hrs.

Aircraft was intercepted by a night-fighter and struck the ground at a very fine angle and high speed as wreckage was scattered over nearly a mile. Markings: U5+WJ, the W was in black outlined in light green. Works number 2338. Black camouflage on lower surfaces, the remainder of the aircraft being dark green.

Major Kurt Heintz Ritterkreuz, Gruppen Kommandeur (F) (Killed Folkestone, Kent).

St Fw Otto Runge (Bf) (Killed NKG) Believed to lay in a grave next to Heintz marked as an unknown airman.

Major Kurt Heintz (left) and St Fw Otto Runge (right) who died when their Me410 crashed on the Lydd Ranges in Kent.

Ju188 2/KG6 3E+MK WNr 260327

Failed to return from a sortie to London, probably shot down by a night fighter.

Oblt Rudolf Haschke, Staffel Kapitan (F) (Missing), Uffz Jaroslav Chobot (B)(Missing), Uffz Jürgen Koch (Bf) (Missing), Fw Gerhard Fürch (Bs) (Missing).

Ju88 6/KG6

Zeebrügge. Crashed during a sortie to London

Uffz Wolfgang Schmidt (F) (Missing), Fw Ernst Argast (B) (Inj), Uffz Werner Seidler (Bf) (Missing), Uffz Theodor Rehn (Bs) (Missing).

Ju88 6/KG6

Crashed at Lacres, south of Samer, France, during a sortie to London.

Fw Arno Kohl (F) (Killed), Uffz Siegfried Kruse (B) (Killed), Ogefr Johann Sussner (Bf) (Killed), Gefr Hans-Georg Dashe (Bs) (Killed).

Ju88 6/KG6

Crashed near St Omer.

Uffz Werner Stark (F) (Inj), Ogefr Kurt Saulich (B) (Inj), Ogefr Heinz Völmer (Bf) (Inj), Uffz Gustav Petershagen (Bs) (Inj).

Ju88 A-4 6/KG 30 4D+EP WNr 550414

Rail embankment, Hop Pocket Pub, Paddock Wood Station, Kent. 04.32 hrs.

Shot down by Sub Lt J. A. Lawley-Wakelin (RNVR) in a 96 Sqn Mosquito.

Started from Eindhoven at 02.20 hrs to attack the Charring Cross area of London. After take off the route was Beauvais, cross the coast at St Valery, gradually climbing, landfall being made near Eastbourne. Over Tonbridge, while at 1,500 ft. aircraft was hit by AA in the starboard engine, although an examination of the wreckage revealed 20 mm strikes in the tail from dead astern and level. The engine failed and in the ensuing chaos the observer baled out. The aircraft crashed with the remaining crew. The survivor joined 6/KG 30 on the afternoon of 21st January and was captured with a broken leg in the small hours of the following morning on his first and last war flight.

Wreckage fell partially in a pond and the rest on marshy ground in the village, most of it being buried.

Lt Hans-Joachim Petzinna (F) (Killed Maidstone, Kent), Fw Conrad Scherer (B) (PoW seriously injured), Gefr Günther Lotz (Bs) (Killed Maidstone, Kent), Ogefr Oswald Schweigel (Bs) (Killed Maidstone, Kent).

He177A-3 2/KG 40 5J+ZL WNr 2231

In sea 6 miles south-east of Hastings, Sussex. 04.29 hrs.

Shot down by F/O Nowell in an 85 Sqn Mosquito.

Started from Chateaudun. Whilst on its way to the target one engine failed and the order to bale out was given. When the observer and bordmechaniker left the aircraft it was over the sea at 20,000 ft. but the wind carried them over land. The remainder of crew either came down in the sea or perished in the aircraft. It is believed that the prisoners from this aircraft gave the names of two men from Lt Melcher's crew that had crashed on return from the first raid (Ogefr Hoffmann and Uffz Schlagkamp) to their interrogators in the place of Uffz Stanjewski and Gefr Morbitzer. Both men were missing and these prisoners are assumed to have been trying to protect their identities, should they be on the run.

The bordmechaniker held the Silver (60) War Flights Badge.

Ofw Alfred Billing (F) (Killed Folkestone, Kent), Fw Heinrich Beitter EKII. (B) (PoW), Fw Otto Hirschfeld (Bf) (Killed Folkestone, Kent), Ofw Franz Andrae EKI (Bm) (PoW injured), Uffz Josef Stanjewski (Bs) (Missing), Gefr Alfred Morbitzer (Bs) (Missing).

Ju88 1/KG54 WNr 550297

Failed to return from a sortie to London.

Uffz Peter Emrich (F) (Missing), Ogefr Johannes Bohrenfeld (B) (Missing), Uffz Helmut Kirschnick (Bf) (Missing), Ogefr Kurt Eschholz (Bs) (Missing).

Ju188 E-1 2/KG66 Z6+CK WNr 260174

Landed at Montdidier airfield with combat damage. 05.45 hrs.

Uffz Albrecht Fröhlich (F) (Inj), Uffz Johannes Müller (B) (Inj).

Ju88A-4 1/KG 76

In sea off Worthing, Sussex. 04.35 hrs.

Hit by AA fire over the coast. Pilot lost control and gave the order to bale out. Two men baled out, but then the pilot regained control and returned safely to base. Started from Varrelbusch to attack London.
Uffz Hermann Hollmann (Killed Littlehampton, Sussex). Gefr Heinz Anskat (Killed Littlehampton, Sussex).

Ju88 A-4 Trop 3/KG 76 F1+BL WNr 822577

Lower Chantry Lane, Canterbury, Kent. 04.50 hrs.

Started from Laon at 02.30 hrs to bomb London. The crew first flew south-west to Beauvais, then to St Valery-en-Caux and from there set course for landfall near Eastbourne. The flight plan allowed for an ETA over the target at 05.00 hrs at a height of 18,000 ft. Crossing the Sussex coast on the way in the aircraft was hit by AA and dived away to starboard, all the crew baling out. The observer was found handing dead from an oast house. The survivors did not know whether the crash was due to fighters or AA fire. The aircraft passed low over Canterbury from the south-west with its engines spluttering and crashed into an area of the town that had previously been devastated by bombing. It burst into flames on impact and the wreckage scattered over a fairly wide area.
Markings: each spinner had a yellow band consisting of a series of triangles very close together and from the nose of the spinner backwards there was a red spiral. The aircraft was camouflaged black on the lower surfaces with blue and green mottle on the upper.
The crew were all newcomers to the unit, this being their second War Flight.
Uffz Kurt Matschin (F) (PoW), Uffz Andreas Marliot (B) (Killed Folkestone, Kent) - found handing dead from an oast house. Ogefr Bernhard Lügering (Bf) (PoW), Ogefr Werner Clauss (Bs) PoW).

Ju88A-4	3/KG76	F1+HL	WNr 300383

Failed to return from a sortie to London.

Lt Ernst Schmidt, (F) (Missing), Ofw Wilhelm Schneider (B) (Missing), Fw Werner Schröder (Bf) (Missing), Ofw Ernst Dierks (Bs) (Killed).

He177 A-3	3/KG100	5J+DL	WNr 332198

Span into the ground after control had been lost 15 km south-east of Dieppe.

Oblt Hans-Werner Von der Dovenmühle (F) (Killed), Uffz Justin Teschner (B) (Killed), Fw Gustav Hanning (Bf) Killed), Fw Rudolf Krützner (Bw) (Killed), Uffz Theodor Patt (Bs) (Killed).

RAE report on He177/F8: -H, dated 23 January 1944 - Technical features

The following preliminary report was issued by the Farnborough staff in respect of the first He177 to come down on British soil;

This He177 was an A-3 variant with DB610 engines (coupled-DB605s)

Armament

Five machine guns were discovered being; one MG151/20; three MG131s; and one MG81.

The MG151/20 is belt-fed and percussion fired. It was fitted within a hand-operated bullet-proof mounting directly behind the rudder. The mounting is reminiscent of, but very much larger than, the type of dorsal mounting found in Ju88s. The armoured portion was approximately 12mm thick and the bullet-proof glass was 3 in. thick. Owing to the mounting's damaged condition it is not possible to give an estimation of its arc of fire. About 150 to 200 rounds were carried for this gun and the loading order was; one HE/I/T/SD and one HE/SD repeating.

One MG131 was situated in an electrically-operated turret on the fuselage top about midway between the main-plane trailing edge and the tail-plane leading edge, which is exactly the same as those fitted on the Do217. Two fixed MG131s were found which may have come from the ventral position. This is the first time fixed guns of this type have been found in bombers and it is probable they were remotely controlled. The position of the MG81 could not be determined. It is probable that other armament will be found when the wreckage is lifted.

Bomb Carriers

Two ETC 2000/XIIAs were fitted, one each under the wings outboard of the engine nacelles. There were two studs, each 1 ¼ in. in diameter projecting from each carrier; on one was painted 'X' and the other '293'. No internal carriers were found but two plates were recovered, which gave the following information;

'Rear support' (by which it is presumed the rear set of bomb carriers in the mount)

SC1000
PC1400
SC1700
SC1800
LMB III

'Forward support' (A type of carrier found on the Do217 that takes eight x SC50 Bombs)

Geruest 8/50
SC250
SC500
SD500
PC1000
LMA III

Armour

Large quantities of armour plate were lying about; so far the only pieces identified are as follows;

i) Pilot's protection that consisted of an 8mm armoured seat with side pieces coming up to the nape of his neck.
ii) A 5mm lid that fitted the dinghy recess.
iii) MG131 turret protection similar to the Do217.
iv) The 12mm plate in the tail gun mounting.

Internal equipment

Apart from the following wireless equipment, very little could be identified;

i) FuG 10 W/T set fitted with a short-wave unit spanning 6 - 12 Mc/s.
ii) Peilgeraet 6 H/F, D/F receiver spanning 150-1200 Kc/s.
iii) FuG 17Z (VHF communications and D/F set) spanning a range from 42.1 to 47.9 Mc/s. This is a new piece of equipment that differs from the FuG 17 in that it has an external D/F loop for (probably) homing onto submarines. A separate wireless report will be issued on this installation.
iv) FuG101A radio altimeter that reads from 0-150 m and 0-750 m.
v) Lotfe. 7D/1 that is used in conjunction with Hs293 units; it was in very bad shape.
vi) Radar equipment - none was found.

Special remarks

A balloon cable-cutter similar to that applied to Ju88s was fitted in the main-plane's leading edges. Hot air de-icing, led from the engine nacelles into the leading edges via a 5" diameter asbestos-lagged pipe. Tail unit de-icing system could not be ascertained.

Fully flexible self-sealing tanks were found in the wings.

The crew all wore electrically-heated clothing and parachute harnesses that had a new type of release mechanism; this will be subject to a separate report. Single-seater dinghies were also worn but no trace of a large dinghy was found.

Author's Notes

i) The investigators clearly confused the MG131 paired weaponry with the MG81Z that was the standard fitting for the ventral position, although they were correct in the assumption that the guns were remotely controlled – in this case from the forward dorsal turret location. Nor were they aware at this stage that the single MG81 was located in the cockpit nose.

ii) The FuG101 original equipment provided a very poor and therefore potentially lethal impression of the aircraft's height in the lower height band as recorded in the section dealing with internal equipment.

A Heinkel 177 5J+HL of 3/KG100 which crashed on 24th January 1944, one day after the RAE report on the new type was issued.

Non Operational Losses 24th to 25th January 1944

He177 A-3 3/KG100 5J+HL WNr 332217

24/1/44 Crashed 15 km north-east of Antwerp during a non-operational flight; possibly shot down by AA fire.

Oblt Heinz Kröcher (F) (Killed), Uffz Karl Fritz (B)(Killed), Uffz Gerhard Schmidt (Bf)(Killed), Uffz Johann Fischer (Bw) (Killed), Ogfr Hans Werner Rülke* (Bs) (Inj), Fw Heinrich Middeke (Bs) (Killed), Uffz Heinz Gerhard Kurt Raczek (1 wart) (Killed), Ogfr Leonhard Maier (Fallschirmwart) (Inj).

** Rülke was captured later in the war and was still detained in the UK in 1947.*

Ogfr Hans Werner Rülke (left) who survived the crash of He177 5J+HL only to end up as a POW later in the war (right).

Do217K-1 7/KG2 U5+HR WNr 4494

25/1/44 Crashed at Osnabrück during a night time non-operational training flight.

Oblt Erich Hellwig (F) (Killed), Uffz Johann Klarmann (Bf) (Inj), Fw Karl-Heinz Henne (Bs) (Inj).

Opposite page: Coastal gunners examine the shattered canopy of a Ju88 brought down off Tilbury on 29th January 1944.

CHAPTER FOUR

Still Groping in the Dark

Chapter Four

'Still Groping in the dark'

28th-29th January 1944

Although the overall operational strength of the *'Steinbock'* Gruppen was still high following the 21st/22nd raid the bombers remained on the ground for all but one of the ensuing six nights. Even then the raid launched on the 28th was minuscule in terms of numbers dispatched, which were sixteen Me410s and ten FW190s. The attackers swept in over Kent to deliver their attacks in a twenty-minute spell, and returned home with just one Me410 of V/KG2 damaged. Squadron Leader Parker-Rees of 96 Squadron made a claim for an Me410 damaged, he fired 400 rounds, but two cannons jammed and he was forced to break off his chase.

Fighter Command lost a Mosquito and its two crew when Sub Lieutenant Blundell and Sub Lieutenant Parker of 85 Squadron reported at 22.40 hours they were abandoning their Mosquito over the Channel due to an engine fire. Despite a search they were not found.

RAF Intelligence summary of bombing 28-29 January 1944

Twenty-two aircraft flew over south-east England and East Anglia at well separated points. One aircraft was plotted over London.

Bombing Reports:

Essex:

Southend - 1 HE, slight damage to the pier.

Southminster - HE, 6 houses seriously damaged, 5 seriously injured.

Kent:

Tonge - 1 HE.

Bishopsbourne - 1 HE slight damage to a farmhouse.

Yalding - HE 4 houses damaged, 2 seriously injured.

Bexley - House damaged by AA shell.

WEEKLY APPRECIATION OF DAMAGE TO KEY POINTS AND PROGRESS OF REPAIRS.

Period from: 09.00 hours Wednesday 26th January 1944.
To: 09.00 hours Wednesday 2nd February 1944.

GENERAL

Land-targets in this country were attacked on two nights during the past week.

On Friday/Saturday night (28th/29th January) a mixed force totalling 22 aircraft made penetrations over parts of East Anglia and South-Eastern England, but they accomplished almost nothing.

Early on the following night Saturday/Sunday (29th/30thJanuary) there was an attack intended for London which, by present standards, may be called heavy. The force overland is estimated at 100 long-range bombers, and the total in operation on this night at 161, the largest effort on any one day or night since the enemy`s reaction to the Combined Operations at Dieppe on 19th August, 1942 (when he flew 175 sorties). As in the attack on London on 21st/22nd January of this year, there was a considerable spill, mostly in South-Eastern England and in the Southern part of East Anglia. The heavy A.A. barrage appears to have deterred most of the enemy pilots from pressing home their attacks: there was considerable cloud on this night, and visibility was reported as "moderate to good." None the less, the enemy met with rather more success on this night than on 21st/22nd January: the key-point picture is similar to that for the night of the 21st/22nd but civilian casualties are higher. On this night, 343 fires were attended by the N.F.S. The enemy`s losses in aircraft were 5% compared to over 17% for the night of the 21st/22nd. On this night the Kent Coast was shelled in reply to our own batteries.

Damage to the essential war-effort during the week involved 17 key-points including 3 Air Ministry properties: in addition, there were 6 railway incidents. Except perhaps for a ten-pump fire at the Surrey Commercial Docks on 29th/30th, none of the damage so far reported has proved of a major character.

Civilian casualties during the week (all on the night of 29th/30th) total 51 fatal and 124 serious: of those, 41 fatal and 116 serious occurred in London.

Luftwaffe Non Operational Loss

Ju52 I/KG6 G6+MU

29/1/44 Shot down with 23 men on board by a night fighter. Crashed near Spa, Belgium, while ferrying ground crew of 1 and 2 Staffel KG6.

Ofw Herbert Stuhr, Fw Helmuth Thorn, Gefr Karl Wiegand, Fw Werner Rothenberg, Uffz Fritz Jänisch, Ofw Fritz Kreidler, Fw Ehrard Binner, Gefr Wolf-Dieter Gerlach, Uffz Jozef Pichler, Ogefr Alfred Hecht, Uffz Willi Riegel, all killed.

Major Bomber Command Operations

22nd to 29th January 1944

27-28 January Berlin	567 killed	530 aircraft	33 lost
28-29 January Berlin	*	677 aircraft	46 lost

* number of dead unknown, but 'considerable'.

29th-30th January 1944

It was fully eight days before the second *'Steinbock'* thrust was launched, with an obvious hope that better success would attend its completion than on 21st/22nd January. This time a total of eleven Gruppen would participate. II/KG2 was making its debut, but the Ju88s of II and III/KG30 would not again feature in the campaign until 14th/15th March. The He177s of I/KG40 were now to be permanently withdrawn. In addition I/KG100 and the FW190s of I/SKG10 were absent from the night's battle order. I/SKG10 had operated along with the Me410s of KG51 the night before, a possible reason for their absence.

The War-time Diary of Miss J. M. Oakman – Chelsea Saturday 29 Jan 1944

20.15 sirens. Guns soon afterwards, as loud as the old days. Odd planes passed over – various fires showed round about from afar distant. Saw some flares and "fire pot" blow up E of Victoria. Shrapnel bits fell about like hail.

21.37 all clear. Three planes came down by gunfire.

I/KG54

At 16.30 hours on 29th January thirty crews of I/KG54 congregated at their holding airfield of Wittmundhafen were briefed for the second *'Steinbock'* raid on London. Hauptmann Sehrt (Gruppenkommandeur) conducted the main briefing with a separate briefing for the Bordfunkers carried out by Leutnant Quaiser (Gruppennachrichtensoffizier). The area to be attacked was east of Tower Bridge, with Hackney as the epicentre; bombs would all be released within nine minutes of the 21.00 hours ETA over the target area. An *'Ablauflinie'* would be laid, but specified Gruppe crews would supplement the target markers by flying to the right of the *'Ablauflinie'* before depositing their incendiary loads above the right-hand boundary of the marked-out zone. According to PoW interrogations made subsequent to this raid, I/KG76 were reputed to have bombed earlier with the aid of skymarkers.

The course to London was initially made to a *'Drehscheinwerfer'* (rotating searchlight) at Dalen, after which a further navigational aid would be provided by *'Lux'* buoys dropped in the sea north of Ostend. The bombers would be at 5,000 metres on crossing in over East Anglia with Colchester as a reference point. A quick course change from west to south would then be reversed northwards towards the target area. Once bombing was completed, the pilots having descended 1,000 metres after crossing-in, the bombers would continue north and then east out over the Essex coast. However, their destination would now be an un-named airfield near Rheims, with the bombers turning over the North Sea, from where they would complete the final leg.

Take-off commenced at 18.30 hours with all thirty crews (a figure representing one-sixth of the total attacking force) getting airborne. Among the 3 Staffel crews was that led by Unteroffizier Heinz Goergen in B3+AL, which bore two AB 1000 wing-mounted containers and ten SC50 bombs in the bomb-bay. This bomber was normally flown by the Staffelkapitän, but was allotted to Goergen on this occasion since his usual aircraft, B3+IL was un-serviceable.

Goergen duly reached Dalen and commenced to climb; then when reaching two points close to either side of the 'Lux' buoy indicator Unteroffizier Zehetner took two additional fixes on Sonne 5 and a *Funkfeuer* beacon. A final fix procedure was carried out short of the Essex coast after Goergen informed Unteroffizier Sprenger that the bomber was passing through the equi-signal of a *'Knickebein'* beam (probably from the station at Calais), whereupon the Beobachter took a fix upon this as well as Sonne 5.

The briefed weather conditions of reasonable visibility proved to be well astray and in fact Goergen's first indication that he had crossed-in was the reflection of searchlights. At this stage the aircraft's altitude of 4,000 metres was well below the briefed height and a further complication lay in the fact that the crew was ahead of schedule and also believed to be off course.

A confusing situation became critical when the bomber was homed in upon by a Beaufighter up from Coltishall flown by Flight Sergeant Neal. He had sighted his target against the moonlight, but having closed to 150 yards, he missed with his first burst of fire. However, the violent evasive manoeuvring now indulged in by Goergen availed him nothing, because a second and third burst struck home with the latter causing the starboard engine to explode. The last sight of the Ju88 was of it plummeting steeply into a cloud layer, followed shortly after by a flash and glow.

On board the stricken machine Goergen had promptly dumped his mixed incendiary/bomb load and swung onto a reverse course for home, but to no avail. Fire had taken firm hold and the crew was ordered to bale out, an action that only Goergen failed to survive when the Ju88 plunged into the ground at Barham near Ipswich.

Belts of 20mm cannon shells are loaded into a night fighter Beaufighter for the coming night's operations.

Combat Report

Flight Sergeant L.W. Neal, 68 Squadron Beaufighter

F/Sgt. Neal and F/Sgt. Eastwood* took off from Coltishall 1811 hours for G.C.I. and S/L Co-operation, and at 2025 hours were vectored 180 degrees to intercept hostile 52E. They flew on this vector at 12,000 ft. for approximately 10 minutes, were then vectored 260 degrees and obtained a contact at a mile and a half at 2030 hours, position M7395. The Beaufighter closed in and from 1,000 ft. saw an E/a, which was identified as a JU188 when silhouetted against the moon. F/Sgt Neal had closed to starboard and slightly underneath at 15,000 ft, I.A.S. 190/200; he dropped back to 150 yards and gave a half second burst of cannon fire 10 degrees to starboard but missed the target.

Violent evasive action by the e/a did not shake off the Beaufighter which, however, began to lose ground. With a second burst at 250 yards our pilot obtained strikes on the fuselage causing the e/a to turn steeply to starboard. Our aircraft followed at 300 yards fired again for two seconds 30 degrees to port, allowing two rings deflection. The starboard engine was hit and blew up, the e/a continuing its turn, with smoke issuing from it. It disappeared in cloud, diving steeply and the Beaufighter crew observed a vivid flash from the ground, with subsequent glow.

Confirmation of the claim was provided when Suffolk Police found the wrecked aircraft at Shrubland Hall, position M5870, N.N.W. of Ipswich. Three of the crew are believed to have been captured.

**F/Sgt Neal and his navigator were on their first operational flight, Neal having thus realised an ambition that dated from January 1941 when he joined the Squadron as an AC1 electrician. He left after a few months and returned three weeks ago as a pilot.*

Documentation found on the crashed I/KG54 bomber yielded further information on Luftwaffe navigational aids. Visual assistance was provided as follows:

Searchlights	(Time of operation)
Kette 3 and 4	X-60 to X-20 minutes
	X+30 to X+70 minutes
Searchlight dome (Rotterdam)	X-60 to X-20 minutes
	X+30 to X+70 minutes
Schraube 1 and 2	X-50 to X-20 minutes
Schraube 3 and 4	X-10 to X+40 minutes
Bremen (Perpendicular searchlight)	X+75 to X+130 minutes
Münster/Handorf	
(Two intersecting searchlights)	X+55 to X+110 minutes

'Kette' and *'Schraube'* were low-powered directional searchlights operating in pairs, which dipped continuously in the direction of pre-determined points on the British coast. These were also available for the bombers' homeward route but not on the initial *'Steinbock'* raid.

Notes on *'Knickbein'* were also unearthed, on this occasion involving four frequencies between 30.4 and 31.7 Mc/s. Unteroffizier Zehetner claimed one was from a transmitter based in the Pas-de-Calais region, laid on a bearing of 2 degrees and believed by his interrogator to relate to the station at Boulogne.

KG6

KG6 had a disastrous time on this raid. During the day a Ju52 transport aircraft had been caught on a transfer flight by prowling fighters and shot down; eleven of the 23 groundcrew aboard were killed. By the following morning KG6 had lost seven aircraft and 23 men.

Vechta was the start-point for II/KG6 on 29th/30th January, when thirty crews were called to a briefing outlined by Hauptmann Maier (Gruppenkommandeur). Although details of the briefing gathered by RAF intelligence were very sparse it was likely that the Gruppe's course to London generally paralleled that of I/KG54. Unlike the Wittmundhafen-based unit, the II/KG6 airmen having completed their bomb-runs would then head southeast towards their regular operational airfield at Le Culot.

This Gruppe took off from 19.00 hours onward, but each pilot flew at a specified speed and climb-rate that was intended to bring the entire unit together in a loose formation before crossing-out over the North Sea. Oxygen-level altitude was not apparently reached until around 90 minutes after take-off.

Unteroffizier Stapelfeldt was the Bordfunker aboard a II/KG6 Ju88. He believed the outward route took his Ju88 over France and that he saw a succession of flares over 'the Channel' as well as a later mix of white, green and red flares in the direction of London.

According to him, the bomber had just crossed-in when it was attacked by a night fighter. The apparent scale of damage to the tail section induced the pilot, Leutnant Berstecher, to order his crew to jump. Stapelfeldt, the Bordfunker, and gunner Unteroffizier Schilde jumped. However, the recorded bale-out time of 21.09 hours near Biddenden, Kent, in British records would have accorded with the bomber being on the way back, as opposed to inbound, especially since the Gruppe's target ETA was roughly 20.00 hours.

The 96 Squadron Mosquito pilot who submitted his report identifying this Ju88 as the one he attacked referred to the two airmen baling out and at a time close to that stated in the A.D.I.(K) report. Stapelfeldt's crew were approaching their twentieth operational sortie and so were hardly inexperienced in operational flying, a factor which further intensifies, rather than clarifies, the mystery.

Stapelfeldt and Schilde had baled out on orders from Leutnant Berstecher who then successfully regained control of the Ju88. The fourth crewmember was killed when 3E+ON was abandoned near St. Omer; this was Unteroffizier Kitlaus (Beobachter) whose parachute failed to open.

The morale of the two PoWs was assessed as 'very high' since no information was gleaned after 24 hours solid questioning. However, gunner Schilde was further described as 'an exceptionally unintelligent type', a status that was unlikely to yield positive results for the interrogators. A second comment in the report assumed that security must have been tightened within Luftwaffe ranks since all the PoWs captured from the 29th January sortie displayed similar resistance. By the time a follow up report was issued dated 17th February A.D.I.(K) (the interrogators) had succeeded in their task. The report contained four full pages of information on II/KG6 activities and staff during 1943, so the initial reticence displayed by these two men was of little consequence!

I/KG76

All available crews were to hold themselves in readiness for a briefing on a London raid that was duly held at 17.00 hours. Taking off from Varrelbusch, the crews were to head for a W/T beacon *(Funkfeuer)* near the Dutch border, after which the navigators were to rely on D/R methods to reach their target. The return leg would be to Varrelbusch unless adverse weather intervened, in which case a diversion into Laon/Couvron was recommended. The target area would be marked out by pathfinder aircraft, and indicated by an approach line of seven white flares followed by three red target marker flares. A line of green and white flares would be laid at right angles across this first line between the last of the white flares and the first red target marker flare. Any variations on this flare pattern were to be ignored. As with I/KG54, the entire Gruppe was to complete bombing within fifteen minutes of the 20.10 hours ETA. Bombing was to be conducted from 6,000 metres in a shallow dive.

Sixteen crews took off at 60-second intervals around 18.30 hours. Feldwebel Türke's Ju88 - F1+AK made unexpectedly fast time, so much so that he was forced to circle east of London having arrived too early for the briefed ETA. The errant bomber was picked upon by one or two night-fighters according to Unteroffizier Rinke, the Bordschutz. The twin AB 500 containers were jettisoned. A further severe strike induced the pilot to call for a bale out, to which Rinke and Feldwebel Zillmann responded; Zillmann's parachute failed and he fell to his death, but Rinke landed safely. RAF intelligence believed that the Ju88 exploded and the remains fell into the Thames estuary, taking Türke and Unteroffizier Dernberg to their deaths, but the pilot successfully regained control and crash landed at Grevillers, France.

Feldwebel Rinke's subsequent interrogation contained an interesting comment as regards the use of *'Düppel'*. He was the second KG76 PoW to assert that his crew had been alerted to scatter the metal strips particularly when a scratching sound was picked up over the intercom, this being ascribed to the British ground stations and/or night-fighter radar systems having locked onto the aircraft!

Summary

To the single loss over England during this raid were added 16 more aircraft and crews lost at sea or crashed in occupied Europe. Considering that the recorded number of bombers reaching London was between 15 and 30, this loss must have been extremely disappointing to General Peltz and his staff. On the other hand a measure of destruction had been inflicted upon several inner-city boroughs with 145 fires attended to by the NFS, although casualties were 'light' at 41 dead.

Bombing Incidents

In Valance Wood Road, Dagenham, two families were sheltering in Morrison Shelters when bombs struck. 38 year-old Mrs Florence Hodson passed her young son and a neighbour's two children through the wreckage to rescue workers. Sadly her bravery cost her her own life as she died shortly after from burns received during the rescue; her husband was serving with the army in Italy at the time. Nearby a young soldier home on leave, 19 year old Private Buckley, was hit by shrapnel and died the next day.

In Ilford the Dane School in Melbourne Road was hit by incendiary bombs resulting in a blaze that was put out by the Fire Brigade. Next day Mr Saunders the headmaster caught two boys stealing from his study, the culprits were handed over to the Police. Later the school's unsafe bell tower had to be demolished.

Nearby in Cranley Drive nine people were killed when an HE bomb demolished several houses.

An HE bomb exploded at Ramsden Heath and demolished a hut on an army camp. According to various reports the number of soldiers killed in the incident was either 3 or 23.

Luftwaffe Losses 29th-30th January 1944

Ju188E-1 5/KG2 U5+FN WNr 260241

Left engine caught fire and crew baled out near Soesterberg.

Uffz Kurt Schneider (Bs) (Killed). Rest of crew safe.

Do217M-1 9/KG2 U5+FT WNr 2899

Failed to return from a sortie to London.

Fw Kurt Kiessling (F) (Missing), Uffz Karl-Heinz Noss (B) (Missing), Ogefr Hans Gossner (Bf) (Missing), Uffz Werner Bals (Bs) (Missing).

Uffz Karl-Heinz Noss, who was aboard Do217M U5+FT when it went missing on the 29th January raid on London.

Ju188 2/KG6 3E+PK WNr 260325

Failed to return from a sortie to London - probably shot down.

Uffz Heinz Gaffke (F) (Missing), Karl-Heinz Damaschke (B) (Missing), Günther Dietrich (Bf) (Missing), Gefr Franz Berger (Bs) (Missing).

Ju88 4/KG6

Crashed at Ulbeck nr Hasselt, Belgium, on return from London.

Uffz Heinrich Oppermann (F) (Killed). Rest of crew baled out safely.

Ju88 5/KG6 3E+ON WNr 550426

Possibly attacked by F/O Hibbert in a 96 Sqn Mosquito. 21.09 hrs.

Started from Vechta at 19.30 hours. While flying above cloud at 12,000 feet the aircraft was attacked by a night-fighter and after being hit in the tail unit the pilot appeared to loose control, giving the order to bale out. The two crew who did so were captured near Biddenden, Kent, but the pilot and observer regained control and made it to St Omer where they baled out. Uffz Kitlaus was killed when his parachute failed, but Lt Berstecher landed safely – He was killed on his next operation on 4 February

The wireless operator was on his second war flight.

Lt Hans Berstecher (F), Uffz Kitlaus (B), Uffz Peter Stapelfeldt (Bf) (PoW), Uffz Heinz Schilde (Bs) (PoW).

Ju88 6/KG6

Crashed on take off for London at Vechta airfield.

Uffz Leo Bytomski (F) (Killed), Uffz Richard Singer (B) (Killed), Uffz Rudolf Emminghaus (Bf) (Killed), Uffz Kurt Lindner (Bs) (Killed).

Ju88 8/KG6

Failed to return from a sortie to London.

Ofw Arnold Jach (F) (Missing), Uffz Friedrich Schückler (B) (Missing), Ogefr Wilhelm Hinderkopf (Bf) (Missing), Gefr Gerhard Brandmeyer (Bs) (Missing).

Ju88 9/KG6

Crashed and exploded after take off 20 km north of Diepholz.

Hpmn Helmut Schüttke (F) (Killed), Uffz Martin Bitriol (B)(Killed), Uffz Max Seidel (Bf) (Killed), Uffz Johann Tessner (Bs) (Killed).

Ju88 **9/KG6**

Failed to return from a sortie to London.

Uffz Franz Lizon (F) (Missing), Fw Heinz Hermann (B) (Missing), Uffz Herbert Nissel (Bf) (Missing), Gefr Gustav-Adolf Grafe (Bs) (Missing).

He177A-3 **1/KG40** **CJ+FV** **WNr 535748**

Crashed at Münster on return from London.

Oblt. Günter Kampf (F) (Killed), Gefr Willi Horn (B) (Killed), Ofw Gerhard Kromer (Bf) (Killed), Uffz Kurt Zinsmeister (Bm) (Killed). Rest of crew safe.

Ju88 **3/KG54** **B3+GL** **WNr 800652**

Failed to return from a sortie to London.

Uffz Heinz Egon Götz (F) (Missing), Fw Bernhard Günther Göllen (B) (Missing), Uffz Heinrich Jastack (Bf) (Missing), Uffz Augustin Emilian Maierhofer (Bs) (Missing).

Ju88A-14 **3/KG54** **B3+AL** **WNr 300228**

Shrubland Hall, Codenham, Suffolk. 20.40 hrs.

Shot down by F/Sgt L W Neal in a 68 Sqn Beaufighter on his first operational flight.

Based at Wittmundhafen, but for this raid moved to a Dutch base, from which the whole Gruppe took off to attack London. Some twenty-five to thirty aircraft of I/KG 54, including nine of the 3rd staffel took part in this raid. Whilst on the way to the target this aircraft was attacked from above by a night-fighter and the port engine put out of action, the bombs were jettisoned and the pilot headed for home. Soon after the aircraft caught fire and the pilot gave the order to bale out. The aircraft exploded on hitting the ground.

Markings: A in black outlined in yellow, L in black outlined in white. Camouflage on the upper surfaces was a dark green with wavy grey lines. The under surfaces were a dark grey. Call sign PI+SV.

Uffz Heinz Paul Josef Goergen (F) (Killed CC1/43), Uffz Joachim Fritz Hermann Sprenger (B) (PoW injured), Uffz Alois Zehetner (Bf) (PoW), Uffz Wolfgang Gerd Brüning (Bs) (PoW).

Ju88 **4/KG54** **B3+FP** **WNr 3862**

Crashed on operations near Dinant Houx in Belgium. Possibly shot down by a night fighter.

Uffz Max Schöpner (F) (Killed), Uffz Ferdinand Ruess (B) (Killed), Ogefr Max Reissmann (Bf) (Killed), Gefr Herbert Diebold (Bs) (Killed).

Ju88 6/KG54 B3+WP WNr 801385

Failed to return from a sortie to London.

Uffz Rudolf Baumgartner (F) (Missing), Uffz Josef Poster (B)(Missing), Uffz Johannes Scholz (Bf) (Missing), Ogefr Siegfried Madritsch (Bs) (Missing).

Ju88S-1 3/KG66 Z6+CL WNr 140598

Failed to return from a sortie to London.

Uffz Karl Ludwig Hoffmann (F) (Missing), Ogefr Erich Hege (Bo) (Missing), Uffz Werner Courtois (Bf) (Missing), Uffz Johann Platzer (Bs) (Missing).

Ju88A-4 2/KG 76 F1+AK WNr 1226

Whilst on its way to London, the aircraft was hit by AA fire or a night-fighter and the pilot gave the order to bale out. The gunner was captured uninjured, but the wireless operator fell 100 yards away from his opened parachute near Tilbury, Essex at 21.50 hrs. The survivor claimed sixty-six war flights. There was no trace of the aircraft, which led RAF Intelligence Officers to assume that it may have come down in the Thames Estuary. The pilot actually successfully crash landed at Grevillers, France.

Fw Türke EKI (F) (Safe), Uffz Dernburg EKI (B) (Safe), Fw Siegfried Zillmann EKI (Bf) (Killed CC 1/378), Uffz Adolf Rinke EKI (Bs) (PoW).

Ju88A-4 3/KG76 F1+CK WNr 142379

Crashed near Athies, France, during a sortie to London.

Fw Franz Christel (F) (Killed), Ogefr Heinrich Holthaus (B) (Killed), Ogefr Christian Fischer (Bf) (Killed) Ogefr Franz Gleissner (Bs) (Killed).

Fighter Command Claims, not attributable to a particular loss

A claim was made for a Ju88 destroyed at 20.44 hrs near Needham-Market by Lt R P Cross (RNVR) in a 68 Sqn Beaufighter.

Major Bomber Command Operations
30th January to 3rd February 1944

30-31st January Berlin-1,000 killed* 534 aircraft-33 lost

*** approximate figure.**

February 1944

Falling numbers of serviceable aircraft, compared to the opening raid on 21st/22nd January, coupled with very poor bombing results and high losses boded ill for the ultimate success of *'Steinbock'*. However, General Peltz must have sensed even prior to the start of the campaign that the net effect upon the British war effort could be no more than a temporary blip upon its advancement. The central areas of London, although containing a notable degree of war production as well as a key dockland system, provided but a small element of Britain's overall military output. Even if London could be regularly attacked, the sheer scale of the city's spread would probably defeat the available bomber force's bombing effort, even should its strength in aircraft and crews be maintained at its initial peak. In the meanwhile, the remaining industrial zones within Britain could continue to function unhindered, while the build-up to 'D-Day' that the Germans were well aware of would also proceed unhindered. *'Steinbock'* had been created as a 'revenge' campaign in the face of the Allied combined bombing offensive, and to date was not even achieving that emotionally-pitched end!

The Dornier 217E was already outdated by early 1944, however a few examples were pressed into service with KG2 alongside the later K and M variants.

3rd February 1944

The first major operation of the month was briefed on the third day of February, with ten of the eleven Gruppen involved in the previous raids being joined by I/KG100 and SKG10. I/KG100, having flown the 21st/22nd January sortie from Chateaudun, was now based at Rheine, from where it would take-off and return, the other units flying out of their usual assigned airfields. This raid was to be conducted in two waves, with the first launched between 19.00 and 19.30 hours. Once again the number of bombers releasing their loads over the capital was very small in relation to the overall force, which itself was modest. The last bomber cleared London a mere 40 minutes after the attack began. The units taking part in the first raid comprised just 26 Me410s and nineteen FW190s, which released a mix of SC250 and SC500 bombs.

Luftwaffe Losses 3rd February 1944

FW 190G-3 **3/SKG10** **WNr 160465**

Crashed on return from England at Amiens-Pierre.

Uffz Hermann Wurster (Killed).

FW 190G-3 **2/SKG10** **Wnr 160822**

Crashed at Les Essarts, 5 km west of Fourmont, Neufchatel.

Lt Friedrich Engel (Killed).

The body of the pilot was found with an unopened parachute on 6th February.

3th-4th February 1944

The War-time Diary of Miss J. M. Oakman – Chelsea Friday 4 Feb 1944

04.50 sirens. Good gunfire later.

06.10 all clear. The barrage was good and heavy and flares green and yellow – all round – also the "dropping rain" – (big IB. firepot blowing up in air). Planes could be heard diving and then clearing off. 70 planes crossed the coast – 20 reached London and 5 were brought down. (One up Estuary). There were two big fires – one NE was burning well after 7 o'c – the other was E.

No greater degree of success attended the second raid that developed in the early hours of the 4th from 04.25 hours and lasted 95 minutes. German records again paint a positive image; "During the second part of the night 210 out of 235 bombers dispatched were over London. Weather 7/10 cloudy with good view above clouds. Defences were weak. Attack as a whole regarded as satisfactory as the majority of bombers dropped bombs on lit-up areas. Heavy fires were observed. 500 kg scattering fire-bombs were used". The reference to 'lit-up areas and heavy fires' must have extended well beyond London's boundaries in the light of British reports.

A similar pattern of geographically widespread bombing was seen as in the previous raids. Minor incidents were reported from as far from London as Gloucestershire (where the village school at Upper Slaughter was set alight by incendiaries) Wiltshire, Bedfordshire and Suffolk. The wanderings of the crews could easily be ascribed to an indifferent to poor standard of navigation. However, General Peltz had decided to ignore Göring's stricture that all raids be conducted during the periods of maximum moonlight. The quality of the pathfinder effort, primarily by I/KG66, was another key issue, since accurate marking was crucial to the success or failure of the planned attack.

25 tons out of the 190 tons of bombs released over south-east Britain fell on London. Five bombs landed in the borough of Wimbledon, but their effect was notable since they were estimated to be in the SC500 category at least. Twenty-seven houses were destroyed, 48 seriously damaged and over 320 received minor damage. Casualties in Wimbledon were five killed and six seriously injured. Individuals suffered the inevitable bad or good fortune. One fatality involved an elderly woman who was visiting, while a man survived the destruction of his house, but his daughter was killed. In contrast, a sleeping man was revealed to the public after the entire front of his house was blasted away. A family that normally occupied their Anderson Shelter in raids had taken the option of remaining in their house – the shelter was destroyed! Several domestic animals thought killed in bombed out houses appeared out of wreckage days after the raid to the relief of their owners. One dog was found by rescuers as they began to dig for survivors in the rubble of a house because they saw its tail wagging. A cat dug itself out the wreck of its former home after being buried for four days.

The danger from above was never totally confined to Luftwaffe' bombs, as a tragic incident in Croydon demonstrated on this night. AA shells did not always explode in the air; rather these (fortunately rare) exceptions described a deadly arc back to earth. In this instance a shell struck one end of the Brighton Road, killing two civilians outright and fatally injuring a third.

The total casualties reported were 31 killed and 88 injured, of which 16 killed and 45 injured were in Greater London.

For the Luftwaffe a disturbing, and potentially demoralising, aspect of the raid related to the casualty rate. Of the fifteen bombers that were lost just one had fallen in Britain, an astonishing eleven 'vanished' completely and are presumed lost at sea, and three crashed in occupied Europe. One of the pilots from 5/KG6, whose Ju88 crashed near Malmedy in Belgium, was Leutnant Berstecher. He had survived the loss of his bomber near St. Omer when returning minus two of his crew on 29th/30th January raid, but was killed on this occasion.

Mixed Fortunes for 488 (NZ) Squadron

488 (NZ) Squadron Operational Record Book
Bradwell Bay

3.2.44 01.45 F/Sgt Watson.K.J. (Pilot) and F/Sgt Edwards. E.F. (Nav/Rad) both New Zealand, were killed during an exercise with searchlights near the airfield, possibly due to dazzle and momentarily losing control. This was a most promising crew and a great loss to "B" Flight and the Squadron.

4.2.44 04.30 F/Sgt Vlotman C.J. (Dutch) and Sgt Wood.J.L. (British) intercepted and destroyed a Dornier 217; after a long chase the e/a was shot down into the sea 40 miles East of Foreness. The first success by an N.C.O. crew and by the only Dutch Night Fighter Pilot in the Royal Air Force made a most popular "victory".

Essex Police reported.

05.30 hrs 6 HEs landed on a military camp at Grays damaging huts and injuring one soldier, IBs damaged shops at West Tilbury.

05.40 hrs 4 HEs at Vange killed 5 people and injured 41 more 16 of them seriously, 11 bungalows were destroyed and a shop and 34 houses badly damaged.

05.45 hrs IBs at Brentwood caused major fire at a school with lesser damage to 21 shops a pub, and 130 houses. At Upminster 2 HE's damaged 240 houses (16 seriously) 14 shops and a school.

06.10 hrs. IBs destroyed the Tilbury Hotel.*

**At the time of the attack about 120 people were staying in the hotel. Being made largely of wood it burnt fiercely, but all the guests bar one were thought to have escaped. In April, as the wreckage was being cleared, the body of an army captain was discovered. He was identified as Captain W. E. Bridge who had last been seen calling for help from a balcony.*

Luftwaffe Losses 3rd-4th February 1944

Ju188E-1 | 6/KG2 | U5+KP | WNr 260216

Maplin Sands, 2 miles east of Shoeburyness, Essex. 05.40 hrs

Failed to return from a sortie to London, after taking off from Münster Handorf at 03.25 hrs. The aircraft dived steeply into the sand and disintegrated, being only just visible at low water. At the time police found parts of an aircraft and bodies as well as an ID disk No 58215/198, which later research shows belonged to Ogefr Werner Zwintschert.

Uffz Franz Flamme (F) (Missing), Ogefr Werner Zwintschert (B) (Missing), Uffz Wolfgang Niemayer (Bf) (Missing), Ogefr Willi Piller (Bs) (Missing), Ogefr Johann Malacha (Bs) (Missing).

Uffz Franz Flamme

Do217M-1 | 7/KG2 | U5+JR

Failed to return form a sortie to England.

Fw Gottlieb Schnebel (F) (Missing), Uffz Oskar Seiler (B) (Missing), Uffz Karl May (Bf) (Missing), Uffz Hermann Witzel (Bm) (Missing).

Do217M-1 | 8/KG2 | U5+CH | WNr 40728

Failed to return form a sortie to England.

Uffz Erich Schewe (F) (Missing), Gefr Karl Kliever-Lorenz (B) (Missing), Ogefr Helmut Kräuter (Bf) (Missing), Uffz Franz Bemmerl (Bs) (Missing).

Ju188E-1 | 2/KG66 | Z6+DK | WNr 260178

Failed to return from operations.

Lt Werner Exner (F) (Missing), Uffz Walder Reimer (B) (Missing), Uffz Joachim Bialas (Bf) (Missing), Uffz Ernst Schreer (B) (Missing), Uffz Werner Zieske (Bw) (Missing).

Ju188 3/KG6 3E+VH WNr 260333

Failed to return from a sortie to London-probably shot down.

Fw H. Winter (Missing), Fw Ehrhardt (Missing), Fw Max Gunther Xylander (Missing), Fw Ottenjams (Missing), Flgr Herakleitos (Missing).

Ju188 3/KG6 3E+CL WNr 260218

Failed to return from a sortie to London- probably shot down.

Lt Berhard Ostendorf (F) (Missing), Ofw Kurt Bartsch (B) (Missing), Uffz Heinz Götte (B) (Missing), Fw Walter Kaczerowski (Bs) (Missing), Ogefr Willi Müller (Bs) (Missing).

Ju188 3/KG6 3E+BB WNr 260363

Crashed shortly after take off for London due to engine fire at Leuze, Belgium.

Fw Richard Pietsch (B) (Died of injuries on 5 February). Rest of crew safe.

Ju88 5/KG6

Crashed at Rötgen / Malmedy on return from a sortie to London.

Lt Berstecher had been involved in the incident on 29-30 January when he was the only man in his crew to return.

Lt Hans Berstecher (F) (Killed), Gefr Erich Bayer (B) (Killed), Uffz Heinz Held (Bf) (Killed), Gefr Wilhelm Kramm (Bs) (Killed).

Ju88A-4 5/KG6 3E+NN

Made an emergency landing at Gilze-Rijen.

Lt Ruhland (F) (Safe), Ogefr Josef Primas (Bs) (Injured), rest of crew safe.

This crew had been interned by the Turkish authorities on 14 October 1943 when their Ju88 crashed near the island of Leros. They returned in November 1943 and went back on operations in time for their unit to move from the Mediterranean theatre to take part in operations against Britain.

Lt Ruhland returned to duty while Josef Primas recovered from his injuries. On 13-14/2/44 Lt Ruhland's luck ran out; his crew with a new gunner were shot down and crashed near Whitstable, Kent.

Ju88 7/KG6

Failed to return form a sortie to London.

Uffz Ernst Fickentscher (F) (Missing), Uffz Herbert Schmidt (B) (Missing), Uffz Ottmar Nehmeier (Bf) (Missing), Gefr Gerhard Wellmann (Bs) (Missing).

Ju88 **8/KG6**

Failed to return from a sortie to London.

Uffz Luis Schepock (F) (Missing), Fw Ernst Schlichting (B) (Missing), Uffz Heinz Werner Scheepers (Bf) (Missing), Uffz Erich Zatzkowski (Bs)(Missing)

Ju88 **1/KG54** **B3+OH** **WNr 550452**

Failed to return from a sortie to London.

Uffz Heinrich Hannappel (F) (Missing), Uffz Paul Dewes (B) (Missing), Ogefr Ferdinand Sauer (Bf) (Missing), Gefr Rudolf Veckenstedt (Bs) (Missing).

Ju88 **2/KG54** **B3+EK**

Failed to return form a sortie to London. This aircraft was discovered by the Dutch Air Force in the Zuider Zee when it was drained in the 1970s.

Uffz Helmut Friedrich Weihs (F) (Missing), Uffz Franz Wenzel Prinke (B) (Missing), Uffz Herbert Georg Gustav Garske (Bf) (Missing), Uffz Alfons Auerbach (Bs) (Missing).

Uffz Weihs and his crew pose with members of their ground-crew in front of B3+EK. They were lost for over 25 years before their aircraft was discovered in the Zuider Zee in the 1970s.

Ju88A-4 **2/KG54** **B3+BK** **WNr 800657**

Failed to return from London.

Lt Rolf Stockert (F) (Missing), Uffz Georg Brehl (B)(Missing), Uffz Fritz Beyer (Bf) (Missing), Uffz Alfred Forstner (Bs) (Missing).

Ju88 **6/KG54** **B3+CP** **WNr 8850**

Failed to return from a sortie to London.

Lt Hans-Joachim von Krieg (F) (Missing), Uffz Herbert Holznagel (B) (Missing), Uffz Florian Lasthoffer (Bf) (Missing), Uffz Michael Meister (Bs) (Missing). The body of Uffz Meister was washed ashore at Texel and buried on 17/5/44.

Fighter Command Claims, not attributable to a particular loss

A claim was made for a Ju88 destroyed at 05.50 hrs off Southwold by F/O K Seda in a 68 Sqn Beaufighter.

A claim was made for a Ju88 damaged at 20.54 hrs near Tonbridge by Lt J Raad in an 85 Sqn Mosquito.

A claim was made for a Do217 destroyed at 04.50 hrs 20 miles east Walton on the Naze by F/O H B Thomas in an 85 Sqn Mosquito.

A claim was made for a Ju88 damaged at 05.15 hrs near Stapleford Tawney by F/O W G Dinsdale in a 410 Sqn Mosquito.

A claim was made for a Do217 destroyed at 04.50 hrs 40 miles east of Orfordness by F/O E S P Fox in a 410 Sqn Mosquito.

A claim was made for an enemy aircraft destroyed at 20.52 hrs 40 miles near Tours airfield, France, by F/Lt J C Anderson in a 418 Sqn Mosquito.

A claim was made for a Do217 destroyed at 04.52 hrs 40 miles east of Foulness by F/O C J Vlotman in a 488 Sqn Mosquito.

A claim was made for an enemy aircraft damaged at 06.56 hrs near Chievres airfield, France, by F/Lt A D Wagner in a 605 Sqn Mosquito.

WEEKLY APPRECIATION OF DAMAGE TO KEY POINTS AND PROGRESS OF REPAIRS.

Period from: 09.00 hours Wednesday 2nd February
to: 09.00 hours Wednesday 9th February 1944.

GENERAL

Enemy air-activity during the past week occurred on two nights, a total of 111 sorties being plotted overland. No serious damage was done to the essential war-effort, and considering the scale of activity, civilian casualties were small. The enemy is reported to have lost 19 aircraft (8%)

On the first of these nights, Thursday/Friday (3rd/4th February) 80 long-range bombers and 15 fighter-bombers operated overland. The attack was conducted in two phases, the first from 2040 to 2120 and the second from 0425 to 0610. About a third of the total force operated in the first phase over South-East England, and two thirds in the second over East-Anglia. In the first phase 5 aircraft succeeded in reaching London, and in the second 12. No Key-points were seriously damaged. Civilian casualties in London were 17 fatal and 12 serious, and elsewhere 16 fatal and 22 serious.

On Saturday / Sunday (5th / 6th February) 16 long-range bombers crossed the South Coast between 0547 and 0625 and operated over South Eastern England. A single machine reached London. Bombing was trivial.

The total civilian casualties for the week were 33 fatal and 35 serious. 9 Key points were affected, and there were also 4 incidents involving railways.

6th to 12th February 1944

The staccato nature of *'Steinbock'* operations continued into February with three small-scale attacks on London up to mid-month. During the early hours of the 6th fourteen Me410s crossed the Channel and returned home unscathed. Then between 19.55 and 20.03 hours on the 11th a force of 25 aircraft consisting entirely of Me410s and FW190s flew through heavy cloud, thirteen were credited with attaining their goal; Luftwaffe records state that one FW190 crashed. Twenty-four hours later sixteen Me410s and nine FW190s completed similar sorties with no losses.

Luftwaffe Losses 5th to 12th February 1944

Two FW190s of Erg St (nacht) 1/SKG10

5/2/44 Destroyed by a bombing attack on the airfield at Tours.

Ogefr Kurt Rinnert and Ogefr Friedrich Heinrichs killed.

FW 190G-3 1/SKG10 WNr 160460

11/2/44 Crashed whilst on operations 6 km south of Rosiers, France.

Fw Karl Seele (Killed).

Do217M-1 3/KG2 U5+GL WNr 26258

12/2/44 Shot down by fighters during a transfer flight to Vannes carrying two groundcrew. The aircraft was chased at tree-top height and pulled up after being hit to allow six men to bale out. Crashed at Josselin, France.

Uffz Hans Pakulla (Bs) (Inj), Uffz Bruno Fiedler (Bw) (Killed), Uffz Josef Thiel (Bm) (Inj).

13th-14th February 1944

II/KG54 and SKG10 were not on the battle order for the large-scale *'Steinbock'* thrust at London on 13th /14th February, but the other ten Gruppen on hand were called upon. 150 crews took part according to British intelligence, but the Luftwaffe records claim that 230 crews as participated.

KG100's Woes

I/KG100's two available Staffeln were again visited by General Peltz before this operation. During his conversation with the crews he again emphasised the importance of maintaining a strict course and adhering to the briefed times for each stage of the sortie. One surprising aspect of his talk was the playing down of the night fighter threat. As an example he cited the 'fact' that on 3rd/4th February a bare thirty RAF crews were airborne, of which only a third were under GCI Control. Although the overall force available to RAF Fighter Command was smaller than its Nachtjagd counterpart policing the continental skies, its bomber adversaries were arriving in much smaller numbers than Bomber Command's four-engine 'heavies'. Consequently, Peltz's remark could be regarded as a psychological morale booster for his personnel rather than one based on firm fact.

On 13th February, I/KG100 had major problems with its He177s such as this one, 6N+SK of the second staffel.

The He177s were readied for take-off, a process that included a 'cold start' procedure in view of the low temperature – a necessary activity that was to have dire consequences. One bomber remained on the ground after bursting a tyre, but the other thirteen rose majestically and headed west into the darkness. The General's frustration must have therefore been hard to contain when over a period of time no less than eight pilots declared they were 'aborting' the operation. The reason was over-heating engines that in some instances actually caught fire, but were thankfully extinguished.

I/KG100's overall performance was but a foretaste of the raid's almost total failure to render any impact upon London. Although no less than 70% of the overall force was tracked in over the coast, according to intelligence sources of the time a laughable figure of five bombers was judged to have released their loads within the capital's boundaries. In post-war accounts these figures have been revised to 70 and 15 respectively; but even if the latter statistics are correct, the end result would have been of no more comfort to General Peltz.

I/KG66

The dispersed nature of the *'Steinbock'* raid this night would inflict punishment on a number of locations well distant from London. The former holiday resort of Clacton-on-Sea, nestling on the Essex coast, was badly hit and a cinema and several commercial premises were destroyed or heavily damaged. Incendiaries also burnt out farm buildings, with severe loss of life among the livestock, one farmer lost six horses, 30 cows and 17 ewes.

No less than five of the Luftwaffe's losses came from the ranks of KG66. A Ju88S-1 from I/KG66 became one of the three losses confirmed by British records. Z6+HH was brought down near Havering-atte-Bower, Essex, at 21.10 hours by heavy AA guns. This night, the *Y-Verfahren* system was apparently in use by I/KG66 according to the sole survivor, Unteroffizier Niedack. He asserted that *"the bomber's speed and the precise dropping points of the flares were controlled by radio beam from France."*

Uffz. Havering Neidack, the sole survivor of Z6+HH

Niedack recalled that his crew had been briefed that their markers would be homed-in upon by the Dutch-based Gruppen whose inward course was directly up the Thames Estuary. The GM-1 engine booster system was in use, but was casting back a thin vapour trail. The pilot, Unteroffizier Ehling, was advised to switch it off as it was a clear indication to the searchlight cone that had picked them up. Scarcely had the aircraft been caught by searchlights than what he said was an AA shell struck home, no reference to a night fighter attack was made. The bomber's spinning motion initially held Niedack firmly in place, but then the rear canopy detached and he was thrown out into mid-air. His worst injury was a broken left arm, which was caused when he was entangled in an ammunition belt. He landed safely in a back garden.

The crash made the front page of the local newspaper.

GUNNERS DESTROY A RAIDER

Fire Guards Capture Nazi Airman

German aircraft which raided S.E. England and the London area on Sunday night were met by a terrific barrage. Five machines were brought down. One of them, a Junkers 88, which crashed on the outskirts of a village, was the first of the five victims, and its crash was observed by large numbers of people as it spiralled down from a cone of searchlights, in which it had been caught, to finish in a field, where it burst into flames and was destroyed.

Two members of the crew were killed, but a third, who had baled out, landed in a village behind some shops and was captured by two Fire Guards, who took him to a Warden's Post, whence he was removed to hospital suffering from injuries to his head and to one of his arms.

Pieces of his aircraft were broken off while it was still in the air. A large piece of the fuselage came down on the village green close to some ancient stocks.

The aircraft was one of the first to come in and met very spirited opposition. Searchlights picked it up and silhouetted it. Suddenly the bomber was seen to fall out of the cone of searchlights, obviously in trouble. The whine of the wind through the propellers and fuselage as it spiralled earthwards could be heard for miles, and then observers saw the aircraft come to earth and burst into flames. It was obvious from the start that it was doomed, as were anybody who were left in it.

Found by Fire Guards

A short time afterwards, however, Mr. A. Willis and Mr. W. Willis, who are brothers and members of the Fire Guard, heard groans and went to the spot and found a German airman, who had injuries to one of his arms and in his head. It was soon apparent that he could not speak English and when found by the Fire Guards he was entangled in his parachute. His captors released him and then, helped by Mr. Hardcastle, and Petty Officer L. W. J. Butcher, R.N., who was home on leave for the night, they escorted him to the village and handed him over at a Warden's post.*

Mr A. Willis, who is a shopkeeper in the village, described his experience to our representative.

"I saw the plane coming and told our wives to get into the shelter" he said. "A short time afterwards somebody was screaming and moaning. He was in a field near our houses, and was crying out, 'Doctor.' We found that he was a German and started to

**The airman was Uffz Helmut Niedack, who returned to Havering-atte-Bower in 1986 and was given his flying helmet that had been taken from him.*

take his parachute off as he was tangled up in it. We escorted him to the Warden's post, Mr. Hardcastle carrying the parachute. The German's arm was broken and his head was hurt. He didn't seem to be able to speak any English but kept calling 'Doctor.'"

Niedack's bomber was but one of ten aircraft dispatched by I/KG66 that night. The performance of the other nine crews in gaining a path to London and carrying out their marking duties is unclear. The fact that such a small proportion of the main force did achieve their objective does not necessarily mean that the target marking was similarly deficient, however.

WEEKLY APPRECIATION OF DAMAGE TO KEY POINTS AND PROGRESS OF REPAIRS.

Period from: 09.00 hours Wednesday 9th February
to: 09.00 hours Wednesday 16th February 1944.

GENERAL.

Enemy aircraft attacked land–targets in this country on three nights during the past week, a total of 127 sorties being flown overland. In each case London was the main target, but only 22 aircraft (17%) succeeded in reaching it, and bombing was scattered and ineffective. No serious damage was done to the essential war-effort and fatal civilian casualties totalled only 7. Eight aircraft (6%) are known to have been destroyed.

Early on Thursday/Friday (10th/11th February) two aircraft reconnoitred wide areas of Scotland for about an hour. One came in at Fraserburgh and went out at Stonehaven, and the other came in at Duncansby Head and went out at Wick.

On Friday/Saturday (11th/12th February) two long–range bombers and ten fighter-bombers crossed the South Coast at a high altitude and operated over Kent, Sussex, Essex and Suffolk for about 45 minutes. Four machines penetrated to London. Incidents were of little account.

On Saturday/Sunday (12th/13th February) five long-range bombers and ten fighter-bombers crossed the coast between Hythe and Hastings and operated over Kent, Sussex, and Essex for about half an hour. Three reached the Greater London Area. None of the incidents merits special mention. It is however interesting to note that all the bombs dropped on this night were H.E., and that in no incident was more than one bomb dropped.

On Sunday/Monday (13th/14th February about a 100 long-range bombers made landfall between North Foreland and the Harwich/Orfordness area: probably fifteen reached London, the remainder operating over Essex and South Eastern England. Activity lasted for about two hours. There were clusters of incidents on the North side of the Estuary and in areas River Colne/Colchester/The Naze and Dartford/Maidstone/Sevenoaks/Knockholt. A considerable proportion of the bombs were incendiaries, but the fire situation amounted to only 14 medium and 84 small, mostly in East Anglia. Casualties in London totalled 1 fatal and 6 serious, and in the whole country 7 fatal, 11 serious and 2 missing believed killed.

2 Key-Points were affected by enemy action during the week: in addition, 1 railway and 1 airfield were affected

Capital Defences

The perceived potency of the Capital's ground defensive system, as opposed to poor navigational ability, may have been the reason for more crews not releasing their loads over the briefed zones. Those crews completing their bombing runs were beginning to report a steady increase in the concentration of gun fire, although this was seemingly not being matched by a noticeable increase in losses due to the gunners' efforts. De-briefing notes stated that pilots were claiming they were taking no special evasive action even when shells were bursting in their immediate vicinity. The sites for several 'Z' batteries of rockets within the City were readily identified and naturally avoided whenever possible, although the Hyde Park battery was well placed to cause problems in making an un-impeded bombing run, in theory at least, since some of the raids were directed against the surrounding region. The rocket spread was reported as covering an area 1½ to 2 miles in diameter with the salvoes repeated at approximately four-minute intervals.

There is little doubt that the sight of AA fire of any intensity was off-putting, especially to novice crews who were naturally un-versed in the experience. As a possible antidote to prevent a crew asserting that it had bombed the briefed target when in fact it had released the load indiscriminately, the de-briefing sessions involving pilots and Beobachters were vigorously conducted in respect of sightings of flares and any other special observations. Moreover, psychology sometimes came into the equation, with the release of flares or flare of a different colour to that briefed being included in the marker clusters - this was done to further check the veracity of the crews' claims to have bombed as briefed!

After the raid on the night of 13th February, the German radio claimed that 'several hundred aircraft' had dropped 180,000 incendiary bombs and several thousand high-explosive bombs, 'in a concentrated attack on London'. In fact the number of aircraft used was 230 according to Luftwaffe records; less than four tons of bombs fell on London, about 157 tons in Kent and Essex. The number of bombs counted on land was 57,525, of which the vast majority were small incendiaries.

The War-time Diary of Miss J. M. Oakman – Chelsea Sunday 13 Feb 1944

20.36 Sirens. Some very heavy gunfire for a long time. Fire S. believed to be Streatham way. Heard some heavy bits falling about – one large piece fell in Walton Street.

21.49 all clear. Planes were diving about singly – it was chiefly an I.B. raid. 5 more were brought down. Heaviest gunfire for some months. Moon was not up – cloudy. 60 planes came over and 15 reached London and 8 were brought down.

Luftwaffe Losses 13th-14th February 1944

Ju88A-4 Stab II/KG6 3E+DC WNr 63868

Burgess Farm, Bogshole, nr Blean, Kent. 20.43 hrs. Shot down by W/Cdr Crew in a 96 Sqn Mosquito.

After sustaining damage from the Mosquito and AA fire, the pilot stalled the aircraft at low altitude and it pancaked onto the ground.

Markings: DC in black, outlined in blue. Call sign KG+KJ and works number from log book 088043868 manufactured by Henschel AG, Schonfeld bei Teltow. The camouflage was most unusual as both top and bottom surfaces were the same, namely dark green mottled with a light greenish blue.

The sole survivor, the wireless operator, baled out from 1,500 feet and sustained a broken leg. Another crew member baled out, but was killed. This is the crew to which Ogefr Primas was attached when he was injured on 3-4 February 1944. Because he was recovering from his injuries, he was replaced on this mission by Walter Orlieb. All crew men were on the strength of 5/KG6.

Lt Egon Ruhland (F) (Killed CC 1/407), Ogefr Karl Keim (B) (Killed CC 1/408), Uffz Eberhard Fichtner (Bf) (PoW), Uffz Walter Orlieb (Bs) (Killed CC 1/409).

Ju88 4/KG6

Failed to return from a sortie to London.

Uffz Herman Weisserth (F) (Missing), Fw Siegfried Henze (B) (Missing), Ogefr Franz Wagner (Bf) (Missing), Ogefr Martin Thiele (Bs) (Missing).

Ju88 6/KG6

Failed to return from a sortie to London.

Fw Oswald Reich (F) (Missing), Ogefr Hermann Eich (B) (Missing), Ogefr Werner Helke (Bf) (Missing), Gefr Fritz Spierling (Bs) (Missing).

Two of the KG6 crewmen lost on this night. Left is Ogefr. Martin Thiele who went missing in a 4/KG6 Ju88 and right is Ogefr. Karl Keim who was killed in Ju88 3E+DC.

Ju88 **7/KG6**

Failed to return from a sortie to London.

Fw Walter Hillebrecht (F) (Missing), Uffz Gerhard Böttcher (B) (Missing), Lt Hans-Joachim Nack (Bf) (Missing), Uffz Rudolf Willkomm (Bs) (Missing).

Ju88 **8/KG6**

Failed to return from a sortie to London.

St Fw Ernst Kothe (F) (Missing), Ofw Werner Zabel (B) (Missing), Fw Werner Hartung (Bf) (Missing), Uffz Friedrich Meyer (Bs) (Missing).

Ju88 **8/KG6**

Failed to return from a sortie to London.

Uffz Ernst Nolden (F) (Missing), Gefr Xaver Bauer (B) (Missing), Ogefr Max Hofstetter (Bf) (Missing), Ogefr Erich Runge (Bs) (Missing).

Ju88S-1 1/KG 66 Z6+HH WNr 140606

Havering-atte-Bower, nr Romford, Essex. 20.50 hrs. Shot down by 3.7 inch AA guns.

En-route to London this aircraft was coned by searchlights and the pilot took evasive action which became so violent that he lost control. There was a loud explosion, the cabin seemed to collapse and the wireless operator baled out, he landed with a broken arm ¼ mile from the aircraft and was taken to Oldchurch Hospital. The two remaining crew were killed in the aircraft when it crashed and burnt out.

Markings: Call sign RF+MV. The camouflage of the lower surfaces was the normal black, but the upper surfaces were unusual in that the background was greenish-grey, onto which irregularly shaped patches of black had been sprayed.

The crew was on its third war flight. Neidack had previously flown Bf110s with ZG101 over Russia.

Uffz Herbert Ehling (F) (Killed CC 1/45), Fw Josef Weikert (B) (Killed CC 1/46), Uffz Helmut Niedack (Bf) (PoW).

Ju188E-1 2/KG66 Z6+AK WNr 260246

Crashed in the town of Lille on return from London after elevators had been damaged by AA fire. 22.21 hrs.

Fw Hermann Sigg (F) (Killed), Uffz Helmut Kleine (B) (Killed), Ogefr Hartwig Berndt (Bf) (Inj), Uffz Hans Meyer (Bs) (Killed), Gefr Günther Sittig* (Tb) (Died of injuries 15 February).

* Truhe Gerät (Gee) operator.

Ju88 Verbandsführerschule KG101

Crashed into the sea off Clacton. 21.16 hrs.

Probably shot down by S/Ldr Somerville (RCAF) in a 410 Sqn Mosquito. The aircraft was seen to blow up and break in two. Also claimed by the Clacton 3.7 inch AA guns and the Ack-Ack ship 'Royal Eagle'.

Uffz Konrad Fisahn (F) (Missing), Gefr Kurt Urban (B) (Killed CC), Uffz Ernst Sölkner (Bf) (Missing), Gefr Adolf Threin (Bs) (Missing).

The body of Gefr Kurt Urban was found at Foulness, Havingore, Essex.

Ju88 Verbschule KG101

Uffz Karl Bachus (Bs) (inj) during an attack on London.

Fighter Command Claims, not attributable to a particular loss

A claim was made by the Dover AA guns for a Do217 that was seen by many observers to fall in flames into the sea 5 miles south-west of Dover at 21.26 hrs.

A claim was made by S/Ldr Sommerville in a 406 Squadron Mosquito for a Ju188 damaged over Essex at 21.00 hrs. Strikes were observed on the fuselage and return fire was experienced from the rear gunner. This claim has been associated with the loss of Z6+HH at Havering-atte-Bower, as this crash is refered to in the combat report, but this seems unlikely.

A claim was made by F/O Schultz in a 410 Sqn Mosquito for a Ju188 destroyed over the Thames Estuary at 21.50 hrs. The Mosquito was damaged by return fire that stopped the port engine. This was possibly Z6+AK that landed at Lille with combat damage.

A claim was made for an enemy aircraft destroyed at 22.05 hrs near Chievres, France, by F/Sgt F Cassidy in a 605 Sqn Mosquito.

Under Interrogation

Operational flying held its fair share of risk for all airmen, but the mind-set of the majority of crewmen considered only two of the three possible scenarios likely to confront them during a tour of duty - either surviving the number of operations comprising the tour, or being killed or injured in the process. The third possibility – being shot down over enemy territory, but surviving the experience to end up in captivity, was rarely envisioned.

Personnel in all air forces were usually thoroughly lectured on how to behave should they be captured, especially when facing the initial stage of incarceration, namely the ‘grilling’ carried out by what were often very experienced interrogation staff. The ‘Name, rank and serial number’ restriction in divulging details that was stressed during training lectures was a vital cornerstone of the (relatively) unfortunate airman’s required reaction in such basically harrowing circumstances. This of course was a logical and comforting response when sat in a room among one’s fellow-airmen, but it was totally divorced from the stark ‘twilight world’ of imprisonment.

The transformation from one minute being enclosed within the familiar if Spartan fuselage of a bomber along with the comforting presence of one’s crewmembers, to seeking salvation through baling out into the black void of the nocturnal sky and hanging under the swaying motion of a parachute, was shocking enough. Once on the ground, and assuming an injury-free landing had been made, the knowledge that one was now in a totally unknown and hostile environment meant that his sense of apprehension was hardly lessened when being immediately or soon afterwards apprehended. Would the arms-bearing soldier or civil authority restrict their action to arrest or - worse? Even when constrained in a prison cell, could the risk to one’s life be dispelled, especially when given the reported activities of the infamous Gestapo or some elements of the German armed forces.

The perception of Luftwaffe airmen as well-drilled, but unimaginative individuals in the mould of the Germanic character still persists in the minds of many of their former adversaries. It is certainly true that until the final 18 months to two years of WWII the average Luftwaffe airman was as well, if not better, versed in the skills of operational flying than their Allied contemporaries. Flugzeugführer (pilot) candidates proceeded through A and B-Schule courses lasting anything up to two years, while Beobachters (navigator/bomb-aimers) underwent training over a similar time-period. Nor were the duties of Bordmechanikers (flight engineers), Bordfunkers (Radio operators) or even Bordschützers (air-gunners) impressed upon trainees in other than lengthy spells of instruction. So it was that Luftwaffe personnel entered the field of combat quite well able to match their adversaries in operational efficiency.

How did the Luftwaffe PoWs fare in comparison to the RAF/USAAF experience? On the question of interrogation following their capture, there was little or no distinction to be discerned, as instanced by the reports of the British Intelligence Service available over the period of Operation 'Steinbock'. Having 'arrived' either by parachute or occasionally through surviving their bomber's crash-landing, the arrested airman would go through the normal procedure of being searched and medically examined before being dispatched to an Interrogation Centre, the main one being at Cockfosters in North London.

Interrogation techniques

During a PoW's initial period of incarceration, disorientation techniques such as raising and lowering cell temperature or switching on and off lights at inconvenient hours were certainly practiced by Luftwaffe interrogators. Whether or not the same de-stabilising methods applied in British centres is an open question, but could well have been applied. Certainly variations on this theme were applied by interrogators during the recent lengthy spell of IRA activity in Northern Ireland, so there seems little reason why the foregoing psychologically-disturbing methods would have been eschewed during the arguably starker conditions of WWII. The fitting of hidden microphones in the rooms did catch out a number of personnel in unguarded conversation with fellow airmen. A major 'information spill' picked up in this manner involved not a member of the Luftwaffe but the Wehrmacht's General Von Thoma, who in March 1943 talked at incriminating length to General Cruewell (his fellow-captor from North Africa) about the retarded progress of rocket research at Peenemünde, expressing surprise that the offensive against London in particular had not yet commenced, since he had heard no explosions!

Physical maltreatment should a PoW not be forthcoming with answers was rarely threatened, directly or indirectly, although the occasional 'roughening up' of an individual was later claimed by some Luftwaffe personnel after WWII.

A Luftwaffe bomber crewman is escorted into captivity, his boots and socks being removed to discourage any attempt to make a run for it. Ahead of him lies an interrogation followed by a long journey to a PoW camp, possibly overseas.

Verbal interrogation of a PoW was generally regarded as being more productive if couched in a persuasive manner, rather than one that was hectoring or bullying. On the other hand, the initial 'softly, softly' verbal approach of one interrogator, including the handing out of cigarettes or even alcoholic drink, could be interchanged by the harsher presentation of a second interrogator. This technique was likely entertained in cases where the subject appeared to be in a confused or hesitant state of mind.

The divulging of information to a PoW about his unit's activities was regularly done at some stage of an interrogation. The sources for such revelations, that often shook the PoW's confidence in handling the situation, were assembled via several channels. The major ones were;

(a) Carelessly-handled documents, etc, carried by airmen. In one instance a comprehensive diary was borne aloft by an airman; the fact that he was killed probably saved him from bearing the shame of this blatant and unforgivable breach in security regulations. A similar case involved Leutnant Kuttler, 2/KG2's Staffelkapitän, on whose body was discovered the operations order for the previous night's raid launched on 23rd/24th February. In addition maps and documents were sometimes unearthed from the remains of crashed bombers.

(b) General information on Luftwaffe activities was obtained via neutral sources; a principal source relating to both units and personnel lay in access to the major Nazi propaganda magazines such as Signal and Der Adler.

(c) To a lesser extent details were gained thanks to observations regarding unit movements, etc, arising from SOE operations.

PoW reactions

Among the ranks of those 'Steinbock' personnel ending up in British hands, there was a relatively small group of airmen who still believed in the Führer, the Nazi Party and therefore in ultimate victory for Germany. As regards the majority of PoWs, an element proved just resolute in their unwillingness to answer questions, and expressed no such political reactions in the course of their interrogations. The interrogators' opinion of their captives ranged from regarding most as 'polite' to those exceptions who were regarded as taking up stances that rendered them 'thoroughly unpleasant types'.

One individual clearly falling into the latter category was Obergefreiter Grün, the Bordschützer and sole survivor from his 4/KG6 Ju88 3E+LM captured on 21st/22nd January. The 21-year old airman was on his first sortie and had been seriously injured. He not only remained extremely reticent when questioned, but also came across as a thoroughly indoctrinated Nazi – not surprising when given the fact that his upbringing had been made following the assumption of autocratic national control by Hitler. He spoke of retribution to come 'not from the air alone' as a vague expression of confidence in Germany achieving its 'Endseig' or final victory.

On the other hand, in contrast to Grün's attitude, there were one or two of his fellow airmen who asserted that they were motivated to remain silent by the fear of being brought to Nazi justice should they talk. Rumours of several PoWs being faced with court-martial on return to a 'victorious' nation because their superiors had gained knowledge that they had divulged vital information were mentioned by some PoWs as circulating among their ranks. One case involved a captive seized by paratroopers during the Bruneval raid of February 1942. Personnel from 2/KG2 said they had heard that he had been condemned and sentenced to death 'in absentia' for breaches of security.

In between these stances could arguably be placed the bulk of Luftwaffe airmen. The fact that an individual was intelligent did not mean that he was less likely to buckle under subtle pressures applied by his questioners. On the contrary, the more perceptive German could perhaps be induced to consider that his nation's stance on the conduct of the conflict was not only far from perfect, but even open to genuine doubt. In such cases the feeling that honest expression of one's opinion could be indulged in could and sometimes was, perhaps ironically, of benefit more to the interrogator than his subject – such was the tangled web of intelligence gathering!

The extent of previous operational experience did not always equate with the degree of resistance put up in the face of interrogation. The twilight world of captivity was a whole new and generally unsettling scenario for any individual to live through. A percentage of Luftwaffe airmen falling in the 'operationally experienced' category did provide accurate answers to both general and detailed questions. On the other hand it could be argued that men shot down after a single, or handful, of sorties may not have possessed very much information to divulge in the first place.

Such a mixture of responses can be gleaned from reports on the first 'Steinbock' crew survivors to come into British hands following He177 F8+ ?H's demise on 21st/22nd January:

The Beobachter, Obergefreiter Bikker (22) was a replacement for an Hs293-trained airman, who had arrived from 3/KG40 (Trondheim) with his crew at Fassberg in early 1943. He joined the Luftwaffe in 1941 and entered the Beobachterschule/ Hoersching late that same year. He was posted in the summer of 1943 to IV/KG30 but later was sent to zBV 25 to serve on that unit's He111s and Ju52s flying transport sorties to and from Italy. Having returned to operational flying, he was posted to 1/KG40 at Fassberg.

The Bordmechaniker, Oberfeldwebel Six (31) joined KG40 from the Austrian Army in 1939 and remained until 1942. He then spent one year at A/B Schule/Wels as an Oberwerkmeister before joining 3/KG40. He had flown 66 operations.

The surviving Bordschützer Obergefreiter Doge (23) had volunteered for combat to boost his income. A short training spell at Trondheim was completed prior to joining a 3/KG40 crew, but three months later (September 1943) he transferred to the present crew without having attended a regular gunnery school (Bordschützerschule). Oberleutnant Waterbeck (Flugzeugführer), Oberfeldwebel Jursach (Bordfunker) and Oberfeldwebel Six had flown together for around two years on Norwegian-based FW200s.

Intelligence recorded that the morale of Bikker and Jursack (31) was high; the latter held the EK (Eiserne Kreuz) I and II and the Golden War-Flight Badge for 65 completed reconnaissance sorties over the Atlantic. In contrast both Six and Doge's morale was assessed as 'very low'. It is clear that neither age nor operational experience held an advantage in this instance. Oberfeldwebel Six may well have been a married man, with the natural concern of becoming parted from his wife and family for an unknown period of time being an extra burden in comparison with unattached contemporaries. In the course of being interrogated either this trio or their two contemporaries from F8+?K did divulge a fair to good degree of material on the structure, operations and movements of their Gruppe as well as information about senior officers. Also revealed was the fact that KG100 was converting to the He177.

Luftwaffe Losses 14th to 16th February 1944

Ju188E-1 4/KG2 U5+CM WNr 260364

14/2/44. Crashed at Nordlich-Vohren near Warendorf / Westfalen after engine failure during a training flight.

Uffz Helmut Schiltze (F) (Killed), Uff Horst Riedel (B) (Killed), Uffz Johannes Wolf (Bf) (Killed), Ogefr Johann Ludwig (Bs1) (Killed), Uffz Herbert Knispel (Bs2) (Killed).

Ju290A-5 2/FAGr5 9V+FH WNr 0175

16/2/44 16.50 hrs. Shot down near convoys OS68, ONS29 and KMS42 south-west of Ireland by F/Lt R R Wright in a Beaufighter Mk. X of 235 Sqn Coastal Command.

Lt Eberhard Elfert (F), Ofw Conrad Oberhauser (F), Lt Albert Pape (B), Ofw Albert Holzmann (Bf), Uffz Rudolf Dreissig (Bs), Ofw Otto Zech (Bm), Ofw Wilhelm Hausmann (Bs), Ofw Gustav Schlatthaus (Bs), Fw Erich Barlau (Bs), Ogefr Albert Pfeffer (Bs). All missing.

Ju290A-5 2/FAGr5 9V+DK WNr 0177

16/2/44 10.05 hrs. Shot down by Lt E S Erikson and Lt W C Dimes in Wildcat Mk. IVs from HMS Biter into the Atlantic west-south-west of Ireland at 53.31N 14.46W.

Hptm Karl-Friedrich Bergen (StKp) (F), Oblt Kurt Baumgartner (F), Lt Martin Glöckhofer (B), Ofw Heinz Felleckner (Bf), Fw Heinz Schacht (Bf), Uffz Gottfried Beninde (Bm), Ofw Ludwig Ebner (Bs), Uffz Jakob Daniel (Bs), Ogefr Karl Zinke (Bs), Ogefr Josef Neubauer (Bs), Referendar Werner Cordes (Wetterdienst). All missing.

Major Bomber Command Operations

3rd to 18th February 1944

15-16 February Berlin-500 killed* 891 aircraft-43 lost

*** approximate figure.**

Opposite page: The wreckage of Ju88 B3+KK which fell to earth at Selhurst, Croydon on 20th February 1944.

CHAPTER FIVE

The 'Baby Blitz' begins to bite

Chapter Five

The 'Baby Blitz' begins to bite

General Peltz's expectations for any, let alone a notable, degree of success for '*Steinbock*' had simply not been realised to date. Not only had a good proportion of the attacking crews failed to bomb the primary target; a serious scale of loss in bombers had undoubtedly provided an added damper to the overall proceedings. However, the situation was about to take somewhat of a turn for the better, at least during the remainder of February, commencing on the night of the 18th/19th.

18th-19th February 1944

According to British intelligence 175 crews from ten Gruppen were on hand for the assault upon London on 18th/19th February. This total was rounded up to 200 in German accounts of the raid, with 184 bombers getting as far as the target. This raid heralded an almost nightly series of major attacks on the Capital that lasted until the 23rd/24th of the month, the exception being the 21st/22nd. In addition, the raids would witness by far the greatest degree of material damage and destruction as well as human casualties to be inflicted during '*Steinbock*'.

The crews of I/KG100 were to take off from Rheine but return to Evreux, while records indicate that II/KG2 and III/KG2 were to operate from Coulommiers and Bretigny as opposed to their regular Dutch airfields of Soesterberg and Gilze-Rijen. All other participating units were listed against their normal operational locations.

By the time the bombers had departed for their airfields 480 fires were recorded, while no less than 180 citizens were dead or dying. A particularly distressing incident involved a soldier home on leave and due to be married next day. The occasion called for a family party in Hampstead. Even when the sirens sounded, their dire message did not halt proceedings. A mere 60 minutes later all but one of the celebrants were dead. A bomb blew the flat apart and created a fire that thwarted all rescue attempts by Civil Defence personnel to extricate anybody who might have survived the initial blast. A further sixteen persons were killed in a separate incident close by.

Hospitals were particularly vulnerable to Luftwaffe assault. On this occasion two bombs fell on or very close to the Queen's Road Home. Two whole blocks were wrecked along with the children's ward and the nursing staff quarters. Of the nine adult fatalities, seven were dead when found by Civil Defence and ARP personnel; the other two later succumbed to their injuries. More positively, only one of the child patients was in any manner affected and he received a degree of bruising, this despite the ward's extreme proximity to where the bomb hit. Wimbledon recorded several serious incidents. The most harrowing involved a row of houses, two of which were Catholic Rest Homes occupied by elderly residents, that were wholly or partially demolished. In a twelve-hour marathon of digging in very cold conditions, and after removing an estimated 80 tons of rubble, rescuers managed to bring out all but five of the people alive, although a number were injured. Bombs were dropped on or near several airfields. At 01.00 hours two HEs and an IB container fell at Earls Colne airfield, two AB1000 containers and eight SC50 bombs fell in a wood just south of Debden and at 01.15 hours IBs fell on the US airfield at Willingale. Airfields at Panshanger and Nuthampstead, and the RAF Balloon Establishment at Chigwell, reported bombing incidents. Essex Police also reported black strips found all over Essex.

Total reported casualties were 179 killed, 484 seriously inured and 65 missing.

Around 120 bombers had been plotted over the southern British mainland, but not all would gain the security of their airfields.

'Intruder' Strike

Operational flying demanded a high degree of physical and mental energy from the moment an airman approached his aircraft until he was safely back on the ground. Added to the dangers posed by an opponent's fighters and AA defences over its territory was the looming presence of enemy aircraft over or around one's own airfields on return from an operation. This was at a time when individuals were approaching a nadir in their likely response to danger and simultaneously relaxing at the thought of touching down, with de-briefing, a meal and then a spell in bed as tension-releasing sources.

During 1940/41 a handful of Ju88s and Do-17Z crews from I/NJG2 had made their presence felt over Bomber Command's bases along England's eastern coastal zone. They had created a threat out of proportion to their numbers, but fortunately Hitler had ordered their withdrawal in October 1941, reportedly on the basis that the German population wanted to witness the bombers' destruction overhead, not depend on statistics that even if accurate could not be confirmed! It was to be the final year of WWII before any form of 'intruder' operations would be resumed, by which stage the die was cast for Nazi Germany's ultimate defeat.

In 1942/43 the burgeoning daylight presence of RAF Fighter Command over Western Europe – in concert with its 8th USAAF contemporary - was by now extended into the hours of darkness, in the shape of 'intruder' operations mounted by Mosquito and Beaufighter-equipped units. One of these was No. 418 (Canadian) Squadron, which at 01.15 hours on

19th February dispatched Flight Lieutenant Kipp and Flying Officer Hulotsky from RAF Ford in their Mosquito Mk. VI, with the intention of infiltrating the homeward-bound Luftwaffe bomber stream.

Kipp set course for Laon/Athies and noted several airfields lit up while en-route. He noted three searchlights southeast of his primary destination and almost immediately sighted the navigation lights of an aircraft heading south from Laon to Juvincourt; Flying Officer Hulotsky had simultaneously noted a red flare shot up from Laon, which was regarded by both RAF airmen as a diversion signal to their potential prey. While taking up the pursuit one Merlin engine momentarily failed due to fuel starvation, but a swift switch-over to the inner tanks rectified the situation and what had been identified as a Me410 was caught again two miles north of Juvincourt whose NE/SW runway was lit up.

The Luftwaffe crew was now flying at 2,800 feet and 250 IAS, doubtless anticipating a safe landing within the next few minutes, and seemingly oblivious of their nemesis directly astern. The Mosquito almost over-shot at one point and Flight Lieutenant Kipp was forced to lower his undercarriage, close his throttles and open the radiator flaps in order to avoid doing so. He then closed to 200 yards and delivered a four-second burst, but with little discernable effect since his reflector-sight was flickering on and off despite having replaced the bulb several minutes before. The 'Me410' pilot now doused the white light located underneath while Kipp again closed to 200 yards to deliver a 'blind' second burst of fire in the approximate direction of the target, since the sight bulb had burnt out completely. Fortune favoured him because the cannon shell and machine-gun fusillade landed squarely on the fuselage of the bomber, which climbed slightly before sharply reversing its attitude and diving into the ground.

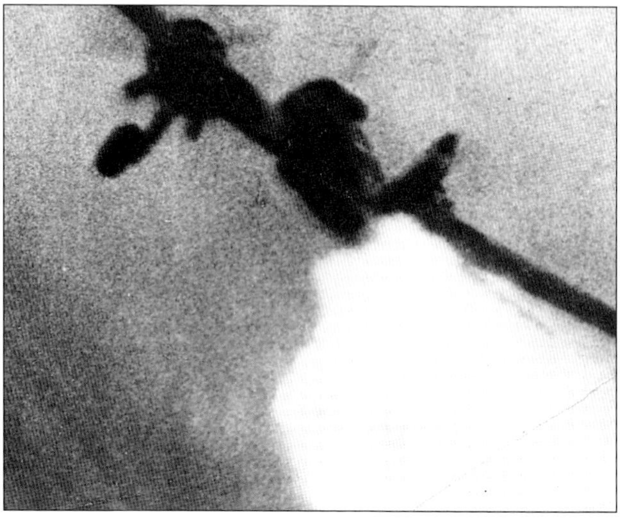

Although Kipp and Hulotsky claimed two Me410s, post-war research indicates that the aircraft shot down were actually Ju88s similar to this one.

The Kipp and Hulotsky team were still watching their victim descend when both caught sight of another bomber straight ahead and west of the airfield. This pilot was also displaying navigation lights, which were not doused even after the explosion of the other bomber that should have alerted him to danger in his vicinity! The Mosquito, still with its landing gear down, tracked in behind its second 'Me410' with a replacement reflector-sight bulb in place. The Luftwaffe aircraft was now circling south of the airfield with the evident intention of lining-up with the SE/NW runway but would never achieve its goal. Kipp struck home with another four-second burst of fire that caused both engines to ignite with a terrible explosion. The resultant crash along with its predecessor, created a blaze effect so fierce that the Mosquito crew could pick out every ground detail for a considerable distance in all directions. Once again two Luftwaffe crews had been granted no reprieve, having been brought face to face with the fact that the nocturnal skies over Europe were becoming almost as lethal as those over the British Isles.

The two aircraft shot down by Flight Lieutenant Kipp can now be identified as two Ju88s belonging to 3/KG54 flown by Uffz Heinrich Framing and Uffz Rolf Backofen.

The War-time Diary of Miss J. M. Oakman – Chelsea Saturday 19 Feb 1944

1st Fire Raid

00.38 alert. A spectacular night of red flares, fires and heavy gunfire. Most trouble was N and SW areas of London. Heard one HE. N of King's Road.

01.47 All clear. Sky red with fires. Tate and Lyles of Garrett Lane had fire. 2 fires at Kensington – mews and flats near "Adam and Eve" P.H. and Queen's Gate. Bad trouble. Bad fire at Putney where Gibraltarian refugees were billeted. Finsbury had a bad time.

Chemical works at Barnes was burnt out.

Luftwaffe Losses 18th-19th February 1944

Do217 2/KG2 U5+CK WNr 40722

Crashed near Antwerp whilst engaged in an attack on London, but not due to enemy action.

Lt Karl Schröder (F) (Killed), Uffz Hans Witte (B) (Killed), Uffz Heinz Seelig (Bf) (Killed), Uffz Karl-Heinz Mazcholleck (Bs) (Killed), Lt Paul Klose (Kriegsberichter) (Killed).

Ju88 **6/KG6**

Failed to return from a sortie to London.

Fw Werner Vogt (F) (Missing), Fw Hubert Majchrzak (B) (Missing), Ogefr Helmut Klein (Bf) (Missing), Uffz Alfred Philp (Bs) (Missing).

Ju88 **9/KG6**

Crashed at Oudenbosch north of Rosendahl on return from operations.

Oblt Erhard Grundmann (F) (Killed), Uffz Gustav Schreer (B) (Killed), Uffz Paul Wilde (Bf) (Killed), Gefr Richard Frischholz (Bs) (Killed).

Ju88 **3/KG54** **B3+AL** **WNr 5556**

Shot down by F/Lt Kipp in a 418 Sqn Mosquito (who identified it as an Me410) on return from London. Crashed 5 km south of Juvincourt.

Uffz Heinrich Framing (F) (Killed), Ogefr Rudolf Kretschmann (B) (Killed), Ogefr Wolfgang Fischer (Bf) (Killed), Ogefr Walter Bludau (Bs) (Inj).

Ogefr Kretschmann baled out, but his parachute failed. Ogefr Fischer baled out but came down in the Aisne Canal and drowned

Ju88 **3/KG54** **B3+VL** **WNr 142409**

Crashed in flames after being shot down by F/Lt Kipp in a 418 Sqn Mosquito (who identified it as an Me410) on return from London. 02.26 hrs.

Uffz Rolf Backofen (F) (Killed), Ogefr Günther Dube (B) (Killed), Uffz Ernst Hautumm (Bf) (Baled out but injured), Gefr Wilhelm Röhr (Bs) (Killed).

Ju88S-1 **1/KG66** **Z6+LN** **WNr 301152**

Crashed 3 km south of Le Culot on return from operations due to fuel shortage and radio failure. The crew all baled out.

Fw Volkher Kottmann (F) (inj), Uffz Helmut Werner (B) (inj), Fw Franz Buxan (Bf) (inj).

Ju188E-1 **2/KG66** **Z6+IK** **WNr 260202**

Crashed into the town centre of Montdidier shortly after take off for London. 23.45 hrs

Fw Werner Köhler (F) (Killed), Uffz Heinz Kreul (B) (Killed), Uffz Karl Rachfat (Bf) (Killed), Uffz Kurt Sawatzki (Bw) (Killed), Ogefr Karl Heese (B) (Killed).

Ju188E-1 **2/KG66** **Z6+FK** **WNr 260189**

This a/c took off at 23.42 hrs but failed to return from a sortie to London.

Lt Jens Herdtle (F) (Missing), Uffz Johann Förstl (B) (Missing,) Ofw Helmut Leuthold (Bf) (Missing), Ofw Ernst Fehr (Bw) (Missing), Uffz Erwin Ahlf (B) (Missing).

Ju88S-1 **E Staffel I/KG66** **Z6+IN** **Wnr 30061**

Failed to return from a sortie to London.

Lt Walter Steinebronn (F) (Missing), Uffz Matthias Pohl (B) (Missing), Uffz Walter Obermüller (Missing).

20th February 1944

From the earliest days of the war a constant eye had been kept of the Home Fleet at anchor in Scapa Flow and around the Scottish coast. 29 year-old Helmut Quednau from the reconnaissance unit 1(F)120 was making his lonely way across the North Sea from his base in Norway at 30,000 feet for Scapa Flow. A lonely dot in the huge expanse of sky over five miles above the North Sea was unlikely to be intercepted, but Helmut Quednau had the misfortune to be picked up on radar and have two eagle-eyed Spitfire pilots spot him.

Luftwaffe Loss

Me109G-6 **1(F)120** **A6+XH** **Wnr 20357**

Shot down on a reconnaissance of Scapa Flow by P/O J Blair in a 602 Sqn Spitfire 50 miles east of the Orkney Islands. Oblt Helmut Quednau (F) (Missing).

An unusual loss today was a single seat Me109G up near the Orkney Islands.

Combat Report

602 (City of Glasgow) Squadron

Red Section No. 602 (City of Glasgow Squadron) 2 Spitfires Mk. VII took off 12.30 hours and one Spitfire Red 2 landed 13.26 hours (Red 1 force landing on island of Stronsay, Category E. due to glycol leak). Ordered to intercept Raid X556. When about 50 miles E. of Orkneys flying due east at 32,000 feet were given vectors of 120° 130° 090° 080° 100° when they saw smoke trails at 30,000 feet about six miles away. E/A did 180° turn to starboard and made off down sun, thence dived at great speed at 4,000 feet and was identified as Me. 109 Long Range. Red 2 followed and during dive noticed his I.A.S. was registering 400 at 25,000 feet. Red 1 dived and states his I.A.S. was registering 420 at 25,000/20,000 feet - during dive gave 2 short bursts from Starboard side, range 1,000 yards. Red 2 then fired a long burst from Starboard when about 200 yards ahead of Red.1 at range 300 yards closing to 50 yards. Red 2's ring sight, however, failed, but he thinks he got one hit on Port radiator of E/A, but did not see any strikes and makes no claim, and broke off as Red 1 passed under his port wing. Red 1 gave a two second burst at 100 yards after which four feet of enemy aircraft, starboard wing broke off and E/A spun into sea in flames where it exploded leaving only burning wreckage on water, no sign of pilot.

There was no return fire from E/A.

Both pilots consider a perfect interception was made.

Weather:- Visibility unlimited, cloud base estimated at 15,000 - 20,000 feet.

Camouflage:- E/A coloured dirty grey with letters thought to be either A.K. or A.H. in very feint black lettering on fuselage - Black crosses were also on wings and fuselage.

Red 1. P/O J. Blair, D.F.M., claims one Me. 109 Long Range destroyed.

Red 2. F/Lt Bennetts makes no claim.

Major Bomber Command Operations

19th February to 20th February 1944

19-20 February	**Leipzig***	**823 aircraft-78 lost**
	*** casualties not known**	
20-21 February	**Stuttgart-125 killed**	**598 aircraft-9 lost**

WEEKLY APPRECIATION OF DAMAGE TO KEY POINTS AND PROGRESS OF REPAIRS.

Period from: 09.00 hours Wednesday 16th February

to: 09.00 hours Wednesday 23rd February 1944.

GENERAL.

During the past week the G.A.F. attacked land-targets in this country on four nights, on the first two and on the fourth with considerable weight and on the third with little. The three big attacks (18th/19th, 20th/21st, 22nd/23rd February) were all aimed at London. The other (21st/22nd February) was on a small scale and confined largely to South Eastern England.

The three big attacks on London were the heaviest since May 1941, and were all of short duration. Provisionally it is estimated that 120 bombers operated overland on the first occasion, 95 on the second, and 150 on the third: probably a larger proportion than in recent attacks reached London. H.E. and I.B. were dropped more or less simultaneously. In the first attack there were 480 fires in London and 24 outside, in the second 606 in London and 50 outside, and in the third 235 in London and 34 outside. On all these occasions the Dock area received little attention. There was no great concentration on any one borough, but on the whole South-West London received the main weight of all these attacks. Little of moment occurred outside London except on the last night when Colchester received a weight of bombs. Fatal civilian casualties in London in these attacks were as follows : first attack 182, second 216 and third 29.

The minor attack (21st/22nd February) was made by 15 aircraft which, except for a single penetration as far as Beckenham, operated over Southern and South Eastern England and did negligible harm.

The total fatal civilian casualties for the whole country for this week amounts to 442: in addition 995 people were seriously injured and 67 are missing. Enemy losses in aircraft amount to 20 (5.5%)

The following have been reported;

18th/19th February	23 Key-point incidents	10 railway incidents
20th/21st February	23 "	16 "
21st/22nd February	Nil "	Nil "
22nd/23rd February	14 "	7 "

No Key-Points were seriously damaged except on the night of 20/21st when Latimer Engineering Co (radio apparatus) Marconi`s W/T Co (Wireless equipment) and Integral Auxiliary Equipment Ltd (hydraulic pumps) suffered damage which appears to be substantial.

KEY POINTS AFFECTED AND OTHER INCIDENTS

ATTACK ON LONDON

Fri/Sat 18th/19th Feb. Night

Shortly after 0030 hours 120 long-range bombers crossed the coast between Happisburgh and the Thames Estuary, the majority penetrating to Greater London, where 56 boroughs were involved. There were also incidents outside London, mostly within the area bounded by the Buckinghamshire – Bedfordshire border/ Colchester/Thames Estuary. A provisional estimate of the places affected is as follows: London 78, Essex 50, Hertfordshire 20, Suffolk 5, Cambridgeshire3, Norfolk and Buckinghamshire 1 each.

THE FOLLOWING KEY POINTS WERE AFFECTED

FACTORIES

1) G. BEATON & SON LTD, 27 Telford Way and 31 Brunel Road, Westway Estate, East Acton W.3

Production: Airframe Components.

Ministry Interested: Ministry of Aircraft Production.

H.E. caused blast damage to roof and glazing. Production slightly affected for 2-3 days.

2) BUCK & HICKMAN LTD, 407 Hornsey Road, London N.19

Production: small tools, jigs, fixtures and gauges.

Ministry Interested: Ministry of Supply.

A nearby H.E. caused superficial damage to the roof. Production was slightly affected.

3) A.C.COSSOR LTD, Cossor Valve Works, 22 Highbury Grove, Highbury, London N.5

Production: Wireless valves and apparatus.

Ministries Interested: Ministry of Aircraft Production, Ministry of Supply.

H.E. fell nearby causing damage by blast to the roof and wall. Production was stopped for a few days.

KEY POINTS AFFECTED AND OTHER INCIDENTS

ATTACK ON LONDON

Sun/Mon 20/21st Feb. Night

Shortly after 2130 92 long-range bombers crossed the coast between Orfordness and the Northern fringe of Kent. Probably not less than 25 reached London, where 63 boroughs were affected. There was a spill to the North and South of the Estuary and in particular within the areas Epping/Halstead/Shoeburyness and Dartford/ Tonbridge/ Faversham. A provisional estimate of the places affected outside the London area is as follows: Essex 32, Kent 16, Suffolk and Surrey 2 each, and Wiltshire 1. At about 0330 hours three other aircraft came in over the South Coast and penetrated to the outskirts of London: they dropped no bombs and may have been engaged in reconnaissance.

THE FOLLOWING KEY POINTS WERE AFFECTED

FACTORIES

1) ALUMINIUM PLANT AND VESSEL CO., Northfield House, Point Pleasant, Wandsworth, S.W.16

Production: W/T and A/S apparatus.

Ministry Interested: Admiralty.

Only slight damage was caused and the effect on production was negligible.

2) FORD MOTOR CO.LTD., Dagenham, Essex

Production: I.C. Engines, Lorries, Rolled Steel products, tank tracks.

Ministries Interested: Admiralty, Ministry of Supply, Ministry of Fuel & Power, Ministry of Works, Crown Agents for the Colonies.

H.E. fell damaging a small gas main. Production was not affected.

ENEMY ACTION

KEY POINTS AFFECTED AND OTHER INCIDENTS.

ATTACK ON LONDON

Tues / Wed 22/23rd Feb, Night.

At about 0015 hours 150 long-range bombers began to cross our coast, some over East Anglia and the Estuary and others over the South Coast. The number reaching London is not known but 36 boroughs were bombed. There was a more widely scattered spill on this night, and incidents were reported from the following places: Essex 22, Berkshire 11, Suffolk 10, Surrey 7, Kent and Hertfordshire 6 each, Sussex 3, and Bedfordshire and Hampshire 2 each.

THE FOLLOWING KEY POINTS WERE AFFECTED

FACTORIES

CHAMBON LTD, Reo, Riverside & Vencourt Works, Beaver Lane & Standish Road, Hammersmith, London, W.6.

Production: Small tools, jigs and gauges, rifle components.

Ministry Interested: Ministry of Supply.

Some damage was caused by a fire started by I.B.`s at 0046 hours.

20th-21st February 1944

This attack was the sixth mounted during *'Steinbock'* that could be regarded as falling into the 'major' category and was to feature the involvement of twelve Gruppen providing a total of 165 aircraft; this figure included fifteen FW190s from SKG10. II/KG54 would operate from Varrelbusch and I/KG100 from Rheine in Germany. Wittmundhafen and Münster/Handorf were recorded as the start point for I/KG54 and II/KG2 this evening, although Juvincourt, Soesterberg and Coulommiers were the airfields linked with these units during *'Steinbock'*. The other participating Gruppen were recorded as starting from the clutch of airfields scattered across Holland and France.

II/KG54, I/KG100, I/KG54 and II/KG2 were to take off in a staggered sequence that would see them link up over the Dutch coast using *'Funkfeuer' 2* at Noordwijk. I/KG2 operating from Eindhoven would also head for this M/F beacon. Take-off time for II/KG54, with between 28 and 30 bombers participating and coming down from its more northerly airfield of Varrelbusch, was around 20.00 hours, compared to 20.30 hours for II/KG2 heading out from the more westerly location at Münster/Handorf. Between them the five Gruppen would dispatch a force in the region of 90 to 100 bombers. The North Sea crossing would culminate in a landfall skirting the Essex side of the Thames Estuary. The absence of any route markers meant that the crews were expected to navigate using D/R methods, make their final bombing approach slightly north of the target area, then bank left and make their runs from west to east - at least according to subsequent interrogation of PoWs. Navigation notes found on a 2/KG54 bomber lost this night revealed four *'Knickebein'* transmitters and two *'Sonne'* units were available; as it was, all the PoWs captured from the raid later denied either using the systems, or even being aware of the bearings on which the beams were laid!

I/KG100 and I/KG54 were to be in the van of this stream since their ETA over London was timed for 22.02 to 22.12 hours, while I/KG54 was to commence bombing from 22.12 hours onwards. II/KG2's ETA was probably the same as for I/KG54.

He177 6N+KK from I/KG100 was one of between ten and thirteen bombers that flew out over Noordwijk at 21.11 hours and 27 minutes later was part of the Gruppe formation droning westward above the Noord Hinder light vessel. A further thirteen minutes passed before landfall was made ENE of Southend with the target just over ten minutes distant.

The He177s were believed to be carrying four SC1000 *'Hermanns'* but apart from several SC500s loaded into selected II/KG54 Ju88s, the other bombers were due to release AB1000 and/or AB500 incendiary-laden containers, along with 50 kg (Brand C 50) phosphorous bombs. Bombing altitude would vary between 13,000 and 16,000 feet.

The War-time Diary of Miss J. M. Oakman - Chelsea Sunday 20 Feb 1944

21.38 sirens

22.36 all clear

Second raid of fire. Very heavy barrage again. Heard UXB East at 21.58. A cold night and strong wind. Red glow in N and NW areas – counted 7 "going" after the "all clear" – (2 with big flames). Flares of red dropped over the same area NW as during previous raid.

Major pathfinder changes.

A major alteration in target-marking procedure was introduced at this stage of Operation *'Steinbock'*. Hitherto, I/KG66 had used the appropriate variation of 'Ablauflinie' or 'Leuchtpfad' flare layout for the attacking force's benefit, depending upon the degree of visibility. Now, both systems would be suspended in favour of a simple flare pattern laid over the target zone, with a different colour combination used on successive raids, and with the altitude at which the flares were ignited also regularly altered. Amber or white flares with which to provide enhanced identification of the target zone were sometimes used.

The abandonment of the more precise flare systems seems to have been a further indication of the Luftwaffe's switch-over to the equivalent of 'area bombing' marking methods employed by their British contemporaries. The pathfinder crews were to take off and reach the target at three-minute intervals in order to maintain a regular flare pattern; the first crew was actually timed to arrive three minutes ahead of the ETA.

Another change in procedure that affected the target-marking sequence related to the incorrect positioning of any of the flare patterns. Up to now any pathfinder crew that picked up such a failure would have attempted to rectify the situation by releasing its flare load in the correct location. Now, the mislaid flares were to be ignored, but a greater concentration of correctly-aligned flares was to be dropped. With this principle applied in sequence by pathfinder crews, it was anticipated that the main force would not be distracted by the inaccurate flare pattern.

On 20th February the British radar screens began to pick up the bombers' 'traces' as they approached in two separate waves that then converged some distance from the English coastline. The attackers were observed to be flying in a loose pattern spread between Harwich in Essex and Hythe in Kent. By 21.30 hours the first marker flares were bursting over the capital, albeit in a very scattered manner and in numbers barely exceeding twenty. The time for initial pathfinder marking of the target, along with the reference to aircraft crossing in over Kent, is a reasonable indication that units based at other than German airfields were involved in this element of the raid. All three Gruppen from KG6 were operating from Belgium

Of the flares released over the London area, roughly half descended along the line of the Thames between the city centre and as far west as Chiswick. In spite of this haphazard and meagre preliminary target marking effort by I/KG66 a fair proportion of the 80 bombers recorded as crossing the British coast won through to drop their loads within the target area. Elsewhere bombing incidents were recorded extending eastwards of the City of London, while some incidents involving more than one aircraft, were recorded from Suffolk, Essex and Kent.

The bombing extended over a near two-hour period and resulted in some 600 fires, demonstrating the wholesale use of incendiaries in concert with bombs ranging from SC500 to SC1000. Fulham, Putney and Chiswick absorbed the bulk of this onslaught with many of the 216 recorded fatalities occurring in these three Boroughs. Serious as the situation had become, matters might have been even worse had a much higher proportion of the attacking force found its primary target and dropped their loads within the designated compact target area. Had this occurred there was a high possibility that a fire-storm might have been created thanks to the thousands of incendiary bombs could not have been discounted.

Reported casualties were 216 killed and 417 seriously inured.

The Luftwaffe Effort

At least two I/KG100 crews got through to central London and released their bombs on marker flares according to the airmen concerned. The hitherto uneventful sortie then began to go wrong for both crews. One suffered a compass failure that finally saw the crew more than happy to land at Marx – almost 100 miles north-west of their airfield at Rheine.

The other crew had experienced W/T failure thanks to a quantity of '*Düppel*' that had wrapped itself around the aerial. Although they got back over the Continent they wandered round until, with fuel almost down to nil, it was brought into the Dutch airfield at Twente/Enschede, some twenty miles west of Rheine.

The return route for the Luftwaffe crews was noted as extending between North Foreland and Dungeness in Kent. The aircraft from Münster/Handorf, Varrelbusch and Rheine were tracked heading out over north-east Norfolk. I/KG100 flew back to Chateaudun from its forward airfield the following day.

The twelve crews of 5/KG2 were flying back to Münster/Handorf, but they arrived there short of one bomber. The Leutnant Bohe's Ju188s was heading in over Essex around 22.00 hours. Stalking the bomber was a Mosquito of 25 Squadron up from Coltishall in the hands of Pilot Officer Brockbank. His Radar Operator/Navigator Pilot Officer McCausland temporarily lost contact, but was brought back on track by the GCI Controller. However, despite closing to 1,000 feet on several occasions, the first visual of the now violently weaving 'hostile' was not gained for some 25 minutes. Two bursts of fire, the second from very close in and directly behind, set the port engine on fire. Scant seconds later as the RAF crew watched their prey as it drooped into a steep dive. On board the stricken bomber the pilot ordered his crew to abandon their charge. The two branches of RAF intelligence differ as to whether Oberfeldwebel Rittgen (Beobachter) baled out or not, but he did not survive.

A Junkers Ju188 in the typical night bomber camouflage of this period.

Combat Report

20/21 February 1944

25 Squadron Mosquito XVII/ AI Mk.X

22.03 hours Braintree

10/10 cloud at 3,500 feet, clear, fine and starry above. Visibility excellent. 1 Ju188 destroyed

Grampus 16 (P/O Brockbank, Pilot and P/O McCausland, Nav/Radio) took off from Coltishall at 21.10 hours. Was handed over to G.C.I. Neatishead, (Sgt. Jefferson, Controller,) and told to go to 17,000 feet. After several vectors was informed that "bandit" was at 20,000 feet and was told to make 21,000 feet. At 21.37 hours contact was obtained at 7 miles range on aircraft crossing from port to starboard in position. 7692. Throttles to 2650 revs. At plus 4 boost and gained gradually on the target, which weaved gently at first and later more violently. Closed in several times to 1,000 feet but target was 20/30 degrees above and no visual was obtained. Contact was lost once but restored after a further vector from G.C.I. Whilst following the target in over the coast, fighter was illuminated by single searchlight beam through cloud gaps and was unable to douse them. Target was then corkscrewing violently and after a chase lasting approximately 25 minutes visual was obtained on exhaust glows at 600 feet range, 11 o'clock and slightly below in position M.3466 and was identified as JU.188. E/a crossed gently from port to starboard and as it was crossing back two short bursts were fired from 10 degrees port at 300 feet with unobserved results. The range was further reduced to 75 feet and visual of JU.188 obtained against dark sky. A further short burst was fired from dead astern point blank range between port engine and fuselage. E/a immediately caught fire and fighter broke starboard to observe results. E/a flew straight and level for a few seconds and as fighter closed in again it started a very steep dive with pieces flying off. In the dive an explosion occurred and when last seen e/a was still diving steeply into cloud blazing furiously. No return fire was experienced.

Extract from the interrogation of U5+LN's crew by ADI(K)

This aircraft was one of twelve of 5/KG2 which took off to attack London. The crews were briefed to return to Münster/Handorf.
The U5+LN was attacked from below by a night-fighter when on the way to the target, and hits were received in the port engine, which caught fire. All members of the crew baled out, and the aircraft crashed in flames.
It will be noted that this aircraft carried a crew of five, the fifth member being an extra gunner.
MORALE: The A/G's morale is low and he has little pretention to security-consciousness; the morale of the remaining three surviving members of the crew is high. The observer and W/T operator hold the E.K.1.

Extract from the crash report on U5+LN by AI(IIg)

Report No.8/36 Ju188E-1 issued 28 February 1944

This aircraft was attacked by a Mosquito at very close range and crashed at 22.10 hours on 20th February 1944 at Park Farm, Wickham St. Paul. Ten 20mm strikes were seen in the tailplane and rear fuselage. The aircraft broke up in the air and was widely scattered, the tail unit and some nine feet of fuselage being found 1 ½ miles from the main wreckage. The cockpit broke away and was fairly complete when first inspected. Unfortunately, this suffered from the attention of looters and all the instruments have since been stolen.

Identification markings

U5+LN (L in black, outlines red)

Works number on fin 260339.

Camouflage

The under-surfaces were black, the upper surfaces being blue-grey sprayed with irregular black lines.

Engines

BMW 801 G-2. These are both badly damaged by fire and are still buried.

Armament

1 x MG 131 in dorsal turret. This turret is a modified one and will be further examined.

1 x MG 131 rear dorsal position.

Twin MG 81s presumably ventral armament, but these guns had been jettisoned and have not so far been found.

MG 151/20 was forward firing armament, but this also is missing. The aircraft was apparently carrying only incendiaries as a large number of 1 kilo incendiary bombs and five U.X. 50 kilo phosphorous incendiary bombs were found in the immediate neighbourhood of the crash.

Armour

The usual type of pilot's fully armoured seat was fitted and the lower half of the oil radiators were protected by armour plates as previously seen on the BMW 801 engines. The dorsal turret was fitted with an internal screen of armour, consisting of three strips each 19 ½" wide x 3 ½" deep and 10mm thick. The hydraulic oil tank in the fuselage was protected by a rectangular piece of armour plate underneath, 26 ½" long x 10" wide x 6mm thick.

Internal equipment

Wireless installation consisted of the FuG 10P, FuG 16 and the FuG 101A. The dial in the cockpit for this instrument had a red mark opposite 50m on the lower scale and 250m on the higher scale. The usual dive bombing equipment, consisting of a Stuvi 5B sighting head with BZA computor, was fitted.

There was also a mounting for the Lotfe 7D horizontal bombsight, but the sight itself was not found.

The automatic pilot was of a new type and is being sent to R.A.E., Farnborough for further examination. A balloon cable cutter was fitted to the leading edge of the mainplane and round the nose of the cockpit. De-icing of the mainplanes and tailplanes was by hot air. The lagging of these hot air pipes, which used to consist of glass wool, was found to be of corrugated cardboard and tin foil. Large quantities of "window" were found around the wreckage.

Crew

Five, one dead in wreckage, four prisoners.

The AA Defences start to bite

Gerhard Klunker and his crew in B3+MP of 6/KG54 had taken off shortly after 20.00 hours, the initial start time for the Gruppe, with the crews orbiting the airfield until all were aloft at 20.20 hours, whereupon course was set for the Dutch coast. The pilot had experienced problems in wending his way to this point thanks to possible British interference with the signal from the Noordwijk beacon. Navigation by D/R across the North Sea did not work out in the crew's favour since landfall was made, not over the briefed Essex coast, but further south over the north Kent coast. It was then that AA fire erupted and bracketed the lone Ju88. The crew on its first operational flight had been told to 'abort' the mission should they encounter severe opposition. They therefore jettisoned their load of incendiaries and banked the bomber round for home. However this action proved in vain as the shells struck the bomber which crashed into the sea close to Whitstable.

As Johann Krettek's 2/KG54 Ju88 approached London from the south it was struck by AA fire over Croydon. The port engine caught fire and Krettek ordered his crew to bale out. The bomber still had its bomb load on board when it plunged into the ground with Johann Krettek at the controls. The fact that he was unable to follow his crew out was not surprising. Although the rear canopy on the Ju88 could be jettisoned, the pilot's location was such that he had to get out of his seat which was enclosed by the fixed forward cockpit frame in order to bale out. In addition the obstruction posed by the control column yoke and base was a notable factor in making a swift exit from the seat awkward, especially when encumbered by flight gear. The *'Steinbock'* record of Ju88s shot down indicate a high mortality rate among pilots compared to other crewmembers.

The wreckage Krettek's Ju88 is inspected by RAF personnel.

Another view of the RAF personnel inspecting the wreckage of Johann Krettek's Ju88.

The Luftwaffe View

Once again Luftwaffe accounts of the raid quoted a higher figure for participating crews (200) as well as crews bombing the primary target (171). The time-span of the raid was stated to have been between 21.24 and 22.18 hours, with six crews in all failing to return and a further two crashing on the continent. In addition the attack was the first of three, albeit the major one in terms of numbers. Between 02.18 and 02.25 hours twelve Me410s from V/KG2 and ten of the thirteen FW190s of SKG10 released a mix of incendiaries and SC500 bombs – Oberleutnant Plate was lost in his FW190. Barely one hour later eleven more FW190s carried out what was described as 'disruptive action' without loss, but equally with no stated effect upon London itself.

A Narrow Escape

Queen Wilhelmina of the Netherlands living in exile in Britain had a narrow escape when a bomb landed near the house she was staying in; two of her staff were killed. At Fulham the local MP assisted in rescue work using his car as an ambulance on several occasions. At Balham a bomb destroyed a stables, however the horses inside were rescued. Next day three pigs were found shivering with fear and sheltering in the bomb crater.

Luftwaffe Losses 20th-21st February 1944

Ju188 E-1 5/KG 2 U5+LN WNr 60339

Park Farm, Wickham St Paul, Essex. 22.10 hrs. Shot down by P/O Brockbank in a 25 Sqn Mosquito.

Started from Münster at 20.30 hrs to attack London. Attacked from below by a Mosquito night-fighter when on the way to the target. Hits received in the port engine which caught fire. All members of the crew baled out and the aircraft broke up in the air and crashed in flames. Markings: L in black outlined in red. Under surfaces were black, the upper surfaces blue grey sprayed with irregular black lines.

The aircraft was carrying two AB 1,000 incendiary bomb containers plus ten 50 kg phosphorous incendiary bombs.

A large quantity of 'Window' was found in the wreckage.

Lt Ewald Bohe injured (F) (PoW injured), Ofw Karl Rittgen EKI (B) (Killed CC 5/318), Uffz Gunther Güldner EKI (Bf) (PoW injured), Uffz Wilhelm Pyttel (BS) (PoW injured), Gefr Hugo Schweitzer (Bs) (PoW injured).

Do217K-1 7/KG2 U5+AR WNr 4592

Failed to return from a sortie to London.

Oblt Wolfgang Brendel (F) (Missing), Fw Bruno Preher (B) (Missing), Ofw Bruno Schneider (Bf) (Missing), Uffz Heinz Grudssus (Bs) (Missing).

Do217M-1 9/KG2 U5+HT WNr 6407

Failed to return from a sortie to London.

Uffz Walter Schmidt (F) (Killed – washed ashore at Texel 2/5/44), Uffz Fritz Frese (B) (Missing), Ogefr Siegfried Briesning (Bf) (Missing), Ogefr Heinz Bodzien (Bs) (Killed – washed ashore at Sint Maartenszel and buried 4/5/44).

Ju88 5/KG6

Shot down near Le Culot during a non-operational flight by an enemy day fighter.

Uffz Wilhelm Geldermann (F) (Inj), Uffz Walter Beck (B)(Inj), Uffz Josef Keferstein (Bf) (Inj), Fw Gottfried Bach (Bs) (Inj).

Ju88 1/KG54 B3+EH WNr 310300

During return flight from London an engine failed and crew baled out.

Uffz Helmut Schmidt (F) (Killed - parachute failed), Gefr Heinrich Hofmann (B) (Inj), Uffz Harry Kastaun (Bf) (Inj), Ogefr Gerhard Bickendorf (Bs) (Inj).

Ju88 A-4 2/KG54 B3+KK WNr 3661

Dagnall Park, Selhurst, Croydon, Surrey. 22.10 hrs.

Started from Wittmundhafen at 20.00 hrs. with two AB 1,000 incendiary bomb containers to attack London. Hit by AA fire at 15,000 ft. over the target in the port engine which caught fire and the pilot gave the order to bale out. The pilot failed to escape and aircraft crashed with the bomb load.

Ogefr Johann Krettek (F) (Killed Brookwood, Surrey), Ogefr Heinz Graf (B) (PoW), Uffz Heinrich Gross (Bf) (PoW), Uffz Franz Serwe (Bs) (PoW).

Heinrich Gross, Heinz Graff, Franz Serwe and Johann Krettek, crew of B3+KK

Ju88 **2/KG54** **B3+GK** **WNr 3661**

Failed to return from a sortie to London.

Uffz Walter Scharf (F) (Missing), Karl Pfefferle (B) (Missing), Uffz Kurt Jeide (Bf) Missing, Uffz Kurt Hantschel (Bs) (Missing).

Ju88A-4 **6/KG 54** **B3+MP** **WNr 301346**

In the sea, 1 mile north of Whitstable, Kent. 21.55 hrs. Shot down by 3.7 inch AA guns.

Started about 20.00 hrs to attack London carrying two 500 kg HE and ten 50 kg incendiary bombs. At about 12,000 ft over the Thames Estuary very intense AA fire was encountered. As crew were on their first war flight and unsure of their position, they dropped the bomb load and headed for home. At that moment the tail was hit by AA fire and the pilot gave the order to bale out, the observer doing so with great speed and came down on the shore near Leysdown, on the Isle of Sheppey. He took shelter in an empty look-out post and gave himself up the next morning. The aircraft was seen to come down in the sea.

Uffz Gerhard Klunker (F) (Missing), Gefr Gerhard Grosspietsch (B) (PoW), Gefr Harald Meyer (Bf) (Killed CC 1/439), Uffz Helmut Schäffer (Bs) (Killed CC 1/180).

Ju188E-1 **2/KG66** **Z6+DK** **WNr 260369**

Crashed at Sailly-Loretto after take off for England. 21.20 hrs.

Uffz Alfred Swillims (F) (Killed), Ofw Josef Vollmer (B) (Killed), Uffz Ludwig Neuhaus (Bw) (Killed), F Franz Claes (Bf) (Killed), Uffz Max Kopka (B) (Killed).

Fighter Command Claims, not attributable to a particular loss

A claim was made for an He177 destroyed at 22.36 hrs 50 miles east of Lowestoft, by F/Lt J Singleton in a 25 Sqn Mosquito.

A claim was made for an enemy aircraft damaged at 23.45 hrs near Soesterberg, Holland, by W/Cdr B R O'B Hoare in a 605 Sqn Mosquito.

A claim was made for a Ju188 damaged at 22.09 hrs near Staplehurst, by W/Cdr J Cunningham in an 85 Sqn Mosquito.

A claim was made for a Ju188 probably destroyed at 22.00 hrs near Lydd, by F/Lt B J Thwaites in an 85 Sqn Mosquito.

21st-22nd February 1944

London was granted a reprieve from a major Luftwaffe assault, since the main bomber force remained on the ground. A token effort was made to attack London by the fast-flying FW190s and Me410s, One Me410 was damaged and an FW190 lost.

The War-time Diary of Miss J. M. Oakman - Chelsea   Tuesday 22 Feb 1944

02.56 sirens

03.28 all clear. One burst of gunfire, a bunch of orange flares and our fighters "up". A few searchlights about. Some bombs were dropped.

Tuesday 22 Feb 1944

23.56 sirens

Wednesday 23 Feb 1944

01.24 all clear. About the heaviest barrage we've ever had was put up. Three bombs (HE) fell followed by 1 UX – in SE direction. One green flare appeared in E bright and green and gently drifted right over to W way. Red tracer bullets tried to pick it off – one in fact knocked a bit of it off – but it gently glided on and eventually burnt itself out. Other bunches of white flares (candelabra fashion) were all over the sky. Two fires of some dimension showed up – one in NE and other SE.

Shepherd's Bush Gaumont and Market were hit. Lot of trouble Battersea and Hounslow way.

Luftwaffe Losses 21st-22nd February 1944

Me410 **13/KG2**

Returned damaged.

Ofw Bolten safe.

FW190G-3 **2/SKG10** **WNr 160851**

Failed to return from a sortie to London.

Oblt Helmut Plate (Missing).

22nd-23rd February 1944

The citizens of London were probably glad of a respite from aerial attack the previous night. However any thought that the Luftwaffe might have spent its force was quickly dispelled when the air-raid sirens churned out their shrill and distinctively eerie note as midnight was fast approaching.

Several hours previously 155 *'Steinbock'* crews had been called to their latest briefing. II/KG54 did not take part, but the three Gruppen of KG6 put up ten extra crews (50 compared to 40). German records show that just over half the number of operational aircraft were available this night compared to the first raid. Luftwaffe records also show times over target between 00.28 and 00.50 hours. 166 of the 185 aircraft reached London, 13 of which were lost.

V/KG2's Me410s were operating for the second consecutive night and late that evening duly dispatched fifteen aircraft from Vitry-en-Artois. Leutnant Müller was piloting one of the Me410s that, by 00.45 hours was plotted north-west of London. Unfortunately for Müller and his Bordschütz Karl-Heinz Borowski their course took them near to a major 3.7 inch gun battery, whose predicted fire struck home fatally. The 16 Staffel machine was finally seen flying at low level over the village of Radnage, before it dived into the ground.

I/KG100 was briefed for this operation by the Kommandeur, Hauptmann Gotthelf von Kalkreuth, who undoubtedly hoped that his particular He177 would carry him through to the target, unlike his 'aborted' sortie nine nights before. This time all fourteen bombers got away from 20.37 hours onward, having previously lined-up at the runway-end in designated take-off order. Such was the emphasis on precision that if any crew was more than three minutes outside their allotted take-off time they would not be allowed to proceed! The bomb loads were entirely high explosive and included SC1800 and SC1000 bombs, two of each being reportedly borne in the aircraft of the more experienced pilots. The remaining He177s carried four SC1000s. Each bomber had its tail light on and this was switched off as soon as it was airborne, this being a 'runway clear' signal for its successor. Finally, the aircraft circled the airfield in a left-hand pattern at 3,000 feet before setting course at the briefed time.

At this stage of *'Steinbock'* the original Staffeln strength of fourteen aircraft (2/KG100) and eleven (3/KG100) established between December and the start of operations had shrunk noticeably, although five of 2/KG100's He177s had been transferred to I/KG40. The average serviceability figure for the Gruppe had been between twelve and fifteen, barely half of available strength.

The current freedom from loss over Britain enjoyed by I/KG100 was of some comfort to Oberfeldwebel Ruppe's crew as they headed out in He177 5J+QL. As they closed in on the Suffolk coast they had no way of knowing that Flight Lieutenant Baillie, who had been carrying out practice interceptions in combination with the GCI Station at Neatishead, was now under guidance from Happisburgh and flying a north/south course on more intense business. Around midnight the GCI Station informed Baillie it had a 'contact' on a westward-heading 'bogey' and he banked his Mosquito in its direction. The controller managed to bring his charge within a three mile range before he informed Baillie that no further guidance could be provided. Fortunately, Flying Officer Simpson's Mk. X radar set proved equal to the task in picking up not one but two 'traces' two miles to port and 10-15 degrees above at 17,000 feet. Range was closed to some 2,000 feet, at which point the rear flying 'bogey' banked to port and the other aircraft turned in the opposite direction. Baillie fastened onto the latter machine, but experienced a degree of frustration at being illuminated by searchlights that were only doused after several minutes had elapsed.

The 'Do217' (as identified at the time) was weaving gently out to the Mosquito's port side when finally picked out visually at a mere 400 feet range. The night fighter banked in behind its prey and a two-second burst of fire was delivered with immediate and shocking effect, since the bomber disintegrated. A measure of retaliation from the downed machine took the form of debris striking the Mosquito, as a result of which the starboard engine began to overheat. Course was immediately set for 25 Squadron's airfield at Coltishall on which the pilot safely set his charge down at 00.25 hours. Many miles to the south the smouldering remains of his 'kill' lay scattered near Yoxford, Suffolk. Only Obergefreiter Imm, strapped into the tail turret, had somehow survived the descent of the severed tail section some two miles distant from the main crash site. He had suffered two broken legs and was subsequently assisted out of his position by a Mr Kiddie, whose Samaritan act included the administration of a cup of tea from his Thermos flask! Oberfeldwebel Ruppe and the other four crewmembers enjoyed no such good fortune.

German records at the time quoted a greater number of losses (13) compared to the nine listed in contemporary British records. Five of the latter were lost over British soil and included a second Me410, this time from 14/KG2, that lost its encounter with a 96 Squadron Mosquito flown by Squadron Leader Caldwell operating out of West Malling. The crash at Framfield in Sussex left neither Unteroffizier Eggers nor his gunner Obergefreiter Bednorz alive. Around 25 minutes later, at 00.30 hours an AA battery located near Stebbing in Essex locked onto a 6/KG2 Ju188 flown by Unteroffizier Elster. A shell hit the port engine and almost immediately the bomber fell steeply away. Whatever efforts were made to bale out

Ogfr Emil Imm, the only survivor of He177 5J+QL which was shot down by a 25 Squadron Mosquito over Yoxford, Suffolk.

by the five-man crew, success only attended Feldwebel Heimann, and even he only managed to squeeze out into the slipstream scant seconds before the bomber slammed into the ground.

The fifth and final bomber that failed to clear British shores was B3+JP, a Ju88A-4 from 6/KG54 that came down in the Thames Estuary south of Brightlingsea, Essex, having probably been downed by AA fire. One body was later washed up on the Essex coast, another drifted across the North Sea and was found on the Dutch coast five months later, in July.

Among a number of boroughs affected by the raid, Hammersmith, Camberwell and Feltham received the worst of the punishment, although little if any long term damage was experienced. 230 fires were reported, one in the Victoria Dock took several hours to bring under control. The total of 29 casualties was away down compared to the previous two assaults.

81 tons of bombs fell on the Capital with 75 tons in Essex and Kent. Widespread bombing in London caused damage. Harrow Boys' was school damaged by incendiaries with the tuck shop burnt out. An incendiary container was found next day in the school orchard. Three children were killed when an AA shell fell on a house in Albert Road, Leyton. Five more shells fell in the area without causing damage. Essex police reported three HEs at Hornchurch airfield with three RAF personnel injured, two of them seriously.

Combat Report

96 Squadron

One Mosquito XIII A.I. Mark VIII PILOT S/L P L Caldwell OPERATOR F/O K P Rawlins took off from West Malling at 2335 hours on patrol under Wartling G.C.I. (Controller S/O Legge) The pilot reports that :-

"I was patrolling over the Channel at 24,000 feet under Wartling Control when I was warned of a bandit 15 miles South at 21,000 feet on a vector of 290°. I obtained contact crossing port to starboard, range 5 miles slightly below. E/a now on Northerly vector. At 2,000 feet I obtained visual of blue exhausts. Evasion was regular and hard. I was forced to break away to avoid overshooting and momentarily lost contact. This was regained at 2,000 feet after e/a had been seen to pass beneath at 40 to 50 feet, speed 220 ASI. I closed to 800 feet and fired a burst with 1 ½ ring deflection, no strikes resulted. I was temporarily illuminated by S/L's but bandit was not apparently aware of our presence. I closed to 4/500 feet and fired second burst with ½ ring deflection. Strikes and flashes appeared, followed by an explosion and sparks, in what was believed to be starboard engine. Time 0013 hours, height 15,000 feet. E/a turned starboard and dived vertically, soon afterwards I saw an explosion on the ground to starboard."

R.O.C reported crash in Q9235 square 0015 hours.

1 Me. 410 claimed as destroyed.*

Armament report: Rounds fired : 20 mm SAPI. 60
" HEI. 60
Total 120

**This was Me410 U5+CE that fell at Framfield.*

The War-time Diary of Miss J. M. Oakman - Chelsea   Wednesday 23 Feb 1944

22.07 sirens. Most awful barrage – and a most spectacular sight of flares, rockets and gunflashes.

22.34 four bombs fell all together. The World's End got blown down.

23.12 all clear

Got sent to Guiness Trust SW10 which had had a heavy bomb on the third wing from the E side front and gas main in Kings Rd was alight in crater full of water. The other two bombs were Upcerne Road and Lamont Road. It was truly an awful night – the Guiness wing was one awful heap of rubble and the other wings terribly blasted. It was reckoned 200 people were underneath trapped and to crown it, the heap was smouldering all night with piles of smoke. The gas main was later got out. Work proceeded on the Guiness all night. There were queues at F.A.P.'s* of injured – rest centres were soon full up with the homeless – and supplementary ones opened up. We were all up all night doing whatever job came along – at any time. The big shelter has been used and nobody was killed in it.

* First Aid Post

Luftwaffe Losses 22nd-23rd February 1944

Ju188 E-1   6/KG 2   U5+IP   WNr 260312

White House Farm, Stebbing, Essex. 01.35 hrs.

Started from Münster / Handorf at 23.00 hrs carrying ten 50 kg incendiaries internally and two large incendiary bomb containers externally, to attack London. The aircraft was hit in the port engine by AA and after a steep dive crashed and burned out. The wireless operator managed to bale out at 500 metres and landed at Stebbing, he then walked seven miles to a hospital in Braintree where he gave himself up to a gate porter. On his journey to Braintree he had tried to surrender to a publican, who told him to 'clear off'. The rest of the crew was killed in the crash. It is believed the pilot was trying to make a belly landing, but came in too steeply. A bomb exploded destroying all but the tail end of the fuselage.

Markings: Squadron markings; the U5 was painted in dark grey letters 5 inches high. The letters IP were in black, outlined in yellow. Painted on the fin was the works number 260312 and aircraft letters IP.

An interesting point was the recovery of an elevator counter balance weight made of glass. It was 10 inches long and 5¾ inches wide x 3 inches deep and weighed approximately 15 lbs.

Uffz Reinhard Elster (F) (Killed CC 1/191), Gefr Harry Dornio (B) (Killed CC 1/192), Fw Adolf Heimann EKII (Bf) (PoW), Uffz Ernst Neu (Bs) (Killed CC 1/186), Fw Bernd Gronau EKII (Bs) (Killed CC 1/185).

Me410A 14/KG 2 U5+CE WNr 20463

Bentley Farm, Framfield, Sussex. 00.15 hrs.

Shot down by S/Ldr Caldwell in a 96 Sqn Mosquito.

This was one of four aircraft, which was flying about 23,000 feet on a north-westerly course when it was attacked by a night-fighter and set on fire. The aircraft went into a steep dive and exploded on impact with the ground, wreckage was scattered over a wide area.

Markings: C in black, outlined in white. Upper surfaces were two shades of grey, the sides of the fuselage were a mottled grey and undersurfaces black.

Uffz Bernhard Eggers (F) (Killed CC 9/45), Ogefr Stefan Bednorz (Bf) (Killed CC 9/45).

Me410A 16/KG 2 U+?Q

Andridge Farm, Radnage, Buckinghamshire. 00.45 hrs. Claimed by AA site SM7's 3.7 Inch guns.

Aircraft was observed approaching from the north at low altitude. The engines were heard to rev up and the aircraft suddenly dived into the ground and caught fire. There was no explosion, but the wreckage was scattered over a wide area.

Lt Felix Müller (F) (Killed 5/422), Gefr Karl-Heinz Borowski (Bs) (Killed CC 5/421).

Ju88A-4 6/KG6

Crashed near Ligny, France, on return from a sortie to London.

Lt Walter Petrasch (F) (Killed), Uffz Heinz Matz (B) (Killed), Ogefr Norbert Cyron (Bf) (Killed), Uffz Ludwig Mackel (Bs) (Killed).

Ju88 9/KG6

Failed to return from a sortie to London.

Uffz Friedrich Bieberstein (F) (Missing), Fw Heinrich Ernst (B) (Killed), Fw Karl Landenberger (Bf) (Missing), Uffz Heinz Exner (Bs) (Missing).

The body of Heinrich Ernst was washed ashore on 6 May near Groote Keeten, Holland, and was buried two days later at Bergen.

Ju88 5/KG54 B3+EN WNr 550291

Failed to return from a sortie to London.

Uffz Horst Hechler (F) (Missing), Uffz Harry Möbius (B) (Missing), Uffz Adolf Seitz (Bf) (Missing), Ogefr Heinz Twittenhoff (Bs) (Missing). The body of Ogefr Twittenhoff was washed ashore in Holland on 12 June.

Ju88 6/KG54 B3+JP WNr 01436

Buxey Sandbank, 10 miles south Brightlingsea, Essex. 00.15 hrs.

Shot down by AA guns.

The wreckage was only exposed for a short while at low tide, only being found on 24th February.

Markings J black outlined in yellow. Black lower surfaces, the upper surfaces being dark green with grey wavy lines superimposed.

Engines: Jumo 211 J, works number on one 1046064132.

Equipment: FuG 10P, FuG 16, FuB1 2f. A balloon cable cutter was fitted to the leading edge of the wing.

The body of Uffz Langer was washed ashore in Holland on 17 June. The body of Uffz Kihle was found off the Essex coast on 9 May and buried at sea.

Oblt Alfred Simm (F) Killed CC 5/412), Uffz Ewald Langer (B) (Killed), Uffz Erich Kihle (Bf) (Killed), Uffz Gerhard Daut (Bs) (Killed CC 5/411).

He177 A-3 3/KG 100 5J+QL WNr 32227

Welseley, Yoxford, Suffolk. 00.12 hrs.

Shot down by F/Lt A S H Baillie in a 25 Sqn Mosquito.

After a single burst of cannon or MG fire had been heard from the ground, this aircraft crashed and the wreckage was spread over a wide area. The tail unit, containing the rear gunner, landed some two miles away. The gunner came down in tail unit and was seriously injured.

Markings: The only letter seen was a white Q on a black shield apparently from the side of the nose. Upper surfaces greyish blue sprayed with black strokes. Lower surfaces black.

Ofw Wolfgang Ruppe (F) (Killed CC 1/294), Uffz Georg Lobenz (B) (Killed CC 1/292), Uffz Friedrich Beck (Bf) (Killed CC 1/295), Gefr Georg Markgraf (Bm) (Killed CC 1/293), Uffz Ernst Werner (Bs) (Killed CC 1/291), Ogefr Emil Imm (Bs) (PoW injured)

FW190G-3 3/SKG10 Wnr 160459

Failed to return from a sortie to London.

Uffz Max Seidel (Missing).

Fighter Command Claims, not attributable to a particular loss

A claim was made for an Me410 destroyed at 00.45 hrs off Dungeness by F/Lt B A Burbridge in an 85 Sqn Mosquito.

A claim was made for a Ju188 probably destroyed at 00.50 hrs off Dungeness by F/Lt D Dixon in an 85 Sqn Mosquito.

A claim was made for a Ju188 damaged at 01.00 hrs off Dungeness by F/Lt D Dixon in an 85 Sqn Mosquito.

A claim was made for an Me410 destroyed at 00.32 hrs off Dungeness by F/O E R Hedgecoe in an 85 Sqn Mosquito.

A claim was made for a Ju88 destroyed at 23.43 hrs off the Suffolk coast by S/Ldr C A S Anderson in a 410 Sqn Mosquito.

A claim was made for a Ju188 destroyed at 00.03 hrs off the Suffolk coast by S/Ldr C A S Anderson in a 410 Sqn Mosquito.

A 29 Squadron Mosquito MkXIII. Despite the Mosquito crews having all the advantages over the bombers, danger lurked in the darkness for them too. On this night the squadron lost its C/O Wg Cdr Mack DFC and the squadron navigational leader Flt Lt Townsin, when they failed to return from a patrol.

A claim was made for an enemy aircraft damaged at 01.50 hrs near Coulommieres by F/Sgt H William in a 418 Sqn Mosquito.

A claim was made for an Me410 destroyed at 01.53 hrs near Coulommieres by F/Sgt H William in a 418 Sqn Mosquito.

A claim was made for an enemy aircraft damaged at 02.30 hrs near Eindhoven by F/Lt W A Bird in a 605 Sqn Mosquito.

A claim was made for an enemy aircraft destroyed at 01.45 hrs near Melsbroek by F/O B F Miller in a 605 Sqn Mosquito.

29 Squadron Operational Record Book

Ford 22.2.44

There was hostile activity overland again early in the night and the Squadron had a piece of very bad luck W/Cmdr R.E.X.Mack DFC. And F/Lt. B.C.Townsin, the Squadron's Nav/Radio Leader, not returning from Patrol. They were scrambled at 23.02 hours and gave contact 25 miles south of Beachy at 00.10 hours. A hard turn to port was apparently made after which nothing more was heard. S/Ldr.Arbon and F/O.Jarvis both had contacts, the latter getting two. Neither got visuals, although F/O.Jarvis had closed to 2,000 feet on his second chase when the French coast was reached.

23rd-24th February 1944

Having conducted what was considered as a concentrated assault upon Britain's Capital less than 24 hours previously, General Peltz's crews were again alerted. The bomber serviceability levels for this raid would reflect a continuing severe decline in comparison with the onset of *'Steinbock'*.

V/KG2's Me410s were removed from the battle order for the first time since $18^{th}/19^{th}$ February and while most Gruppen would put up the same number of aircraft as on the previous night, I/KG6's strength was to be reduced from 15 to 10. In all, 130 crews (161 as stated in Luftwaffe records) were to head across the Channel and begin their attack at 22.00 hours following the release by I/KG66 of white target flares fused to burst at 10,000 feet. The inward route (for all but III/KG6 flying out of its Belgian airfield) was via Evreux and Le Havre, and would finally involve a course reversal from 345 degrees to 110 degrees, the turning point being marked by four red flares northwest of High Wycombe.

The briefed target area, code-named *'Hamburg'*, was in the vicinity of the Isle of Dogs in London's East End. This was where several of London's major docks were located, so the prospects for creating a degree of economic damage, as opposed to primarily striking at the civilian population, were reasonable-to-good.

Yellow flares would be released over the target to ignite at around 11,000 feet and bombing runs would be conducted from 13,000 feet, a height reduction of 3,500 feet compared to the crossing-out altitude at the French coast, with the descent commencing at the English coastline. This steady loss of height would be continued all the way back to the French coast, which would be crossed at just 500 feet.

The III/KG6 crews were briefed to head for Boulogne before adopting a north-westerly course to the target. On their return the II/KG2 crews would return to Coulommiers, rather than their base airfield at Soesterberg in Holland, and III/KG2 would set course for Lille and thence to Eindhoven after crossing the English coast at Dungeness.

The use of star shells as a further navigational aid off five points on the coast between Ostend and Le Havre, along with the same facility inland at Cambrai, Montdidier and north-west of Paris, was now being adopted. The shells were fused to burst marginally above any cloud layer existing at the time. Combinations of up to four shells would be fired during pre-determined times that coincided with both the outward and homeward flights of the bombers; furthermore the shell pattern could be either horizontal or vertical in presentation.

KG2's three Gruppen were reportedly providing between 30 and 45 crews on this occasion. I/KG2 sent fourteen crews in eleven 2 and 3 Staffel bombers along with two aircraft from Stab elements. U5+AK, U5+EL and two Stab machines were loaded with four SC500 and four BC50s and these would take off first. Incendiaries carried in AB 1000 and two AB 500 containers were allotted to the other bombers and comprised the remaining loads. The outward route was almost due west to Evreux before heading west-north-west; first to St. Valery-en-Caux, then Eastbourne and finally the target, which was briefed to be attacked between 22.30 and 22.42 hours. The route back to Melun was via St. Valery-en-Caux, while descending steadily to cross over the French coast at less than 1,000 feet.

One of the Do-217M-1s from 2/KG2 was in the hands of Oberfeldwebel Stemann, who was the fifth of the Staffel crews to take-off between 21.16 and 21.20 hours. He and his

Obfw Stemann's Do217 which, despite the crew abandoning it over London, flew steadily on in a shallow glide and made a smooth belly landing near Cambridge!

crew had progressed from Melun without incident and an hour or so later were over-flying London's north-west suburbs when matters took a dramatic turn. The aircraft was engaged by AA battery fire and seemed to suffer damage to the fuselage, starboard engine and wing. Stemann was sufficiently shaken by this to put his bomber on automatic pilot and order a bale-out that minutes later deposited him and the other three airmen on the ground in Wembley. His reaction was to prove too hasty because, regardless of any damage, the abandoned Dornier flew steadily northwards, albeit in a gentle glide. Some 60 miles from London the aircraft floated in for a relatively soft crash-landing in allotments in the Milton district of Cambridge!

In the 2¼ hour period between the first 'Alert' and the final Luftwaffe bomber crossing-out, barely one-third of the attacking force was recorded as releasing their loads over the London within 15 minutes. Nevertheless, residential property in numerous boroughs was particularly affected, a factor probably reflected in the fatality figure of just under 300. The total of 120 tons of incendiaries and explosives was equally split between London and the counties of Surrey, Sussex and Hampshire.

Evaluation of Oberfeldwebel Stemann's Do217 U5+DK

The virtually intact nature of the Stemann Do217M permitted a good evaluation of the design's final variant by RAF intelligence AI1(g). It was noted on the Crashed Aircraft Report that this was only the second occasion on which a Luftwaffe bomber had made such an unassisted and intact landing. The camouflage scheme was recorded as blue, mottled with green on top with black under-surfaces. A prominent aviation author recalled after visiting the crash-site when still a schoolboy, that the colour scheme caused him to have nightmares for some time afterwards!

The investigation team was well pleased to have a pair of DB603 engines on hand in good condition. Points of note were the positioning of the oil cooler on top of, and the coolant radiator underneath, the cowling. This compared with the Me410 installations where the oil cooler was placed under the cowling and the coolant radiator positioned in the wing. Small projecting castings with forward-facing apertures were borne on the starboard cowling side; flexible pipes linking the apertures to the generators permitted cooling air to be circulated. The pressed steel engine bearers were modified and quite different from those of the Me410. The fact that 600 gallons of fuel and 40 gallons of oil were in the aircraft was regarded as of benefit to the Farnborough 'Boffins' in bench-testing the DB603s.

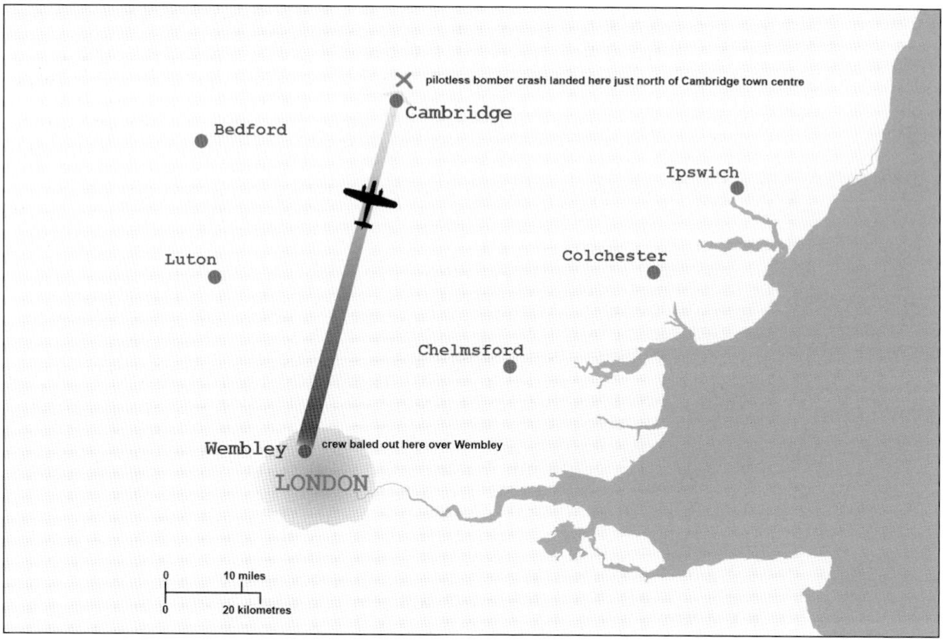

The route taken by the pilotless Do217 after being abandoned over London.

Another view of U5+DK showing what a superb landing the pilotless bomber achieved on the allotments near Milton Road.

Examination of the bomb load in the single AB1000-2 and two AB500-1 containers revealed the content of the former unit to be a mix of incendiary bombs and IBSENs compared to the normal load of up to 590 1kg IBs. The container had four sub-compartments containing IBs and IBSENs in alternate order.

In the nose compartment a Stuvi 5B bomb sight was used in conjunction with BZA dive-bombing equipment. The Beobachter was provided with an electrically-heated windscreen when acting as bomb-aimer.

In the cockpit, a clear-vision panel was fitted in front of the pilot, which was protected by a Perspex wind deflector that prevented air entering when the panel was in use. The pilot had a shaped and fully protected armoured seat, but no other form of either armour plate or bullet-proof glass existed in the forward nose area. The dorsal gunner was protected by armour plate located around the turret sides. There was no armour plate in the cockpit roof, while protection for the ventral gunner could only be confirmed or otherwise when the Do-217 was raised from its crash-landed attitude.

The full range of radio, direction-finding and blind-landing equipment was fitted, although only the frame for the FuG 214 tail-warning radar equipment was found.

Colchester in Flames 23rd-24th February 1944

Incendiaries and eight phosphorous bombs fell on the St Botolph's shopping area of Colchester. In a few seconds the whole town was lit up by huge fires. Machinery in two clothing factories fell through the upper floors of the buildings and firewatchers saw incendiaries, 'pouring through the roofs as like a handful of peas tossed through a sieve.'

A furniture depository, a furniture store, an ironmongers and the Plough Hotel were among the businesses ablaze. When the roof of St Botolph's Church was seen to be alight fire guards assisted by two 'plucky schoolboys' climbed a rickety iron ladder carrying buckets and stirrup pumps. Three fires were extinguished and the church saved. The Empire Cinema also had a lucky escape when seven incendiaries were successfully extinguished. A witness remarked of the incendiaries, *'They were like a lot of red hot metal coming down and then they seemed to spray away in all directions.'*

Fire-fighters broke down doors to gain access to buildings where incendiaries had fallen. The insecure buildings led to four soldiers being fined for 'looting'.

The fires lit up the surrounding area for miles around. 15 properties were destroyed and 99 seriously damaged. It was estimated that 1,400 incendiaries had fallen. There was a single casualty; seventy year-old Mrs Bertha Nunn was in bed when an incendiary fell through her roof and onto her bed, causing her serious burns.

Seventy fire pumps were in use and pumped nearly 2 million gallons of water onto the fires, which were successfully contained and did not spread to neighbouring buildings.

Luftwaffe Losses 23rd-24th February 1944

Do217 M-1 2/KG 2 U5+DK WNr 56051

Milton Road Allotments, Cambridge. 22.40 hrs.

Started probably from Orleans to bomb London. Only incendiary bombs carried.

This aircraft was over the NW suburbs of London, at a height of about 10,000 feet when it was engaged by the London AA barrage. This caused no little consternation and panic amongst the crew so that when the pilot thought the aircraft had been hit, he immediately gave orders to bale out. The crew left in good order and were duly captured in the Wembley area. The aircraft, flying on "George" proceeded on its course - also in good order - lost height gently and came in to make a perfect belly landing on some allotments in Cambridge.

Markings U5+DK, call sign DM+AW. The compass card gave the works number as 6051 but the main aircraft plate on the port side of the fuselage gave the full number as 56051. The radio card and the plate on the nose section gave the number as 56031. It would therefore appear that this aircraft had been damaged and repaired using parts of another aircraft. The noses of the spinners were white. The undersurfaces were black, the upper surfaces blue, mottled with green with a very rough finish to the paint. On the tail fin was a large white 2.

Two boxes of Window were carried, consisting of black paper strips, metallised on one side, 79.7 cms long x 20 mm broad which were packed in bundles of 350. Each bundle was held together by two 2 inch bands of adhesive brown paper, whilst forty such bundles are carried in a large cardboard box and a single band of baling wire went round the centre of the box to hold the strips firmly round the centre.

A balloon cable cutter was fitted to the leading edge of the main plane and also to the nose of the aircraft.

Ofw Hermann Stemann (F) (PoW), Uffz Walter Rosendahl (B) (PoW), Uffz Hans Behrens (Bf) (PoW), Uffz Richard Schwarzmuller (Bs) (PoW).

Ju188E-1 5/KG2 U5+CN WNr 260315

Crashed at Eindhoven after engine failure from Coulommiers to Handorf – not due to enemy action.

Lt Erich Höhne (F) (Inj), Major Heinz Engel Gr Kpr 2/KG2 (B) (Inj), Uffz Werner Beck (Bf) (Killed), Uffz Herbert Wolf (Bs) (Inj).

Ju188E-1 5/KG2 U5+AN WNr 260222

Landed at Coulommiers after an engagement with a night fighter.

Uffz Johann Triebel (Bs) (inj), Flg Wilhelm Spönemann (Bs) (inj). Rest of crew safe.

Ju188E-1 2/KG6 3E+CK

Lt Lenkeit (Staffelkapitän) (inj), Fw Eder (Inj), Fw Brabant (Inj).

A claim that may relate to this loss was made by F/O Williams in a 605 Sqn Mosquito for a Ju88 shot down at 00.12 hrs 23-24/2/44, on the boundary of Chievres airfield.

Ju88 4/KG54 B3+HM WNr 8808

Uffz Herbert Weberschinke (Bs) (inj) during an attack on London. Aircraft returned safely.

Fighter Command Claims, not attributable to a particular loss

A claim was made for a Ju88 destroyed at 00.12 hrs near Chievres by F/O E L Williams a 605 Sqn Mosquito.

A claim was made for a Ju88 probably destroyed at 22.20 hrs off Beach Head by W/Cdr J Cunningham in an 85 Sqn Mosquito.

WEEKLY APPRECIATION OF DAMAGE TO KEY POINTS AND PROGRESS OF REPAIRS.

Period from: 09.00 hours Wednesday 23rd February

to: 09.00 hours Wednesday 1st March 1944.

GENERAL

The enemy`s air-offensive against this country was continued on the first two nights of the week and on the last night, and in addition bombing of no account occurred on Friday the first daylight incident since 2nd December.

The first two night attacks were made on London by forces estimated at 90 bombers of various types and 10 fighter bombers, which came in over the South Coast. In the first attack only about 15% succeeded in reaching London where the bulk of the bombing occurred within the period 2230/2245: the spill was spread over a triangle Hastings/Isle of Wight/St Albans. In the second attack the number of aircraft reaching London is not known: more boroughs were involved, but the failure to achieve any concentration was very marked, operations extending over a wide area, mostly Southern England. Boroughs in the west of Central London have again been mainly involved in these attacks. There have been isolated incidents involving casualties to the civilian population, but damage to Key-Points, dislocation of railways and utility services, and numbers of fires, all show an appreciable reduction from the previous week.

Activity on the last night was conducted by about 20 aircraft, of which 6 reached London, the remainder operating over South-Eastern England. Incidents were of no particular account and no civilian casualties were caused.

Civilian Casualties for the week total 242 fatal, 54 missing, and 539 serious: of these 234 fatal, 531 serious, and 54 missing are attributable to London. The enemy is reported to have lost 17 aircraft (8%)

The number of Key-Points affected by enemy action is 20: of these 1 was serious. There were also 11 incidents involving railways and 1 an airfield.

The War-time Diary of Miss J. M. Oakman - Chelsea Thursday 24 Feb 1944

08.49 alert. A lovely bright morning, two planes over on reconnaissance.

09.00 All clear

21.42 alert

22.52 all clear. Some suspected phosphorus fell in Hans St and started a fire.

Major Bomber Command Operations
21st February to 25th February 1944

24-25 February	**Schweinfurt**	**734 aircraft-33 lost**

24th-25th February 1944

The pressure, that had been applied to London over three of the previous four nights, was kept up on the $24^{th}/25^{th}$, the night's raid being directed upon what was described as 'the Westminster area of government buildings'. I/KG66 crews would commence releasing white flares at 22.00 hours that were fused to ignite at an altitude of 10,000 feet. The numbers of operational aircraft (170 in Luftwaffe records compared to British intelligence estimates of 135) again demonstrated the huge gap between either of these figures and the original strength available for the campaign.

A new bomb-aiming technique was now in use. The Beobachters for some Gruppen were being briefed to select an individual flare on which to direct their Lotfe bombsight, and furthermore to allow for the angle of lead by releasing the bomb or incendiary load before being actually over the flare. This 'rule of thumb' method was even more pertinent for those bombers not fitted with a bombsight, of which there was a sizeable proportion among the force!

The usual pattern for target approach was briefed. For example, I/KG2 would take off at one-minute intervals which for 2 Staffel would last from 20.33 to 20.39 hours. The initial course was to Evreux and on to Le Havre, by which time the bombers would be flying at 16,500 feet on a heading of 345 degrees. This would be maintained until four red flares would be sighted near High Wycombe, at which point a reverse course of 110 degrees would be taken to the target. Bombing was briefed to commence at 22.00 hours and to be marked by red flares released by I/KG66 that would ignite at 10,000 feet. The return course was out over Dungeness and south-east to Lille, from where a final turn would lead the crews to Eindhoven. II/KG2 would take off from Coulommiers and follow on behind as far as London, however it would return to its home airfield.

The bomber-stream tactic once again did not involve III/KG6, and presumably the two fellow Gruppen, operating out of Belgium. The instructions were for its crews to take up a course for Boulogne from where a direct course to pick up the red flares released near High Wycombe would then be flown. The heightened risk to this relatively small force of being picked upon by RAF night fighters must have been considered by General Peltz and discounted as a threat, otherwise the crews would have been directed to head for Le Havre and link up with the other Gruppen.

A variation in tactics was also carried out by I/KG66 on this occasion. Whereas the Main Force units were to be at maximum altitude by the time they had crossed-out over the Channel, the pathfinder crews were instructed only to commence climbing at the French coast and to reach their operational altitude of 19,500 feet on the other side of the Channel. This altitude was to be maintained as far as London, in contrast to the following crews who would gradually lose 3,000 feet between the English coast and the target.

A similar pattern of mixed success and failure attended the Luftwaffe effort. This time the bulk of the 100 tons of bombs did fall within the city's boundaries, starting around 250 fires and killing 75 people. The Boroughs of Westminster and Wandsworth bore the brunt during the sharp 30-minute assault, and the last bomber headed out over the Channel at 23.00 hours.

Rich 'Harvest' for 29 Squadron

No. 29 Squadron was based at Ford in Sussex and in common with most night fighter units had built up a creditable tally of 'kills' in a steady if unspectacular fashion ever since entering the nocturnal battle against the Luftwaffe bombers in mid-1940. The crews had operated from several airfields along Britain's eastern coast and had arrived at Ford the previous September. It was on 'alert' as the first indications of imminent enemy incursions began to appear on the Channel-based C.H.L. radar screens. Pilots and their navigator/radar operators were either held at 'readiness' in the crew-room or were boarding their Mosquitos.

Despite I/KG66's prime function in the pathfinder role, one of the estimated ten Ju188s dispatched was actually bearing a bomb load totalling 1,500 kg in addition to ten LC50 flares. Unteroffizier Boetsch made a landfall near Beachy Head and successfully guided Z6+HK up to the final turning point for London. Minutes later he had released the two SC500 and ten SC50 bombs, as well as the flares, and took up a southerly heading for Montdidier.

Flying Officer Provan and Warrant Officer Nicol were already aloft in their Ford-based Mosquito Mk. XIII and under control from Tangmere. They had orbited at 25,000 feet and had made several 'contacts' that turned out to be friendly bombers. Then, at 22.15 hours according to his combat report, Provan 'Gauntleted' and headed almost due east towards a searchlight concentration. Nicol picked up a 'contact' to port at 2½ mile range, whereupon the searchlights were doused on request. The initial sight of the target from close in revealed the bomber jinking violently, an action that was swiftly doomed to failure. A short burst of fire from dead astern set Boetsch's port engine on fire. This was followed by four further bursts all over the fuselage, after which the Ju188, that was emitting flames and smoke, turned onto its back and fell inexorably towards its end near Framfield in Sussex.

Extract from AI(K) report

Place, Date and Time:

Great Streele Farm, Framfield, Sussex (Q.9439)

Type and Marks:

Ju.188 Z6+HK Works Number 260185

Unit 2/K.G.66

Start and Mission:

Started at about 19.30 hours from France with two 500 kg. and ten 50 kg. bombs. Düppel was used.

1. This aircraft was one of about ten from the unit which were detailed for the operation. No definite target was given.

2. The Z6+HK made landfall near Beachy Head at 5000 metres flying at 360 k.p.h. The pilot flew to a point West of London, turned eastwards and after releasing the bombs over London set a southerly course for home.

3. When flying on a bearing of about 150° at 5/6,000 metres the aircraft was caught in a cone of searchlights and in spite of evasive action taken, was attacked from the rear by a twin-engined fight-fighter.

4. Hits were received and the aircraft caught fire. The pilot gave the order to bale out. The aircraft crashed and was burned out.

Morale:

Pilot: Morale good but not very security conscious. He was on his second war flight over England and holds the E.K.II.

W/T: Morale poor and not security minded. He was on his eleventh war-flight and holds the E.K.II.

Crew:

Pilot: Unteroffizier Ludwig Boetsch - injured.

Obs: Leutnant Heinrich Köthe- 22 yrs - dead.

W/T: Unteroffizier Helmut Thomale - uninjured.

1st A/G: Oberfeldwebel Albert Schulz - Dead.

2nd A/G: Unteroffizier Helmut Böhm - 23 yrs - dead.

Combat Report

29 Squadron F/O W. Provan (Pilot) W/O. W. G. Nicol (Obs)

24 Feb. 1944. 2230 and 2241 hours

Mosquito XIII AI Mk.VIII. 20 mls N of Beachy (Q8543)

second attack from R.7538 - R4150.

Unlimited Vis. Cloudless. No moon. 1 JU.88 & 1 JU188 destroyed

General Report.

F/O Provan and W/O Nicol took off from Ford 2125 hours landed 2322 hours. Scrambled from Ford at 2125 hours. Controlled by Sector (Tangmere) Controller on Button B. Told to orbit F.O.B. 7 at Angles 25. After several contacts on friendly bombers, Mosquito at Angels 16 Gauntleted 080° (2215 hours) on intersection target not illuminated. Contact gained at port at 2/1/2 miles range. S/L's doused on request and Mosquito closed in to 300 ft. slightly to Port and below E/A. which was identified as a JU. 88, doing violent evasive action, with no bombs in rack. A 2 sec. burst from dead astern, set the port engine on fire, 4 further bursts given and strikes on fuselage seen after all bursts. E/A turned over on its back and dived straight down emitting flame and smoke and hit the ground and burst into flames Position Q8543 at 2230 hours.

Pilot called control for a fix then flew West towards F.O.B.7 and saw an intersection with A/C illuminated 15 miles away to the E. Mosquito "Gauntleted" again and a long chase at 1900ft. took place. E/A turned south and Mosquito cut him off, and closed to 300 ft. and identified E/A as a JU.188. E/A was held by S/L's all the time and was doing violent evasive action on a S.E. course. A short burst was given from dead astern and strikes seen (100 yds range) on fuselage. E/A turned starboard and a slight deflection shot given which set the starboard engine on fire. E/A was given 3 further short bursts as Mosquito followed it in dive from 19,000 ft. to 12,000 ft. Visual contact was enveloped in smoke but A.I. contact held. Mosquito overshot twice even though throttled right back, each time passing close to Port of E/A which was flying in a N.W. direction. Contact was then lost, but the E/A was later seen to explode on the ground. A fix was obtained at 2241 hours from Tangmere. Position R.4150 after Mosquito had flown over position of explosion.

Only one of Flying Officer Provan's claims was confirmed, the other being later 'downgraded' to a 'damaged'. What the RAF air intelligence officers failed to determine was that this aircraft carried the T-Gerät 'Gee' based equipment as well as Leutnant Köthe, the specially trained operator. Later a 15 year-old boy was arrested by local police for taking a pair of binoculars from Hans Köthe's body.

The Provan 'kill' heralded the beginning of arguably the best ever 'bag' of Luftwaffe aircraft to be entered in 29 Squadron's Operational Record Book for a single night's activity. Two Gruppen in particular were to suffer at 29 Squadron's hands, beginning with KG6, whose crews were approaching London at an ever-closing tangent to the main stream. An 8 Staffel Ju88A-4 - 3E+PS - was on the way in, having headed north-west from Boulogne to make probable landfall near Hastings and maintain a direct course for London.

A second 29 Squadron Mosquito flown by Flight Lieutenant Pargeter had followed on one minute behind Provan and was orbiting at 22,000 feet, also under Tangmere Control, when the pilot 'Gauntleted' onto a searchlight concentration that had picked out a 'bogey' heading up from the south. Pargeter closed in to 600 yards to deliver a three second burst of fire, and the bomber promptly peeled off downwards to port. The Mosquito again closed in to 200 yards for a second three second burst that peppered the fuselage and both wing-roots. This interception was the first of three recorded by Pargeter and the time of 21.44 hours in his combat report ties in fairly neatly with the loss of Feldwebel Wudzig's bomber that fell at Withyham, Sussex, at 2150 hours.

Fw Wudzig's Ju88 which fell near Withyham at 21.50hrs.

Flt Lt Pargeter's third victim was Fw Von Pawelsz's Ju188 U5+GP, the fin and rudder of which is seen here lying in a field near Shorne.

Pargeter had only whetted his appetite for success, as a second KG6 crew was soon to experience. Within a few minutes of having taken up a southerly heading he picked out another Ju88 heading in to London. His gunfire was claimed to have set an engine on fire, whereupon the bomb-load was jettisoned and the aircraft was believed to have fallen some 20 miles north-east of Brighton. This 'kill' was subsequently reduced to a 'damaged' status.

Pargeter's third interception again commenced with a visual sighting of a 'bogey' caught by searchlights to the north and this signalled the start of an extended tail-chase. A bomber crew was throwing out regular streams of 'Düppel' – one indication to its pursuer, along with a natural inability to respond to IFF interrogation - that it was 'hostile'. Closing in on his target near Gravesend, Pargeter identified the bomber as an Me410 and administered several short bursts of fire upon the violently jinking target as it flitted in and out of successive bands of searchlight batteries. Finally, the night fighter pulled up from underneath at minimum range; the cannon shells tore into the starboard wing and fuselage. The blazing bomber dropped into a slow spiral and struck the ground at Shorne, just west of the Medway towns of Kent. Feldwebel. Von Pawelsz and two of his four-man crew did not survive their Ju188's fiery demise. Pargeter fixed the location as north of West Malling and stated that identification of his adversaries was difficult due to his Mosquito being illuminated by searchlights. Therc had been a minimum of time to carry out full identification, although the 'Düppel' release by U5+GP and no IFF indicators from all three 'bogies' was a sound guide as to the aircraft being 'hostile'.

Squadron Leader Kirkland had 'Gauntleted' towards a searchlight concentration ten miles to his west, and after several minutes sighted a 'bogey' 2,000 feet lower on a north-easterly heading. In his urge to close-in to firing range Kirkland overshot to port of the target, but identified it against the searchlight beams as a Do217, although two to three miles distant. The range was steadily closed and a two-second burst from dead astern hit the fuselage; a second short burst set the starboard engine and wing ablaze, sealing the bomber's fate.

On board Obergefreiter Schürger, the Bordfunker, promptly baled out after half the tail unit became detached. Obergefreiter Trunsberger, the Beobachter, stayed at his post until he heard Leutnant Kuttler give the order to jump. Barely had he cleared the bomber when it went into a spin to fall at Westcott, west of Dorking, Surrey, at 21.56 hours, still with the other two crewmembers on board.

The substantial wreckage of Do217M U5+EL of 3/KG 2 shot down by Sqn Ldr Kirkland at Wescott near Dorking.

Success on this amazing scale for 29 Squadron was completed by Flight Lieutenant Barry in his Mk. XII Mosquito as I/KG2 was heading home. The Mosquito pilot had taken over the interception of what was described as an 'Me410' from another crew who had run out of ammunition during their pursuit. The aircraft was thoroughly 'hammered' and stated to have gone down into the Channel waters between Eastbourne and Beachy Head, but this claim appears to have been later reduced to a 'damaged' category.

Heading up towards the West Malling area, Barry caught sight of a searchlight-transfixed aircraft heading east as he approached at 19,000 feet. A fair degree of altitude had to be lost as he closed upon what was Do217M - U5+CL - indulging in full evasive manoeuvres, albeit unable to throw off the searchlight beams in the process. Barry over-shot but orbited quickly to port and closed to firing range. He noted that a red downward identification light was switched on by the pilot just before he opened fire. The Do217's starboard engine and

Do217M U5+CL fell in a field near Willesborough leaving little for the investigators to search through.

wing area promptly burst into flame and the bomber staggered away and down to starboard. The final crash-site was at Willesborough near Ashford, Kent, at a recorded time of 22.33 hours. Feldwebel Spiering and two of the other three airmen were the final victims of 29 Squadron's 'turkey shoot' that night.

Completing the Cull

488 (New Zealand) Squadron, based at Bradwell Bay on the Essex side of the Thames Estuary, joined in on the cull of Luftwaffe bombers. Flight Lieutenant Hall was airborne in his Mosquito at 22.00 hours under control from North Weald. He was then handed over to Biggin Hill for freelance patrol at 18,000 feet. Hall pursued several 'bogies' heading southward. One of these was a Do217 going at top speed. Strikes were made on the port engine and fuselage, but Hall overshot on his second attack and lost contact as a result.

Flight Lieutenant Peter Hall of 488 Squadron who claimed two victories on this eventful night.

Nothing daunted, Hall continued patrolling in a north-easterly direction and observed what was described as an 'intersection' slightly below at 13,000 feet. A pursuit of this developed into a head-on visual sighting of what was then taken to be a Ju188, but was actually the He177 - 5J+PK - of I/KG100. The searchlights were doused, but Hall had no difficulty in visually holding onto his prey. Four attacks were delivered after which the bomber's starboard engine caught fire and the aircraft entered a steep dive while shedding parts of its airframe. At around 7,000 feet the bomber was observed to fall into an even steeper dive and strike the ground at 22.40 hours. Hall stated that the crash location was

The remains of Heinkel 177 5J+PK which slammed into the ground near Lamberhurst, Kent.

'east of Wadhurst', marginally south of the actual site at Lamberhurst, Kent. Oberleutnant Hundt, the bomber's pilot, was one of three from his six-man crew killed in the incident. Examination of the bomber's remains revealed an interesting social aspect of Luftwaffe operations from France. Among the technical contents of the fuselage was unearthed several 'non-technical' items, namely bolts of silk cloth. Clearly some of the crew had availed themselves of the opportunity to buy the silk France with the intention of passing on to their families and/or fellow-airmen – the latter doubtless being a source of financial reward for the crewmembers concerned!

To the six crews brought down over British territory was added three more. A second II/KG2 Ju188 simply failed to return, perhaps Provan's 'kill'. One of I/KG66's Ju88S machines was shot down north of Fecamp, while a Ju88 from 4/KG54 crashed on its return. Unbeknown to General Peltz and his crews was the fact that the 'high tide' of *'Steinbock'* operations against London had just passed.

A Further Target-marking Variation

The pilot from Z6+HK revealed under interrogation a further variation in target-marking procedure that was similar to RAF pathfinder operations - the Master Bomber or *Verbandsfürhrer* (Master of Ceremonies). Unteroffizier Boetsch stated that he had flown in this capacity on his last operation and described his function as follows. He had been briefed to arrive over the target simultaneously with the first pathfinder aircraft, but at a higher altitude from where he would orbit the are. Should any of the flares be incorrectly positioned he would drop a single red flare over their location before laying his own flares over what he regarded as the proper target. A further measure to correct errors was for him to inform the leaders of the bombing force by R/T of the change in marking and the need to ignore the incorrect markers. He also revealed that the burn time of the standard single candle flare (LC50) was approximately seven minutes and the ideal time for their renewal by successive crews was six minutes. The normal complement of flares borne by each bomber was eighteen and the crews would release these either in three groups of six or two groups of nine.

'*Knickebein*' – a continuing controversy

'Knickebein' Station Nos. 5, 8, 10 and 11 were operating on the night of 24th-25th February. To date, the system's function had been a source of conflicting remarks from the captured airmen when interrogated by Wing Commander Felkin's team. The Luftwaffe personnel had regularly asserted that their crews had either been unaware of the equipment's availability for any raid or had refrained from its use, even when briefed to use it.

'Knickebein' had been available for operation ever since its introduction in 1940. As it transpired, its use prior to the Battle of Britain, and more significantly the ensuing 'Blitz' campaign, had permitted the British to gain access to its secrets, thanks initially to careless talk by captured personnel. Dr. R V Jones, a brilliant scientist, had ultimately realised that the 'Lorenz' blind-landing equipment from a crashed He111 formed a vital component of the system and was far too refined for its intended primary use as a landing aid.

Radio diathermy sets were hastily utilised to re-radiate the dot and dash sequences that informed the Luftwaffe pilots when they were on the appropriate side of the steady-tone beam indicating the course to be flown. However, these 'reverse transmissions' were neither in regular direct or indirect synchronisation with the 'Knickebein' transmissions, an operational aspect that ironically enhanced rather than diminished the confusion factor. Consequently, it was not unknown for a pilot seeking the main signal to inadvertently stray from one side to the other of the dot/dash boundaries in an involuntary 'weaving' pattern without ever achieving his aim. The comparison with a drunk attempting to steer a straight line is none too inaccurate.

The resultant distrust in the system voiced by pilots so affected was to be further increased by the fear that 'Knickebein' (in common with the 'H_2S' radar and 'Monica' tail-warning equipment in use by RAF Bomber Command in 1944) was capable of being homed-in upon by night fighters, which was never the case. In sad contrast, the 'Monica' sets were open to easy tracking by the Luftwaffe night fighters who would duly close in upon their victims thanks to the 'Naxos' and 'Flensburg' equipment that was specifically designed for this function.

The Village Dornier

On the night of 24th/25th February a Do217 landed at Westcott, Surrey, in the garden of a house in Parsonage Lane. In 1975 villager David Knight started asking people what they remembered. He found they still had many memories that make a unique account.

David Knight, himself then aged 8, recalled being in the air raid shelter at the top of Ashley Road when his father called him out to see a plane coming down. It had its navigation lights on and was spinning slowly like a sycamore seed. He went up to the Common i.e. Heath Rise in the morning to look at the crash beyond Thorndale Cottages, but was told to retire as far as The Sandrock as bombs were still on board.

Mr Batts of Chapel Lane said he went to Parsonage Lane on the morning after the crash with Mr Goult of St John's Road. The door of the plane had been forced off in the crash and they went inside, but an RAF Regiment chap told them to get out as there were still bombs

Above: An RAF airman holds a fragment of wreckage with the Dornier's radio call sign CL+UA.
Opposite: The Dornier came down near houses but as it fell in a flat spin, the houses survived intact.

aboard. He asked for a piece of the plane. The front of the plane was smashed in but an instrument panel was sticking out and he was given a part that looked like a radio circuit on an alloy sheet. On the other hand, Alan Brewer of North Street said that nobody went inside the plane, only himself, as it was too well guarded.

Mrs Jeater, who lived on the main road in Penny Cottage, at the time said that her husband was an ARP warden and was on guard duty while the plane was in Parsonage Lane. He brought home a brass part from the petrol tank that she threw out when they moved.

Dick Brookes was in the RAF in Southern Rhodesia at the time of the crash but it was in his parent's garden that the plane crashed and he had one of the hinges from an aileron.

Mrs Hutchins whose house had been next door to the crash site had a petrol gauge and said her lawn was covered with black-coated silver paper. She also recalled that one of the German airmen had tried to bale out, but left it too late and fell into the trees just behind her house. She thought he must have been alive during the night because she was sure she heard him blowing his nose!

Mr A Rice of Parsonage Lane also visited the crash site and recalled that he had been surprised to see that the plane had Dunlop tyres, whilst Mr J Rice reported that the wings of the plane were cut off by an axe to get at the bombs.

George Sawyers and Reg Rose, of Furlong Road, said they had each broken off a large part of the perspex nose but dumped them later. Bert Upfold had a small red light from the plane and said that the bomb disposal squad corporal also gave him a switch from the bomb aiming equipment. Mr Tugwell had a piece of perspex and Mr Arnold had a small piece of the plane which was given him by Mr A Rice who, apparently, used other pieces to make a base for a garden shed.

Captain Binge of Hill House recalled taking a photograph from the top of his garden near Thorndale Cottages and reported that he had since dug up several pieces of the plane in his garden.

Mr Russell of Furlong Road said that the remains of the plane were put on show outside Canter's Yard because Field Marshal Montgomery was passing through and the wreck disposal people thought he might like to look at it.

works hard and loves her job. Before joining up she kept house for three mistresses of Grafham School.

GERMAN RAIDERS

Captured by Innkeeper

Shortly after 'closing time' at the Wotton Hatch Inn, near Dorking, on Thursday last week, Mr. Charles Pullen (manager) and Mr. Alphonse Malmgambel (waiter), who were standing outside, saw a man coming along the road.

Thinking it a British soldier, the waiter called out, 'Hey, old man—have you missed the bus?'

The man replied, in a thick accent, 'Me German.' He was a young man, about 21, in flying equipment, carrying a Very pistol.

Mr. Pullen put his hand on the breach of the pistol to stop the airman using it, but when the airman said it was to signal his comrades in, he was allowed to do so.

Soon afterwards another young German (aged about 23) appeared, and both were taken to the inn.

A Canadian sergeant who happened to be there disarmed the Germans, and Special Constable Reffell took them in charge.

The airmen had come down by parachute in fields in the neighbourhood. Their plane crashed some distance away and the other members of the crew were killed.

DELAYED ACTION

Incendiary Bomb Injures Eight

The local newspaper's version of the night's activities

Peter Knight could recall the plane on a trailer outside Canter's and had a handle from an oxygen bottle which he managed to acquire when nobody was looking.

Mr Batts said that he was told that the bombs were taken to the range at Bury Hill and acid was poured in to make them safe although Mr Paine who lived in the house next to the old bakery at the time, thought the bombs were taken to Ranmore and defused. He also claimed that when one of the bombs was taken down the lane it started to make a noise and everybody got out of the way and went back later.

Cyril Brown who lived in Thorndale Cottages was home on leave from the RAF at the time and was called in to help guard the plane when it was taken down to Canter's Yard and went with it to the RAF scrapyard. He said that he took the compressor from the plane but that he felt guilty as so much had been stolen that he gave it back and said he found it in his garden. He also claimed to have had two saucepans made from the alloy on the plane but they had long since worn out.

Away from Parsonage Lane, Ted Nash of Furlong Road was a paper boy employed by Parson's the paper shop and recalled seeing one of the engines on the lawn in front of Broomfield House when he delivered the paper on the morning following the crash. Mrs Anscombe said that a large part of the tail fell behind her house in Balchins Lane. Mr and Mrs Tupper of Milton Street said that several pieces of the plane were found in the woods at Hungry Hill. Gerald Chennell said that one of the parachutes used by the German airmen was put on display in Wotton School the day after the crash.

It became apparent that not all the recollections could be relied upon. 'Peggy' Lewer of St John's Road was in the ARP in Westcott during the war. He was convinced that the German crew were all aged 15. In fact the pilot was 23, the two gunners 22 and the observer 21. But Miss Mold of Westcott Street was probably correct when she recalled that the Parish Church was full on the following Sunday (27th) when a Thanksgiving Service was held for the safety of the village.

As for the German airmen, the two dead men were buried at Dorking Cemetery and in 1962 their remains were removed to the German War Cemetery at Cannock Chase near Stafford. From Dorking Police Station, 'Corporal' Schürger was taken to an interrogation centre in London and then to a prisoner of war camp in Scotland. He was then shipped to America where he spent three years harvesting peanuts, cotton, tobacco and sugar cane on the Eastern Seaboard of the USA. He was repatriated to Germany in September 1947 to find that his home had been bombed, but he eventually found a job as an accountant, married in 1950 and was very happy that his nephew was made so welcome when invited by David Knight to visit Westcott in 1975.

Luftwaffe Losses 24th-25th February 1944

Do217 M	**3/KG 2**	**U5+CL**	**WNr 22736**

Willesborough, near Ashford, Kent. 22.33 hrs.

On returning from an attack on London flying at 4,000 metres at a speed of 380 kph, the aircraft was caught by searchlights and hit by AA fire, then attacked by F/Lt Barry on a 29 Sqn Mosquito. Some two minutes later the starboard engine cut out and the tail unit broke away and the aircraft went into a dive. All four members of the crew succeeded in baling out and the aircraft crashed and was burned out.

Markings: U5+CL, C in black outlined in yellow. A large 3 was painted on the fin. Undersurfaces sprayed black while the upper surfaces were a greenish blue, mottled with black.

Fw Werner Spiering EKI (F) (PoW injured), Fw Heinrich Bogeholz EKI (B) (PoW injured), Fw Martin Vogel EKI (Bf) (Died 25/2/44 Folkestone, Kent).

Do217 M **3/KG 2** **U5+EL** **WNr 56126**

Parsonage Lane, Westcott, near Dorking, Surrey. 21.56 hrs. Shot down by S/Ldr C. Kirkland in a 29 Sqn Mosquito.

Ogfr Georg Trunsberger

Started from Evreux at 20.54 hrs to attack the 'Hamburg' area of London. Having just reached the target area, half the tail unit disappeared without warning or noise. The wireless operator, taking a poor view of this, baled out. The observer remained in the aircraft a few minutes longer until he heard the pilot give the order to bale out. In this he was successful. As he left the aircraft it went into a sudden dive and spin, the port engine breaking away. The aircraft crashed into an outhouse, but there was no fire and under the circumstances was not very badly smashed. At the time of the crash the aircraft had its navigation lights on. No cause for the crash could be ascertained from the wreckage.

Markings: U5+EL, E in yellow, L in grey. On the fin was a large white 3. Call sign CL+UA. The spinners had white noses. The upper surfaces and sides of the fuselage were a dull blue with black wavy lines superimposed. The undersides and sides of the fin and rudder were black.

Engines: DB603 A-2, starboard works no. 01600361 maker HST and port 01600019 Maker HST.

Bomb Load: Four 500 kg and four 500 kg phosphorus incendiaries were carried. Seven UXBs were found with type 55 fuses and four Sprengbrand C 50 (incendiary bombs).

The bodies of the pilot and gunner/mechanic were found amongst the wreckage and bombs.

Lt Walter Kuttler EKII (F) (Killed CC 1/432), Ogefr Georg Trunsberger EKII (B) (PoW injured), Ogefr Julius Schürger EKII (Bf) (PoW injured), Uffz Erwin Brieger EKII (Bs) (Killed CC 1/431), Uffz Siegfried Erschwig EKI (Bm) PoW injured).

Ju188E-1 **5/KG2** **U5+GN** **WNr 260359**

Started from Coulommiers at 20.51 hrs and failed to return from a sortie to London.

Ofw Albert Daxenberger (F) (Missing), Uffz Rudolf Schmidt (B) (Missing), Uffz Kurt Scheffler (Bf) (Missing), Uffz Ernst Kwapis (Bs) (Missing), Ogefr Georg Preissner (Bs) (Missing).

A claim for a Ju188 shot down off Beachy Head by F/Lt Ward of 96 Sqn may relate to this loss.

Ju188 **6/KG 2** **U5+GP** **WNr 260321**

Queen's Farm, Higham, nr Gravesend, Kent. 22.35 hrs.

Shot down by F/Lt Pargeter in a 29 Sqn Mosquito.

This aircraft started from Coulommiers at 20.44 hrs and was approaching the coast of Kent when a fire occurred in the tail unit. The wireless operator and mechanic baled out and the aircraft crashed with the pilot and observer still on board. According to local reports, some cannon or machinegun fire was heard in the air shortly before the aircraft was seen to crash.

Markings: G outlined in yellow.

Equipment: Remains of torpedo dropping equipment found in wreckage.

Lt Friedrich-Wilhelm von Pawelsz (F) (Killed CC 5/56), Ogefr Bruno Schievelbein (B) (Killed CC 5/57), Uffz Michael Hofmockel (Bf) (PoW), Uffz Fritz Otto (Bm) (PoW), Gefr Adalbert Thimian (Bs) (Killed CC 5/55).

The crew of U5+GP Mechanic, Michael Hofmockel, Friedrich-Wilhelm von Pawelsz, Bruno Schievelbein and Fritz Otto.

Ju88 A-4 **8/KG 6** **3E+PS** **WNr 710409**

Hale Farm, Lyewood Common near Withyham, Sussex. 21.58 hrs.

Shot down by F/Lt Pargeter in a 29 Sqn Mosquito from dead astern. Crashed in flames into a small hollow and burnt out.

Markings: 3E+PS, the P black outlined in red. Black underneath, sides of fuselage and top wing surfaces were olive green with greeny grey wavy lines superimposed. On the lower half of the fin and rudder the wavy lines were a blue grey.

The wireless operator and gunner baled out while the bodies of the pilot and observer were found in the wreckage.

Fw Gerhard Wudzig EKI (F) (Killed CC 9/44), Uffz Albert Hessmann EKI (B) (Killed CC 9/44), Uffz Eberhard Wulf EKI (Bf) (PoW), Ogefr Albert Grundler EKI (Bs) (PoW).

Ju88 **4/KG54** **B3+CM** **WNr 550271**

Crashed on return from operations.

Uffz Willi Steckhan (F) (Killed), Ofw Heinrich Kneermann (B) (Killed), Uffz Werner Rüsch (Bf) (Inj), Uffz Richard Otte (Bs) (Killed).

Ju88S-1 **1/KG66** **Z6+MH** **WNr 300623**

Shot down by a night fighter during a sortie to London and crashed 40 km north of Fècamp.

Uffz Jurgen Schroiff (F) (Missing), Uffz Werner Wiede (B) (Missing), Uffz Herbert Höckendorf (Bf) (Missing).

Another view of Fw Wudzig's Ju88.

Ju188 E-1 2/KG66 Z6+HK WNr 260185

Great Streele Farm, Framfield, Sussex. 21.50 hrs. Shot down by F/O Provan in a 29 Sqn Mosquito.

Started at about 19.30 hrs from France. Duppel was used. This aircraft was one of about ten from the unit which were detailed for the operation. No definite target was given. Landfall made at Beachy Head at 5,000 metres flying at 360 kph. The pilot flew to a point west of London, turned eastward and after releasing the bombs over London set a southerly course for home. When flying on a bearing of about 150° at 5/6,000 metres the aircraft was caught in a cone of searchlights and in spite of evasive action taken, was attacked from the rear by a night fighter. Hits were received and the aircraft caught fire, the pilot giving the order to bale out. The tail unit disintegrated, the outer mainplanes broke up and the remainder of the aircraft span into the ground almost vertically and was burned out.

Three of the crew baled out. The pilot landed with two broken legs, the wireless operator landed safely, but the observer, Lt Köthe, was found dead half a mile from the crash site.

It was noted that the leading edge of the fin was made of plywood doped over with fabric. The large dinghy contained yellow hooded capes made of rubberised fabric, almost identical to the British model.

Uffz Ludwig Boetsch EKII (F) (PoW injured), Ofw Albert Schulz EKI (B) (Killed CC 1/8), Lt Hans Heinrich Köthe (T-B) (Killed CC 1/10), Uffz Helmut Thomale EKII (Bf) (PoW injured), Uffz Helmut Böhm EKI (Bs) (Killed CC 1/9).

He177 A-3 3/KG 100 5J+PK WNr 2222

Chequers Farm, Lamberhurst, Kent. 22.40 hrs. Shot down by F/Lt P F L Hall in a 488 Sqn Mosquito.

Started from Chateaudun at about 21.00 hrs to bomb London, Duppel being used. Whilst approaching the target at a height of about 12,000 ft. the aircraft was held by searchlights and attacked by a nightfighter. The underside of the fuselage caught fire and the aircraft crashed at a shallow angle in flames. The observer, wireless operator and bordmechaniker baled out. It is estimated that two large bombs exploded on impact and the wreckage was completely destroyed.

Olt Wilhelm Hundt (F) (Killed CC 1/5) ,Uffz Wolfgang Michaelis (B) (PoW), Ogefr Adolf Kreiser (Bf) (PoW), Uffz Konrad Keusch (Bm) (PoW injured), Uffz Rolf Luce (Bs) (Killed CC 1/4), Fw Ernst Graf (Bs) (Killed NKG).

Fighter Command Claims not attributable to a particular loss

A claim was made by F/Lt Cox in a 29 Sqn Mosquito for an 'He177' shot down 30-35 miles south of Beachy Head at 21.15 hours. Cox followed the target from the French coast at 18,000 feet and closed to 200 yards before he fired two short bursts. In his second attack the starboard engine and fuel tanks exploded, pieces fell of the aircraft and it went down into the sea on fire.

A claim was made by F/Lt Barry in a 29 Sqn Mosquito for an 'Me410' probably destroyed off Beachy Head at 22.28 hrs. A searchlight crew at Beachy Head reported something burning on the sea between Eastbourne Pier and Beachy Head.

A claim was made by F/O W W Provan in a 29 Sqn Mosquito for a Ju88 shot down near Shorne at 22.30 hrs.

A claim was made by F/O W W Provan in a 29 Sqn Mosquito for a Ju88 damaged near Shorne at 23.41 hrs.

A claim was made by F/Lt B J Thwaites in an 85 Sqn Mosquito for a Ju188 probably destroyed 15 miles SSW of West Malling, at 22.25 hrs.

A claim was made by F/Lt Ward in a 96 Sqn Mosquito for a 'Ju188' shot down off Beachy Head at 21.44 hrs. The Mosquito returned covered in oil, blistered by heat and damaged by parts of the exploding aircraft.

A claim was made by S/Ldr A Parker-Rees in a 96 Sqn Mosquito for an He177 probably destroyed over, Sussex, at 23.00 hrs.

A claim was made by F/Lt D A McFadyen in a 418 Sqn Mosquito for an Me410 shot near Wurzburg airfield at 02.45 hrs.

A claim was made by F/Lt C C Scherf in a 418 Sqn Mosquito for a Ju88 shot down near Ansbach airfield at 02.30 hrs.

A claim was made by F/Lt C C Scherf in a 418 Sqn Mosquito for a Ju88 shot down near Ansbach airfield at 02.39 hrs.

A claim was made by F/Lt P F L Hall in a 488 Sqn Mosquito for a Do217 damaged near Plumpton, Sussex, at 22.25 hrs.

A claim was made by F/Lt G A Holland in a 605 Sqn Mosquito for an aircraft damaged near Melsbroek, at 23.30 hrs.

A claim was made by Lt J O Armour (RM) in an FIU Mosquito for a Ju188 damaged over, Sussex, at 23.00 hrs.

25th-26th February 1944

A Little Knowledge….

The final February raid cast up a sardonic comment on the individual's ability to assess the size of Luftwaffe bombs. A number had fallen but remained intact on Wimbledon Common. An ARP Chief Warden established the impact point of what he identified as an SC1000 that had sunk into the soil. Being of the opinion that these were dropped in pairs as well as not being fitted with delayed-action fuses, he realised the combination of darkness and heavy bracken made a further search useless until the morning. The impact point of the second suspected 'Hermann' was duly discovered, but just then a Sergeant Major accompanied by an ATS girl appeared. The Warden explained what he was doing, and the girl asked him if the bomb was very large – to which her companion asserted that the crater size indicated a weapon no greater than an SC50. He solicited the Warden's opinion on the subject and was stunned into silence, before beating a very hasty retreat when he was informed of the weight and unexploded nature of what lay within the crater!

The Hodgson Diary

A lady named Vene Hogdson, who lived in an un-disclosed west London district north of the Thames, kept a detailed diary that later formed the basis for a book; the title 'Few Eggs and no Oranges', was an apt comment on the scarcity of numerous food items compared to normal times. This witness's notes display a deceptively flippant, albeit not irresponsible air. The gun barrage may have pepped up her spirits as well as limiting the noise effect of any bombs dropped in her vicinity. There was no apparent sense of fear. For example on 20th/21st February when she was in initially at risk from shattering glass from the window out of which she viewed proceedings – and more so when she was totally exposed through going up on the roof! However, she tends to outline sensible precautions to be taken during the raids.

21st January; "Terrific barrage. Went to front door but it was a bit too hot – sky lit up and shrapnel fell. Again in the middle of the night; stuck it for a time then went downstairs. Found Miss Lambert there, but as she always starts on the Pope I did not stop but descended to see how the fire-watchers were getting on. Heard one great swish – seemed as if near St. Mary Abbots Church".

30th; "Terrific display of gunfire. I had a visitor when the warning went. Noise deafening, so retired to landing, and heard ping, ping on roof but no shrapnel through my skylight, glad to say."

6th February; "Terrific raid last Thursday and Friday. Had a good view of the star flares. Most were gold – some blue – like glorious fireworks. Barishnikov says they are not ours. Our guns kicked up an awful din – deafening. Sat up and watched hoping nothing would drop on me. Seems there was a bomb on Harrow Road – comparatively near here. Lines of shops done in. Southend and all the Thames Estuary towns also had it bad, so they say. Dymchurch Police Station was hit. "Two more raids on Frankfurt. Berlin will soon be like Carthage I should think and we shall end by ploughing it up!"

20th/21st February; "Had not heard the warning and was wakened by the guns; they were so noisy that I soon left my bed. Whole sky as light as day, festooned with three red star flares throwing amazing colours over Campden Hill. Shots going for the flares – occasionally little bits fell off and dropped like falling stars. Stood at a window with another lady; a great red glow filled the sky. We hopped too and fro for an hour. Once a roar filled the air and she called; "Come away, that's a bomb". I did not seem to be frightened and I can honestly say I saw it flash down it seemed on Notting Hill Gate. Heard some glass go as if it was the skylight – but still I did not worry. Finally we went up on the roof using the fire escape. Sound of fire in Portobello Road direction with other fires round about. We deserved pneumonia since there was a white frost but could not resist such an amazing sight from where we were".

Further post-raid notes refer to several incidents of bombed commercial and private property, and the tired and grimy appearance of the AFS personnel as they collected in their hoses. Mention was also made of a group of children trying to 'salvage' items from a burnt-out confectionery shop! The latter incident was concluded; "An invalid woman had kept the shop for years; now she had lost home and business at one swoop".

21st /22nd February; "Warning came; could see searchlights probing the sky, with one seeming to pin something down and move overhead. I shouted to the others that he was above, then the whole house shook from head to foot, the windows and doors rattled amid the deafening noise. Incendiaries had fallen around. I galloped to the top of the house but all seemed intact. Huge fires reddened the sky all round - Shepherds Bush and Bayswater. Then all went quiet and we went outside. One end of Pembridge Square was ablaze, including the United Diaries store. Lady Montague's house was also on fire. Second warning at 3.30 a m – we cursed it, but no guns, and I slept again".

Several days later this lady enquired about the loss of the United Diary building. She was informed that all the horses were safely evacuated with one horse reportedly engaged in busily stamping out the flames that ignited the straw-covering to the stable floor!

Ms. Hodgson was apparently elsewhere during the London raids of February 22nd/23rd and 23rd/24th although she refers to their continuing 'horrifying but short' nature. She was not that blasé about the raids and the risk factors attending these events. She accepted that in the event of being buried under rubble, the carrying of whistles would act as a valuable 'trace' for would-be rescuers. In her words; "A useful idea – and if necessary I shall whistle with all my might!" Despite the casual tone of her comments in the fore-going quotations, she was facing up to the possibility of being killed, but added that if she had to die it would be better to be in company rather than alone.

She also mentioned a sensible course of conduct to be taken by the fire-watching party during raids, namely to take shelter during periods of heavy AA fire in order to minimise the risk of being injured or killed by falling fragments of shell casing. This basic matter cropped up during one raid when, a fire-watch meeting concluded, she recalled; "No sooner was the meeting over than the barrage set up in an horrific manner; chandelier flares, rocket guns and star flares filled the sky back and front. I watched at the front door and then shut it instantly as I thought a bomb was about to drop on the drive – it seems like this at times. I left near midnight and stepped into peace and calm. It does not seem possible it is the same world".

The 'Baby Blitz's' malign effect upon London's population was now evident in one obvious respect. The Underground system had proved its value during the sustained Luftwaffe assault almost three years previously with its thousands of nocturnal occupants leading a basically safe but uncomfortable and troglodyte life. Now, Ms. Hodgson noted;

"Queues for the Tube start at 4 pm... old people, children, prams. At Holland Park there are bunks for 500 people, but 1,500 were there this week, many sleeping on the platform with the trains passing; one night the train was sent on as the passengers could not alight among the mass of sleepers".

Propaganda was a vital subsidiary weapon in WWII, little better expressed than through the medium of the cinema. Ms. Hodgson recalled on 28th February how she had gone to the cinema and was impressed by 'San Demetrio, London'. The film, although pitched in a spirited nationalistic manner, was not pure propaganda since it was based on a true incident. The vessel was an oil tanker that had been abandoned during a convoy action on 5th November 1940. The Armed Merchant Cruiser 'Jervis Bay' had been sacrificed in a largely successful attempt at diverting the attention of the Kriegsmarine battle-cruiser *Admiral Scheer* away from the vulnerable convoy until they were cloaked by the shroud of darkness. The tanker's crew had subsequently discovered their charge still afloat, boarded her and sailed her into the Clyde after a protracted voyage.

A week later (5th March) she viewed another classic film 'First of the Few'. Her remarks unconsciously highlight a major and often sad irony arising from any conflict, namely having had prior positive relationships with individuals now on the opposing side; *"R J Mitchell died before the war but he did as much as anyone to win the Battle of Britain... I was especially interested in the Schneider Trophy. One year the Italians won it - it was Major de Bernardi with great rejoicing; a nice modest hero he was...I knew the family well in Florence".* She had watched the final race and acknowledged that at the time she regarded the expenditure on the event as financial folly with no perceived benefit of any kind to Britain. A similar sentiment arises on the 19th when she records; *"Frankfurt bombed twice this week. I do not care tuppence about Berlin, but am sad for Frankfurt and only hope that Mrs. Remy and her children have left the town".*

The final references to 'Steinbock' assaults are on 19th and 26th March;

"Tuesday night (14th), Mr. H and I just finished letters.....paid no attention at first. When guns began to fire, donned my rubber boots in which I feel – for some reason – powerful and competent. Took action stations.... Hullabaloo was terrific. Great blaze by Campden Hill, also near the Albert Hall".

Then, the three successive raids commencing 22nd/23rd raid are observed.

"Paddington Station took quite a biff....Bombers were turned back....Same on Thursday....Friday a long and noisy raid; we stood at the door, what a sight are the rocket guns, of which we seem to have a lot and they fill the sky with showers of flame – then a bang! Very cold and the racket was enormous. All Clear at 1.00 am".

Luftwaffe Non-operational Losses 25th February 1944

Ju188E-1 4/KG2 U5+IM WNr 260344

Shot down at Monchy, north-west of Compiegns, France whilst on a ferry flight from Coulummiers to Handorf. 13.30 hrs

Lt Wolfgang Andratschke (F) (Killed), Hptmn Walter Pult Stab IX Flieger Korps(B) (Killed), Uffz Ludwig Russ (B) (Killed), Ogefr Emil Jehns (Bf) (Killed).

He177A-3 1/KG100 WNr 2655

Crashed at Eger while on a non-operational flight after engine failure.

Fw Karl-Ferdinand Felbermeyer (F) (Inj), Uffz Heinrich Jokish (B) (Inj), Ogefr Alois Andessner (Bf) (Inj), Uffz Erich Fritsch (Bw), (Inj) Uffz Rudolf Kastner (Bs) (Inj).

He177A-3 3/KG100 5J+AL WNr 332159

Shot down by Lt F. Fearnley in a 331 Sqn Spitfire 12 km north-west of St Trond on a non-operational flight. Lt Fearnley was a leading Norwegian ace and was killed when he was hit by AA fire near St Trond. 11.00 hrs.

Ofw Arno Scholz (inj), Ofw Walter Helbig (Inj), Ogefr Kurt Quick (Inj), Uffz Horst Moche (Inj).

Major Bomber Command Operations
25th February to 29th February 1944

25-26 February Augsburg 594 aircraft-21 lost

The War-time Diary of Miss J. M. Oakman - Chelsea   Tuesday 28 Feb 1944

21.30 alert. 5 flares over Battersea – some gunfire.

22.00 all clear. A great many more folks go into the shelters.

Oberst Dietrich Peltz talks to returning bomber crews after a mission over England. Despite their best efforts, the effectiveness of Operation Steinbock was fading as the RAF night fighter force slowly took its toll of Peltz's experienced crews.

Opposite page: When F/O Hedgecoe of 85 Squadron landed back at base in the early hours of 25th March 1944 it was clear that he had seen some action! His Mosquito was scorched from nose to tail with paint removed and canopy blackened, the result of flying through a fireball as his target exploded in mid-air. The likely victim was Z6+HH a Ju88S-1 of 1/KG66 which was lost over the Channel without trace.

CHAPTER SIX

Ever-diminishing Returns

Chapter Six

Ever-diminishing Returns….

29th February 1944

The steam appeared to have again been taken out of *'Steinbock'* operations because the 24th/25th February raid on London was the last to be conducted either in any sizeable numbers or, more vitally, with any great measure of success for several weeks. In reality, the strength and overall quality of the bomber resources allotted to General Peltz were to prove inadequate for the task at hand – a key factor in the ultimate demise of the 'Baby Blitz'.

The nomadic existence of the Gruppen continued to lay crews open to often lethal assault, especially when transferring during daylight hours. On 29th February, Major Fuhrhop (I/KG6 Kommandeur) took off from Chievres around mid-morning; accompanying him in a second bomber was Unteroffizier Meier. Their destination was Dreux, west of Paris, but their progress was summarily ended near Cambrai. A group of Typhoons on the prowl descended on their prey and shot them out of the sky. Fuhrhop was one of the confirmed fatalities; with him aboard the Ju188 were his two Boxer dogs, Chica and Ciro. Fuhrhop had flown in the Spanish Civil War and had been attacked by fighters that put 65 bullet holes in his aircraft on 13 June 1938 – on that occasion he also had a dog with him – 'Peter' who was killed by the bullets.

The loss of Major Fuhrhop

Flying Officer Charles de Moulin was on patrol with fellow 609 Squadron Typhoon pilots over Belgium and France. He recalled in his book 'Firebirds':

"At 14.05 hrs Johnny turns slightly left and leads us into France, hoping that around Beauvais airfield we will meet with better luck – and suddenly, we hit a snow storm. Very poor visibility, down to a few yards, compels us to fly in close formation. I stick to Smithy and Jaspis, while the other five Typhoons are with Johnny Wells to our left.

Major Helmut Fuhrhop's funeral

Major Helmut Fuhrhop

"We fly at about 150 feet, and barely manage to keep together through the snow. Dark patches alternate with short clear spaces.

"Suddenly, two shadows cross our path, just above us, and then disappear to our left into broken cloud. Not fast enough to prevent me from identifying two fat, juicy Ju188s.

"The three of us, at great risk of collision, make a sharp turn after the shadows, without waiting for the other Typhoons to join in the chase. It's free for all. Full throttle, screaming engine and fingers on the gun button, we go flat out after the Ju188s and within a few seconds come upon them in a clear patch of sky.

"Fire! No waiting! My distinguished colleagues are not about to do me any favours – everyone's appetite is whetted.

"In front of me a multi-coloured ribbon streams towards my Typhoon and I can see the rear gunner of the second bomber throwing tracer at me. A little rudder to correct and his turret becomes mute as the gunner crumples on his seat.

"It's the moment chosen by the first bomber's rear gunner to bring us under cross-fire, the bullets pass over my cockpit. This is not cricket, pal, and a little rudder to left brings my burst home. Streaks on the fuselage, left engine on fire – the ball is in full swing. But the place is getting rather crowded, with eight Typhoons now keen to join in the kill, with guns all firing at the same time. If this goes on much longer we are going to shoot each other down, because everyone wants a share. In fact, we are killing the dead, for the two Junkers are fully ablaze and tumbling down. Two seconds later they explode on the ground, which we miss by a narrow margin.

"The Typhoons reform above cloud to cross the nearby coast at Hardelot. Only seven of us. One Typhoon is missing. It's Shelton, Johnny Wells' No.2. In the shambles nobody saw what happened, and nobody heard a thing.

"When we land at Manston the clock shows 2.27 pm. On that 29th of February. Nothing will ever be heard about Mike Shelton, a charming fellow, whose loss is keenly felt. Our victories have a taste of blood, and we share the first Ju188 among three of us, while the second is credited to the other four. It was a collective effort, and everyone contributed willingly."*

*Flying Officer Shelton's body was found and he was buried at Cambrai, he had been brought down by Flak.

Luftwaffe Non-operational Losses

Ju188 1/KG6 3E+KH

Shot down by 609 Sqn Typhoons and crashed at Bohain, 18 km north of St Quentin. 13.30 hrs

Uffz Wilhelm Meyer (F) (Killed), Uffz Eberhard Bräutigam (B) (Killed), Uffz Rudolf Zimmer (Bf) (Killed), Fw Karl Priegler (Bs) (Killed), Gefr Erich Pankratz (Bs) (Killed), Fw Heinz Generlich (1 Wart) (Killed), Oblt Rolf Hailbronner (I Gr T.O.) (Killed).

Ju188 Stab I/KG6 3E+AB

Shot down by 609 Sqn Typhoons whilst on a flight from Chievres to Dreux and crashed at Seboncourt, 18km north of St Quentin. 13.30 hrs

Major Helmut Fuhrhop (Geschwader Kommandeur) (F) (Killed), Ofw Alfred Schubert (B) (Killed), Ofw Alfons Eichschmidt (Bf) (Killed), StFw Walter Rehfeldt (Bm) (Killed), Ufw Wilhelm Schachtshabel (Bs) (Killed), Fw Arnold Büttner. (1 wart) (Killed).

Fighter Command Claims not attributable to a particular loss

A claim was made by F/Lt Prinavsi in a 96 Sqn Mosquito for an 'FW190' shot down 20 miles south of Brighton at 22.28 hrs.

A claim was made by F/Lt Farrell in an 85 Sqn Mosquito for an 'He177' shot down 50 miles south of Brighton at 21.37 hrs.

New German Bombs

One minor improvement in the conduct of the raids was the increased explosive power of some of the larger-calibre bombs from 500 kg upwards. What was known as the 'England mix' consisting of Trialen and Hexogen formed the content of these heavier bombs. Fortunately, the original directive from Göring back on 3rd December had required that some 70% of the overall loads be incendiary in nature.

However, the use of these enhanced-performance bombs was in sufficient quantity and regular enough for no less a personality than Churchill to have his attention drawn to the fact and then to express concern for the well-being of one category of Britain's defensive force, namely the AA gunnery crews. On 28th February he wrote and forwarded a minute to the appropriate authorities:

"There is no doubt that the blast effect of the new German bombs has increased. In these circumstances, and indeed on general grounds, would it not be well to provide, so far as is possible, slit trenches and blast or splinter-proof cover for anti-aircraft personnel not on duty during the air raids? Each raid is likely to be short on account of the enemy's reliance on

'Window', and the anti-aircraft personnel (a large proportion of who are women) should be directed to use the slit trenches when not otherwise employed during the raids. In most cases the batteries should be able to do the bulk of the work themselves if materials are provided. Where outside assistance is required, priority should be granted to the most exposed positions".

The nature of gun and searchlight batteries, which determined they were largely positioned in open areas, accordingly left their men and women operators with only their steel helmets as protection. Therefore they constantly faced an increased risk of injury or death in the event of a near or direct bomb strike – or even to some extent the shrapnel fall-out that inevitably resulted from the explosion of the shells. The overall situation for these personnel was clearly exercising the mind of the Prime Minister. In addition he revealed that he was primarily not chauvinist in nature, since the Minute made specific reference to the vulnerability of the female members serving alongside their male contemporaries. The sex of an individual was not generally a determinant as to whether one combatant should be granted extra protective measures over one's contemporaries, such as was raised in the fore-going Minute. The current conflict had inexorably expanded into one that was 'total' in nature. Regardless of this development, and equally sadly, was the fact that injury or death as the ultimate sanction was to go hand-in-glove with those called to serve the military in WWII. At least Churchill's suggestion went some way, however marginally, to easing the problem for the women in question in this instance.

March 1944

1st-2nd March 1944

The first full night of March witnessed no more than seventy Luftwaffe crews crossing into hostile territory with barely double-figures recorded over London. Once again these statistics were far below the German record of 131 out of 164 crews dispatched 'getting through to the target'. Bomb incidents were recorded across an extended region encompassing Kent and Hampshire. Civilian casualties were light with 34 fatalities; ironically the worst incident involving deaths occurred not within London, but at Rochester. A terrace row in Rochester was devastated and eighteen people lost their lives. Among the survivors later dug out of the rubble were three people whose Anderson shelter had remained intact, even though it was bare feet distant from a bomb crater.

KG100's 2 and 3 Staffeln were participating in reasonable numbers, including 6N+KK flown by Leutnant Goetze. He had taken off around 01.30 hours as one of fifteen He177s from I/KG100 armed with four 1,000 kg bombs. According to a captured map, the briefed course was up to *'Funkfeuer* 8' at Cherbourg and from there direct to a point west-south-west of Watford, before turning on to a heading of 116 degrees to London. The target area north of the Thames, calculated to be around Victoria Station according to markings on the map, was to be marked by red flares. From there the crews were to head south-east towards Maidstone and then directly back to Chateaudun. '*Lux*' buoys dropped in the Channel and the availability of three specific *'Knickebein'* and *'Sonne'* Stations were further navigational aids. That was the theory, at least for the Goetze crew, before the RAF intervened.

Wing Commander Goodman had assumed command of the Colerne-based 151 Squadron in October 1943 and that night at 01.30 hours, the same time that Goetze left Chateaudun, commenced what developed into a two-hour sortie. He was directed by Sopley GCI to head south of the Isle of Wight to intercept a 'bogey' approaching at 16,000 feet. Following several vectors, Goodman's radar operator Flying Officer Thomas picked up a 'trace' at 1 ½ miles, crossing from port to starboard, but at an appreciably lower altitude. The aircraft was jinking and when closed upon was identified by night-vision binoculars as a Ju88. A short burst of fire hit the fuselage and port engine, with debris seen to fly in all directions, after which the victim was reported as spiralling down in flames into the sea.

Goodman was then ordered on a 'freelance' patrol and soon picked up a Do217 that was taking violent evasive action and releasing what turned out to be a 'Window' screen that proved of value when the Mosquito lost its adversary's trail. What was good fortune for one Luftwaffe crew would not prove true for its successor. While the Mosquito waited, Thomas gained another 'contact' at 16,000 feet 2 ½ miles away heading northward. The night fighter closed swiftly and Goodman identified a 'Ju188'.

Leutnant Goetze was flying his He177 on a straight and level course when the cannon shells exploded. Goodman had opened fire from an estimated range of 75 yards. The effect was cataclysmic. The aircraft simply disintegrated and the He177's remains plunged into the ground near East Grinstead. Surprisingly enough only Goetze and one of the other four crewmembers lost their lives, although two of the survivors were injured.

The complete disintegration of the bomber was not instant, since one survivor stated under interrogation that he had ascribed the initial explosion and the aircraft catching fire to an oxygen bottle having been struck. The bale out order was swiftly issued and responded to, while the flaming mass of the He177 only began to fall apart on the way down. The attacking crew were fortunate since the resultant stream of debris cast across the Mosquito's path did no more than shatter the cockpit frame's upper area, although Thomas was injured in the process. Goodman called up RAF Ford for an emergency homing, but landed there with no difficulty.

Combat Report

Wing Commander G. H. Goodman. F/O W. F. E. Thomas (Nav/Rad)

151 Squadron Mosquito XIII (Mk VIII A.I)

Cloud 9/10ths at 5,000 feet. Visibility good. ¼ Moon.

One Mosquito Cat 'B' One JU 88 Destroyed One HE 177 destroyed.

Wing Commander G. H. Goodman (Pilot) with F/O W. F. E. Thomas Nav/Rad. Left Colerne on Defensive Night Patrol at 01.30 hrs and landed at Ford at 03.20 hrs. Call sign Limber 63.Sopley G.C.I. ordered them, after being scrambled, to patrol south of Isle of Wight at 22,000 feet. Soon after this Bandits were reported coming in from the South at 16,000 feet and pilot was directed on to a Bogey with orders to investigate with caution. Various Westerly vectors followed and then a contact was obtained at 1 1/2 miles range, well below, and crossing port to starboard. E/A speed was about 220 I.A.S. and there was moderate jinking in elevation. Range was closed without difficulty and a visual of a silhouette was obtained at 1,000 feet. With the aid of Ross glasses A/c was identified as a JU 88. On closing to 175 yards the JU 88 exhaust characteristics could be seen. A short burst from astern at about 150 yards range caused an explosion in the fuselage and the port engine caught fire. Large pieces of the A/C flew off and it spiralled down and burnt on the sea for some time. No return fire but "window" had been experienced, though not of a very severe intensity.

Orders were then received to freelance in the area and soon a contact was obtained at 2 miles range, followed by a visual of a Do.217 taking extremely violent evasive action. The visual was lost after a violent peel off at 2,000 feet range and contact was not regained owing to severe "window". Pilot was now ordered to orbit slowly and while flying at 16,000 feet a Contact was received at 2 ½ miles range of an A/C flying north. Its direction then changed south, speed 240 I.A.S., and Mosquito closed rapidly. Visual came at 5,000 feet range and A/C was thought to be a JU 188, but the remains have since been recognised as part of a HE 177. It was taking no evasive action and a three second burst from astern 100 yds to 75 yds caused a violent explosion and the A/C disintegrated. The Mosquito flew through the debris which shattered the top of the cockpit and wounded the operator. In this case "window" was also experienced. Emergency homing was then requested and the Mosquito landed at Ford.

Wreckage from Lt Goetze's He177, shot down by Wg Cdr Goodman of 151 Sqn. Top is the upper tail fin and above, the burnt remains of one of the engines.

***'Knickebein'* – A Poisoned Chalice?**

The navigational and blind-bombing aid 'Knickebein' had been compromised by British counter-measures soon after the sets' introduction into service in 1940. Nevertheless, the current provision of a number of 'Knickebein' stations had meant that crews were well aware of the facility and indeed had been encouraged to utilise the beams guidance, regardless of any electronic interference that might arise. It was by now clear in British intelligence circles that the use of 'Knickebein' was being regularly eschewed by many crews, and apparently on grounds other than the equipment's efficiency being compromised.

It appears that the Luftwaffe airmen were convinced that 'riding the beam' invited the attentions of RAF night fighters who were reputed to be able to home onto the system and therefore effect an interception of the bomber or bombers involved. Unlike the 'jamming' to which 'Knickebein' was constantly liable to run into, the night fighter aspect of interception via the system was simply a myth, but one that the British would have pushed to the limit had they been aware of the almost phobic mind-set of their aerial adversaries on the subject.

A consequence of this was that navigators were relying evermore on 'dead' reckoning once they had taken full advantage of the beacons, searchlights and flak star-shell aids on departure from and return to the Continental shores. Some captured airmen had also stated that the pin-pointing of London was easy thanks to the city's massive AA barrage and searchlight concentrations. The latter assertion was by now somewhat contradictory given the reduced numbers of crews crossing into southern England compared to the total dispatched. Even more blatant was the extremely scattered bomb pattern ranging many miles distant from London's boundaries on nearly half the occasions when a major raid had been launched. It therefore appears that either those airmen interrogated were sound exceptions to the rule in terms of their navigational capability, or they were covering for their previous lack-lustre or downright poor performance in this key role!

Luftwaffe Losses 1st-2nd March 1944

Do217M-1 **I/KG2**

Abandoned by crew on return from London in bad weather. Crew safe.

Ju188E-1 **6/KG2** **U5+NP**

Crashed at Coulommiers on return from London in bad weather.

Uffz Hans Engelke (F) (Safe), Ogefr Hanns Refardt (B) (injured), Uffz Hans Konrad (Bf) (injured), Uffz Erich Lichtenfeld (Bs) (injured), Ogefr Karl Gross (Bs) injured).

Ju188E-1 **II/KG2**

Crashed on return from London in bad weather. Crew safe.

Ju88 **9/KG6**

Crashed at Britigny after take off for operations.

Fw Bruno Kappel (F) (Killed), Uffz Josef Haupt (B) (Killed), Uffz Eugen Mürb (Bf) (Killed), Uffz Wilhelm Schemman (Bs) (Killed).

Ju88 **2/KG54** **B3+IK** **WNr 550573**

Failed to return from a sortie to London.

Uffz Heinrich Karmann (F) (Missing), Fw Karl Faitzhofer (B) (Missing), Uffz Mathias Merten (Bf) (Missing), Ogefr Engelbert Hubert (Bs) (Missing).

Ju88S-1 **E Staffel I/KG66** **Z6+DN** **WNr 140589**

Shot down by night fighter whilst on operations, crashed 20 km west of St Omer.

Obfw Rolf Stoop (F) (Killed), Obfw Rudi Nuss (B) (Killed), Uffz Theodor Körner (Killed).

A claim for an 'Me410' shot down near Boulogne submitted by F/O Gough of 96 Sqn at 03.00 hrs may relate to this loss.

He177 A-3 **2/KG 100** **6N+KK** **WNr 332260**

Hammer Wood, 3 miles east of East Grinstead, Sussex. 03.15 hrs.

Shot down by W/Cdr G H Goodman in a 151 Sqn Mosquito. The target exploded in the air and a piece of wreckage shattered the top of the Mosquito's cockpit canopy, injuring the AI operator F/O Thomas.

Started from Chateaudun at about 01.30 hrs to attack London. When flying over Sussex at about 20,000 ft. on its way to the target there was a sudden loud explosion and the aircraft caught fire. The upper gunner thought that the explosion was an oxygen bottle having been hit. Orders were given to bale out and the observer, mechanic and tail-gunner were captured. The pilot and wireless operator were killed. Willi Fischer, the upper gunner, was found at Oak Farm, Flimwell, with one foot and part of his other leg missing; it is possible that he

Ogefr Willi Fischer

had the misfortune to be hit by Goodman's Mosquito. He was taken to Tunbridge Wells Hospital and was later repatriated via Sweden. The aircraft came down in flames; it commenced to break up before it hit the ground and wreckage was scattered over an area of half a mile square. Two 1,000 kg bombs were found in a wood.

Markings: KK black outlined in white but one document and a prisoner gave the markings as 5J+KK. Call sign TI+FQ. Under surfaces spray painted black, sides and upper surfaces spray painted a mottled grey blue.

Lt Kurt Goetze (F) (Killed CC 1/13), Uffz Friedrich Emmerich (B) (Pow), Uffz Andreas Stuckenberg (Bf) (Killed CC 1/14), Uffz Heinz Pohl (Bm) (PoW injured), Ogefr Willi Fischer (Bs – upper) (PoW injured), Uffz Ferdinand Klari (Bs – tail) (PoW injured).

Another view of the widely scattered wreckage of 6N+KK

Ju88 KG101

Crashed at Courvon on return from operations. Ofw Rudolf Zimmermann (Bf) (inj).

Fighter Command Claims not attributable to a particular loss

A claim for a Ju88 destroyed south-east of Selsey Bill at 02.20 hrs was made by F/Lt Stevens in a 151 Sqn Mosquito. The cockpit was hit and the port engine burst into flames, before the aircraft dived vertically and was seen to crash into the sea.

A claim was made by Wg Cdr G H Goodman in a 151 Sqn Mosquito for a Ju88 that crashed in sea off Sandown, Isle of Wight, at 02.25 hrs. Goodman closed to 150 yards and saw an explosion in the enemy aircraft's fuselage and its port engine caught fire. Large pieces detached from aircraft and it spiralled down and burnt on the sea for some time.

A claim for a Ju188 destroyed 30 miles south of Bournemouth at 02.50 hrs was made by S/Ldr R H Harrison in a 151 Sqn Mosquito. The port engine exploded and the gunner returned fire. On the second attack the starboard engine threw out burning fragments and the aircraft dived almost vertically with flame and sparks coming from its starboard engine. It disappeared into cloud at 7,000 ft. and a few seconds later a red glow was seen in the cloud.

A claim for a Do217 damaged near Ford at 03.05 hrs was made by P/O R W Richardson in a 456 Sqn Mosquito.

A claim for a Bf110 damaged north of Paris at 04.19 hrs was made by F/Sgt V J Chipman in a 605 Sqn Mosquito.

A claim for an enemy aircraft destroyed near Laon at 04.20 hrs was made by S/Ldr M Negus in a 605 Sqn Mosquito.

A claim for an enemy aircraft damaged north of Paris at 03.30 hrs was made by S/Ldr M Negus in a 605 Sqn Mosquito.

Non Operational Luftwaffe Loss

Ju188E-1 **II/KG2**

2/3/44 Crashed on transfer flight from to Coulomiers to Evreux. Crew safe.

The War-time Diary of Miss J. M. Oakman - Chelsea Thursday 2nd March 1944

02.40 sirens

03.33 all clear. A very noisy time. Flares and guns. Big fires S and SE chiefly (Flares were mostly S.) Fires at Streatham, S Norwood and the Docks area. 100 planes crossed the coast line, raids were widespread and 5 planes were brought down. One odd plane kept diving about overhead, made one feel uncomfortable and conspicuous – tin hat felt too small by far.

Luftwaffe Losses 4th to 7th March 1944

Me 410A-1	13/KG2	9K+OX	WNr 236

4/3/44 Failed to return from a night-time internal flight.

Uffz Franz Joppen (F) (Killed), Ogefr Ruppert Ehret (Bf) (Killed).

Ju88D-1	1(F)120	A6+BH	WNr 430576

5/3/44 16.00 hrs Crashed into sea off Holm of Beosetter Island, Lerwick, Shetland Islands during a photo reconnaissance of Lerwick Harbour.

Shot down by Lerwick AA defences who fired a total of seventeen 40mm rounds at it, causing the port engine to catch fire. The aircraft landed in sea and three crew took to a dinghy.

Fw Eugen Margraf (F) (PoW), Oblt Alfred Cardaun (B) (PoW), Uffz Anton Reisch (Bf) (PoW), Uffz Bruno Lindner (Bs) (Missing).

Last Flight of A6+BH - extract from ADI(k) report

At about 1530 hours on March 5th, two aircraft of 1(F)120 took off together from Stavanger/Sola. The A6+BH was to take oblique photographs of Lerwick harbour, whilst the other, piloted by a Feldwebel Schantze, was to make a reconnaissance of the Orkneys.

The two aircraft flew together at a height of 50 feet over the sea, keeping about 10 yards apart, to a point 50/60 km. North-East of the Shetlands, where they parted company. The A6+BH turned West and then South and skirted the western side of the Shetlands until it reached the vicinity of Foula. It then headed North-East across Mainland towards Lerwick, having by this time increased height to about 800 feet.

Whilst over the channel between Lerwick and Bressay Island the pilot tilted the aircraft to enable the obliques to be taken. Immediately afterwards the aircraft was engaged by light A.A. and was hit in the port engine, which burst into flames. The pilot turned East and ditched the aircraft just North of Bressay. The crew managed to scramble out and three of them were picked up by an Air/Sea Rescue launch; the gunner was drowned.

He177A-3 3/KG100 5J+AL WNr 332214

5/3/44 Shot down at Chateaudun whilst on a non operational flight.

Lt Wilhelm Werner (F) (Killed), Uffz Kolomann Schlögl (B) (Killed), Uffz Gustav Birkenmaier (Bw) (Killed), Uffz Alfred Zwieselsberger (Bs) (Killed), Uffz Josef Kerres (Bs) (Killed).

A claim was made by W/Cdr E F F Lambert for an He177 destroyed 8 miles west of Melun at 21.47 hours. Lambert was on detachment from 605 Squadron, flying a 515 (Bomber Command) Sqn Mosquito.

Lt Wilhelm Werner, the pilot of He177 5J+AL and the graves of him and his crew.

FW190 Stab/NAG13

7/3/44 Crashed on Guernsey during a reconnaissance mission.

Oblt Gottfried Heinrich Bitterlich (Killed).

Possibly the aircraft engaged 35 miles SSE of Start Point at 17.45 hours by two Spitfire Mk.XIVs of 610 Sqn.

Major Bomber Command Operations
30th February to 15th March 1944

1-2 March	**Stuttgart-125 killed**	**557 aircraft-4 lost**
2-3 March	**Meaulan-les-Meureaux, Paris**	**123 aircraft-none lost**
6-7 March	**Trappes, France**	**267 aircraft-none lost**
7-8 March	**Le Mans, France**	**304 aircraft-none lost**
13-14 March	**Le Mans, France**	**222 aircraft-1 lost**

WEEKLY APPRECIATION OF DAMAGE TO KEY POINTS AND PROGRESS OF REPAIRS.

Period from: 09.00 hours Wednesday 1st March

to: 09.00 hours Wednesday 8th March 1944.

GENERAL.

The G.A.F. attacked land-targets only on the first and sixth nights of the past week. On the first occasion 70 aircraft crossed the South Coast: 10 succeeded in reaching London, the others scattering over Hampshire, Surrey, Sussex and Kent. The attack was poorly conducted, little damage was caused and civilian casualties were light. On the second occasion an aircraft, at the time unidentified, caused a minor incident at Selsey Bill.

The only other activity to report occurred on Sunday afternoon when one aircraft (which was destroyed) reconnoitred the Shetland Isles and another the Orkneys.

Civilian casualties for the week total 36 fatal and 90 serious. The G.A.F is reported to have lost 7 aircraft (10%)

Damage to Key Points amounts to 5 factories in London and 1 in Kent where a Research establishment was also affected: in addition there were 3 railway incidents (not Key – Points), 1 in London and the other two in Kent. Except in the case of one of the factories in London where production was affected, none of the damage was serious.

ENEMY ACTION

KEY POINTS AFFECTED AND OTHER INCIDENTS.

ATTACK ON LONDON AND SOUTH EAST ENGLAND

Tues / Wed 1/2nd Mar. Night.

A force estimated at 60 long-range bombers and 10 fighter-bombers crossed the South Coast between Hastings and the Isle of Wight: 10 aircraft reached London. The attack which was mostly concentrated into half an hour, involved 13 London boroughs, 46 places in Kent, 15 in Sussex and 2 in Surrey.

THE FOLLOWING KEY POINTS WERE AFFECTED

FACTORIES

1) L.P.S ELECTRICAL CO. LTD, Ealing Road, Alperton, Wembley, Middx

Production: Electrical equipment and cable.

Ministry Interested Ministry of Aircraft Production.

Blast damage to buildings, roof and windows. Production was temporarily suspended, but is now approximately 50%.

2) SIEMENS BROS & CO.LTD, Woolwich, London,S.E.18

Production: smoke bomb machining, relays for mines assembly, electrical equipment.

Ministries Interested: Ministry of Aircraft Production, Admiralty, Ministry of Supply, General Post Office, Crown Agents for the Colonies.

I.B.`s caused a fire affecting the top floor of "L" building. Production was not affected.

3) GLACIER METAL CO., Ealing Road, Alperton.

Production: Plain bearings, Tube pressings, brass billets.

Ministries Interested: Ministry of Aircraft Production, Ministry of Supply, Admiralty.

H.E. blast on 2.3.44 damaged roof and windows. Production not affected

14th-15th March 1944

The War-time Diary of Miss J. M. Oakman - Chelsea Tuesday 14th March 1944

22.32 sirens

23.43 all clear. A bad raid with unusual barrage, low diving planes, peculiar green flares, and big fires. HE fell at Clivedon Place in road causing hundreds of windows to break and a good deal of blast to nearby property. Water, gas and sewer mains "went". It seemed to have been a widespread raid – 13 planes were brought down.

WEEKLY APPRECIATION OF DAMAGE TO KEY POINTS AND PROGRESS OF REPAIRS.

Period from: 09.00 hours Wednesday 8th March

to: 09.00 hours Wednesday 15th March 1944.

GENERAL.

Enemy aircraft attacked land targets in this country on five nights of the past week.

The attack on the night of 14th/15th March, which was the only one of importance, was made by about 140 aircraft, 80 of which, it is estimated, concentrated their attack on London. The others caused incidents in Kent, Surrey, Sussex, Berks, Herts, Essex, Suffolk and Norfolk.

During the week 5 Key-point factories were affected (all on the night of the 14th/15th March) and 3 railway incidents occurred. Two of the factories were seriously affected, causing suspension of production: work at the other 3 factories was not interrupted.

Diversionary Forces

The already faltering progress of *'Steinbock'* between the end of February and the beginning of March now only worsened with no major operation launched until the 14th of the month. A handful of FW190s made attacks on the south coast while incidents were recorded over the southern counties on four separate nights.

The attention of the Luftwaffe crews on the 14th was directed against central London, including Whitehall and Buckingham Palace, as the briefing notes for personnel of III/KG6 flying out of Brussels/Melsbroek stated. The outward route was initially to the north-west to a bomber-stream collecting point over the North Sea that was also north-west of Rotterdam (52.21N – 03.08E); by then the bombers were to be at 5,000 metres altitude. Leiston on the English coast and a point fifteen miles east-south-east of Cambridge, the latter marked by four red flares, featured as turning points to the target. Once the bombing runs were completed a further series of headings would bring the crews out over the Channel at Beachy Head with a further map reference turning-point that would head them directly back to Melsbroek. A similar routing-pattern to the target was briefed for I/KG54, whose crews were informed that the raid would entail a 'maximum effort' by all available *'Steinbock'* units.

Concentration of numbers over the target was now the established norm for operations; each Gruppe had a specific time-period in which to complete its bombing effort. That night, for example, I/KG54 and III/KG6 were allotted a twelve-minute spell commencing at 23.00 hours in which to bomb. The need to adhere to the briefed flight-plan was further emphasised; should a crew find itself behind or ahead of the ETA laid down for each turning point it was to adjust air-speed accordingly to reach the next turning-point on time.

So far Luftwaffe attempts to deceive the British defences appeared to have been restricted to the wholesale use of *'Düppel'* to obscure the ground and AI radar screen presentations. On this occasion the briefings included a reference to the pilots of SKG10. They were to fly a sortie to attack Plymouth with the ETA over that city timed for fifteen minutes ahead of the London raid. Flares would be released by the FW190 pilots to further delude the defenders into thinking that Plymouth was the intended target.

However, there were flaws in this aspect of the raid. First, by the time the FW190 diversionary force was closing on Plymouth the vanguard, if not the bulk, of the main attacking force was already over the mainland or closing the English coast. The scale of radar screen activity, however inhibited by *'Düppel'* deployment, indicated that a major raid was developing from the east. Second, the smaller number and faster airspeed of the SKG10 contingent alerted the British to its diversionary function.

The raid duly went ahead with a good proportion of the attacking force recorded as dropping their loads over London. Disappointingly for the Luftwaffe the results were in no way commensurate with this effort, since no significant scale of damage was inflicted. More telling were the losses suffered, with no less than six crews downed over Britain and a further eleven entered into the 'missing' column or crashing on the Continent. KG30 *'Adler'* Geschwader was particularly hard struck with six aircraft losses. A seventh KG30 Ju88 - 4D+DM - came back, not to Varel, but Melsbroek less one crewmember. Leutnant Wolf's bomber had come under attack either by AA or a night fighter. A shell had blown away the lower gondola and cast Unteroffizier Wiesmaier out into mid-air; amazingly, he was not killed but managed to pull his parachute ripcord and descend onto Essex soil near Althorne. His immediate interrogation proved almost impossible, however, since he had sustained an injury to his mouth. Meanwhile his three fellow-airmen and their bomber staggered back to a crash-landing from which they emerged unscathed. This was an operationally experienced crew with 25 sorties to date, mainly flown over Italy; time was fast running out for them.

Another KG30 machine was lying, a smashed wreck, at Dorking following the Ju88's dispatch by Flt Lt Head in his Mosquito. Squadron Leader Bunting of 488 Squadron added to his steadily growing tally of confirmed 'kills' when he shot down Leutnant Becker's Ju188 - U5+BM - near Great Leighs in Essex. Bunting and Flight Lieutenant Reed were lost on 30th /31st July when their Mosquito was downed by flak over Normandy – his final tally was nine enemy aircraft destroyed.

Junkers 188 U5+BM which was shot down on this night by Sqn Ldr Bunting of 488 Sqn

Combat Report

14th March, 1944

488 (NZ) Squadron Mosquito XIII. AI Mk VIII

23.03 hours.

Great Leighs. M.1735

Fine. Patches cloud. 8/10,000 ft. Vis good.

One JU 188 Destroyed.

One Mosquito XIII (AI VIII) S/Ldr E. N. Bunting DFC (Pilot) (Br) and F/Lt C. P. Reed DFC (Nav/R) (Br) was airborne Bradwell Bay 2155 hours under North Weald control (Controller F/Lt. Fox-Male) landed base 2359.

On going over to searchlights Pilot gave Gauntlet and investigated an area of several beams, picking up a contact with the e/a dropping Window. S/Ldr Bunting continues as follows:-

"I climbed from 16,000 to 20/21,000 on making contact which was at three miles range, 25° above, 20° off and estimated the enemy aircraft to be travelling at 160/170 mph. During the chase I was lit by searchlights many times, but closed in and obtained a visual at 300 yards of a JU 188 doing mild evasive. I opened fire from 120 yards, dead astern with a 2 ½ second burst observing strikes on the starboard engine and a big fire started on the wing outboard of the starboard engine. The starboard engine began to burn and the e/a went down vertically to starboard. The fire went out temporarily but shortly afterwards there was a large flash from the ground. I orbited and gave fix which control confirm as M1735 and this is now known to be the position at which a JU 188 has been found near GREAT LEIGH.

I claim a JU 188 Destroyed."

Pilot further reports that at 2315 hours he observed an a/c hit by ack ack fire, going down in flames in the NE area of the I.A.Z.

Ammunition. Cannon HE/SAPI. 25 rounds each. No stoppages.

The art of navigation by 'dead' reckoning could only be perfected by regular practice, and the risks to crews of straying off course were ever-present, as one novice team from 8/KG6 discovered. Unteroffizier Schönleitner lifted off from Melsbroek 45 minutes behind his briefed time. This meant that, in the absence of any indication that the bombing ETA of 23.00 hours had been put back, a much faster speed to the target was needed.

The Beobachter (Unteroffizier Baumgard) carried out his duties of navigation with his limited experience as his pilot guided 3E+LS across the North Sea and then through a succession of searchlight concentrations. All the time the pilot was taking what was later described as 'violent evasive action' and maintaining full engine boost in order to keep to schedule. The evasive action was kept up with great vigour because the crew was of the opinion that it was under imminent threat of interception by a night fighter.

Barely had the Ju88 reached what was taken to be the outskirts of London when both engines began to splutter in quick succession. The pilot ordered the AB1000 container and ten SC50s mounted in the bomb-bay to be jettisoned. Shortly after, the starboard engine burst into flames and the bale-out order was issued. Three men took to their parachutes, but Schönleitner went down with his bomber.

Far from being in the region of their target they had descended near Devises in Wiltshire – well over 100 miles to the west of London! During subsequent interrogation Baumgard asserted that the briefed wind-speed at bombing altitude (70 mph from WNW) was far too strong, hence the reason for the positional error. Since he had over-shot by a distance that would have involved at least 30 minutes flying time for the Ju88, it seems that he had not adhered to this aspect of the briefing. The constant use of engine boost and consequent over-strain on the Jumo 211s was also regarded by one or more of the survivors as a major contributor to the aircraft's demise.

Unteroffizier Heide's crew were on their eighth operational sortie. Their debut on 14th/15th February had been anti-climactic when technical problems forced a return and diversion into Brussels/Melbroek. Five of the following six sorties were flown according to plan, but the seventh, although completed, entailed a diversion into Le Culot owing to an over-crowded circuit at the briefed airfield of Juvincourt.

Flying in Ju88 B3+CK they had been the third crew of their Staffel to take off, at around 21.00 hours. Also flying on this occasion was Oberstleutnant Riedesel (KG54 Kommodore). The bomber was carrying two AB1000 containers and flew the prescribed outward course without incident. 10/10 cloud over Ijmuiden did not prevent the crew sighting the navigational aid provided by Flak star shells and as the English coast was approached packets of *'Düppel'* were released at 30/40 second intervals.

By 23.00 hours Heide was seeking the red target markers and, being convinced he was over London, commenced to orbit. At this point he was some distance south-east of the city centre, near Tonbridge in Kent. It was now that Lieutenant Harrington, a USAAF officer flying with 410 Squadron, pounced with his Mosquito and landed 20mm strikes on the unsuspecting Ju88. The starboard engine burst into flames, forcing Heide to call for the containers to be jettisoned on 'safe' and for the crew to bale out. Although the pilot and one other airman were injured, all four airmen parachuted safely to the ground.

Civilian viewpoint

An eye-witness account coming from Westminster Borough, a region that was the central focus for some of the *'Steinbock'* raids, provides some insight into the attitude of the population towards the offensive. Whereas the 1940/41 raids were often of many hours duration, now they were relatively infrequent and of very short duration. In the London Blitz the raids affected everybody to some degree and created a common sense of 'resigned composure' to the attacks. Now, in contrast, one person wrote; *"Raids consumed a great proportion of each 24-hours by which time was measured. Now, into a 24-hour period the raid bursts suddenly, twists and prods its hot barb for one vicious hour, and then there is silence - a terrible interruption but no more than that. People adjusted to the pace of the working day. So it was in the city, except for isolated patches involving a bombed building over-flowing into the street, maybe with rescuers tunnelling waiting for the slightest sound – and at the next corner a man suddenly appears with a load of oranges, a queue forms, and the goods are swiftly gone!"*

The fact that the raids were largely scattered and short-lived affairs did not ease the sense of apprehension. The unspoken fear was that these might only have been the harbinger of a greater and more concentrated effort by the Luftwaffe; to approach if not match the punishment being handed out to its nation's cities. If so, a return to "the old misery, the cold long nights of dust and fear and fire, the resumption of the past" as noted by the same eye-witness, would strike a severe blow at the people's morale.

The preponderance of incendiary loads was also commented on, as was the thankful reflection that there had been no incidence of *'Butterfly'* bombs having been encountered. In essence, the eye-witness suggested; *"This is not to say that the London morale had lost its old obduracy; people were merely more tired and the perverse vivacities and do-or-die ebullience emanating out of the old 'Blitz' were less evident – this little 'Blitz' was a glum business, and nerves were impatient of it"*.

Belgravia Bombs 14th-15th March 1944

At 23.03 hours HEs exploded in the Belgravia area of London. Damage was caused to Clivedon Place, Eaton Close, Eaton Terrace, Bourne Street, Cardine Terrace and Eaton Terrace Mews.

One of the fatalities of these incidents was 35 year old model Muriel Wright, lover of author Ian Fleming. At the time Fleming was working for naval intelligence at the Admiralty, where Muriel worked as a despatch rider. The two socialites had met in 1935 during a skiing holiday in Austria and had carried on a stormy relationship ever since. Fleming, like his later James Bond character, had many affairs with other women, which lead Muriel's brother to threaten to horse-whip him. He was reportedly 'distraught' to hear that a bomb had fallen through the roof and killed her.

ADI(K) Intelligence Report 117/1944
RAF Station, Friston, Sussex (Q.9616)
Do.217
(III?)/KG2

The local A.A. state that they engaged this aircraft at a height of about 23,000 feet and that after catching fire, it dived into the ground at high speed. The wreckage was buried in a deep crater and burned for many hours; consequently few documents of value were recovered.

The aircraft was presumably in its way to the target since the remains of an ABB500 were found.

The unit could only be established as K.G.2 by the Ausweis, which is that of IV/K.G.2, but a food ticket which was found had been issued at Gilze Rijen and from this slender evidence it is possible that the aircraft belonged to Gruppe III. The names of the crew were unknown to P/W of Gruppe I.

CREW:

W/T Gefr. Albert Rasch…. 15th Nov.1923 … Dead
? Ofw. - Hofmann … 29th Sept.1916 … Dead
Remainder of crew unknown - assumed dead in wreckage.

Zur frommen Erinnerung im Gebete an

Albert Rasch

Uffz. u. Bordfunk. in ein. Kampfgeschw.

geb. am 15. Nov. 1923 zu Hallstadt
gef. am 14. März 1944 über London

Above: The shattered remains of Albert Rasch's Do217 which came down near Friston.

Right: Rasch's death notice.

Combat Report

14/3/44. 23.12 hours. 68 Squadron Beau VI. AI. VIII
L10 [Gants Hill, nr Ilford, Essex.]
Clear but very dark. One Ju 88 or Ju 188 destroyed.

W/Cdr. Hayley Bell, Pilot, and F/O Uezzell, Navigator, took off from Fairwood Common at 2215 Hrs., handed over through sector to Casey, then Punter and then East Hill. Vectored into where there was considerable flak, ordered to Angles 20. While fighter was climbing at 20,000, V. 060, we saw approaching from the North and above, a machine carrying a green and white light, estimated about 3 ft. apart. Fighter turned round behind it and obtained AI. contact. The operator noted there was no I.F.F. showing and it was throwing out window. Target was jinking extremely hard, diving and climbing up to 5,000 ft., and altering speed from 140 to 230, doing 360 deg. Turns. Fighter followed target visually; the lights remained fairly constantly on, switching off only occasionally, not more than 10 secs at a time. The light appeared to be underneath the machine; there appeared to be no signalling from these lights, but were only left on by mistake.

Fighter closed to 500 ft., speed about 230, height roughly 16,000ft., and fired 2 second burst at the lights. There was no return fire. The camera gun which had a night film is exposed two feet. The port engine immediately exploded and strikes were observed crossing the pilot's cabin onto the starboard engine which also exploded. The machine went into a steep dive port, and the fighter went through the smoke of the burning engines. When the machine was fairly close to the ground, and well alight from wing-tip to wing-tip, it appeared as if both engines fell out. The machine was seen to explode on the ground at 2312 hrs.

Weather was clear but very dark. Visual was not obtained on the machine which was not identified as a ju 88 or 188 until it was on its way down on fire, when it was temporarily illuminated by incendiaries burning on the ground. There was considerable flak in the combat area, but no S/Ls which helped fighter.

One of 151 Sqdn heard W/Cdr. Hayley Bell report that target was destroyed and this was also seen by him.

One Ju.88 or 188 is claimed as destroyed by W/Cdr. Hayley Bell and Flying Officer Uezzell.

The aircraft shot down at Gants Hill was actually a 6/KG6 Ju88A-14. The wreckage fell in the centre of the town, much to the interest of the residents

More photos of the Gants Hill Ju88, an engine and mainwheel are visible above, the tail fin with the usual squiggle camouflage is below.

Luftwaffe Losses 14th-15th March 1944

Do217	3/KG2	U5+AL	WNr 326252

Shot down by S/Ldr H. Negas in a Mosquito of 605 Sqn and crashed into a farm yard at Veldhoven, near Eindhoven. 00.20 hrs

Lt Josef Ott (Killed), Uffz Gustav Renziehausen (Killed), Uffz Helmuth Class (Killed), Ogefr Hermann Stark (Killed).

Ju188 E-1	4/KG 2	U5+BM	WNr 260238

White House Farm, Great Leighs, nr Chelmsford, Essex. 23.03 hrs.

Shot down by S/Ldr E. N. Bunting in a 488 Sqn Mosquito on its way to target at about 16,000 ft. The aircraft broke up in the air. The port wing, engine and the tail were found reasonably intact, the rest dived vertically into the ground on fire, wreckage being spread over a wide area.

Markings: U+B- the forth letter was indecipherable.

Camouflage: Upper surfaces dark green with wavy grey lines superimposed, the undersurfaces spray painted black.

Remains of eight 50 kg phosphorous incendiary bombs were found in the wreckage.

Lt Horst Becker (F) (Killed CC 5/155), Uffz Gerhard Bartolain (B) (Killed CC 5/158), Uffz Albert Lange (Bf) (Killed CC 5/154), Uffz Gunther Goecking (Bs) (Killed CC 5/157), Ofw Heinz Litschke (Bs) (Killed CC 5/156).

Another view of Junkers 188 U5+BM which crashed at Great Leighs near Chelmsford, killing the four crew members including Heinz Litschke (above).

Do217 M-1 7/KG 2 U5+MR WNr 6335

Nr RAF Friston, Eastbourne, Sussex. 22.25 hrs.

Engaged by 3.7 inch guns at Newhaven at a height of about 23,000 ft. It dived into the ground at high speed and exploded. The wreckage was buried in a deep crater and burned for many hours.

Uffz Herbert Ballweiser (F) (Killed CC 9/62), Ofw Werner Hofmann (B) (Killed CC), Uffz Albert Rasch (Bf) (Killed CC 9/62), Uffz Helmut Lenz (Bs) (Killed CC).

The youthful crew of U5+MR who all died when their Do217 crashed near Friston.

Ju88 A-14 6/KG 6 WNr 550509

Shot down by W/Cdr Dr. D Hayley-Bell in a 68 Sqn Beaufighter. Woodford Avenue, Gants Hill, nr Ilford, Essex. 23.15 hrs.

Attacked by a night fighter, several 20mm HE and AP as well as .303 AP strikes were found in the tail unit and aft end of the fuselage, all from about 5 degrees starboard quarter and slightly below. Aircraft caught fire in the air and crashed, the wreckage falling on a row of empty shops that collapsed onto the burning aircraft. Two of the crew baled out, the observer died the next day and the wireless operator was seriously injured.

Markings: Undersides spray painted black whilst the upper surfaces were duck egg blue over which wavy black lines had been painted. The spinners had a 1½ inch green band painted near the propeller blades; further forward there was a 1½ inch black band and then a 1½ inch red band with the remainder of the spinner black.

Lt Paul Kohn (F) (Killed CC 1/390), Uffz Claus Prodehl (B) (Killed CC 1/375), Uffz Hans-Rolf Eger (Bf) (PoW seriously injured), Uffz Gerhard Donzyk (Bs) (Killed CC 1/374).

Ju88 A-4 8/KG 6 3E+LS WNr 0141152

Rendles Farm, All Cannings, Wiltshire. 23.30 hrs.

Started from Brussels / Melsbroek at 21.45 hrs to bomb London. The course for the attack was to take this aircraft across the English coast in the neighbourhood of Colchester, after a run from the north to south across the target area the aircraft was to cross the coast again at Selsey Bill and return to Melsbroeck. The crew was on its first operation and had evidently joined the unit within the last week or two. The pilot had taken off late and flew at full throttle to make up time. They missed their turning point north of London and whilst approaching London from a north-westerly direction, one of the engines went out of action. The bomb load was jettisoned. Later the starboard engine caught fire and the order was given to abandon the aircraft. Three members of the crew baled out and the aircraft crashed at high speed and was completely wrecked. The prisoners could only account for the fact that they were badly off course by suggesting that this was due to evasive action.

Markings: L in black outlined in red. Undersurfaces were lamp black over light blue. Upper surfaces greenish grey.

Engines: Jumo 211.

Armament: one AB 1,000 and ten 50 kg bombs carried.

Uffz Hans Schönleitner (F) (Killed Bath 39/H/233), Ogefr Helmut Baumgart (B) (PoW), Ogefr Alfons Harnisch (Bf) (PoW), Gefr Gerhard Grünewald (Bs) (PoW).

Ju88 A-4 4/KG30 4D+DM WNr 301491

While on operations to attack London, having made landfall at about 16,000 ft, the aircraft was attacked by a night fighter from behind and below. Gunner Josef Wiesmaier, who held the Bronze (20) War Flights Badge, was precipitated into the air when the lower gondola was shot away and he landed by parachute at Althorne, Essex. 22.30 hrs.

Aircraft and three remaining crew returned and made a belly landing at Melsbroek. The three men that returned were lost over Essex on the night of 21-22 March.

Lt Eginhart Wolf (F) (Safe), Ogefr Hans Möller (B) (Safe), Uffz Hans Ober (Bf) (Safe), Uffz Josef Wiesmaier (Bs) (PoW).

Ju88 4/KG30 4D+MM WNr 144679

Crashed approx 5km north of Abbeville at Caors on return from London.

Lt Eugen Schillinger (F) (Killed), Uffz Eduard Buchwinkler (B) (Killed), Uffz Franz Maier (Bf) (Killed), Ogefr Erwin Renner (Bs) (Killed).

Ju88 A-4 6/KG 30 4D+FP WNr 40099

Blackbrook, Holmwood Common, Dorking, Surrey. 23.05 hrs.

Shot down by F/Lt Head in a 96 Sqn Mosquito. After cannon fire had been heard in the air this aircraft was seen to be on fire, after which it dived into the ground at a steep angle and was completely wrecked. Some HE and incendiary bombs were jettisoned in the neighbourhood shortly before the aircraft was seen to crash. These were estimated to be four of 250 kg and four of 50 kg; one of the latter was a phosphorus bomb. Fragments of Czech and German money were found and ration cards were stamped 'Fliegerhorst Varel' and 'Standort Kommandantur Nancy'.

Markings: Upper surface was a light blue grey mottled with dark green. The undersides were spray painted black, while the engine cowlings were yellow with wavy lines of black.

Uffz Gerhard Straube (F) (Killed CC 9/33), Uffz Alfred Schiffmann (B) (Killed NKG*), Uffz Hans Sing (Bf) (Killed NKG*), Gefr Heinz Wende (Bs) (Killed NKG*).

* These three men are believed to be buried in Cannock Chase as 'unknown airmen'.

Uffz. Gerhard Straube

Uffz. Hans Sing

Gefr. Wilhelm Wetteborn

Ju88 6/KG30 4D+GP WNr 142085

Failed to return from a sortie to London.

Obfw Herbert Flaminger (F) (Missing), Uffz Anton Landgraf (B) (Missing), Ogefr Erich Schönfelder (Bf) (Missing), Gefr Wilhelm Wetteborn (Bs) (Missing).

Ju88A-4 7/KG30 4D+LR WNr 301535

Failed to return from a sortie to London.

Ogefr Rudolf Hasenberger (F) Missing), Uffz Karl Schäfer (B) Missing), Gefr Friedrich Jakoblich (Bf) (Missing), Ogefr Hans Selzer (Bs) (Missing).

Ju88A-4 7/KG30 4D+KR WNr 301528

Failed to return from a sortie to London.

Uffz Fritz Kugel (F) (Missing), Gefr Rudolf Odendahl (B) (Missing), Ogefr Erich Dittes (Bf) (Missing), Uffz Jonas Trümner (Bs) (Missing).

Ju88A-4 8/KG30 4D+IS WNr 144626

Crashed at Le Couquet on return from London.

Uffz Heinze Henke (F) (Missing), Uffz Willi Vinkemöller (B) (Killed), Uffz Alfons Mai (Bf) (Killed), Ogefr Berthold Heger (Bs) (Killed).

Ju88 9/KG30

Landed at St Omer on return from London.

Ogefr Johann Ehgleitner (Bf) (Killed) rest of crew safe.

Ju88 A-14 2/KG 54 B3+CK WNr 550299

Marchants Farm, Hollanden Park, Hildenborough, Kent. 23.25 hrs.

Shot down by Lt Harrington (USAAF) in a 410 Sqn Mosquito. The aircraft broke up in the air, wreckage being widely scattered.

Markings: C in grey white outlined in red, K in black outlined white. Call sign VR+FU. Undersurfaces black which had been sprayed over light blue. Upper surfaces dark green and the sides greeny grey with thick wavy grey lines. Spinners light greeny blue.

Uffz Hans Heide (F) (PoW injured), Uffz Ewald Schneider (B) (PoW), Uffz Kurt Schneider (Bs) PoW), Uffz Hans Oberle injured (Bs) PoW injured).

Me410 1/KG51 9K+FH WNr 420298

Crashed near St. André.

Oblt Werner Pape (F) (Killed), Ogefr Georg Löpel (Bf) (Inj).

Me410 2/KG51 9K+KK WNr 420420

Crashed into a wood at Beauvais attempting an emergency landing on return from operations.

Lt Horst Eppendorf (F) (Killed), Uffz Günter Zabrodsky (Bf) (Killed).

FW190 2/SKG10 WNr 2691

Shot down and crashed at Villers-La-Fosse, approx 5 km north-west of Soissons.

Ofw Adolf Wucherpfennig (Baled out injured).

FW190	**2/SKG10**	**Red 2**	**WNr 160866**

Hit another aircraft upon landing on return from operations at Amy near Roye-en-Santerre.

Ofw Karl Niemann (Killed).

FW190	**2/SKG10**	**Red 4**	**WNr 1417**

Failed to return form a sortie to England. Oberfähnrich Peter Schmiedinger (Missing).

Fighter Command Claims not attributable to a particular loss

A claim was made by F/Lt Singleton in a Mosquito of 25 Sqn for a Ju88 shot down 4 to 5 miles east of Southwold, Suffolk, at 22.10 hrs. Singleton delivered a burst of fire and saw the port side of fuselage explode. Burning fiercely enemy aircraft then broke in two, passed through the cloud layer, and exploded in the sea.

A claim for a Ju188 destroyed over the Channel at 22.30 hrs was made by F/Lt N S Head in a 96 Sqn Mosquito.

A claim for a Ju88 probably destroyed near Althorne at 0.52 hrs was made by S/Ldr W P Green in a 410 Sqn Mosquito.

Claims for two Ju88s destroyed near Boblingen airfield at 00.27 hrs were shared by S/Ldr R A Mitchell and F/Lt A G Woods in 605 Sqn Mosquitos.

Flt Lt Head of 96 Sqn who claimed two victories on this night.

Major Bomber Command Operations
15th to 19th March 1944

15-16 March	**Stuttgart-88 killed**	**863 aircraft-37 lost**
18-19 March	**Frankfurt-421 killed**	**846 aircraft-22 lost**

19th-20th March 1944

Target-Switch

To date the focus of *'Steinbock'* operations had been on London. There now transpired the first switch in target choice; to the northern city of Hull, a key commercial seaport on England's eastern seaboard. Although the target's location near the mouth of the river Humber provided a sound geographic reference for navigation, the Luftwaffe crews faced a prolonged flight over the featureless North Sea, greater than they had regularly traversed between Holland and the Thames estuary.

The losses suffered by KG30 during the previous thrust at London appear to provide a partial explanation as to why only II/KG30 was scheduled for this night's assault against Hull. A similar diminution in KG6's presence to only its I Gruppe was not so readily explicable. As it was, the eight participating units dispatched a total of around 130 bombers according to German records; barely two-thirds of that for the 14th/15th, even according to British intelligence statistics. I/KG66 had transferred from Montdidier to Soesterberg for this attack; the other seven Gruppen were mainly flying out of their normal airfields, but would cross-out over the Dutch coast at three separate points spread over approximately 40 miles between Noordwijk, Ijmuiden and Petten (I/KG6, I and II/KG2 and I/KG100 respectively used these navigation references). The actual stream assembly point was at 53.32N-02.35E; a procedural change lay in varying instructions as to what altitude was to be attained at this stage. Some units were briefed to be at their operational height, whereas the remainder were instructed to commence climbing only when reaching the stream assembly point. Further aids to stream assembly were:

1) The availability of two *'Knickebein'* beams on bearings of 296.5 degrees from Station 3 and 336 degrees from Station 5.

2) The laying of '*Lux*' buoys.

3) Red sky markers.

The sky markers were intended to counter the anticipated thin cloud-layer that might obscure sight of the buoys. From the stream assembly point a direct flight to Hull would be made, although a right turn near the target was a common briefing point, with Grimsby over-flown by all participating Gruppen, except I/KG100. I/KG100 was directed to head marginally further north, between Spurn Head and Withernsea, and in addition the He177 crews would navigate back to the original stream assembly point (53.32N – 02.35E) passing over Terschelling Island before turning south-east to Rheine.

The approximate distance to be flown from the Dutch coast to Hull was 250 miles, with the bomber-stream assembly point almost halfway. On this occasion it appears that the almost extravagant deployment of further *'Lux'* buoy markers was made at four grid square points between the assembly point and the target, according to a document unearthed from the wreckage of Z6+EK shot down almost one month later. This showed a course from Soesterberg to Den Helder as well as the following details.

Grid Square	Map reference	Buoys	Time (- or + X, with X the target ETA)
2449	53.32N – 02.55E	4	X-65 minutes
2468	53.17N – 02.45E	3	X-60 "
2487	53.02N – 02.35E	3	X-55 "
0445	53.37N – 00.45E	9	X-15 "
2449	53.32N – 02.55E	4	X+10 "
2468	53.17N – 02.45E	3	X+15 "
2487	53.02N – 02.35E	3	X+20 "

Examination of the fore-going record casts up an apparent contradiction regarding the route target. This is that the first 'Lux' buoy location (2449) lies to the east of the stream assembly point; the marker's function would therefore appear to be redundant in view of the following fact. Instead of pursuing a straight course towards Hull, the map-reference locations for nos. 2 and 3 buoys' release directed the pilots in a south-westerly angle that took their bombers to a point off the Norfolk coast north-east of Cromer. A sharp north-westerly turn was then made to a point off the port of Grimsby at the mouth of the Humber estuary marked by buoy No. 4 (0445); this ties in neatly with the distance from No. 3 buoy (2487) and the allotted flight-time of forty minutes. The Grid Square references for Nos. 5 to 7 buoys are logical in respect of the left-hand column but totally inapplicable as regards the right-hand column, since these are pitched in the same westward sequence as for the inward route; also the Grid Square reference are the same as for the inward route! However, if the right-hand column figures are reversed in sequence the map-references at least would tie in with a logic return flight-path. The navigators' task was to be made harder in achieving accuracy by tracing a dog-leg route to Hull, as well as prolonging the overall flight-time - clearly, a situation not tailor-made for any novice Beobachter among the formation's ranks!

The target-marking procedure demonstrated a return to earlier methods, with I/KG66's efforts being supplemented by a separate unit, in this case II/KG2. Selected bombers such as Ju188 U5+EN, were also carrying LC50 flares that were white in colour when exposed, in

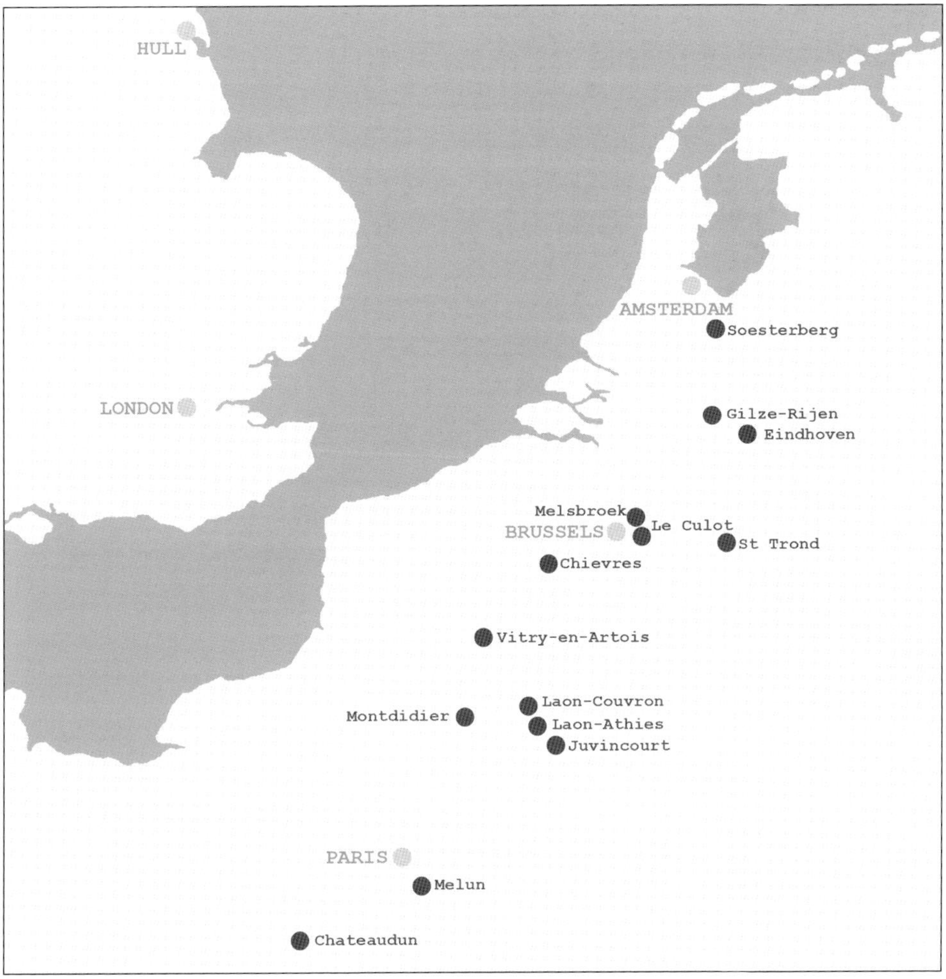

The main forward operating bases used by the Lufwaffe bomber force during Operation Steinbock.

addition to AB1000 and AB500 containers. In the event, and regardless of what provisions for target-marking had been made, the citizens of Hull were to remain blissfully ignorant of what was intended for them - because the Luftwaffe's effort was totally unsuccessful.

The first aircraft from among a force of 131 bombers were to have opened the attack at 22.02 hours and the last bomber leave by 22.33 hours, according to post-war examination of Luftwaffe records. In fact the initial red markers sighted by approaching crews were blossoming out over north Lincolnshire, well to the south of Hull.

A number of bombers made landfall further to the south, along the Lincolnshire coast, rather than the mouth of the Humber. One crew from I/KG54 stated they had pin-pointed their position by the Humber before sighting any flares. Two very powerful white flares were seen to the south; these were treated as either British decoys or flares released by a pathfinder crew endeavouring to identity the target - several bombers dropped their loads on these flares. The same crew claimed to have gone on to drop their load without any marker assistance and that it was only at 22.12 hours, when they had already turned for home, when a sighting of target marker flares was recorded. A more specific, albeit equally inaccurate claim, emanated from U5+EN's crew. Its members claimed to have made a landfall north-east of Hull at 13,000 feet and headed south towards a group of red marker flares while dropping down to10,000 feet to release the incendiary element of its load. Then the pilot circled and lost a further 4,000 feet before adding the LC50 flares to this group of primary markers.

P/O Brochocki of 307 (Polish) Squadron who shot down He177 6N+OK.

103 Luftwaffe crews claimed to have crossed the coast, double that recorded by British observers!

He177 - 6N+OK - came down in the North Sea off Skegness, a victim of a Polish pilot, Pilot Officer J Brochocki, flying a 307 Squadron Mosquito; none of Hauptmann Müller's crews survived. Do217M - U5+RL - piloted by Unteroffizier Jakob was lost over Lincolnshire. Already up from Church Fenton was Flying Officer R L J Barbour in his 264 (Madras Presidency) Squadron Mosquito. 264 Squadron had taken up night fighting with Defiants in 1940 and was by now well practiced in the art of nocturnal 'hunting'. While approaching Orbit Beacon G, Flying Officer Paine picked up a 'contact' crossing from port to starboard at three miles range and 18,000 feet. When closed in upon the outline of a Do217 was confirmed, whereupon the Mosquito was slid in directly behind and two bursts of cannon fire delivered that smothered the fuselage and set the port DB603 and its fuel tanks ablaze. The stricken bomber's vertical descent ended 100 yards from the vicarage of Leybourne. The tail section was later found on a railway line about one mile distant from the main crash site. Gefreiter Meinel, the Bordschützer, was the sole survivor among the four-man crew.

Wolfgang Krum, Walter Schmitt, Otto Samus and Günther Stuve pose with their Ju88. This crew went missing on this night, believed to be the aircraft claimed shot down by Humber AA guns that went into the sea 5 miles north of the Humber Light Ship.

Flight Lieutenant Singleton and Flying Officer Haslem operating with 25 Squadron out of Coltishall submitted a claim for three bombers shot down. They had taken off in their Mosquito HK255 at 20.55 hours and came under the initial directional control of Neatishead GCI Station, whose staff requested a course of 080 degrees and rapid climb to 16,000 feet be followed. The CHL Station at Happisburgh took over and a course alteration almost due north was issued. Flying Officer Humphreys at the CHL Station advised Singleton that around twelve 'bogeys' crossing from starboard to port were ahead. Sure enough the night fighter's Mk. X radar set picked up a 'trace' at eight miles range that materialised into a Ju188, flying marginally higher than its pursuer. Closing to minimum firing range Singleton delivered a short burst of fire that caused a big explosion, against the garish light of which a swastika was clearly outlined. Debris spattered the Mosquito's airframe despite its being pulled up sharply. While its crew orbited the scene they witnessed the terrible end for both bomber and crew as the airframe broke up prior falling in the sea some 55 miles north-north-east of Cromer.

Haslem had already picked up another 'trace' maintaining the same north-westerly course. When closed upon the 'bogey' was identified as a 'Ju188' flying in a straight line. Once again a single short burst of cannon fire sealed the Luftwaffe crew's fate when their bomber burst into flames and plummeted vertically into the sea; this time Neatishead GCI confirmed the crash location as 65 miles noth-north-east of Cromer.

Almost immediately another 'trace' on the same heading appeared on Haslem's screen, but the pilot of what was again identified as a 'Ju188' was taking violent evasive action. The frightening destructive power of the 20mm cannon shell was demonstrated for the third occasion. First the starboard engine caught fire under the impact of the first burst of fire; then as the bomber drooped into a shallow dive the airframe was shredded and also caught fire. Burning parts of debris were ejected into mid-air as the aircraft continued an inexorable downward path towards the frigid North Sea on whose surface it spread itself 50 miles noth-north-east of Cromer. Three down in 13 minutes!

The sortie had been exciting enough, but now became fraught with danger. Singleton noted the port and starboard engine radiator temperatures had risen to 140 and 120 degrees respectively. He feathered the port engine that was emitting a shower of sparks, but soon found that the extra pressure on the functioning Merlin forced a rapid temperature rise. He un-feathered the port engine and flew with both motors throttled back to a level that still permitted a bearable loss of altitude. The Norfolk coast was safely crossed and Coltishall was called upon to light the flare-path. This was done, but as the final approach was being made the starboard engine burst into flames. Singleton had already decided upon a wheels-up landing, but as he increased power to the port engine it too seized up. Fortunately the Mosquito levelled out of its approach before it struck the airfield's surface and skated to a swift halt, with both airmen vaulting out of the overhead hatch. Small persistent fires around the cylinder heads were extinguished by basic means – gathering up and throwing of earth upon the cowling-less engine blocks! Later examination confirmed that the glycol tanks had undoubtedly been punctured by debris from the first or second Luftwaffe victim; the scale of damage to HK255 was sufficient for it to be 'written off'.

Further Evaluation

The single Luftwaffe bomber to fall on British soil that night provided specific information on the aerial signalling/identification system used on the Do217, according to Crash Report 229/23.3.44; this was in spite of the aircraft being almost totally destroyed following its steep impact with the ground. The evaluation was as follows;

DORNIER 217M

The Do-217M is fitted with two extra signalling lamps, positioned in the nose and tail-cone and angled downwards. Each fitting mounted in colourless Perspex contains a 25 watt filament lamp as also features in the side navigation lamps. The lights can be seen from a maximum clear visibility distance of 5 miles down to around 2 ½ miles if coloured Perspex is fitted.

A modified form of the intercomm. ADB11 switchbox operates the lights. A three-position switch is selected as follows;

1) Ein = On

2) Morsen = Morse

3) Getrennt Morsen = Divided Morse

A second main selector switch determines the lamp to be used;

1) Hinten = Aft

2) Hinten + Vorn = both

3) Vorn = Forward

A push-button switch marked 'Ruf' (call) flashes the lamps when depressed. The switchbox indicator lamps are in parallel with the signal lamps and indicate to the pilot which signal he is sending.

The signal variations are;

(a) Either lamp separately, or both lamps, on continuously.

(b) Either lamp separately or both lamps keyed by the push-button switch, the lamps being off when the switch is not depressed.

(c) Either lamp continuously on, with the other being flashed through use of the push-button switch. In this case when 'Hinten' is selected the nose lamp lights continuously with the rear lamp flashing; the reverse situation applies when 'Vorn' is selected.

A further note was made regarding the standard downward-angled ID lights (Zuzatzlichte). These had 15 watt lamps within coloured Perspex and could also be used as signalling units, since a switch was on hand to activate the lamp circuit.

ADI(K) Report 126/1944

Vicarage Fields, Leybourne, near Louth, Lincs. (A.8304).
19th March 1944, 2215 hours.
Do.217 U5+RL
2/K.G.2

Start and mission: Took off soon after 2100 hours to attack Hull; incendiary bombs only. Place of start refused.

This aircraft was attacked from astern by a Beaufighter [sic] which the crew saw too late. Two bursts set the port engine and wing tanks on fire and the aircraft crashed and was burnt out.

The gunner baled out and was captured; the other three members of the crew are assumed to have perished in the aircraft.

The crew was evidently flying a borrowed aircraft. P/W states that he belonged to 2/K.G.2 and he gave the F.P.N. of the 2nd Staffel. The pilot was shown on a recently captured operational order as being detailed to take part in the attack on London on the night of February 23rd/24th, flying the U5+MK.

MORALE: Fair only.

A Dornier 217M similar to U5+RL which crashed near Louth. The M version looked identical to the K version apart from the engines. The M having inline engines and the K radials.

Combat Report

F/Lt Greaves, DFC (Pilot) 19/20 March, 1944.

25 Squadron. Mosquito XVII/AI.Mk.X.

(i) 2128 hours.

(ii) 2148 hours.

(i) C.1300 35 mls. N.N.E. Cromer.

(ii) B.4303 30 mls. N.N.W. Cromer.

No cloud - very dark but starlight.

(i) 1. Do. 217 Destroyed. (ii) 1. He. 177 Destroyed.

We took off from Coltishall at 2055 hours and were taken over immediately by G.C.I. Neatishead, given vector of 080° and told to climb to 18000 feet. When at 12000 feet we were told to remain at that height and informed the bandits were coming in on a North-Westerly course. Contact was immediately obtained at a range of 4 ½ miles crossing from starboard to port at about 2000 feet above. We closed in without difficulty to 1000 feet and obtained a visual. (Nav/Rad. Identified E/A, with aid of night binoculars as a Do. 217). Closed in to 50 - 60 yards and fired a 2 sec. burst from dead astern; E/A took no evasive action. Fuselage caught fire and the E/A fell away to port. A further 2 sec. burst, with one ring deflection, scored more strikes and caused the E/A to burn furiously. E/A dived down and hit sea where it was seen to burn.

We went back to G.C.I. at 14000 feet and was given a fresh vector. Another contact was obtained at 4 ½ miles range crossing from starboard to port, 4000 feet above. Closed in, climbed and obtained visual at 1000 feet and identified E/A as a HE.177. E/A took no evasive action. Closed in to 50-60 yards and gave a 3 - 4 sec. burst from dead astern. Strikes were scored on the fuselage and port motor and E/A started burning furiously, dived away to port and was seen to explode on hitting the sea.

G.C.I. Controller. F/O. Black.

WEEKLY APPRECIATION OF DAMAGE TO KEY POINTS AND PROGRESS OF REPAIRS.

Period from: 09.00 hours Wednesday 16th March

to: 09.00 hours Wednesday 22nd March 1944.

GENERAL.

The G.A.F has attacked land-targets in this country on four nights during the past week. On the first two the scale was small and of no consequence: on both the last two they were of appreciable size, but only on the last did the enemy accomplish anything worthy of mention. In addition the Kent Coast was shelled on two occasions during the week.

On Wednesday / Thursday (15th/16th March) 8 long-range bombers and 7 fighter-bombers crossed the South Coast; 5 aircraft penetrated to London. On Friday/Saturday (17th/18th March) 10 long-range bombers and 5 fighter-bombers crossed the South Coast; 6 aircraft penetrated to London. The results of the bombing on both nights was trivial.

On Sunday/Monday (19th/20th March) 90 long-range bombers came overland. The bulk of the incidents occurred in Eastern Lincolnshire and there was some scattered bombing in Northern Norfolk. The enemy claims to have attacked Hull. No bombs fell on Hull, and on this night negligible harm was done by air activity. Buildings were, however, damaged at Dover by Cross-Channel shelling, Dover was also attacked on the following night, when part of the town`s electricity supply was interrupted.

On Tuesday/ Wednesday (21st/22nd March) a force of aircraft provisionally estimated at 95, came overland at about 2345, mostly across East Anglia and the remainder over the South Coast. The majority are believed to have passed over London, where the boroughs affected lay mostly within the triangle Hammersmith/Orpington/Waltham Holy Cross. Outside London incidents were scattered within an area bounded by Cosham/Slough/ Harwich/Lowestoft. The attack appears to have been primarily incendiary and caused 247 fires in London; there were two fire zones, one of 50 pumps in Islington and the other of 20 in Tottenham and in addition there were fires of 40 pump dimensions in the area of Millwall Dry Dock, of 30 pump dimensions at Winkleys Wharf, Millwall and at May & Baker, Dagenham, and 5 10 pump fires, four of which occurred in dock areas of London; all fires were under control by 0435.

Civilian casualties, almost entirely confined to last night, are at present estimated at 39 fatal and 225 serious, the great majority of them in London. The G.A.F. is known to have lost 17 aircraft (8%).

The damage by enemy action has been done to 5 Key-Points; in addition there have been 11 incidents affecting railways and 2 airfields.

Luftwaffe Losses 19th-20th March 1944

Do217M 2/KG2 U5+RL WNr 56055

Vicarage Fields, Leybourne, nr Louth, Lincs. 22.04 hrs.

Shot down by F/O R. L. J. Barbour in a 264 Sqn Mosquito.

Markings: On the tail fin U5+RL, in small 6 inch high grey letters. Superimposed over the swastika was a large figure 2 in white paint. On the side of the fuselage was a very badly burned marking 55+RL (sic), the R and L in grey paint and normal 2 ft high letters. The 55 were in grey paint and 3½ inches high. The undersurfaces were spray painted black, whilst the upper surfaces were greenish blue mottled black.

Uffz Hans Jakob (F) (Killed CC 3/190), Yffz Kurt Dölling (B) (Killed CC 3/191), Uffz Ludwig Osterhuber (Bf) (Killed CC 3/192), Gefr Werner Meinel (Bs) (PoW).

Do217M-1 7/KG2 (a/c from 8/KG2 crew from 7/KG2) U5+FS WNr 6262

Failed to return from a sortie to Hull.

Uffz Johann Glombitza (F) (Missing), Uffz Herbert Kallabis (B) (Missing), Uffz Heinz Oehme (Bf) (Missing), Uffz Heinz Vetters (Bs) (Missing).

Ju88 5/KG30 4D+NN WNr 550742

Failed to return from a sortie to Hull.

Ofw Werner Weil (F) (Missing), Ogefr Gerd Schipke (B) (Missing), Fw Konrad Meyer (Bf) (Missing), Fw Ludwig Leibig (Bs) (Missing).

Ju88 5/KG30 4D+GN WNr 883970

Failed to return from a sortie to Hull.

Fw Fritz Stenutz (F) (Missing), Ogefr Albert Vogt (B) (Missing), Uffz Walter Schmidt (Bf) (Killed), Uffz Willi Mühlendhaupt (Bs) (Missing). The body of Walter Schmidt was recovered from the sea.

Ju88 5/KG30 4D+LN WNr 800966

Failed to return from a sortie to Hull.

Ufz Ulrich Gerlach (F) (Missing), Ogefr Gerhard Zobler (B) (Missing), Ogefr Karl-Heinz Fischer (Bf) (Missing), Gefr Günther Baus (Bs) (Missing).

Ju88 1/KG54 B3+CH WNr 0142293

Failed to return from a sortie to Hull.

Lt Ferdinand Stadtmüller (F) (Missing), Uffz Willi Boderke (B) (Missing), Uffz Rudolf Heman (Bf) (Missing), Uffz Walter Plate (Bs) (Missing).

Ju88 6/KG30 4D+AP WNr 550143

Failed to return from a sortie to Hull.

Fw Rudolf Junger (F) (Missing), Ogefr Helmut Westerworth (B) (Missing), Ogefr Alfred Müller (Bf) (Missing), Gefr Helmut Barth (Bs) (Missing).

Gefr. Helmut Barth, missing in 4D+AP

Uffz. Wolfgang Krum missing in Z6+EK

Ju188E-1 2/KG66 Z6+EK WNr 260310

Believed to be the aircraft claimed shot down by Humber AA guns at 8,000 ft and crashed in sea 5 miles north of the Humber Light Ship. Crash witnessed by several local trawler crews.

Hptmn Walter Schmitt Stkp (F) (Missing), Lt Josef Antwerpen (B) (Missing), Uffz Wolfgang Krum (Bf) (Missing), Uffz Günther Struve (B) (Missing), Fw Otto Samus (Bf) (Missing).

He177 A-3 2/KG100 6N+OK WNr 2375

Shot down by P/O J Brochocki in a Mosquito from 307 Sqn and crashed in sea off Skegness during operations to Hull. The claim was confirmed by an ROC post situated at Skegness. 21.46 hrs.

Hptmn Heinrich Müller (F) (Missing), Ogefr Fritz Küchler (Bo) (Missing), Uffz Ernst Gündner (Bf) (Missing), Uffz Eberhard Hockauff (Bm) (Missing), Uffz Heinrich Rodenstein (Bs) (Missing), Ogefr Werner Utikal (Bs) (Missing).

Two views of KG30 Junkers 88s photographed by Helmut Barth shortly before his death in a similar aircraft off the north-east coast of England.

Fighter Command Claims not attributable to a particular loss

A claim for a Ju188 destroyed was made by F/Lt J Singleton in a 25 Sqn Mosquito in the sea approx 55 miles north-north-east of Cromer at 21.20 hrs.

A claim for a Ju188 destroyed was made by F/Lt J Singleton in a 25 Sqn Mosquito in the sea approx 65 miles north-north-east of Cromer at 21.27 hrs.

A claim for a Ju188 destroyed was made by F/Lt J Singleton in a 25 Sqn Mosquito in the sea approx 50 miles north-north-east of Cromer at 21.33 hrs. The starboard engine of the enemy aircraft was hit and burst into flames, it went into a shallow dive before it hit the sea and exploded.

A claim for a Do217 destroyed was made by F/Lt D H Greaves in a 25 Sqn Mosquito in the sea approx 35 miles north-north-east of Cromer at 21.27 hrs.

A claim for an He177 destroyed was made by F/Lt D H Greaves in a 25 Sqn Mosquito in the sea approx 30 miles north-north-west of Cromer at 21.48 hrs.

A claim was made by S/Ldr D. J. Williams DFC in a 406 Sqn Beaufighter for an He177 shot down in the sea 20 miles south–west of Alderney, Channel Islands at 23.32 hrs. He closed to within 300 feet and opened fire, whereupon both engines of the Heinkel exploded and whole aircraft burst into flames and dived into the sea, where it burnt for about 30 seconds.

A claim for a Ju88 destroyed was made by F/Lt G A Holland in a 605 Sqn Mosquito near Rhine at 23.45 hrs.

21st-22nd March 1944

The War-time Diary of Miss J. M. Oakman - Chelsea Wednesday 22nd March 1944

00.46 sirens

01.53 all clear. A very noisy time, with guns going, flares and rockets and diving planes – sounding uncomfortably close. The shelters are getting fuller up – There was a big fire at Newspaper Offices in Vauxhall Bridge Road. Somewhere in the regions of NE was another big fire. 100 German planes flew in behind our returning bombers. 9 were brought down. A block of tenement flats had a hit. HE in Paddington Station goods yard.

Whereas the Luftwaffe and British intelligence figures for bombers participating and/or gaining their targets had been noticeably different during the initial stages of *'Steinbock'*, recent statistics had begun to produce almost comparable details. For the Hull raid the figures for aircraft dispatched had been 131 and 120 respectively although there was still a wide divergence on those even gaining British territory (103 to 50). The 21st/22nd March effort that returned to London involved 144 aircraft, of which 123 were to be granted sortie 'credit', compared to British intelligence reports of 95 aircraft crossing-in with no specified equivalent for crews gaining the target. However the key point of this raid, as with several of its predecessors, lay in the greatly diminished numbers of bombers operating in relation to the original strength at *'Steinbock's'* inception. The overall campaign was having little or no effect, neither upon its adversary's war effort, nor upon its civilians' morale. The brutal fact was that the undoubted gallantry of the Luftwaffe airmen, regardless of the quality of their navigational and bombing efforts, was providing not even a short-term benefit to their sadly-misguided nation's bid to stem the Allied advance.

However dispirited the Luftwaffe airmen may have been, they still mustered for briefing. At Varel, where III/KG30 had just arrived that afternoon from Tulln, near Vienna, any prospect of relaxation for the personnel was excluded when they were ordered to hold themselves ready for an operation. Briefing was at 20.30 hours, 3 ½ hours after I/KG30 based at Zwischenahn. Both units, along with nine others, were informed that the Isle of Dogs in London's East End was the focus of attack, which would be marked by what were described as 'Mark 50' red flares (presumably the LC50). Bombing would be conducted from 14,500 feet by both Gruppen, commencing at 01.00 hours.

The initial course was to a point slightly north of the '*Niete*' 3 and 4 searchlights near Ijmuiden, at which stage the minimum altitude hitherto flown was to be increased to reach an operational level by the time the collection-point at 52.21N-03.08E was attained. This would be indicated either by *'Lux'* buoys or white flares depending respectively upon clear or restricted visibility. Once over enemy territory the crews would head for a flare-marked point near Newmarket, and approach London from due north. '*Knickebein'* Stations 3 (257 degrees/0030-0110)) and 5 (276 degrees/0040-0120) would be laid on to assist in target approach, while 10 (025 degrees/0030-0130) marked the actual target. The return route angled out towards Beachy Head and across to St. Valery-en-Caux; from here II/KG30 would head for Orly, whereas III/KG30 crews were given the choice of four airfields, widely spread between Bretigny and Brussels/Melsbroek

KG30 records indicate that upwards of 40 crews participated in almost equal Gruppen numbers. Several hours later the bulk of the bombers landed back on the continent, less two crews. A week previous Leutnant Wolf's aircraft had lost its gondola to AA fire or a night fighter's cannon shells; Unteroffizier Wiesmaier had been precipitated into mid-air, but managed to deploy his parachute and land safely. Wolf had jettisoned his load and headed back via Boulogne to Brussels/Melsbroek where a belly-landing had to be made thanks to the undercarriage refusing to lower. Now Wolf and Unteroffizier Rakowski, having survived the incident, were closing on their target when their Ju88 was intercepted and shot down by Flight Lieutenant Surman of 604 Squadron. The bomber smashed into the Essex soil near Latchington, killing Wolf and Rakowski - the two airmen's continued tenure on life had been sadly brief.

The Luftwaffe effort was spread over a large area extending from Hammersmith to Orpington, with Lambeth and Croydon particularly affected. Up to twenty SC-type bombs fell across the Croydon region, half of them in South Norwood, to cause a significant degree of destruction. An entire family buried within the ruins of their house were among the fourteen fatalities out of an overall total of 61 casualties. It was noted that there was an increased blast effect from the bombs compared to those of earlier in the war; a sound indicator that these weapons contained the Trianol/Hexagon mix providing this enhanced effect.

Security Measures– What Security Measures?

The perceived ability of the intelligence staff among the major WWII combatants to present PoWs with stunningly comprehensive details concerning their Gruppen and fellow-airmen's activities was often made easy. This was primarily due to numerous airmen taking a laissez-faire attitude to security. There was a classic poster displayed in the briefing rooms on RAF bomber airfields; this showed an airman standing in front of a French brothel - underneath are the words, "Avant partir en operations, videz vos Poches!" (Before departing on operations, empty your pockets). This was a humorously risqué approach to what was the vital need for aircrew to ensure that they were not bearing anything on their person that could indicate their specific airfield, squadron, etc. Sadly, such a requirement was often not fully complied with or was even studiously ignored, the latter instances probably relating to airmen who were imbued with a feeling that they were never going to suffer the fate of being downed over enemy territory.

One of the KG6 aircraft operating this night was Ju188 3E+BK, flown by Leutnant Lahl. The bomber was probably on the way into the target around 01.10 hours when its 'Düppel' trail appeared on the radar screen of a Mosquito in the hands of Squadron Leader Bunting. This night fighter 'Ace' was directed by Flight Lieutenant Reed onto the 'trace' that quickly materialised into a bomber. The searchlights that suddenly latched onto the Mosquito were quickly doused, but not before Lahl started to take violent evasive action. Bunting experienced difficulty in hitting his target throughout the first three or four manoeuvres, which resembled the 'corkscrew' pattern used by RAF bomber pilots, exercised by Lahl. He was forced to regain contact via the radar. Finally his cannon fire scored strikes on the cockpit and port wing. Fire immediately took hold and the Ju188 slipped steeply to port. Shortly after an explosion on the ground confirmed the aircraft's demise, along with four of the five-man crew.

Combat Report

21/22 MARCH. 1944. 488 (NZ) SQUADRON
Mosquito XIII AI VIII 0045 and 0110 hrs. 22nd.
(a) CLARE. (B) GT.WAKERING.
Thin cloud 5/10ths 4,000. Visibility excellent.
One JU 88 Destroyed.
One JU 188 Destroyed.

PILOT. S/Ldr E N BUNTING DFC. NAV/R. F/Lt C.P.REED DFC.

I was scrambled from Bradwell Bay at 2335 under North Weald Control for searchlight interception (Controller F/Lt DAY).

We went on to Orbit "D" at 18,000 ft, and after one unsuccessful gauntlet we investigated a cone to the East and obtained a contact at 1 ¾ miles, slightly above and I immediately went below. We throttled right back and closed rapidly to 2,000 ft with e/a 45° below. I lost height at 170 IAS and saw a searchlight flick over e/a which was 3000 ft ahead at the same level. We were then coned by s/ls and e/a made a diving turn to starboard. We obtained a douse on DRL and followed e/a through medium evasive action. Visual obtained at 350 yards 10° above and e/a steadied into mild weaving. Throughout the interception he had been dropping WINDOW. The e/a was identified as a JU 88 or 188 and I opened fire from dead astern 200 yards range. Strikes seen on port engine and wing root, resulting in fire. I gave him another short burst from 300 yards 10° deflection, hitting the fuselage and starboard engine and increasing the fire. E/A fell over to port and I took a camera shot of him going down. He turned over on his back and went down blazing. Shortly after we saw the reflection of the explosion on the ground where we saw the wreck burning. F/Lt Reed observed e/a jettison his bombs after my first attack. We orbited the position of the crash and gave a fix which was NW of SUDBURY, at 0042 hrs. The wreckage of a JU 88 has been found near CLARE and is reported to have crashed at 0041 hrs.

We returned to orbit and shortly afterwards gauntleted south east. F/Lt Reed reported Window and eventually obtained contact on an aircraft dropping Window at 3 ¾ miles range. We closed fairly fast to 4000 feet range when we were illuminated by s/ls. We obtained douse but e/a began very violent evasive action. We nearly overshot beneath him and saw his exhausts 80° above, our speed was then 130 IAS. I saw him begin to peel off to port so turned hard port and regained contact at about 4000 feet, and followed him partly visually and partly on AI through a hard climbing turn to starboard. He steadied for a moment and then dived very steeply to port. I took a quick shot but could not get on enough deflection, 300 yards range: we followed him down and through another starboard turn and steep climb getting into position 250 yards astern. He began a turn to port and I opened fire 1 ½ rings deflection 250 yards, observing strikes. I therefore decreased deflection to one ring and saw many strikes on port wing and cockpit. E/a, which was recognised from its painted wings as a JU 188, immediately burst into flames and went down steeply to port burning very fiercely. An explosion was observed on the ground and we saw a burning wreck. We gave two fixes, one of which was at M.3909. A crashed JU 188 is reported at Butler's Farm, Rochford.

The issue of security – or rather the gross lack of it in this case – was illustrated when the wreckage of the Lahl bomber was investigated. The Bordfunker had neglected to leave his diary behind before take-off and the document would provide a small fund of information both regarding his crew's operations and details of the Gruppe personnel. For example, the first operational entry was as follows:

"21 January - First sortie. Take off from Chievres with 2 x AB1000 and 10 x SD 70. Feldwebel Strebe failed to take off. Intercom. Trouble; turned back halfway over Channel. Landing 2230 hours at St. Dizier. Recognition signal red".

The next three entries on 22nd, 24th and 26th January respectively indicate a return to Chievres via Rheims and Laon, a morning departure for Ahlhorn with six bombers and a note that Oberleutnant Haschle (Staffelkapitän) was lost on the second wave attack on the 22nd.

The 29th January entry was fulsome and went so:

"At 1630 hours a briefing for large scale operations against London – a repetition of 21st January. Approach from Ahlhorn via Beacon Nora marked with flak star shells (Leuchtspucker). Attack from 6,000 metres; over the English coast at 7,000 metres; nose down and evasive action. Throw out 'Düppel' a little before the coast and approach night fighters without firing; twin-engine – white – probably Whirlwind. Fairly considerable flak from the coast onward and searchlights under the 10/10 cloud at 500/1500 metres. Gave no real trouble. Over London itself unbelievably heavy flak and searchlights. Light of fires clearly visible through cloud cover. Searchlights and Lamps – green, red, yellow and white. Good (target marker) lighting provided by us over the cloud. No night fighters over London. Saw one aircraft shot down. Our bombs in the target area at 21.00 hours. Returned flat out over the Thames Estuary then south over Ostend direct home making good landing (Chievres) as first aircraft home. Take off at 19.08 and landing at 21.55 hours. Unteroffizier Gaffke did not return.

Our Ju52 shot down over Aachen. (Oberfeldwebel Kreidler, Oberfeldwebel Stuhr, Feldwebel Rothenburg, Unteroffizier Janisch, Feldwebel Biner dead; Gefreiter Möller injured)".

During the early hours of 4th February the crew headed for their 'Caesar' but were still seeking it out at 03.45 hours, ten minutes prior to briefed take-off; the resultant late take-off at 04.15 was made *'in foul weather'*. On the way over the North Sea 'Rudi', gunner Rudolf Budrat, called in a night fighter whose attentions the pilot managed to evade. Bombing with the two AB1000 containers' content was made at 05.40 hours in the face of *"an astonishing amount of flak"* while searchlight concentration came through the 6/10 to 8/10 cloud cover.

Also noted apart from *'many fires and explosions'* was *'a fine bundle of flak cloudbursts that passed us by – dammed close!'* It then appeared that the pilot overshot Chievres on return since the Bordfunker commented, *'we thought we had come too far and were to the right of the airfield – then we got an astonishing QDM of 121 degrees and there we were!'* After joining the circuit a smooth landing was made, but he noted *'the flak was still firing away at night fighters!'*

Notes on social events dominated the diary up to the 13th with an observation (5th) concerning a B-17 straggler crossing over the airfield and out of which five crewmembers jumped clear; it flew on but apparently was subsequently brought down by fighters 'scrambled' to pick it off.

The sortie on 13th/14th February was completed, but the pilot had to take a short cut to London thanks to engine boost problems. Landing back at Chievres was accomplished on the third attempt, but this difficulty was placed in the minor category in comparison with two Do217 crews whose bombers were described as *'falling down'* on the airfield. Then an 'intruder' appeared and brought about what was stated to be *'a devil of a blaze and monster fire-work display on the perimeter'*.

The crew flew the next two sorties but were left on the ground on the 23rd; their 'Caesar' being taken over by Leutnant L* (Staffelkapitän), an act that was probably a fortunate one for the airmen. The following morning the Senior NCO informed them that on return, as Leutnant L was in the circuit, his bomber was shot down and the machine 'written off'; two of the crew were wounded, but the pilot's fate was not confirmed.

Toothache prevented Leutnant Lahl from flying next evening and it would be 14th March before the next sortie was completed; in the interim period several sorties were 'aborted' including one to Plymouth and another when the crew was at the runway-end, but received a 'red' barring them from following the others thanks to 'intruder' activity.

The circular route up to a line with Rotterdam, over to Cambridge and back over the Channel to Chievres was regarded as *'a crazy approach'* as regards the outward leg. One night fighter was avoided while *'very powerful searchlights, ground marking for night fighters between Norwich and Cambridge'* (probably airfield landing lights) and *'colossal rocket flak and AA flak'* were noted comments. The clear weather deteriorated to solid cloud from the target onwards and the crew, having lost the artificial horizon instrument were relieved to land safely. On taxiing in they discovered they had landed at Abbeville, 30 minutes away from Chievres. Back at Chievres next day their meal was rudely interrupted by a bomber raid that destroyed the repair hangars among other facilities and probably finished off their Ju188/3E+MK stranded out in the middle of the bomb concentration. Their

* *'Leutnant L' was Leutnant Lenkeit of 2/KG6 shot down in 3E+CK shot down at 00.12 hrs 23-24/2/44, on the boundary of Chievres airfield.*

last Ju188 - 3E+BK - was first flown on the 17th and next day the Gruppe transferred to Brussels/ Melsbroek. The penultimate sortie was to Hull (19th/20th) and was recorded as follows;

> *"To Hull via Nora and sea turning point. Low level approach over Holland, then quite low over sea to the climbing point. Climbing with 1.2 boost over the turning point (well marked but too far to the left) about 4,000 metres; 'Knickebein' further to the right. In this way we got to the coast too early, south of Hull, somewhat north of the Wash. Here we stooged around using valuable fuel until ten minutes after zero hour (2200), when lighting was laid over Hull. We see it far away to the right and fly off to 33 for the bombing run. We were the last to drop our load into the town which was burning at every corner. We now had only 800 of our 2,900 litres fuel left and flew direct to Nora. Made a good landing at 23.47 hours".*

The bombers left behind them a measure of destruction that, although not too severe, still caused something approaching a headache for the Civil Defence in general and AFS personnel in particular. No less than 247 fires were recorded with major incidents in several central boroughs from Dagenham across to Islington, while bombs also fell in outer regions such as Orpington and Waltham Abbey Cross. Paddington Station sustained a direct hit and housing in Lambeth and Croydon was badly hit. Overall casualties, mostly borne by those within London, amounted to 62 dead and nearly 250 seriously injured.

Walt Captures a German

Even a Jeep May Sport a Swastika

U.S. Army Air Force Photo

The swastika on this jeep doesn't, naturally, signify one enemy aircraft destroyed. It does, however, stand for the parachuting German airman whom MP S/Sgt. Walton Reed, of Boise, Idaho, and his jeep captured when a Ju88 fell in flames near his Ninth Air Force Marauder base.

Captain Young, the 'C' detachment commander of the 1192nd Military Police Co, was at Braintree Police Station as news of three enemy aircraft coming down in the area was received. One was at Cavendish, another on Earle's Colne airfield and a third at Latchington. It was believed that several airmen had baled out and were still at large; Staff Sergeant Walton 'Walt' Reed was sent out from his HQ at Gainsford House outside Braintree in a Jeep to search for the men. He found Josef Zimmermann, gunner from Ju88 that had fallen on Earls Colne airfield, and took him into custody. A picture of Walt in his Jeep with a swastika painted on its side soon appeared in several US newspapers.

Major Bomber Command Operations
19th to 25 March 1944

22-23 March	**Frankfurt-948 killed**	**816 aircraft-33 lost**
24-25 March	**Berlin -180 killed**	**811 aircraft-72 lost**

Luftwaffe Losses 21st-22nd March 1944

Ju188 E-1 2/KG 6 3E+BK WNr 260326

Butlers Farm, Shopland, nr Rochford, Essex. 01.10 hrs. Shot down by S/Ldr E N Bunting in a 488 Sqn Mosquito.

Started from either Melsbroek or Laon / Couvron. Attacked by a night fighter at 18,000 ft. The aircraft broke up in the air and crashed in flames with bombs still on board. One crew member succeeded in baling out.

Markings: Call sign RM+UE. Underside spray painted black, the upper surfaces a mottled blue.

Lt Günther Lahl (F) (Killed CC), Uffz Julius Fromm (B) (Killed CC 1/67), Ogefr Erich Schiml (Bf) (Killed CC 1/65), Uffz Erwin Kosch (Bm) (PoW injured), Uffz Rudolf Budrat (Bs) (Killed CC 1/66).

Ju88 7/KG6

Failed to return from a sortie to London; cause uncertain. The body of Rudolf Trabant was found in a dinghy washed up on the Norfolk / Suffolk coast on 23/3/44.

Oblt Richard Knödler StKp (F) (Killed), Uffz Gregor Harzheim (B) Killed), Ofw Gunther Becker (Bf) (Missing), Fw Rudolf Trabant (Bs) (Killed CC).

Ju88 A-14 8/KG 6 3E+GS Wnr 301185

Earls Colne USAAF airfield, Essex. Shot down by F/Lt J A S Hall in a 488 Sqn Mosquito. 00.50 hrs.

Started from Brussels / Melsbroek to bomb London. This aircraft was on its way to the target when it was held by searchlights; in spite of evasive action it was effectively attacked by a night fighter. The gunner was the only member of the crew to bale out and the aircraft crashed in flames with the rest of the crew still on board onto a Marauder. One 500 kg bomb exploded, scattering wreckage across the airfield and destroying three Marauders. The Ju88 crashed on B-26 'Perkatory' a 69 mission ship of the 386th Bomb Group normally based at Gt. Dunmow. The B-26 groups were on a base rotation exercise in preparation for proposed moves to forward bases in the invasion.

Markings: The call sign was CR+CK. The upper surfaces were a greenish grey whilst the undersurfaces had been sprayed black over yellow. The spinners were dark green with alternate red and light green bands.

One 1,000 kg HE, one 500 kg HE and ten 50 kg bombs carried. One 1,000 kg HE bomb was found on the airfield.

Oblt Hans Diblik (F) (Killed Brookwood, Surrey), Uffz Egon Staufenberg (B) (Killed Brookwood, Surrey), Uffz Hermann Kamradt (Bf) (Killed CC 5/326), Fw Josef Zimmermann EKI (Bs) (PoW).

USAAF personnel examine the wreckage of JU88 3E+GS which crashed on Earls Colne airfield in Essex.

Ju88 A-4	4/KG 30	4D+AM	WNr 0500

Stanford's Farm, Latchingdon, Essex. 00.52 hrs.

Shot down by F/O S B Huppert in a 410 Sqn Mosquito.

Target London. Whilst on the way to the target this aircraft was attacked by a night fighter at 12,000 ft. The aircraft caught fire and the pilot gave the order to bale out, the observer being the first to jump, the remainder of the crew were killed in the ensuing crash. The aircraft dived vertically into the ground, being almost completely buried.

Markings: Only a large letter D in black found on the fuselage. The works number ascertained as 088300500. Camouflage on upper surfaces mottled green with wavy black lines, while the engine cowlings were yellow with black wavy lines. The undersurface had been sprayed black over light blue paint.

This crew had recently had a new gunner to replace the one who baled out over the same area on 14th March and was captured.

Lt Eginhardt Wolf (F) (Killed CC 5/371), Ogefr Hans Möller (B) (PoW), Uffz Richard Ober (Bf) (Killed CC 5/370), Uffz Theo Rakowski (Bs) (Killed CC 5/369).

A KG30 Junkers 88 in flight showing the Gruppe's diving eagle emblem on the nose.

Ju88 A-4 9/KG 30 4D+AT WNr 301522

Blacklands Hall, Cavendish, Suffolk. Shot down by S/Ldr E N Bunting in a 488 Sqn Mosquito. 00.45 hrs.

Started at 22.55 hrs from Varel to bomb an area north of the Thames, immediately to the west of the Isle of Dogs in the London Docks. The whole of III/KG 30 took part in this operation. The aircraft was attacked by a Mosquito at a height of about 18,000 ft. whilst on its way to the target. The port engine caught fire and the aircraft dived in flames at high speed after the bombs had been jettisoned, two members of the crew baled out and the others perished in the crash. This was only III/KG 30's second operation against England - the first was on the night of 14th March - since the Gruppe returned from Italy. The unit moved to Italy in October 1943 and had been inactive at Leck during the past five months.

RAF pilots examine the hole in the ground created by the crash of Ju88 4D+AT at Cavendish in Suffolk.

This was a very experienced crew, the pilot being the longest serving member of III/KG30 and had sunk 25,000 tons of shipping in 181 war flights.

The pilot had the Deutches Kreuz and Gold (110) War Flights Badge, the observer had the Silver (60) War Flights Badge and the gunner the Gold (110) war Flights Badge.

Markings: Camouflaged with the usual blue grey mottled upper surfaces, whilst the undersurfaces were spray painted black.

Ofw Nikolaus Mayer (F) (Killed CC 1/42), Fw Kurt Maser EKI (B) (PoW), Ofw Willi Szyska (Bf) (Killed CC 1/461), Fw Karl-Heinz Elmhorst EKI (Bs) (PoW).

Me 410-1 2/KG51 9K+IK WNr 420435

Crashed east of Le Havre, France. 00.40 hrs.

Uffz Willi Krause (F) (Killed) Uffz Gunther Onderka (Bf) (injured).

Ju88A-4 4/KG 54 B3+SM WNr 550425

In the Thames Estuary, north of Herne Bay, Kent. 01.05 hrs.

Shot down by F/Lt J C Surman in a 604 Sqn Mosquito near Chelmsford. The canopy and the wireless operator were discovered near Southend. The bodies of the pilot and observer were washed ashore at Halfway Houses.

The jettisonable cockpit cover fitted with one MG 131 and one MG 81 was found on land.

Uffz Willi Fritzenkötter (F) (Killed CC 1/336), Ogefr Karl Friedrich Ahrens (B), (Killed CC 1/335), Ogefr Alfons Walgern (Bf) (PoW), Uffz Kurt Schick (Bs) (Missing).

Ju88 4/KG54 B3+FM WNr 800962

Failed to return from a sortie to London.

Fw Richard Fuchs (F) (Missing), Ofw Otto Hoffmann (B) (Missing), Uffz Franz Maul (Bf) (Missing), Uffz Heinz Lange (Bs) (Missing).

Ju88 6/KG54 B3+BP WNr 8836

Failed to return from a sortie to London.

Uffz Eberhard Egle (F) (Missing), Uffz Hans Götz (B) (Missing), Uffz Martin Stumpf (Bf) (Missing), Uffz Ludwig Keitel (Bs) (Missing).

Ju88S-1 Stab1/KG66 WNr 140577

Crashed on operations 4 km north-west of Soesterberg. 23.46 hrs

Ofw Fritz Karau (F) (Killed), Ofw Max Schiffbauer (B) (Killed), Uffz Walter Heinze (Bf) (Killed).

Fighter Command Claims not attributable to a particular loss

Two claims were made by F/Lt R D R Davies in a 25 Sqn Mosquito.

At 00.15 hrs a Ju188 was shot down at 12,000 feet and seen to disintegrate at 7,000 feet. Two parachutes were seen and the crash confirmed by the Navy 35 miles south-west of Lowestoft.

At 00.33 hrs a Ju188 was shot down at 18,500 feet. A white flash was seen from the starboard engine and shortly after a vivid flash was seen on the sea where a fire lasted 2 or 3 minutes. This was confirmed by the ROC and Navy 25 miles south-west of Lowestoft.

A claim for a Ju88 damaged south of Shoreham at 01.25 hrs was made by F/Lt R H Farrell in an 85 Sqn Mosquito.

A claim for an Me410 damaged over Kent at 00.40 hrs was made by F/O C K Nowell in an 85 Sqn Mosquito.

A claim for an FW190 damaged over the Thames Estuary at 00.50 hrs was made by P/O W J Gough in a 96 Sqn Mosquito.

A claim for a Ju88 destroyed off Rye at 01.12 hrs was made by F/O K. A. Roediger (RAAF) in a 456 Sqn Mosquito. The aircraft was hit in the port wing at 16,000 feet, went onto its back and was seen to dive into the sea by a searchlight post at Rye.

A claim for an FW190 damaged 50 miles south of Beachy Head at 00.44 hrs was made by Lt D G Thornley (RN) in a 456 Sqn Mosquito.

A claim for a Ju88 destroyed 15 miles off Bawdsey at 00.20 hrs was made by F/Sgt C J Vlotman in a 488 Sqn Mosquito.

A claim for an enemy aircraft destroyed off Herne Bay at 00.55 hrs was made by F/Sgt C J Vlotman in a 488 Sqn Mosquito.

Luftwaffe Losses – Non Operational

He177 A-3 3/KG100 6N+TL WNr 840045

22/3/44 Shot down by fighter on a transfer flight to Chateaudun and crashed south of Rheine.

Oblt Karl-Heinz Reper (F) (Killed), Fw Heinz Dittmann (B) (Killed), Uffz Erich Bauer (Bf) (Killed), Ofw Heinrich Karl Zarzitzky (Bs) (Killed), Uffz Karl Bierbrauer (Bs) (Killed), Uffz Richard Kristen (Electrician) (Killed), Ogefr Viktor van Kuil (Mechanic) (Killed), Gefr Erwin Grönner (Mechanic) (Killed), Gefr Kurt Schwarz (Mechanic) (Killed).

Common Operational Experiences

Since WWII, many airmen who flew in Bomber Command have been convinced about the Germans' use of two counter-measures to the Command's incursions over the Nazi hinterland, namely the 'master searchlight' and the 'scarecrow shell'. In the former instance the beam that initially picked out a bomber and onto which the other battery lights then focused was said to be blue in colour, hence its 'master' status. As for the shell, it was said to burst with such intensity that the airmen were convinced it was deliberately increased in explosive effect in order to simulate a bomber blowing up.

Interrogation of veteran Luftwaffe prisoners during '*Steinbock*' elicited similar impressions. The beam power of the searchlights were said to have become evermore powerful and penetrating. In addition, the airmen had been advised that they should look out for searchlight beams that were blue, since these were deemed to possess enhanced lighting effect and therefore more difficult to evade should the bomber be picked out. De-synchronising the engines or momentarily switching one off altogether (the latter action very much a last resort, especially if the bomb load was still on board) was regarded as a possible effective counter-measure. The AA fire was, in general, not regarded as having increased in accuracy, there was one exception to this in what was termed the 'Flieger-schreck'. This was reported as a shell which, when exploding, developed into a number of smaller bursts. As far as the German military was concerned there was no such specialist ordnance as a 'scarecrow shell'. It seems clear that what the Bomber Command crews were seeing was all too often the disintegration of a Lancaster, Halifax or Stirling that usually killed most or all aboard. The Flak guns ranging in calibre from 88mm up to 128mm were more than capable of handing out direct punishment, apart from which their numbers steadily increased as the conflict progressed.

Nor has any evidence come to the fore from British sources regarding the use of 'Flieger-schreck'. The British 3.7 and 4.5 inch AA guns, although never deployed in anything like the numbers of Flak guns in Germany, were of a calibre and performance that would provide a sound deterrent effect at least. As for the searchlights, the general effect of a beam falling directly into one's line of sight was deemed to alter the beam's tone from white to something approaching blue. It is ironic that the airmen of both sides 'enjoyed' a common if natural misconception in aspects of operational flying.

The provision of tail-warning equipment with which to avoid an approaching 'bogey' or 'bandit' night fighter was introduced by both the RAF and Luftwaffe Bomber Commands. In the RAF the equipment, code-named 'Monica', was positioned below the rear turrets on Lancasters, Halifaxes and Stirlings. It proved to be a very mixed blessing, since it merely

Neptun aerials in the port wing of a Do217

picked out the presence of an aircraft whether it be friend or foe. Worse still, the Germans, having examined the equipment on a shot-down bomber, developed 'Flensburg' sets with which to 'home-in' to the signals cast out by 'Monica'.

In the Luftwaffe's case, the parallel types of equipment were FuG214 and FuG216 - code-named 'Neptun'. Examination of crashed aircraft during *'Steinbock'* revealed only the presence of the mountings for the equipment in most instances. On the other hand, interrogation of some prisoners elicited the complaint that, even when installed, there was the same inability to pick out 'hostile' from 'friendly' aircraft.

22nd-23rd March 1944

With *'Steinbock'* now in its second month, it was a sobering fact that just thirteen raids that could in any way be called 'major' had been directed at London – an average of just one raid every four to five nights. In addition the returns from these attacks had been no more than desultory.

Recourse to small-scale attacks by the Me410s of I/KG51 and the FW190s of SKG10 was made by the Luftwaffe on 22nd/23rd and 23rd/24th. SKG10 lost two FW190s, both were claimed by night fighters in interceptions off the Sussex coast. Leutnant Krahner's G-2 went into the Channel near Pevensey late on the 22nd; then just after midnight on the 24th Hauptmann Heisig was the likely victim of an 85 Squadron Mosquito off Hastings.

WEEKLY APPRECIATION OF DAMAGE TO KEY POINTS AND PROGRESS OF REPAIRS.

Period from: 09.00 hours Wednesday 22nd March

to: 09.00 hours Wednesday 29th March 1944.

GENERAL.

Enemy air-activity over this country has occurred on four nights, on each of which land-targets were attacked, and on one day, when reconnaissance sorties were flown.

On Wednesday / Thursday (22nd/23rd March) 10 long-range bombers and 10 fighter-bombers crossed the South Coast between Beachy Head and Dungeness; probably 4 aircraft reached Greater London. Bombing was of no account.

Early on the afternoon of Thursday (23rd March) 3 aircraft made a brief reconnaissance of the Falmouth area.

On Thursday / Friday (23rd/24th March) 9 long-range bombers and 8 fighter-bombers came overland, apparently under cover of our own returning bombers; 5 penetrated to Greater London. At Feltham some damage was done to Gresham Transformers Ltd, but other incidents were of no account.

On Friday / Saturday (24th/25th March) 120 long-range bombers came overland. Activity extended over an area bounded by Portsmouth/Oxford/Southwold, but about half of the aircraft are believed to have reached Greater London. Some of them went out over the Estuary, and others over the South Coast. Activity lasted about an hour and fifty minutes. Twenty–three London boroughs were affected, mostly South of the River. According to reports to hand, the damage was not commensurate with the scale of effort. There was however a 70 pump fire in West Norwood, a 56 pump fire in Fleet Street, and a 28 pump fire in Croydon. There were 81 fires in Croydon and 60 in Beckenham. Civilian casualties on this night totalled 39 fatal and 118 serious.

On Monday/Tuesday (27th/28th March) a force of about 112 aircraft operated overland for about two hours. The great majority crossed the Coast between Plymouth and Weymouth and scattered over an area bounded by Lands End/Cardiff/Banbury/Reading/Selsey Bill; the remainder made shallow penetrations over South-Eastern England. So widespread and ineffectual were these operations that it is difficult to tell from the bombing what the target was. The enemy claims Bristol and also London, although in fact no bombs fell on either.

Civilian casualties for the week total 54 fatal and 141 serious. The G.A.F. is known to have lost 21 aircraft (8%)

During the week 4 Key-points were affected by enemy–action, 1 of them relatively seriously. In addition, there were 5 incidents affecting railways.

The War-time Diary of Miss J. M. Oakman - Chelsea Wednesday 22nd March 1944

21.27 alert - 21.21 all clear. Some little gunfire – not a great deal. A few planes came over for spying purposes.

Friday 24th March 1944

00.02 purple. Heard a plane flying low and it dropped some flares before sirens went and then hopped it.

00.03 sirens. A few guns afar. - 00.30 all clear. One bomb fell at Sudbury. Two planes were brought down.

23.22 sirens again.

Luftwaffe Losses 22nd to 24th March 1944

FW190G-2 Stab 1/SKG10 WNr 840045

22-23/3/44 21.20 hrs. Failed to return from a sortie to London.

Lt Wolfgang Krahner (Missing).

Believed to be the aircraft that crashed in the sea south-east of Pevensey, Sussex, shot down by F/Lt N S Head in a 96 Sqn Mosquito.

FW 190G-3 3/SKG10 WNr 160934

23/3/44. Non-operational. Aircraft crashed on landing at Ahlhorn / Oldenburg airfield.

Uffz Emil Zeitz (Killed).

6/KG6

23/3/44. Injured in a fighter attack on Melsbroek.

Uffz Heinz Winter (B) (Inj).

Ju88 S-1 E. Staffel I/KG66 Z6+KN WNr 300635

23/3/44. Attacked by a fighters and left engine set on fire. Aircraft made a forced landing at Senlis near Creil. The fighters then strafed the aircraft and injured two men; Eduard Zech was hit in the head and Friedrich Grove in his left leg.

Ofw Eduard Zech (Bf) (Killed), Uffz Friedrich Grove (1 wart) (Inj).

FW190G-3 **1/SKG10** **WNr 160498**

23-24/3/44 00.12 hrs. Failed to return from a sortie to London.

Hptm Helmut Heisig (Missing).

Believed to have crashed in the sea off Hastings, Sussex. Shot down by S/Ldr B J Thwaites in an 85 Sqn Mosquito.

24th-25th March 1944

The War-time Diary of Miss J. M. Oakman - Chelsea. Saturday 25th March 1944

01.34 all clear. Noisiest night for some time and also longest raid. Night was dark, and there were few searchlights. Rocket batteries roared into action amid shouts from people. IB's and HE's were dropped. Planes were flying high to avoid the terrific barrage, and only dived to drop red flares. It was a raid of fire chiefly. Some churches were hit. There were 2 DA's dropped at Trinity Road and Croydon "caught it". Fleet St had IB's and lost a church.

It was back to business for the Luftwaffe bombers on the evening of the 24th with 143 crews attending briefings at ten airfields. Three nights before the attackers had come in and out from East Anglia and the Sussex/Kent region, and a similar split pattern of attack appears to have been used for the raid of March 24th-25th. For the personnel of KG6 flying out of Melsbroek and Le Culot the operation was to involve a roughly oval flight-pattern. The outward leg over-flew Le Havre and Selsey Bill to London, but then turned north-east to Saffron Walden and then south-east to Flushing. In contrast, III/KG2, II/KG30 and I/KG100 were operating out of Achmer, Zwischenahn and Rheine; British intelligence reports subsequently recorded Southwold as a second crossing-in point, which would tie in with the separate approach (and likely withdrawal) routing for these Gruppen.

The target was once again the Westminster/Whitehall area (code-named 'Hamburg' for retribution propaganda purposes, following the RAF's perceived 'terror bombing' of that city in July 1943). The time over target for the entire force would be compressed in the usual manner, in this case over a period not exceeding 40 minutes. Details obtained from II/KG6 prisoners revealed an interesting variation in the timetable laid down for each stage of the outward leg. Approximately 20 crews were assigned with the times to be strictly adhered to as follows;

Stage	Time-span
1) Lt Culot (take-off)	2148 – 2203 hours
2) Climbing Point	2227 – 2239 hours
3) Le Havre	2305 – 2315 hours
4) Selsey Bill	2338 – 2345 hours
5) Target	0001 – 0012 hours

The sixteen-minute period permitted for take-off gradually shrunk to twelve minutes at the climbing point, and eleven minutes at Le Havre; barely eight minutes was allowed to cross-in over Sussex, but this figure rose again to twelve minutes for the bomb-run. The bombers were to climb to attain 16,000 feet over Le Havre, marked by a searchlight cone and flak star shells fired at intervals of 60 seconds. This altitude would be maintained until Selsey Bill (marked by LC50 red flares) when a gentle descent to 15,000 feet would coincide with the bomb-run. LC50 red flares would also mark the target, after which a further 2,000 feet would be gradually lost in order to pick up airspeed – steadily increased from 250 to around 300 mph- until out over the North Sea.

The third crew off, at 21.50 hours, was led by Leutnant Besser in 3E+AM. He flew one of the badly out-dated Ju88A-4s that were due for replacement with Ju188s when the Gruppe re-equipped – but there was no sign of new aircraft. Besser's crew, who had been together for around twelve months, were operational veterans having participated in most if not all of the *'Steinbock'* raids to date. Progress to the English coast was uneventful, but once over England the bomber was regularly bathed in light from searchlight beams. Heavy AA fire was encountered. Over London as the load of two SC500 and ten SC50 bombs was released on the red target markers. The chaos of flares, searchlights and gunfire was being left behind as the aircraft crossed east London, but at a reduced altitude, thanks to the pilot taking evasive action from the AA gunners. It was then that the Ju88's tail was blown off by an AA shell. The Ju88 whipped out of control, but three men were able to bale out before it disintegrated upon impact near Chigwell, Essex. The body of its pilot, Leutnant Besser, was found in the crushed cockpit.

One of the Melsbroek-based Ju88s, 3E+HT flown by Unteroffizier Lütcke, was following a similar route away from the target and was crossing east London when it too was crippled by AA fire. The mass of metal that was once a Ju88 smashed into a house in Ilford. The semi-detached house was occupied by Lance Bombardier Murray's wife and his two children - they stood no chance when the bomber turned their house into a pile of rubble.

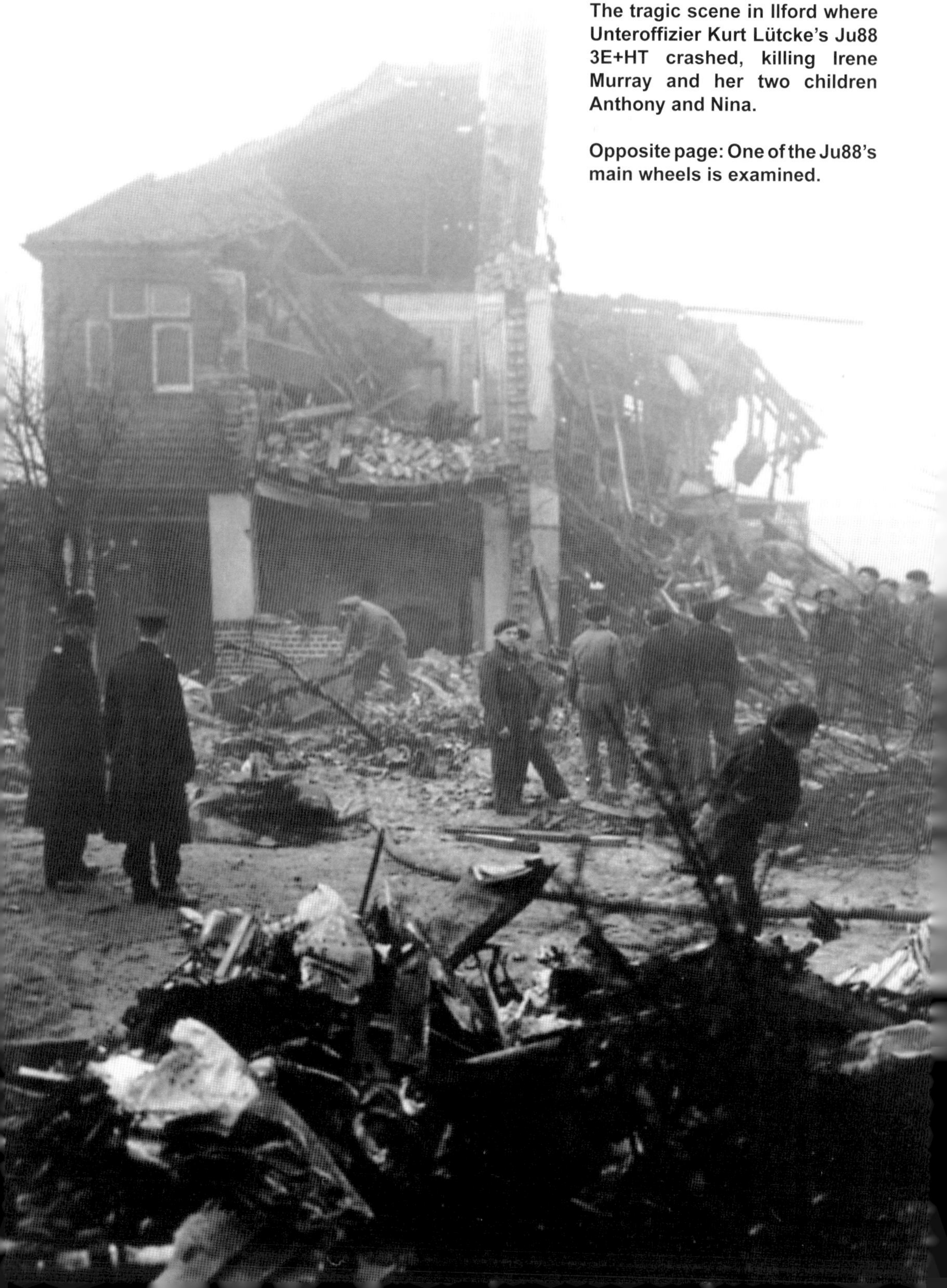

The tragic scene in Ilford where Unteroffizier Kurt Lütcke's Ju88 3E+HT crashed, killing Irene Murray and her two children Anthony and Nina.

Opposite page: One of the Ju88's main wheels is examined.

The third of four bombers to come down on or close to British soil also belonged to KG6. Hauptmann Oeben, the Operations Officer for II/KG6, was flying 3E+AP and was approaching the Sussex coast at around 23.40 hours when he was picked up by a Mosquito. Wing Commander Hampshire's 'Nav/Rad' Flying Officer Condon had the Ju88 on his tiny radar screen. Hampshire was on his second patrol, having been 'scrambled' on reports of 30-40 'bandits' south of Beachy Head and duly tracked the 'bogey' down from the original six miles to a visual 1,000 feet range. The mildly evasive action was of no benefit to the Luftwaffe crew when Hampshire opened fire. The bomber immediately caught fire and the port wing seemed to fall away from the blazing mass. Oeben and the other three airmen either baled out or were thrown out as the stricken machine scattered itself at Walburton, close to RAF Ford. Only the pilot survived the experience, slightly injuring himself when he got hung up in a tree. Unteroffizier Drews (Beobachter) was discovered dead and Feldwebel Bahn (Bordfunker) was discovered alive on the end of one of Ford's runways. He had descended without a parachute and was removed to the Station Sick Quarters, but died shortly after arrival. The fourth airman was Unteroffizier Ehrhardt who, presumably, came down in the Channel since he was never found. Hampshire later paid tribute to the excellent performance of the controller, Squadron Leader Garrett in the face of what he said were difficult 'Window' conditions, so confirming the value of *'Düppel'* distribution in at least hindering night fighter interceptions.

Wing Commander Hampshire and Flying Officer Condon examine the wreckage of their previous night's victim, Ju88 3E+AP which fell near to RAF Ford.

Completing the tally of bombers known by British intelligence to have been lost was Z6+IN from the Erganzungs Staffel of KG66. AA fire punctured its fuel tanks and the last reserves ran out as the Channel coast near Brighton was crossed. Only Gefreiter Rohrhirsch survived the bomber's demise after baling out and spending four hours in his one-man dinghy. The bodies of Unteroffizier Meindl and Leutnant Ohse were subsequently found and buried at sea.

The night's losses for the Luftwaffe added up to sixteen aircraft spread between eight of the participating units; twelve of these were unknown to the British at the time. A Do217 from 8/KG2 was scant miles distant from Evreux after take-off when it crashed, and no less than three Ju88s belonging to KG30 crashed as they arrived back over the Continent. One of the remaining six casualties was a second KG66 'pathfinder' with which contact was lost after it shot down by a Mosquito after departing the English coast.

In some boroughs such as Croydon a period of 20 minutes elapsed between the sirens sounding and the first AA batteries opening up in a sustained barrage lasting at least 60 minutes.

The guns were backed by concentrated searchlight cones that swept the sky in a grim parody of Mother Nature's 'Aurora Borealis' cast up by the Arctic Circle during the winter months. Bombs and incendiaries seemed to rain down on South and East Croydon in particular, although Thornton Heath absorbed a degree of punishment. Separate huge conflagrations in Croydon and West Norwood merited the attendance of 28 and 70 pumps respectively, while numerous other fires created a crimson-tinged backcloth to those witnesses gazing from far afield. A public shelter was totally demolished, but whether it contained any of the sixteen fatal casualties suffered this time is uncertain.

Luftwaffe Losses 24th-25th March 1944

Do217	**2/KG2**	**U5+FL**	**WNr 6253**

One man injured over England during a sortie to London.

Uffz Fritz Lautenschläger (Inj).

Do217	**3/KG2**	**U5+ML**	**WNr 6358**

Failed to return from a sortie to London.

Lt Hans-Günter Hartwig (F) (Killed), Uffz Leo Eisenkolb (B) (Missing), Uffz Albert Schilling (Bf) (Missing), Uffz Erwin Borehard (Bs) (Missing).

Ju188E-1	**5/KG2**	**U5+AN**	**WNr 260382**

Failed to return from a sortie to London.

Uffz Martin Hanf (F) (Missing), Uffz Otto Oberstein (B) (Missing), Uffz Edmund Strobel (Bf) (Missing), Ogefr Heinrich Stein (Bs) (Missing) Gefr Wilhelm Spönemann (Bs) (Missing).

Do217M-1	**8/KG2**	**U5+PS**	**WNr 6336**

Failed to return from a sortie to London.

Uffz Manfred Graf (F) (Missing), Uffz Karl-Julius Levacher (B) (Missing), Uffz Wilhelm Gast (Bf) (Missing), Hptm Hans Summer (Bs) (Missing).

Do217M-1	**8/KG2**	**U5+IS**	**WNr 6224**

Crashed near Evreaux shortly after take off on a sortie to London.

Uffz Josef Schremser (F) (Killed), Uffz Kurt Herrschmann (B) (Killed), Uffz Lorenz Vogtmann (Bf) (Killed), Uffz Josef Zerwas (Bs) (Killed).

Do217M-1 8/KG2 U5+KS

Took off on a sortie to London at 22.40, but crashed at 23.38 after engine failure.

Lt Walter Gehring (F) (Killed).

Ju88 A-14 4/KG 6 3E+AM WNr 550559

Fairview House Farm, Chigwell, Essex. 01.00 hrs.

Started from Le Culot at 21.48 hrs to attack the Government buildings section of London, defined by the code name 'Hamburg'. The aircraft reached the target area and released its bombs, but it was shot down by a direct hit from heavy 3.7 inch guns of the 26 AA Brigade. After having left the target area it was so badly damaged that it broke up in mid-air; the fuselage and tail unit landed 1¼ miles away from the main wreckage on RAF Fairlop. One engine fell in a field ½ mile away.

Markings: 3E+AM, the 3E was in small black letters, while the A and M were in large 2 ft high letters, the letter A being outlined in white. The call sign was DO+LI. The machine was dark green upper surfaces with light green wavy lines. The undersides were black. The starboard spinner was painted dark green with 1½" red stripe round it and the port spinner was dark green with a 1½" white stripe round it.

Three members of the crew baled out. The crew had been together for 12 months and had made 13 war flights over London.

Lt Heinz Besser EKI (F) (Killed CC 1/382), Uffz Johannes Titz EKII (B) (PoW), Uffz Harry Mette EKII (Bs) (PoW), Ogefr Hermann Wissel EKII (Bs) (PoW injured).

Ju88 A-4 6/KG 6 3E+AP

Walberton, nr Arundel Railway Station, Sussex. 23.50 hrs.

Shot down by W/Cdr K M Hampshire in a 456 Sqn Mosquito.

Started from Le Culot at between 21.48 hrs and 22.03 hrs to attack the Government buildings section of London, only incendiary bombs being carried. Shot down by a night fighter at 18,000 ft. when on the way to the target and broke up in the air, the wings and tailplane disintegrated and the fuselage was badly scattered; presumably the wing tanks exploded.

Markings: 3E+AP, the 3E was in small 4" black letters and the A and P were normal size with the A outlined in light green. The aircraft markings from the aircraft compass correction were 8E+BC. The call sign painted just above the wireless operators position was CJ+KP. The upper surfaces were light bluish grey with dark green mottled wavy lines, whilst the underside of the machine was sprayed a very dark green, almost black. The spinners were dark green with bright red and bright green 1¾" stripe painted round them.

The pilot baled out and landed in a tree at Angmering. The observer, whose parachute failed to open, was picked up alive at the end of Ford runway, but died shortly afterwards. The wireless operator was found dead at Binden after his parachute failed. The gunner baled out over the sea, but was not found.

Wg Cdr Hampshire and F/O Condon pose with the cockpit section of Ju88 3E+AP. The official report states that the upper surface camouflage was light bluish grey with dark green wavy lines, but in fact the opposite appears to be the case.

The observer had the Silver (60) War Flights Badge and the wireless operator the Gold (110) War Flights Badge.

Hptmn Anton Oeben EKI (F) (PoW injured), Fw Otto Bahn EKI (B) (Killed - baled out but chute failed. Littlehampton, Sussex), Uffz Gerhard Drews EKI (Bf) (Killed - baled out but chute failed. Littlehampton, Sussex), Uffz H Ehrhardt (Bs) (Missing).

Ju88 A-4 9/KG 6 3E+HT

199, Redbridge Road, Ilford, Essex. 00.30 hrs.

Hit by 3.7 inch AA guns from sites E3 and Z62. The aircraft went into a 45 degree dive and crashed into the lower-front of a house and burst into flames. The house and aircraft were completely destroyed and three people in the house were killed; mother Mrs Irene G Murray, and her two children, Anthony John Murray and Nina F Murray.

Uffz Kurt Lütcke (F) (Killed CC 1/387), Ogefr Hans Witthöft (B) (Killed CC 1/386), Uffz Horst Sinapius (Bf) (Killed CC 1/383), Ogefr Ernst-August Amenda (Bs) (Killed CC 1/379).

Ju88 5/KG30 4D+ON WNr 800967

Whilst on operations an engine caught fire and crew baled out near Dreux.

Uffz Heinz Maiwald (Bf) (Missing).

Ju88A-4 7/KG30 WNr 801361

On return from London radio failed and ran short of fuel over Merzhausen, Taunus. Three crew baled out.

Uffz Fred Geier (F) (Killed), Ogefr Bernhard de Boer (Bf) (baled out, but died of injuries 26/3/44), Gefr Waldemar Skowronnek (Bs) (Killed), Unknown (B) (Baled out).

Ju88 A-4 9/KG30 WNr 884530

Whilst returning from London this aircraft was hit in the left engine and fuselage by AA fire causing it to crash at Abele` Watou, near Ipern, Belgium. The instruments then failed and aircraft caught fire causing three of the the crew to bale out.

Uffz Herbert Kupper (F) (Killed).

Me410 2/KG51 9K+NK WNr 10304

Crashed at Chavigny, 5 km west of St André, not due to enemy action.

Fw Joachim Hübner (F) (Killed), Uffz Hermann Bitzer (Bf) (Killed).

Ju88 3/KG54 B3+XL WNr 301295

Failed to return from a sortie to London.

Ofw Ernst Weible (RK) (F) (Missing), Ofw Herbert Hoppstock (B) (Missing), Uffz Werner Saupe (Bf) (Missing), Ofw Franz Werner (Bs) (Missing).

Ju88 6/KG54 B3+HP WNr 300032

Lt Georg Hahn (F) (Missing), Uffz Karl-Heinz Kaenders (B) (Missing), Uffz Alfred Rebotzki (Bf) (Missing), Uffz Michael Sieben (Bs) (Missing).

Ju88S-1 1/KG66 Z6+HH WNr 370193

Last known location for this aircraft was 40 km south of Brighton. 'Crashed on operations.' Believed to be that claimed by F/O E R Hedgecoe in an 85 Sqn Mosquito at 23.23 hrs.

Uffz Gerhard Hetmann (F) (Missing), Ogefr Hans Mohrmann (B) (Missing), Gefr Rudi Cronauer (Bf) (Missing).

Ju88S-1 E-Staffel I/KG 66 Z6+IN WNr 301228

Sea - off Brighton, Sussex. 01.00 hrs.

Took off from Montdidier to attack London. While homeward-bound the pilot suddenly gave the order to bale out after the fuel tanks were holed by AA fire. The wireless operator baled out, came down in the sea and got into his one-man dinghy. He was picked up 4½ hours later, some 4 miles off Brighton. The bodies of the pilot and observer were found and buried at sea off Brighton by the Royal Navy. When Anton Rohrhirsch was interrogated ADI(K) noted: 'Morale: Very high. Pleasant but extremely security conscious. Refused to even give the names of the rest of the crew.' Felkin's team, however, correctly identified his unit and that he was flying a Ju88S because he gave the ranks of the two men with him – and a Ju88A would have had a four man crew, the S only three.

Uffz Eduard Meindl (F) (Killed), Lt Waldemar Ohse (B) (Killed), Gefr Anton Rohrhirsch (Bf), (PoW).

He177 A-3 3/KG100 WNr 535794

Crashed at Eindhoven on return from operations.

Oblt Rudolf Bernitt (B) (Inj), Uffz Herberts Otec (Bf) (Inj).

F/O Hedgecoe's Mosquito as seen in the chapter heading. His Mosquito was scorched from nose to tail with paint removed and canopy blackened, the result of flying through a fireball as his target exploded in mid-air. The likely victim was Z6+HH a Ju88S-1 of 1/KG66 which was lost over the Channel without trace.

Fighter Command Claims not attributable to a particular loss

A claim was made by F/Lt V H Lithume DFC in a Mosquito of 25 Squadron for a Ju188 in the sea 45 miles east of Lowestoft, at 00.40 hrs. The aircraft had been chased for 50 miles. A vivid explosion was seen and the aircraft flicked on it back and dived vertically into the sea, where it exploded.

A claim was made by F/Lt B A Burbridge in a Mosquito of 85 Squadron for a Ju88 in the Channel off Dover, at 00.20 hrs.

A claim was made by F/Lt B A Burbridge in a Mosquito of 85 Squadron for a Do217 probably destroyed in the Channel off Dover, at 00.52 hrs.

Non Operational Losses 24th-25th March 1944

Ju188 2/KG6 3E+GK

24/3/44. Shot down by own Flak guns at Juvincourt.

Lt Hans-Friedrich Lenkeit (F) (Inj), Fw Eugen Wanner (KB) (Inj), Gefr Eberhard Baumeister (Bs) (Inj), Fw Fritz Detzner (Bs) (Inj), Ofw Max Niebler (Oberwerkmeister) (Inj), Ogefr Ernst Schimmel (1 Wart) (Inj).

Ju188 3/KG6 3E+HL

24/3/44 . Crashed on an internal flight at Crecy-Ensbrie.

Fw Werner Schneider (F) (Killed), Uffz Raphael Simon (B) (Killed), Ogefr Eduard Schott (Bf) (Killed), Gefr Egon Wilhelm Zink (Bs) (Killed), Gefr Wilhelm Lossow (Bs) (Killed), Fw Gottfried Geissler (1 wart) (Killed), Ofw Wilhelm Wissgott (Funkwart) (Killed).

Ju88A-4 9/KG30 WNr 550453

25/3/44 . Crashed at Neuville in France after instruments failed on a transfer flight.

Uffz Walter Reinsch (F) (Killed), Uffz Fritz Hötte (B) (Inj), Ogefr Werner Hössel (Bs) (Killed). The un-named Bordfunker baled out safely.

CHAPTER SEVEN

Debacle at Bristol

Chapter Seven
Debacle at Bristol

27th-28th March 1944

Eight nights earlier the bomber force had been dispatched to Hull, but the sortie had ended in complete failure. Now a second alternative target to London had been selected, this time in the south-west of Britain. The city of Bristol possessed a large seaport at Avonmouth, whose key value to the Allied war effort was enhanced. This was due to the continuing build-up of U.S. Forces and their equipment for the impending Operation *'Overlord'*. A large proportion of the U.S. Army was stationed in the region and therefore the unloading facilities of Avonmouth provided a convenient focal point for equipment of all sorts to be directly channelled to its personnel. The sortie was specifically laid on to hinder this activity since the briefed target was the dock area of Bristol. As might be expected the participating Gruppen were concentrated on airfields in north and north-western France. Guernsey Island was to be the collection point for the force, marked by a cone of six searchlights. From there a due north course would see landfall made at Lyme Bay and 15 minutes later four red flares over the River Usk in South Wales would mark a 90 degree turning point to nearby Chepstow, from where the crews would turn due south towards the target. Bombing runs would be compressed into a twelve-minute spell commencing at midnight and completed from either 11,000 feet or 14,500 feet depending upon the individual unit briefing.

Apart from the River Usk turning point, the target was to be marked by I/KG66 using white flare clusters, but with an extra flare of a different colour, believed to be yellow, also released. The latter provision might well have been included to ensure that false claims of bombing the target could be verified if this variation was not included at the de-briefing reports! I/KG66's efforts were to be backed up by four crews from II/KG2 whose flares would be released at four-minute intervals commencing at 23.58 hours. However, these crews would only release their whole flare and bomb or incendiary loads should the current markers show signs of burning out. Otherwise, they were to retain the flares on the initial bomb-run and then circle for a second flare-release run.

No less than four *'Knickebein'* stations were functioning for the night's sortie as follows:

Station	Frequency	Setting	Time-span
5 (Bergen-op-Zoom)	30.2 m/c	268T	2355-0020
10 (Cherbourg II)	31.5 m/c	332.5T	2335-0010
8 (Caen)	30.6 m/c	345.5T	2345-0040
11 (Morlaix)	30.2 m/c	11.5T	2345-0040

Station 5's beam passed south of Bristol. Station 10's beam intersected 5's at the turning point between Shepton Mallet and Bath, so marking the bomb-run leg's conclusion. This was all very well, but was only usable by those bombers fitted with Fu.Bl equipment. Recent replacement aircraft, particularly the Ju88s, were reported as not having the Lorenz blind approach equipment. In addition the range of *'Knickebein'* frequencies could only be

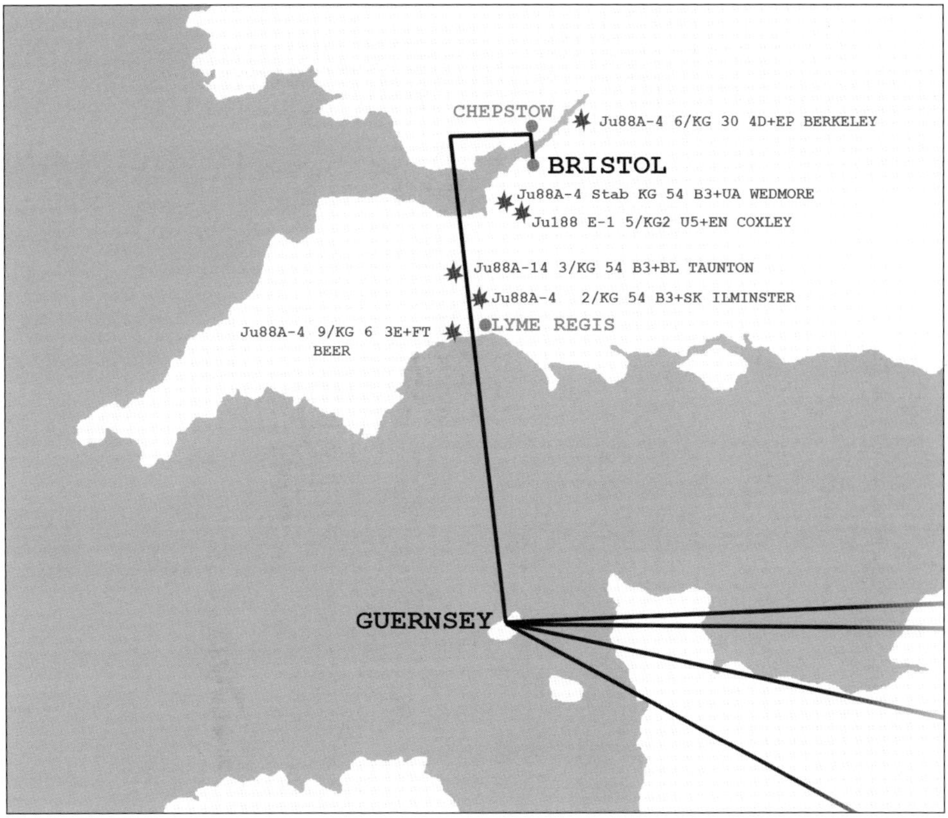

The planned route to target along with the crash locations of the six bombers to fall on English soil that night.

picked up on the Fu.Bl. 2 sets, although Station 10's frequency could be picked up by the original Fu.Bl.1 sets of older aircraft. Such a technical limitation was hindrance enough, but to this could be added a psychological distraction given crews' mistrust of *Knickebein's* efficiency when up against British 'jamming'. It would seem that the successful outcome of the raid could not depend upon *'Knickebein'*. This was all the more ironic since the *'Knickebein'* Station 5 was specifically laid on to pick out the start of the bomb-run rather than rely on the visual assistance provided by flares!

The distance from Guernsey to Bristol involved a flight-time of approximately 40 minutes and the weather conditions were briefed as reasonable in terms of visibility. There appeared little reason why, with accurate marking of the target, the Luftwaffe crews could not inflict a notable degree of damage.

The experiences of two crews, one of which was a target 'backer-up' from II/KG2, would provide pointers to the total failure of I/KG66 to mark the target. Leutnant Siebert was flying in U5+EN, one of twenty crews from the Gruppe, and the second assigned to supplement the primary target-marking effort. The initial route from Vannes to Guernsey and as far as the English coast was uneventful. When searchlights and AA fire were encountered Seibert lost several minutes taking evasive action but carried on towards the turning point. A cluster of white flares was seen but its location was to port, instead of the expected 15-to-20 miles to starboard of the bomber. A heated argument ensued between the pilot and his Beobachter as to whether the bomber had veered off course or whether the flares had been dropped in the wrong location. All attempts to confirm the bearing using *'Knickebein'* were rendered null and void by 'jamming' and so the Ju188 was banked in the direction of the flares. While positioning for a bomb-run a 68 Squadron Beaufighter swept in from behind and Flying Officer Russell delivered a solid burst of fire that hit with the bomber's tail section. The entire load of flares and bombs was jettisoned and a bid made to evade the night fighter; this came to naught when a second pass resulted in cannon shells smashing into the port BMW801 engine and setting it on fire. For once all five crewmembers managed to bale out safely, although Siebert received serious injuries. The bomber fell at Coxley in Somerset – it was almost exactly on the north-to-south bomb-run for Avonmouth, but the crew had already overshot the target by more than 20 miles and were still flying away from the target when shot down!

The falling bomber very nearly claimed the lives of Mrs Cross and her family as it came down. She opened her curtains upon hearing the Ju188's screaming descent and must have been petrified to see its blazing mass heading for her farmhouse. The fortunate presence of a tree less than 100 yards distant that the bomber flew into saved both property and occupants.

The other crew that commented on the failure of the target marking was Leutnant Wolfgang Fritz's from the Geschwader Stab/KG54. The crew was the only one from the Stab to transfer from Marx to Laon/Athies with ten from I/KG54 Gruppe. Specific briefed navigation points from Laon/Athies to Guernsey were Sonne 19 (Beauvais), Funkfeuer 7 (Longueval) and Funkfeuer 9 (Coutances). After climbing to altitude between the last two locations, the route flown to the target was to be the same as for the other units. The Gruppe would bomb from 11,000 feet.

B3+UA took off with two AB1000 containers. The incendiary load appears to have been typical of the loads carried by the force. The incendiaries would be especially effective if they fell among dockside warehouses containing a wide range of volatile imports and would wreak even more havoc than high explosives.

A typical German incendiary bomb, dropped in their thousands over the UK during the war.

Clear visibility over the Channel gave way to a layer of low cloud around Lyme Bay, but Gunther Bärmann, the Beobachter, managed to roughly pin-point his position by reference to searchlight beams. Evasive action put them behind schedule, but the turning point was estimated to be looming up when red flares were seen on a bearing of 320 degrees. Almost simultaneously white flares were observed to starboard. The distance between the two clusters would have been approximately 16 miles on a north-west to south-east line if they had been released as briefed but, both were much closer than this in the surviving airmen's recollections. Leutnant Fritz banked to starboard and took up a zero-degree course for what he took to be Avonmouth.

The incendiaries were dropped on the 'target' and the Ju88 headed back to France. A night fighter was picked out, but a steep starboard turn evidently threw the RAF pilot off the scent. Barely had this threat passed when the cockpit suddenly filled with smoke and a fire took hold in one engine. Fritz and two other airmen reached the ground safely after jumping clear. Unteroffizier Schink was the unlucky one; his parachute failed to deploy and he fell to his death.

Four more of the estimated 112 attackers did not complete the inward leg, with all summarily dispatched by Mosquitos or Beaufighters. Wing Commander Hampshire, Commanding Officer of 456 Squadron, added two to his final tally of seven confirmed 'kills'. Unteroffizier Blaffert was flying his second operation over Britain, his first being to London over two weeks earlier. His Ju88 - 3E+FT - was intercepted over Lyme Bay and the port engine set on fire. Blaffert initially gave the order to jump but then found the controls were responding although height was being lost. He then banked to starboard but on discovering the other engine was now ablaze he jettisoned the cockpit canopy and baled out. The Ju88 hit the top of a hill at Beer, bounced across a valley and crashed into the other side. The bomber completely disintegrated when the load that included a single SC500 bomb promptly exploded. Two of Blaffert's crew remain missing to this day, having most likely baled out and landed in the Channel.

Hampshire's second victim was Ju88 - B3+BL - flown by a Spanish Civil War veteran, Oberfeldwebel. Brautigam. All but Robert Belz, the Bordfunker, got out safely before the bomber broke up in mid-air and tumbled to its destruction on farm grounds at Isle Brewers near Ilminster. In a bizarre postscript to this crew's descent into captivity, two were not immediately apprehended but wandered around until daylight appeared. At this point they walked into Broadfield Farm where Mrs Brown was milking cows. Her initial impression was that they were USAAF personnel from the nearby airfield at Merryfield who had imbibed too well and had spent the night sleeping off the effects in a ditch. Having tried to dispatch them from her premises, it was only when one said 'Morgen, Morgen', allied with closer study of their uniforms, that she realised her visitors were German. Mrs Brown nevertheless kept her calm by bringing them into the house and giving them coffee, while sending her son to the local police station. A policeman duly arrived and took the airmen along to custody in Taunton, several miles to the west.

The British intelligence reports do not provide any indication as to where and how many bombing 'incidents' occurred within the general region on this occasion, nor were the authorities initially aware of what the focal point for Luftwaffe operations had been.

It was only when German broadcasts talked of the swathe of devastation visited upon the city of Bristol that the issue was clarified! A figure of 139 bombers dispatched, of which 116 got through to Bristol and six more bombed alternate sources, was claimed; an unusually honest note in the German written records concerned crews 'aborting' the sortie for which a total of sixteen was listed. Losses were accurately quoted as thirteen declared 'lost'.

What is clear is that the citizens of Bristol were unaware of their impending fate, since not a single explosive or incendiary weapon fell within, or even close to, Bristol's boundaries! A debacle to match, or even exceed, that of the Hull sortie was the harsh result. It is impossible to ignore the failure of I/KG66 to provide the necessary guidance to the target as being a major contributor to the debacle. Although this key unit had lost a steady number of crews since the inception of *'Steinbock'*, there should have been enough expertise remaining among its ranks to ensure a better performance than had been the case to date.

Behind them the raiders had left a score of towns and villages across the northern stretches of Somerset reporting incidents of bombs. Mercifully, recorded fatalities did not rise above double figures but a major headache now arose for the Bomb Disposal Squads. Several hundred UXBs were discovered and the process of dealing with them spanned many months and caused constant disruption to traffic that had to be diverted from each site; indeed the last incidents were not cleared up until the year-end.

The II/KG2 crews tasked with 'back-up' operations were expected to answer the following questions on return;

1) Any visual signals seen during approach.
2) Arrival over the target.
3) Release of their markers on either ground or sky markers (time).
4) Allowance made for drift.
5) How long after the last marking were the markers renewed?
6) If the ground could be seen – how accurate was the placing of the ground or sky markers judged to be?
7) In the event of failure, the reasons were to be given.

The clear assumption is that question 7 must have weighed very heavily upon the minds of the returning crews on this occasion.

Combat Report

27/28th. March 1944. 23.27 hours.

219 Squadron.

Mosquito XVII. Mark 10AI.

Yeovil-Ilminster area.Clear and starlight above. 10/10ths. Cloud at 6000 feet. Vis: good.

1 Ju.88 destroyed.

Aircraft - Noggin 15, Pilot - S/Ldr. Ellis, Navigator - F/ Lt. Craig, of 219 Squadron in Mosquito XVII, Mark 10AI, was scrambled from Colerne base at 23.23 hours, landing Honiley 0045 to intercept hostiles coming in from the South.

Under Sector control (P/O Walton) was ordered to make 12,000 ft. and given a vector of 200° increasing height to 14,000 ft., after 15 minutes controller told pilot bandit 15 miles to port. When closing, pilot was bothered by numerous "window" contacts, and eventually secured contact on target at 3 miles range, height 16,000 ft., chased this contact to the West and closed to 1,500 ft. visual on a twin-engined a/c, believed Ju.88, speed approximately 220 m.p.h. Pilot closed in from astern and below to 150 yards and opened fire with 4 cannons, giving a burst of 5 seconds. Many strikes were seen on port wing and engine causing a tremendous flash and fire broke out in wing and port engine. Return fire was experienced from upper gun position, mostly passing below and starboard, upon later inspection it was found that one round had pierced the Perspex nose and cut an electric cable, causing the A.I. to become unserviceable. The E/A was last seen to roll over to starboard and go down in a vertical dive with flames pouring from it, for some 6-7000 ft., and disappear in cloud.

The Sector Controller took a fix at the time of combat which was in Yeovil area, and it was later established that this Ju.88 crashed near Ilminster.

Relating to the shooting down of Ju88 B3+SK

Combat Report

March 27/28th, 1944.

406 Squadron, R.C.A.F.

Beaufighter VI. - Mark VIII A.I.

00.05 hours

Weather Fine, with fair to good visibility.

Garrick 21 (F/L. H. D. McNabb, pilot, Canadian, and P/O. J.L.N. Hall, English) took off from Exeter at 23.31 hours landing at St. Eval at 01.31 hours.

Under Exeter control, fighter was vectored on 040 degrees at 8000 feet. At 23.40 hours a contact was obtained resulting in visual on Mosquito aircraft. Slight distant window experienced. Immediately after a free lance contact was made, with increasing window on decreasing range. The contact was at 3 ½ miles range and crossing from port to starboard slightly above. After approximately a ten minute chase, a visual was gained at 800 feet range at twelve o'clock, identified as JU.88, taking corkscrew weaving evasive action. Fighter was then at 16,000 feet with target 300 feet above. A one second burst was given, seeing strikes followed by second burst of 3 seconds with slight deflection, when target turned port, no strikes observed. A long third burst with target flying straight and level resulted in port engine and then starboard engine both bursting into flames, revealing German markings by light of fire on port wing. Enemy aircraft remained level for about 3-4 seconds and then spun straight down and was seen to crash on land in flames. Fighter gave fix but received no acknowledgement. After further free lance orbiting, fighter identified one more contact as friendly and then followed another heading north which rapidly pulled away from two to four miles and was abandoned. Fighter then returned to base.

Relating to the shooting down of Ju88 4D+EP

Luftwaffe Losses 27th-28th March 1944

Ju188 E-1 5/KG2 U5+EN WNr 260219

Walnut Farm, Coxley, Somerset. 01.00 hrs.

Shot down by F/O R Russell in a 68 Sqn Beaufighter.

Started from Vannes at 22.32 hrs to bomb harbour installations at Bristol. Eighteen aircraft of II/KG 2 took part in this sortie, having left their base at Gilze Rijen for Vannes earlier in the day. Instructions at the briefing were to cross Jersey at 23.15 hrs and landfall over the English coast was to be made at 23.40 hrs after which course was to be set to a point marked by flares in the neighbourhood of Newport, Monmouthshire. After locating the flares, a 90° turn was to be made, bringing the aircraft to a point due north of Bristol, where another 90° turn was to be made, in preparation for a north to south run over the target. The flight was to be carried out at a height of 5,000 metres (17,000 ft) at an approximate speed of 400 kph. Shortly after crossing the English coast this aircraft was attacked from astern by a night fighter and the port engine set on fire, whereupon the bomb load was jettisoned and the crew baled out. The aircraft crashed and was wrecked.

Markings: E black, outlined in red. N all black. The camouflage on the top surfaces was dark green mottled with pale blue, the lower surfaces black and the spinners green with red centres.

Lt Werner Siebert EKII (F) (PoW injured), Uffz Klaus Holst EKII (B) (PoW), Uffz Matthias Josephs EKII (Bf) (PoW), Fw Hermann Sagel EKII (Bm) (PoW), Gefr Marcel Rozychi EKII (Bs) (PoW).

Do217K-1 7/KG2 U5+GR WNr 4497

Failed to return from a sortie to Bristol.

Fw Emil Krings (F) (Missing), Uffz Hermann Ehrich (B) (Missing), Ogefr Reinhold Banczyk (Bf) (Missing), Uffz Willi Grossmann (Bs) (Missing).

Ju88 6/KG6

Failed to return from a sortie.

Fw Günther Tobor (F) (Missing), Ogefr Karl-Heinz Menzel (B) (Missing), Uffz Theodor Burkard (Bf) (Missing), Fw Gerhard Thon (Bs) (Missing).

Ju88 7/KG6

Failed to return from a sortie to Bristol.

Lt Herbert Blass (F) (Killed), Ogefr Helmut Spaltmann (B) (Missing), Fw Richard Roth (Bf) (Missing), Uffz Gerhard Schiller (Bs) (Missing).

Ju88A-4 9/KG 6

Chelbrough, nr Beaminster, Dorset.

The body of an airman was found at Chelbrough and an empty parachute at Halstock. The aircraft and remaining crew returned. Uffz Alfred Hahn (Bf) (Killed CC 6/22).

Ju88A-4 9/KG 6 3E+FT WNr 44551

Beer, Devon. 23.45 hrs. Shot down by W/Cdr K M Hampshire in a 456 Sqn Mosquito from 15,000 feet.

Started at approximately 21.30 hrs to bomb a factory situated on the western outskirts of Bristol. Bomb load consisted of one 500 kg HE and one incendiary bomb container. After flying in a westerly direction, this aircraft turned northwards towards Lyme Bay and when passing over the English coast was attacked by a night fighter. Hits were almost immediately registered in the port engine, which caught fire and the pilot gave the order to bale out. Three crew landed in the sea, but only the body of the observer was recovered. The pilot then found that, although the aircraft was losing height, it still responded to the controls. He made a turn to starboard, but found that the starboard engine was also on fire, whereupon he himself baled out from a height of 1,500 ft. Onlookers stated that the aircraft dived sharply and crashed into a hill. It then bounced across a valley and blew up, probably owing to the bombs exploding.

Markings: F in black outlined in green; T all black. Upper surfaces dark green mottled with light grey green; undersurfaces black. The spinners were black with two green rings.

Uffz Günther Blaffert (F) (PoW injured), Ogefr Gerhart Harteng (B) (Killed CC 6/247), Ogefr Josef Helm (Bf) (Missing), Gefr Adam Kurz (Bm) (Missing).

Ju88A-4 6/KG 30 4D+EP WNr 550241

Willis Elm Farm, Clapton, nr Berkeley, Gloucester. 23.50 hrs.

Shot down by F/Lt H D McNabb in a 406 Sqn Beaufighter.

Started from Orly at about 21.30 hrs. The crews of II/KG 30 were briefed by the Gruppenkommandeur, Major Pfluger to attack Bristol. All serviceable aircraft from the Gruppe, consisting of about 15 to 20 aircraft, took part of which five were from the 6th Staffel. ETA over the target, which was to be marked by white chandelier flares, was 00.01 hrs and bombs were to be released from a height of 5,000 metres (17,000 ft) from a north to south direction. This aircraft flew by dead reckoning and just after locating the target markers was hit in the fuselage. Two hits in the cabin set the aircraft alight, whereupon the bombs were jettisoned and the crew baled out. The aircraft broke up and crashed in flames.

Markings: Call sign GP+TO. Upper surfaces dark grey with pale grey wavy lines. The undersurface was black, sprayed over light blue. The pilot held the Bronze (20) War Flights Badge.

Uffz Walter Tutschek (F) (PoW), Ogefr Otto Bauch (B) (PoW), Uffz Johannes Wirth (Bf) (PoW), Uffz Karl Wiedner EKII (Bs) (PoW injured).

Ju88A-4 7/KG30 4D+AR WNr 301518

Shot down by a night fighter on return from operations and crashed at Nessy, Cherbourg.

Uffz Helmut Heimpel (F) (Killed), Uffz Ernst Schmidt (B) (Killed), Uffz Mathias Berg (Bf) (Killed), Uffz Werner Neubert (Bs) (Killed).

Ju88A-4 Stab KG 54 B3+UA WNr 1211

Wedmore, Somerset. 23.55 hrs.

Started from Laon / Athies to attack the Bristol docks and carried out an attack from 1,100 ft. It had just left the target area when fire broke out in the port engine; the pilot assumes that this was due to AA fire as the crew had not seen any night fighters. The crew baled out, the pilot being captured unhurt, but the radio operator's parachute failed. The observer and gunner turned up several hours later, having wandered around and slept on the moors. The aircraft crashed into a bog at high speed and was completely wrecked.

Markings: Call sign CE+ZK. Camouflage dark green upper, black lower.

Lt Wolfgang Fritz EKII (F) (PoW), Ogefr Gunther Bärmann EKII (B) (PoW), Uffz Heinrich Schink EKII (Bf) (Killed chute failed. Weston Super Mare, Somerset), Gefr Emil Schwenzer EKII (Bs) (PoW).

Ju88 2/KG54 B3+LK WNr 142276

Crashed on return from a raid on Bristol and came down in the Aisne Kanal at Juvincourt.

Ofw Werner Goertz (F) (Killed), Fw Ferdinand Fuchs (B) (Killed), Uffz Walter Lindner (Bf) (Baled out Inj), Uffz Franz Sitzwohl (Bs) (Killed).

Ju88A-4 2/KG 54 B3+SK WNr 550401

Hestar Combe, Ilminster, Somerset. 23.27 hrs.

Shot down by S/Ldr H V Ellis in a 219 Sqn Mosquito.

Started from Juvincourt at about 21.45 hrs to attack warehouses in Bristol docks area. While over Somerset at about 17,000 ft. on its way to the target the gunner saw a night fighter below and behind. The night fighter opened fire and the gunner gave a short burst in return, but the port engine of this aircraft caught fire and the pilot gave the order to bale out. The aircraft broke up on impact with the ground and wreckage was scattered over a wide area. Leutnant Kerkhof had the cruel misfortune to have his parachute canopy snag upon the cockpit frame and was killed.

Markings: B3+SK, S outlined in red, K outlined in grey. The camouflage on the top surfaces was very dark green with wavy light grey lines superimposed, whilst the undersurfaces were black.

Lt Friedrich Kerkhof EKI (F) (Killed CC 7/226), Uffz Gunther Pfauder EKI (B) (PoW injured), Uffz Rudolf Teismann EKI (Bf) (PoW injured), Ogefr Werner Decho EKII (Bs) (PoW).

Ju88A-14 3/KG 54 B3+BL WNr 0144551

Waldron's Park Farm, Isle Brewers, nr Taunton, Somerset. 23.50 hrs.

Shot down by W/Cdr K M Hampshire in a 456 Sqn Mosquito.

Started at approximately 21.30 hrs to bomb the dock area of Bristol. Instructions given at the briefing were to approach Bristol from the west, then to make a right hand turn and bomb from a north to south direction. After crossing the English coast this aircraft was flying on a northerly course at a height of approximately 10,000 to 13,000 ft. when it was attacked by a night fighter. Immediately the port engine caught fire and the starboard stopped. After jettisoning the bomb load, the pilot gave orders to bale out; the aircraft started to break up and crashed, wreckage being strewn over a wide area, and totally destroyed by fire. The body of Robert Belz was found by a farmer in a water filled ditch on 13th April.

The pilot held the Bronze (20) War Flights Badge and the Spanish Cross, the observer and gunner held the Bronze (20) War Flights Badge.

Ofw Hans Brautigam EKII (F) (PoW), Ogefr Kurt Chalon EKII (B) (PoW), Uffz Robert Belz (Bf) (Killed CC 7/229), Ogefr Alfred Maletzki EKII (Bs) (PoW).

Ju88S-1 E-Staffel/KG66 Z6+FN WNr 301509

Failed to return from operations.

Fw Wilhelm Schmidt (F) (Missing), Uffz Heinz Kunczak (B) (Missing), Uffz Franz Kraus (Bf) (Missing).

Fw. Wilhelm Schmidt with his young wife who was destined to end the war as a widow.

Ju188E-1 2/KG66 Z6+AK

Returned to France after being damaged by AA fire during a sortie to Bristol. Abandoned by crew near Dunkirk after being engaged by own Flak.

Lt Ernst-Karl Fara (F), Uffz Ludwig Konietzka (B), Uffz Gerd Pfeiffer (Bf), Uffz Hermann Visarius (Bm), Ogefr Leo Häusler (T-Gerät specialist).

Fighter Command Claims not attributable to a particular loss

A claim was made by 3.7 inch AA guns at Portland for an enemy aircraft in the sea 6 miles south of Abbotsbury, Dorset.

A claim was made by F/Lt K Kennedy in a 96 Sqn Mosquito for an FW190 in the Channel off Dungeness at 23.42 hours.

A claim was made by P/O R L Green in a 406 Sqn Beaufighter for a Ju188 20 miles south of Plymouth at 00.02 hours. The starboard engine was hit and fire spread along the wing. The aircraft then went down in the sea where it burnt for two minutes.

A claim was made by S/Ldr B Howard (RAAF) in a 456 Sqn Mosquito for a Ju88 50 miles south of Brighton at 01.18 hours. After a blinding flash pieces came off the starboard engine the aircraft then spiraled down to the sea where it burnt.

Major Bomber Command Operations
26th to 31st March 1944

26-27 March Essen-600 killed 705 aircraft-9 lost

30-31 March Nuremberg*-69 killed 795 aircraft-95 lost

***RAF Bomber Command's worst raid of WWII.**

Command Comparisons

The last full week in March 1944 was to witness set-backs for both *'Steinbock'* and the RAF's 'Battle of Berlin' Campaign, but with vastly different effects. On the $24^{th}/25^{th}$ the Luftwaffe's latest foray to London had been indifferent-to-poor. Three nights later had come the total failure of the Bristol raid.

On the other hand, as London was being attacked, a far larger force of Lancasters and Halifaxes set to hammer Berlin was suffering an even greater disaster. Winds of 'jet-stream' proportions tore the bomber stream asunder. The outcome was two-fold; Berlin remained virtually unscathed and, worse still, no less than 72 crews were lost. A sizeable proportion of the losses were claimed by numerous flak batteries as single bombers strayed into the deadly web of searchlights and heavy flak guns.

On the last full night of the month came the disastrous culmination of Bomber Command's 1943/44 campaign. The target was Nuremburg. A combination of clear skies, temperatures that created vapour-trails, and the nightfighters not only left the target unscathed but cost nearly 100 crews.

'Egon' System

The 'Lorenz' blind-landing equipment had been the basis for 'Knickebein' although the results had been disappointing in the light of British counter-measures that inhibited its use as a bombing aid. A similar adaptation of another basic piece of Luftwaffe equipment in the form of the I.F.F. sets (FuG 25 and 25a) brought about the 'Egon Verfahren' (Egon System) a ground-control procedure for crews on bomber operations. In the case of *'Steinbock'* recourse to its use was specifically made by I/K66 whose crews were seeking to mark target zones.

The system was based upon signals radiated by the FuG25 and picked up by two 'Freya' radar sets, the first of whose operators used the signal to plot the aircraft's course, and the second to take over for the final flare-release run. When first introduced the various course alterations to and from the target and direction on the actual flare-dropping run were transmitted by Morse code, and the terminology already in use by the Luftwaffe night fighter force was borrowed.

Prior to take off the crews were given a course to the target and a specific height at which to fly and release their loads. The height was to be rigidly adhered to since it could not be checked by the ground control. A minimum height of 6,000 metres extending up to 8,500 metres over the target was normal. After take-off the FuG 25a was switched on and the No.1 'Freya' took up the duty of plotting the aircraft's course, using the single-letter recognition transmitted from the bomber. The range and bearing was passed by the 'Freya' operator to the plotting table, which closely resembled the 'Seeburg-Tisch' used by night fighters. This took the form of a transparent map of the area of operations laid on a glass screen; the bomber was represented by a red slot of light cast on the screen's underside by a projector connected directly to the 'Freya'. In this manner the aircraft's track could be followed and corrected as necessary. The course corrections were picked up in the aircraft either through the FuG 16 or the T.Z.G R/T attachment to the FuG 10 that reportedly provided greater range than the FuG16.

On approach to the target 'Freya' No. 2 took over, but only in respect of issuing bomb release instructions. Once again the terminology used for this was borrowed from night fighter procedures:

W/T	**R/T**	**Meaning**
(Preceded by the aircraft call-sign)		
1) KKK	Kommen	You are being plotted
2) AAA	Autobahn	Change bearing to….
3) RRR	Rolf	Bearing 5 degrees right
4) 2RRR	Zweimal Rolf	Bearing 10 degrees right
5) LLL	Lisa	Bearing 5 degrees left
6) UUU	Kirchturm	Height
7) CCC	Caruso	Fly straight and level course
8) ZZZ	Pauke Pauke	Open bomb doors
9) -----	-----	Pre-release signal
(3-4 sec. dash)	(W/T dash)	
10) . (dot)	. (W/T dot)	Bomb or flare release signal
11) Not known	Kurfurst	Acknowledge signal is understood (Reply on FuG. 25a)
12) AAA HHH	Autobahn Mat (Heimat)	Set course for home

Signal 1 was passed by control to the pilot to confirm 'Freya' No. 1 had engaged the bomber; the aircraft twin-letter and single number call-sign (eg. CA1) preceded the W/T and R/T detail. On all subsequent occasions only the aircraft number was used. The crew responded by manipulating the FuG 25 – switching off for 3-4 seconds – so confirming signals had been received and understood; a negative response was indicated by repeated switching on and off.

Course corrections were made in multiples of 5 degrees as shown by 3), 4) and 5); for example 'change course 15 degrees right' would be 'Autobahn dreimal Rolf' with left-hand course alterations suffixed by 'Lisa' (The W/T equivalent would be AAA 3 RRR or AAA 3 LLL).

Once the bomb-run was completed following the issue of signals 8) to 10) the pilot signalled 'quitting' by using the Fug 25 switch, after which control gave the order to return and the bomber was vectored back to the airfield.

Interrogation of PoWs disclosed that the 'Egon' system could handle individual aircraft every ten minutes. However, the practice was for the flare-dropping bombers to orbit the target after releasing one cluster before being controlled on a second run approximately six minutes later in order to renew the marking before the first cluster had expired.

When British radio counter-measures began to interfere with messages to the bombers it became Luftwaffe practice to broadcast these both in W/T and R/T format, with the W/T sent over two channels. The R/T details were handled via the FuG16 with one of the W/T frequencies (583 k/cs) sent via thc Peil.Ge 6 (D/F) set, and superimposed upon the Calais 1 Station broadcasting programme; the other unconfirmed frequency was handled by the FuG 10.

A major advance in the 'Egon' system's efficiency occurred when a cathode-ray unit was introduced that was linked to the FuG 25a. The set, which was located between the pilot and Beobachter positions, was similar in size and screen diameter to the 'Lichtenstein' equipment used by Luftwaffe night fighters.

The external aerial was understood to be the same unit used to transmit and receive the FuG 25 set signal. The scale on the cathode-ray screen consisted of a circle divided into equal segments, each representing, and marked with, one of the code-words used above. This inner circle had a surrounding circle marked clockwise from 0 to 9 with the 0 in the 12 o'clock position. The overall screen impression was basically similar to that of a dartboard. A short blip radiating from the screen centre appeared in the segment for the appropriate code-word ie 'Autobahn'. The bearings were indicated by a second central and long blip that appeared against a succession of figures in the outer circle. Course corrections were given by the short and long blips appearing respectively against the 'Rolf' or 'Lisa' segment. In the same way height was indicated by the blip signals appearing against 'Kirchturm' and the appropriate numbers.

British Appreciation of Bombing on London

Date	Sorties Total	Over England	Over London	Bomb Tonnage England	Bomb Tonnage London
21-22 Jan	*270*	*200*	*40*	*270*	*30*
29-30 Jan	*180*	*130*	*30*	*150*	*35*
3-4 Feb	*185*	*130*	*17*	*165*	*25*
13-14 Feb	*150*	*115*	*5*	*160*	*5*
18-19 Feb	*175*	*140*	*90*	*175*	*135*
20-21 Feb	*165*	*110*	*65*	*130*	*90*
22-23 Feb	*155*	*135*	*55*	*160*	*75*
23-24 Feb	*130*	*110*	*30*	*115*	*50*
24-25 Feb	*135*	*110*	*60*	*105*	*80*
1-2 Mar	*100*	*70*	*10*	*95*	*15*
14-15 Mar	*180*	*140*	*70*	*150*	*85*
21-22 Mar	*140*	*110*	*55*	*105*	*65*
24-25 Mar	*130*	*110*	*60*	*105*	*70*
Total	**2095**	**1610**	**587**	**1885**	**760**

Non Operational Losses 28th to 30th March 1944

Me109G-6 5/(F)123

28/3/44. Shot down by fighter 9 km west of Amiens Glisey on return from a reconnaissance of London. Ofw Friedrich Gouter (Killed).

Ju88 3/(F)123

29/3/44. Crashed at Twente, Holland, not due to enemy action. Fw Ernst Mayer (F) (Killed), Oblt Werner Müller (B) (Killed), Fw Gerhard Fischer (Bf) (Killed), Uffz Edwart Neitzke (Bs) (Killed).

Do217M 7/KG2 U5+IR WNr 6128

29/3/44 00.12 hrs. Nienbergen, near Münster. Crashed on a transfer flight from Nantes to Achmer. Lt Gustav Meier (F) (Safe), Ogerf Hans Olm (B) (Safe), Uffz Leo Haring (Bf) (Safe), Uffz Heinz Finkenberg (Bs) (Safe), Uffz Heinrich Offschanny (Bm) (Killed), Uffz Alfred Zecher (1 Wart) (Injured).

Ju188E-1 I/KG2 U5+CB

30/3/44. Damaged on landing at Hesepe. Lt Ortwin Rösner (F) and crew safe. Rösner had flown back from Lincoln on 17-18/8/43 after two of his crew had abandoned his aircraft.

Opposite page: Ju188 3E+LK which came down near Temple Combe, Somerset in the early hours of 15th May 1944.

CHAPTER EIGHT

Advance into Oblivion

Chapter Eight
Advance into Oblivion

April 1944

The prospect of Operation *'Steinbock'* delaying the Allied cause was never a realistic one. The campaign had been launched with too few resources, technical or human, at hand; now by the beginning of April it was a pale shadow compared, even, to the early assaults upon London.

Very little Luftwaffe activity was experienced over the British mainland during the first half of April. Several reconnaissance flights were made by day and night, but the first recorded bombing incidents did not occur until the 13th/14th when a few raiders reached London. The disruption inflicted was infinitesimal, but three civilians did lose their lives.

Major Bomber Command Operations
1st to 17th April 1944

11-12 April	**Aachen-1,525 killed**	**352 aircraft-9 lost**

WEEKLY APPRECIATION OF DAMAGE TO KEY POINTS AND PROGRESS OF REPAIRS.

Period from: 09.00 hours Wednesday 29th March
to: 09.00 hours Wednesday 5th April 1944.
GENERAL.

There has been little enemy air-activity to report and none of any consequence. On Thursday/Friday (30th/31st March) 8 long-range bombers and 7 fighter–bombers operated overland in two phases; in the first 12 aircraft crossed the Sussex Coast, 3 of them penetrating to Greater London, and in the second, 3 crossed the East Coast between Spurn Head and Cromer, making shallow penetrations. The only other overland activity occurred at dusk on Friday (31st March) when a single aircraft made brief landfall in the neighbourhood of Wick without dropping any bombs. Civilian casualties for the week total only two seriously injured. No G.A.F. aircraft have been reported destroyed.

No Key-points or railways have been affected by enemy-action; there has been 1 incident involving an airfield.

Luftwaffe Losses 5th April 1944

Me410	**3/KG51**	**9K+BL**	**WNr 120110**

Crashed near St André, Eure, France. Not due to enemy action.

Lt Walter Renatus (F) (Killed), Uffz Paul Heckel (Bf) (Inj).

WEEKLY APPRECIATION OF DAMAGE TO KEY POINTS AND PROGRESS OF REPAIRS.

Period from: 09.00 hours Wednesday 5th April

to: 09.00 hours Wednesday 12th April 1944.

GENERAL.

Enemy air activity against this country has been negligible this week.

On Sunday night (9th/10th April) one enemy aircraft crossed the coast at Looe in Cornwall and a minor incident was reported from Liskeard.

On Tuesday night, the (11th/12th April), twelve aircraft operated as Intruders over Lincolnshire and East Anglia. Machine-gunning was reported from Stiffkey, Norfolk. One reconnaissance was flown during daylight on Wednesday, the 5th April over the North Sea and one over the South West approaches. Three reconnaissances were also flown over the English Channel on the nights of Thursday, the 6th/7th April and Monday the 10th/11th April.

There were no civilian casualties during this week and no G.A.F. aircraft have been reported as destroyed. No Key-points or railways have been affected during the week.

Luftwaffe Losses 6th to 11th April 1944

Ju88	**IV/KGr101**

6/4/44 Failed to return from a sortie to south-west England.

Fw Johannes Günsch (F) (Missing), Uffz Rudolf Ulrich (B) (Missing), Uffz Joachim Schmidt (Bf) (Missing), Uffz Friedrich Kups (Bs) (Missing).

Ju88	**IV/KGr101**

6-7/4/44 Shot down by own Flak at low level approaching Jersey, Channel Islands after a sortie to the Isle of Wight. Crashed at Eden Chapel, St Saviors, Jersey.

Fw August Spoo (F) (Killed), Uffz Heinz Heimbach (B) (Killed), Fw Wilhelm Bönsel, (Bf) (Killed), Uffz Ferdinand Dür (Bs) (Inj).

He177A-3 **2/KG100** **GN+GK** **WNr 332355**

11/4/44 Shot down by AA fire on a transfer flight, and crashed at Münster-Handorf.

Ogefr Georg Urbanski (B) (Inj), Fw Erich Domke (Bw) (Inj), Uffz Gustav Baumann (Bs) (Inj), Fw Kurt Krüger (Bf) (Killed), Ofw Martin Brünnel (Bw) (Inj).

WEEKLY APPRECIATION OF DAMAGE TO KEY POINTS AND PROGRESS OF REPAIRS.

Period from: 09.00 hours Wednesday 12th April

to: 09.00 hours Wednesday 19th April 1944.

GENERAL.

Enemy air – attacks have been made on land-targets on three nights during the past week. In addition, a single machine flew over the Isle of Wight on Wednesday and was destroyed.

On Wednesday / Thursday (12th/13th April) 12 long-range bombers and 10 fighter-bombers operated over South–Eastern England and Essex; 6 aircraft penetrated to Greater London.

On neither of these nights was bombing of much account. On Tuesday / Wednesday (18th/19th April) a force provisionally estimated at 58 aircraft operated over land; 53 crossed the East Anglia Coast and flew out over Kent and Sussex; the majority of them penetrated to London. The remaining aircraft operated in two other distinct phases over Lincolnshire and Norfolk. Most of the London boroughs affected lay East of a line Cheshunt/Coulsdon & Furley. Civilian casualties totalled 39 fatal, 9 missing and 75 serious. The figures for the whole country for the week are 45 fatal, 9 missing and 89 serious.

The G.A.F is known to have lost 13 aircraft (13%)

2 Key-points were affected by enemy action during the week. In addition there were 2 incidents affecting railways.

12th-13th April 1944

The War-time Diary of Miss J. M. Oakman - Chelsea. Wednesday 12th April 1944

22.53 alert. (very surprising). Plane over almost at once – a bit of gunfire for a short while.

3 flares (orange) almost due S.W. Silence

23.32 all clear. 1 plane was brought down.

Opposite page: The Me410 crews of KG51 were now starting to suffer casualties as they joined the Steinbock offensive.

Luftwaffe Loss 12th-13th April 1944

Me 410A-1	1/KG51	9K+CH	WNr 120017

Failed to return from a sortie to London.

Shot down by S/Ldr A Parker-Rees in a 96 Sqn Mosquito off the French coast at 23.21 hrs. Both engines were set ablaze and aircraft went into a steep dive 3 miles off the coast. Helmut Siol's body was washed ashore in Holland on 14/6/44 and Liehr's body was found on the French coast.

Lt Helmut Siol (F) (Killed), Fw Bernhard Liehr (Bf) (Killed).

The War-time Diary of Miss J. M. Oakman - Chelsea. Friday 14th April 1944

01.23 sirens. 01.57 all clear. Some heavy gunfire from mobile gun. Two planes were brought down.

Luftwaffe Losses 13th-16th March 1944

Me410	2/KG51	9K+CK	WNr 20003

13/4/44 Force landed due to engine failure 15 km south of Pont Audemur, France.

Lt Wilhelm Batel (F) (Inj), Uffz Johannes Ebert (Bf) (Injured).

Me410	3/KG51	9K+HL	WNr 420299

13/4/44 Crashed at Vitry en Artois on return from London. Not due to enemy action.

Fw Karl-Heinz Bargstädt (F) (Killed), Fw Joachim Lenhardt (Bf) (Killed).

Me410A-1 3/KG51 9K+BL WNr 420019

Failed to return from a sortie to London.

Uffz Heinz Zehmisch (F) (Missing), Uffz Heinz Kirstein (Bf) (Missing).

Shot down by S/Ldr A Parker-Rees at 01.38 hrs off the 15 miles west of Hardelot. Parker-Rees reported, *"This resulted in strikes on starboard engine and fuselage, followed by a small explosion in board of the engine, which burst into flames. The e/a slowed down, diving rapidly, with the flames spreading and soon enveloped the a/c. I orbited and watched it crash on the sea, where it continued to burn."* F/Lt D L Ward, also of 96 Sqn, claimed an Me410; at 01.07 hrs over the Channel, but did not see it crash.

Ju188E-1 4/KG2 U5+AM WNr260525

15/4/44 Crashed at Münster-Handorf on a night training flight.

Uffz Herbert Franz (Killed), Uffz Alfred Tiemann (Killed).

Ju88 A-4 4/KG66 Z6+GP WNr 3550

15/4/44 Crashed during a non-operational flight.

Uffz Heinz Bandon (F) (Killed), Fw Hans Trummeter (B) (Killed), Uffz Adolf Kohnhorst (Bf) (Killed), Ogefr Hans Mutter (Bs) (Killed).

Ju188E-1 5/KG2 EM+AB WNr 260398

16/4/44 U/C collapsed on take-off for training flight at Munster-Handorf.

Oblt Georg Kittelmann (F) (Inj), Ofw Wilhelm Schnitner (Bw) (Killed), Ogefr Gerhard Heuer (Bs) (Killed).

Ju88S-1 E-Staffel/KG66 Z6+CN WNr 140573

16/4/44 Crashed on a non operational flight 4 km north of Avord.

Oblt Wolfgang Boehmann (F) (Killed), Ofw Franz Förg (B) (Killed), Ofw Erich Herzberg (Bf) (Killed).

18th April 1944

A bizarre incident occurred over Hampshire on the morning of the 18th. At 07.45 hours Flight Lieutenant Sanders was leading a four-aircraft formation of Typhoons from 266 Squadron back from Exercise 'Smash' to their airfield at Tangmere. The fighters were already in line astern in the circuit at 1,500 feet when the leader's attention was diverted by the sight of several AA bursts ahead. The gunfire was being directed at a twin-engine aircraft flying on a due westerly course that Sanders immediately thought was a Ju188. As the bomber banked to port he followed suit and turned inside its path, whereupon he confirmed its 'hostile' status. Closing in rapidly to 200 feet and only marginally distracted by what he described in his report as 'slight return fire' he loosed off his four 20mm cannon with a small degree of deflection to land strikes on the port wing root and the cockpit. Flame and smoke erupted and as he passed over the bomber he noted pieces falling off. Sanders' No. 2, Flight Sergeant Dodd, now fired two bursts that hit home as the Luftwaffe pilot desperately held a westerly course as far as the eastern coast of the Isle of Wight. At this stage the Ju188 crossed the Solent to crash at a shallow angle close to Beaulieu. The heavy column of smoke observed by the RAF pilots suggested that nobody on board was still alive.

When the investigation team inspected the site its members were amazed at what they found. The normal crew complement of a Ju188 was five, but here the total of bodies removed from the completely burnt-out airframe was seven! The initial reason for this anomaly was based on the assumption that these Luftwaffe airmen were deserters. However, the airmen in question had not fallen into this category, but had suffered a cruel stroke of misfortune. They all belonged to I/KG66 and comprised a standard crew of five along with two mechanics. It appeared likely that the aircraft (Z6+EK) was staging to the Gruppe airfield from which a sortie was due to be launched in the late evening against London. In the course of the flight the pilot had gone very badly off course and strayed into the lethal embrace of the British defences.

Luftwaffe Loss 18th April 1944

Ju188 E-1 **2/KG 66** **Z6+EK** **WNr 260523**

Exbury House, nr Beaulieu, Hampshire. 07.30 hrs.

Became lost when changing base prior to the coming operation on 18-19/4/44. A crew of seven was carried, including two ground crew. It is probable that the aircraft was flying a reciprocal course, and therefore was hopelessly lost. Approached the South Coast at approximately 9,000 ft and was engaged by AA batteries of all calibres, then intercepted by a Lt A V Sanders in a 266 Sqn Typhoon. It hit the ground at a shallow angle, caught fire and burnt out.

Markings: painted on the port side of the fin were the letters Z6+EK, the E was in black, outlined in white. The call sign was RC+RH. The upper surfaces were a mottled green and light blue, showing about 50% of each colour, the under surfaces were spray painted black over light blue.

Uffz Hans Czipin (F) (Killed CC 6/297), Uffz Johann Krauss (B) (Killed CC 6/296), Uffz Robert Schultes (Bf) (Killed CC 6/298), Uffz Hans Ehrhardt (Bf) (Killed CC 6/294), Uffz Eitel Wysotzki (Bs) (Killed CC 6/295), Gefr Kurt Edgar Vester (funkwart) (Killed CC 6/293), Ogefr Leonhard Schwingenstein (1 wart) (Killed CC 6/292).

Uffz. Hans Ehrhardt who was killed in the crash of Ju188 Z6+EK, his rank on the wartime grave is incorrect.

18th-19th April 1944

The War-time Diary of Miss J. M. Oakman - Chelsea. Wednesday 19th April 1944

00.53 sirens

01.42 all clear. Quite noisy again – rockets and guns as usual – mostly odd planes about. The "Daisy" in Brompton Road was hit by a rocket shell. A hospital had four bombs on it with casualties. It was a larger raid than usual and followed our daylight raid over Berlin.

22.26 sirens.

22.52 all clear. Nothing except rain.

Major Bomber Command Operations

18th to 25th April 1944

21-22 April	**Cologne-664 killed**	**379 aircraft-4 lost**
22-23 April	**Düsseldorf-883 killed**	**596 aircraft-29 lost**

The sortie in which Hans Czipin and his hapless crew would have almost certainly have participated featured the monotonous target choice of London; in this instance the London docks with Tower Bridge as the epicentre was selected. The bomb runs would be conducted over a ten-minute spell commencing at 01.00 hours. Target-marking would be the same as for the Bristol raid, with the primary red flare pattern released by I/KG66 and bursting around 8,000 feet and supplemented by white flares from selected II/KG2 bombers laid at a lower altitude of 6,000 feet. Subsequent interrogations of airmen from I/KG54 and I/KG100 confirmed the anomaly of using the white flares, since these men said that no reference to other than red flares over the target had been mentioned during briefing. The alternative suggestion was that the white flares were used to provide enhanced visibility to confirm that the crews were over the target, especially when given the clear weather conditions that night. Whether or not this was the case, the raid would evolve 'according to somebody else's plan'!

Medium-Frequency Beacon *(Funkfeuer)* 'Nora' at Noordwijk on the central Dutch coast would be the converging point for the bomber stream and landfall would be near Leiston in Suffolk. Six *'Lux'* buoys would be dropped at 52.15N-03.05E as an additional navigation check. A turning point near Newmarket marked by four red flares at 10,000 feet would indicate the final target approach. Then, with bombing completed, a steadily descending south-east course would be taken up to the Channel coast at Dymchurch and over to Boulogne, from where the various Gruppen – several of whom were operating from German airfields – would set their final headings.

The provision of *'Knickebein'* Stations 3 (Den Helder) and 5 (Bergen-Op-Zoom) at angles of 257T (00.30-01.07 hours) and 275T (00.40-01.15 hours) would seem to provide additional guidance for any crew electing to tune-in since the beams' convergence was in the final turning-point area; in addition the 30.2 m/c frequency for Den Helder was compatible with the original Fu.Bl.1 blind-landing equipment. The Caen, Cherbourg and Morlaix Stations were also available, with bearings that pointed towards London.

The briefing meteorologists stated that the wind strength would be between 20 and 25 kph from a north-north-east direction and these conditions were expected to prevail during the raid. In Britain the estimated wind speed was 8 kph at 10,000 feet – but from a south-south-westerly direction. Here was a notable operational contradiction that could adversely affect the raid.

Bomb loads were to be a mix of incendiaries and SC250 and 500 explosives, but the nature of the target with dockside warehouses holding vast quantities of material would suggest an imbalance in favour of incendiaries. Oberleutnant Hein, flying in U5+KN, had his Ju188 loaded with a minimal total of ten BC50 phosphorus incendiaries and four LC50 flares. The unit personnel were aware that he was suffering from *'Hals-Schmerz'* (throat-ache), a sardonic Luftwaffe slang term for any airman seeking the award of the Ritterkreuz that hung round the neck when worn! This veteran airman had flown 290 sorties and was treated with scorn for allegedly seeking any measure that would increase his chances of survival, in this instance by bearing a less volatile bomb load. However, there was never any guarantee of immunity from injury or death.

Hauptmann Eichbaum had been appointed Staffelkapitän of 4/KG2 and following the briefing at Münster/Handorf led the Gruppe off at 23.00 hours. The crews headed for London in reasonable hopes of gaining the target, but this did not prove to be the case either for this Gruppe or the force in general. The wind direction was diametrically opposite to the briefing and noticeably lighter than that forecast, probably the 'fly in the ointment' for the raid. The flares were released, but neither over the proper final turning point nor over London. Only 53 of the estimated 125 crews dispatched were recorded as crossing the English coast, although a sizeable proportion of those did appear over London.

One crew that would have probably claimed a degree of success was that led by Oberleutnant Hein in U5+KN. His quest to add the Ritterkreuz to the Spanish Cross and Deutsches Kreuz he had gained for service in the Spanish Civil War was rapidly coming to a tragic end. On the hunt for the enemy bombers was Wing Commander Miller and Leif Lovestad, his Norwegian radar operator. Their Mosquito from 85 Squadron had left West Malling at 00.40 hours and just after 01.00 hours was orbiting a beacon. The radar set had gone U/S, but Miller had been given permission to orbit in the hope of visually picking up some of the 'trade' that had been reported approaching from the north. Sure enough, five miles to the east at a searchlight intersection, Miller picked out a 'bogey' that was Hein's Ju188. The chase was on and shortly after the Mosquito was in a firing position below from where he confirmed the aircraft was 'hostile'. As he dropped back to commence a firing run the ventral gunner opened up, but his shooting was poor as the bullets passed below the night fighter. No second opportunity to retaliate was given as cannon shell strikes caused an explosion. A huge puff of smoke and fire from the starboard engine and cockpit confirmed

The tail of Oberleutnant Hein's Ju188 after crashing near Ivychurch. The codes U5+KN are clearly visible on the fin.

the bomber's demise. It dived steeply and crashed near Ivychurch, close to the Channel coast. Two of the five-man crew survived, but Hein was not one of them. Surprisingly, neither airman had any recollection of being attacked by a night fighter, but only heard a dull explosion whose cause was a mystery before they hastily vacated the aircraft. The mechanics would await the arrival of U5+KN back at its regular Eindhoven base in vain.

The Hein crew appear to have maintained the briefed flight schedule since their bomber crashed at 01.30 hours. In contrast, a second II/KG2 crew, that of Hauptmann Eichbaum, was apparently well behind schedule. U5+DM was approaching the Suffolk coast at around 01.00 hours, and therefore unlikely to reach London until after the end of the briefed bomb-run period. Flight Lieutenant Carr gave no quarter and dispatched U5+DM into the sea off Southwold.

The saying 'troubles come in threes' applied to II/KG2, because U5+BN was also lost. The bomber had got through to London when at 18,000 feet it was caught in a triangle of 3.7 inch AA gunfire from batteries at Chadwell Heath, Wanstead and Enfield. The dying Ju188 tumbled out of the night sky with all five crewmembers hauling themselves out of their aerial tomb. The closely-packed housing estates of the Capital once again provided no chance for the blazing aircraft to come down in open ground; instead it slammed into No. 14 Seven Sisters Road at Ilford. Sheltering in the basement were a married couple and two women.

Whether or not they would have survived the bomber's impact was debatable. As it was they stood no chance when ignited aviation fuel cascaded into the basement and mingled with water from a burst main. All four bodies were later recovered in an unrecognisable state and the only hope was that death was instantaneous. Of the crew, Oberfeldwebel Rögner had been seriously wounded and, although found alive, died two days later. The other casualty was Obergefreiter Hocke who came down in his parachute, but landed on a freshly painted roof, slid off and broke his neck when he fell on a brick wall.

Obergefreiter Hocke landed safely on this building's roof but fell to his death below.

Unteroffizier Brandt's crew from 3/KG54 penetrated the city's defensive ring but paid a price when the port engine and several instruments, including the compass, were put out of action by AA shells. The pilot naturally attempted to head for home, but must have encountered some cloud since no sighting of a coastline, whether British or Continental, appears to have been made over the ensuing 90 minutes. It was then that the landing lights of an airfield were sighted. This, along with the several hundred miles flown in this period, must have convinced Brandt that he was over friendly soil. The blow to the crew's morale when they clambered out of their crash-landed machine and found themselves staring at RAF blue uniforms and insignia must have been stunning. The airfield was Bradwell Bay in south Essex and, far from having succeeded in crossing the North Sea, the bomber had wandered aimlessly over East Anglia!

Interrogation Report

He177 6N+AK 2/KG100

2 miles N.E. of Saffron Walden, Essex.
19th April 1944. 0103 hours.

Start and Mission:

Started from Rheine at about 2318 hours to bomb the Tower Bridge area of London. Twelve 250 kg. H.E. bombs carried.

At about 2000 hours on 18th April, three crews of 2/KG100 and two crews of 3/KG100 were called together for briefing by Hauptmann vom Kalkreuth, the Gruppenkommandeur.

A flight plan, which was amongst the captured documents from this aircraft, shows that the five aircraft were to take off between 2318 hours and 2334 hours, and were to set course for the target at intervals between 2334 hours and 2339 hours, climbing steadily to cross the English coast at 5,500 metres.

The Dutch coast was to be crossed at Funkfeuer II (Noordwijk) and the aircraft were to check their course at a point in the North Sea at 52.15N, 03.05E, which was to be marked with six Lux bouys. After making landfall just north of Orfordness, the aircraft were to make for a turning point for the final leg to London; this point was just east of Newmarket and was to be marked with four red flares at a height of 3,000 metres.

The time of attack for the 6N+AK was to be between 0103 and 0107 hours. The target was to be marked by a cluster of seven red flares at a height of 3,500 metres, and the bombs were to be released in a glide from a height of 5,000 metres.

The return flight to Rheine was to be made via Boulogne and Arnhem, the height of approach to the French coast being 800 metres.

The SN+AK had crossed the East Anglian coast a little to the south of the briefed course on its way to the target, when the crew was taken by surprise by a night-fighter attack; the first burst raked the underside of the fuselage and put the intercomm out of action.

When the rear gunner saw the night-fighter manoeuvring for a second attack, he resorted to the expedient of firing a white Verey signal to attract his pilot's attention.

After another short burst from the night-fighter, the bomb load was jettisoned and the pilot gave the order to bale out. Four members of the crew were made P/W, and the other two were killed in the wreckage.

Morale:

Whilst the pilot, observer and W/T operator were making their best efforts at security, the rear gunner talked quite freely.

The pilot wore the E.K.I and II, and the observer, who had 197 operations to his credit, wore the E.K.I and II and Gold (110) War-Flights Badge. The rear gunner also had the E.K.I and II and the Gold War-Flights Badge, having 179 operations to his credit.

Three views of the wreckage of He177 6N+AK which came down near Saffron Walden after being attacked by F/O Huppert in a 410 Sqn Mosquito.

Combat Report

18/19 April 1944

410 (RCAF) Squadron

Mosquito XIII. Mk.VIII AI.

0100 hours

Clear starlight night. Vis: Good.

Pilot: F/O Huppert (RCAF) Navigator P/O Christie (RAF)

We took off from Castle Camps at 0001 hours to do S/L Co-op Exercises. Under Sector S/L Control ordered to FOB.5. but diverted to 'Z' and informed of trade to the North East. Gauntletted 030 on a good S/L intersection, and obtained contact at a range of 3 miles at 18,000ft. through 'Window'.

Closed in to 2,000ft. and obtained visual on target, travelling west south west then south in gradual Orbit to I.A.Z. Closed to 1,000ft. and identified a HE177. Opened fire with a long burst at a range of approx 300ft, and observed strikes on port wing and motor, with pieces flying off and hitting Mosquito. Accurate return fire from rear turret experienced which hit our starboard wing and aileron. Visual was lost momentarily as E/A peeled off port, but was regained from the glow of the fire which spread over E/A. Closed in again following the E/A down and fired 3 short bursts observing strikes on fuselage and wings. E/A then burst into flames, pulled its nose up for a moment, stalled, and then spun into the ground, exploding as it hit, followed by fire. The time of the combat was approx. 0100 hours. Called for fix which was given as M 1856. I claim this A/C destroyed.

Ammunition used: 20mm 110 rounds S.A.P.I. 111 rounds H.E.I.

At 00.50hrs on 19th April, an Me410 crashed into a churchyard in Brighton scattering wreckage and gravestones far and wide. The following documents tell its story.

Intelligence Report AI2(G)

Report No. 8/118 - Me 410
This aircraft was attacked by a night fighter while still over the sea and crashed in St. Nicholas Church Yard, Brighton at 00.50 hours on 19th April.

Identification Markings
The wreckage was too badly damaged by fire for these to be deciphered.
Works number from fin 420293.
Camouflage on the upper surfaces was a grey blue-green; the under surfaces were sprayed black.

Engines
DB 603, details not yet available.

Armament
The usual guns were carried, namely:-
2 x MG 151/20 and
2 x MG 17, firing forwards.
2 x MG 131 in lateral blisters firing to the rear.

No further information of interest was obtained from the examination.

Crew
Presumed two; pilot killed in crash; Wireless Operator missing.

Intelligence Report ADI(K)

Report No. 175/1944

PLACE, DATE AND TIME:
St. Nicholas Churchyard, Brighton, Sussex.
19th April 1944. 0050.

TYPE AND MARKS: Me. 410 --+F-
Unit: 1/(K.G. 51)
DISC:
One: 65112 (=8/K.G. 51)
FELDPOSTNUMMER:
L. 37119 Brussels (unidentified)
AUSWEIS:
Buff card, issued by Fl. H. Kdtr. E31/XIII
(= (?) Evreux) on 28th March 1944.

This aircraft was crossing the coast on its way to its target when it crashed amongst the tombstones of a churchyard and was burned out. The cause of the crash is unknown, but it is understood that one cannon strike was found in the remains of the fuselage.

The body of the pilot was found; he had baled out but his parachute had opened too late. There was no trace of the W/T operator; it is assumed that he baled out and came down in the sea.

The few papers which have been recovered were not helpful in establishing the unit to which this aircraft belonged, but the fact that the pilot's identity disc is from 8/K.G. 51 and his parachute control card was marked "1st Staffel" would suggest 1/K.G. 51.

A document gave the following list of R/T callsigns:-

	Aircraft	Ground	Tornado
1st Staffel	Braunschweig	Irene	Rembrandt I
2nd Staffel	Tiger	Rembrandt	-
3rd Staffel	(?)	Orion	-

The mention of "Tornado" is of interest, as it is the first time that this has been mentioned in documents carried by aircraft over this country.

The pilot wore the E.K.1 and the Crimea badge. He was known to have been awarded the Ehrenpokal as long ago as March 1942.

CREW:
Pilot: Oberleutnant Richard PAHL 6th Feb. '20 Dead
W/T: name and rank unknown. Fate unknown

Three views of the Me410 wreckage in the churchyard.

Combat Report

Date	Night 18/19th April, 1944.
Unit	96 Squadron
Type and Mark of our a/c	Mosquito XIII A.I. Mark VIII
Time of attack	0048 hours
Place of attack	R.11
Weather	Dark starlight, good visibility.
Our casualties - aircraft	Nil
Our personel - aircraft	Nil
Enemy casualties in air combat	1 Me410 destroyed.

GENERAL REPORT

W/C E.D. Crew, D.F.C., (PILOT) and W/O W.R. Croysdill (OPERATOR) took off West Malling at 0010 hours and landed there at 0230 hours.

"I was patrolling over the Channel at 23,000 feet under Wartling G.C.I. (Controller F/O Powell), when I was vectored on to a course of 340°. Contact was obtained at 4 miles slightly below and crossing port to starboard on an a/c taking slight evasive action. At full speed the range closed easily and I did not use N20 at all. After 4 minutes, range was 1,000 feet and I obtained an indistinct visual of a twin-engined a/c, which, on closing to 3000 feet, I believed to be a Ju. 88. No exhausts were visible. I eased the nose of the Mosquito up and fired a short burst from dead astern, just as the e/a began to dive. This was followed by a large flash from the centre section and cockpit area, and flames. I followed the e/a down and fired again, with more strikes in the same area, resulting in more white flames and e/a dived very steeply to port. A third deflection burst produced more strikes and flashes and e/a disappeared below me. Visual and contact were lost. I noticed that outboard of each engine there was a cylindrical bulge beneath the wing, resembling the long range tanks of the FW. 190. ...cont.

Shortly afterwards I was put onto another contact at 4,000 feet height. This a/c was at 3 ½ miles range, below and to port, flying in a Southerly direction. I turned to starboard as it crossed and followed it down through a steep port orbit. Evasive action and window was being used. As I straightened out of the orbit, an a/c crossed in front at almost collision range, and I had to pull up sharply to avoid hitting it, so that I had no chance to open fire. As it passed below me, I recognised the twin fins and rudders of a Do.217. But though I turned round immediately I could not regain contact, and because of the nearness of the French coast I was told to return on 330°."

Time of combat 0048. Place of combat R.11. At 0050, according to R.O.C., M.G. fire heard to sea, at 0055 and a/c later identified as an Me.410 crashed in Brighton reference Q.72. No ack-ack was heard in the area before 0110, A.I.2(G) report that 20mm cannon strikes have been found in this Me. 410.

This a/c was originally claimed as a Ju. 88 probably destroyed. It is now claimed as an Me.410 destroyed in view of the evidence of the Brighton crash.

W/C Crew states that his Operator said at the time that it was a 410 but he contradicted him and insisted that it was a Ju.88 The inability to see the exhausts from above would also seem to point to its having been, in fact and Me. 410.

Armamnent Report: Rounds fired:

20 mm SAPI	48
20 mm HEI	48
	96

Luftwaffe Losses 18th-19th April 1944

Ju188E-1 4/KG 2 U5+DM WNr 260236

3 miles south of Southwold, Suffolk. 01.15 hrs. Shot down by F/Lt Carr in a 25 Sqn Mosquito.

After a 2 second burst of fire the aircraft went into a vertical spin emitting large quantities of flame and disappeared. It was then seen by an Observer Corps post that reported that the aircraft broke up and fell in the sea. One man baled out and rescued.

Hptm Helmut Eichbaum StKp (F) (Missing), Fw Friedrich Koban (B) (PoW injured), Uffz Joachim Ricklefs (Bf) (Missing), Uffz Hartstack (Bs) (Missing), Gefr Hans-Ulrich Albrecht (Bs) (Missing).

Ju188 E-1 5/KG 2 U5+BN WNr 260391

14, Seven Kings Road, Ilford, Essex. 01.18 hrs.

Probably started from Münster / Handorf. This aircraft crossed the east coast to attack London from the north; the bombs were dropped on red marker flares. The crew carried out two bombing runs on the target, dropping one AB 1000 and two 500 HE on the first run, six LC White on the second from 5,000 metres. They were just turning for home when the aircraft was hit by AA fire from 3.7 inch guns at Chadwell Heath, Wanstead and Enfield. It crashed into a house and burned out with the remains of the house on top of it.

Markings: U5+BN painted on both sides of the tail fin. The camouflage was spray painted black underneath, whilst the upper surface was light blue, mottled with olive green wavy lines.

All five of the crew baled out and three were captured unhurt; the wireless operator was seriously injured and died on 21/4/44. Albert Hoeke, the gunner, landed safely on the roof of the Council yard at Ley Street, Ilford. The roof had just been painted and he slipped off and hit a brick wall, that broke his neck.

Lt Hubert Schymczyk (F) (PoW), Uffz Horst Ziehm (B) (PoW), Uffz Joachim Schulz (Bf) died 21/4/44. (Killled CC 1/385), Ofw Robert Rögner (Bm) (PoW), Ogefr Albert Hoeke (Bs) (Killed CC 1/384).

Ju188 E-1 5/KG 2 U5+KN WNr 260324

Golding's Farm, Ivychurch, Kent. 01.30 hrs. Shot down by W/Cdr C M Miller in an 85 Sqn Mosquito.

Started from Münster / Handorf to attack an area of London west of the Isle of Dogs. The target on this night was to be marked by red flares and one of the duties of this aircraft was to renew the flares at 01.00 hrs. On the return flight the aircraft was held in searchlights and there was a dull explosion and the starboard engine burst into flames. 20mm strikes were found in the tail and rear fuselage from dead astern. The aircraft exploded, the wreckage being scattered over two square miles.

Markings: Call sign RM+UX. On a machine gun belt feed holder was the works number 280073. The figure 6 - 3' high, 18" wide - in white had been painted on the port side of the fin but subsequently covered in dark green paint. On the port side of the fuselage, near the nose was painted 9/50 in 8" high figures. The upper surfaces were blue mottled with dark green, whilst underside spray painted black over light blue paint. The rudder, which appeared to be new, was painted dark green.

The observer, Albert Hein, held the Spanish Cross, Deutches Kreuz and had completed 290 operations. He reportedly always flew with a small bomb load for safety and was out to get the Ritterkreuz.

Fw Helmuth Richter (F) (Killed Folkestone, Kent), Oblt Albert Hein (B) (Killed Folkestone, Kent), Uffz Walter Haberland (Bf) (PoW injured), Uffz Johannes Köhler (Bm) (Killed Folkestone, Kent).

Gefr Karl Leidecker (Bs) (PoW).

Do217M-1 7/KG2 U5+CR WNr 6259

Shot down by P/O B Travers in a 25 Sqn Mosquito near Schiphol, on return from a raid on London. Crew baled out.

Lt Klaus Jäger (F) (Inj), Ogefr Wilhelm Ludwig (B) (Inj), Uffz Wilhelm Dauster (Bf) (Inj), Bf uninjured.

Ju88 4/KG6

Crash landed at Le Coulot on return from London.

Ofw Alexander Lück (Bf) (Inj).

Ju88 A-4 6/KG 6 3E+BP WNr 2537

Coursehorne, nr Cranbrook, Kent. 01.35 hrs. Shot down by P/O C J O Allen in a 96 Sqn Mosquito.

Started from Le Culot at about 23.00 hrs to attack London. The crew was on its first operational flight, having only arrived at Tirlemont (Le Culot) the previous day. The crew flew by dead reckoning, distrusting other navigational aids, to the target which was marked by 15/20 red flares which was duly attacked. When the aircraft was on its homeward flight, it was continually picked up by searchlights and suddenly an explosion occurred that the observer thought was a night fighter attack from astern. The aircraft caught fire and the pilot gave the order to bale out. The pilot and observer landed unhurt, but the other two were found in the wreckage of the aircraft.

The crew of 3E+BP, Harbauer, Gotze, Muhlbauer and Schork.

Markings: The works number on the accumulator was given as 750401 but a works number painted on a piece of armour gave it as 2537. The call sign was GP+GY. The upper surfaces were a pale greyish blue with black wavy lines, whilst the undersides were spray painted black. The spinners were very dark green with three concentric 1¼ wide bands, starting at the nose, red, black, light green.

Uffz Helmut Harbauer (F) (PoW), Uffz Friedrich Schork (B) (PoW), Uffz Hugo Muhlbauer (Bf) (Killed CC 1/32), Uffz Fritz Gotze (Bf) (Killed CC 1/31).

RAF airmen inspect the wreckage of 3E+BP at Coursehorne as locals watch from behind the hedgerow.

Ju88 7/KG6

Crashed on return from London at Valenciennes, France.

Uffz Fritz Überhorst (F) (Killed), Uffz Heinz Müller (B) (Missing), Uffz Bruno Stehr (Bs) (Missing).

Ju88 8/KG6

Failed to return from a sortie to London.

Fw Wolfgang Gollmann (F) (Missing), Fw Heinrich Ackermann (B) (Missing), Uffz Herbert Ilchmann (Bf) (Missing), Fw Heinz Zöllner (Bs) (Missing).

Above left: Another view of the Brighton Me410 in St Nicholas churchyard.
Above right: Fw Heinrich Ackermann who went missing in an 8/KG6 Ju88.

Ju88A-4 9/KG30 4D+AT WNr 884536

Failed to return from a sortie to London.

Uffz Rudi Mann (F) (Missing), Uffz Gerhard Gerlach (B) (Missing), Uffz Horst Kaschinski (Bf) (Missing), Uffz Karl Wilhelm (Bs) (Missing).

Me 410 A-1 1/KG 51 9K+JH WNr 20005

Cooks Farm, Nuthurst, Sussex. 22.28 hrs. Shot down by F/Lt C L Brooks in a 456 Sqn Mosquito.

At 24,000 ft the starboard engine and wing tanks caught fire, the aircraft then dived vertically into the ground and exploded.

Lt Reinhold Witt (F) (Killed CC 9/65), Uffz Ernst Tesch (Bf) (Killed CC 9/65).

Me 410 A-1 1/KG 51 9K+KH WNr 20293

St Nicholas Churchyard, Brighton, Sussex. 00.50 hrs. Shot down by W/Cdr E D Crew in a 96 Sqn Mosquito.

This aircraft was crossing the coast on its way to its target when it was intercepted by a Mosquito at 24,000 ft. One four second burst caused the starboard wing tanks to explode and starboard engine to catch fire. The wireless operator baled out, but landed in the sea and was washed ashore at Friston. The pilot baled out too late and his parachute did not open. It dived almost vertically into the ground and crashed amongst tombstones of a churchyard and was burned out. Remains of candle flares were found amongst the wreckage, so this aircraft was probably a pathfinder.

The pilot held the Crimea badge.

Hptmn Richard Pahl EKI (F) (Killed Brighton, Sussex), Fw Wilhelm Schuberth (Bf) (Killed CC 4/161).

Me410 6/KG51 9K+GP WNr 420414

Returned from operations on one engine and crashed on landing at Bergen, North Holland.

Uffz Heinz Irmer (Bf) (Inj).

Ju88A-4 1/KG54 B3+BH WNr 800659

Failed to return from a sortie to London. Crashed into the sea off Margate, Kent.

Fw Alfred Mach (F) (Killed Margate), Uffz Friedel Lachaise (B) (Killed - buried at sea on 21/5/44), Uffz Helmut Schulz (Bf) (Killed Margate), Uffz Franz von Ahn (Bs) (Killed body washed ashore on 21/6/44 buried at Margate).

Ju88 3/KG54 B3+HL WNr 1769

Failed to return from a sortie to London.

Fw Klaus von Gazen (F) (Missing), St Fw Rupert Gust (B) (Missing), Uffz Josef Christian (Bf) (Missing), Uffz Helmut Fahland (Bs) (Missing).

Ju88A-4 8/KG54 B3+ES

Crashed on take off from Marx – 30% damage. Incendiaries from AB1000 containers scattered over the runway and prevented the rest of III/KG54 taking off for London.

Uffz Horst Baumgart (F) (inj), Ogefr Bruno Sitek (B) (inj), Gefr Ernst Specht (Bf) (inj), Uffz Ernst Kaupa (Bs) (inj).

Ju88 A-4 Trop 3/KG 54 B3+PL WNr 1214

RAF Bradwell Bay aerodrome, Essex. 02.34 hrs.

Started from Wittmundhafen to bomb London. Having bombed target the aircraft was hit in the port engine by AA at 12,000 ft. The engine eventually caught fire and in the ensuing confusion the crew lost their bearings and belly landed at the RAF airfield under the impression that it was Holland. The fire in the port engine was quickly extinguished by the fire tender crew.

Markings: B3+PL, the P being outlined in yellow and the L outlined in white. On the nose bola is the letter F in red 4" high. Call sign CE+ZN. It would appear that this aircraft had recently been involved in an accident as various parts were marked 1083. The upper surfaces were greenish grey whilst lower surfaces spray painted black. The spinners originally had red tips with 2" yellow rings round, but since painted over with gun metal grey paint.

Uffz Heinz Brandt (F) (PoW), Uffz Max Oppel (B) (PoW), Ogefr Walter Kobusch (Bf) (PoW), Gefr Heinz Oberwinter(Bs) (PoW injured).

Uffz. Heinz Brandt, Gefr. Heinz Oberwinter and Ogefr. Walter Kobusch.

Ju188E-1 2/KG66 Z6+GK WNr 260361

Failed to return from an operational sortie.

Uffz Gerhard Guder (F) (Missing), Ogefr Hans Schmid (B) (Missing), Uffz Paul Eichler (Bf) (Missing), Ogefr Johann Hüffner (Missing), Uffz Karl Schwaiger (Bs) (Missing).

He177 A-3 2/KG 100 6N+AK WNr 332379

Butlers Farm, Saffron Walden, Essex. 01.03 hrs.

Shot down by F/O S B Huppert in a 410 Sqn Mosquito.

Started from Rhine at about 23.18 hrs to bomb the Tower Bridge area of London. The target was to be marked with a cluster of seven red flares at a height of 3,500 metres and the bombs were to be released in a glide from a height of 5,000 metres. Having just crossed the East Anglian coast a little to the south of the briefed course on its way to the target, the crew was taken by surprise by a night fighter attack; the first burst raked the underside of the fuselage and put the intercom out of action. After another burst from the night fighter, the bomb load was jettisoned and the pilot gave the order to bale out and four men got out. The aircraft broke in half, the rear falling almost intact, while the forward section was almost burnt out.

Markings: 6N+AK, the figures in white, the 6N being 6" high, the AK normal size. The camouflage was grey mottled blue on the upper surfaces with spray painted black underneath.

The observer held the Gold (110) war Flights Badge although he had achieved 197 operations and the rear gunner also had the Gold (110) War Flights Badge and he had achieved 179 operations.

Fw Heinz Reis EKI (F) (PoW injured), Fw Winand Höck EKI (B) (PoW), Uffz Johann Wehr (Bf) (PoW), Uffz Georg Speyerer (Bm) (Killed Saffron Walden, Essex), Ogefr Fritz Kopf (Bs) (Killed Saffron Walden, Essex), Uffz Werner Heidorn EKI (Bs – rear) (PoW).

Fighter Command Claims not attributable to a particular loss

A claim was made by F/Lt R M Carr in a 25 Sqn Mosquito for a Ju88 probably destroyed off Southwold at 00.30 hours.

A claim was made by P/O K V Panter in a 25 Sqn Mosquito for an Me410 destroyed off the Dutch coast at 04.35 hours.

A claim was made by S/Ldr B A Burbridge in an 85 Sqn Mosquito for a Ju188 destroyed off Sangatte at 01.33 hours.

A claim was made by S/Ldr W P Green in a 96 Sqn Mosquito for a Ju88 destroyed 10 miles north of Margate at 01.40 hours.

A claim was made by F/O L R Snowdon in a 410 Sqn Mosquito for a Ju188 damaged near Braintree at 00.58 hours.

A claim was made by W/O R F D Bourke in a 488 Sqn Mosquito for a Ju88 destroyed 16 miles SE of Trimley at 00.48 hours.

A claim was made by F/Lt J A S Hall in a 488 Sqn Mosquito for a Ju88 destroyed 60 miles east of Bradwell at 01.11 hours.

The statistics for the last six major *'Steinbock'* raids could not have made pleasant reading for General Peltz. These were as follows;

Date	Crews		Losses		Loss Percentage	
	Dispatched	Overland	Total	Over Britain	All	Overland
Mar						
14/15	187	140	14	7	7.5%	10%
19/20	131	90	9	2	6.9%	10%
21/22	144	95	10	4	7%	10.5%
24/25	143	120	15	4	10.5%	12.5%
27/28	139	112	13	6	9.4%	11.2%
Apr						
18/19	125	53	13	8	10.4%	25%
	869	520	74	33		

The scale of effort during this period barely amounted to the figure that RAF Bomber Command was currently dispatching on a single operation. The loss factor was unsupportable high at an average of around 8.5% (aircraft dispatched) and 14.2% (aircraft recorded overland).

London's exposure to actual or potential *'Steinbock'* assaults had come to an end. In the months ahead its citizens would be placed under constant physical and mental pressure approaching, if not equalling, that of the 1940/41 *'Blitz'* as Hitler's vaunted V-Weapons were introduced.

20th-21st April 1944

WEEKLY APPRECIATION OF DAMAGE TO KEY POINTS AND PROGRESS OF REPAIRS.

Period from: 09.00 hours Wednesday 19th April

to: 09.00 hours Wednesday 26th April 1944.

GENERAL.

Enemy air-attacks against land targets during the past week have not been of much account. A total of 196 sorties was flown overland in these attacks, but from provisional reports the emphasis seems to have been on flares rather than bombs. In addition there has been some work by intruders.

On Wednesday (19th April) a high level reconnaissance was flown over the Isle of Wight, and another over the same area on Friday (21st)

On Wednesday / Thursday (19th/20th April) 14 long-range bombers operated over Kent, Sussex, and Surrey, with slight penetration to the Greater London area. Bombing was trivial.

On Thursday/Friday (20th/21st April) 60 long-range bombers operated over an area bounded by Scarborough/York/Peterborough/ Cromer. Some mine-laying off the Humber was suspected. The enemy claims Hull which, however, was untouched.

On Saturday/Sunday (22nd/23rd April) 8 long–range bombers operated over parts of East Anglia and Lincolnshire. One minor incident occurred.

On Sunday / Monday (23rd/24th April) 70 long-range bombers operated over Somerset, Dorset, Wiltshire and Hampshire, with a single penetration to South Wales. Bombing was of slight account. The enemy claims Bristol which was untouched.

On Monday/ Tuesday (24th/25th April) two aircraft operated over parts of East Anglia. There were no incidents.

On Tuesday/Wednesday (25th/26th April) 42 aircraft operated over the Isle of Wight and parts of Hampshire and Sussex. Most of the bombing occurred in an area from Littlehampton to St Katherine`s Point. But the results were slight.

Total civilian casualties for the week are 12 fatal and 16 serious. The G.A.F. is known to have lost 16 aircraft (8%).

Three Key-points sustained minor damage. In addition there were 2 incidents affecting railways and 5 airfields.

The *'Steinbock'* establishment of bombers and crews was still sufficient for targets to be selected for attack on a 'major' basis. On the 20th/21st April some 130 bombers were reportedly sent out to attempt a second assault on Hull. Once again, total failure to even reach the seaport attended the efforts of the sixty crews who were plotted over Britain's eastern coast. To this setback was added no less than five aircraft declared missing and a further five that crashed on return with others damaged.

Mosquito intruder sorties were flown to several Luftwaffe airfields to intercept the returning bombers. Near Handorf, Flight Lieutenant Holland and Flying Officer Wilkinson of 605 Squadron intercepted the Ju188 (U5+BN) of Willi Hartwig and hit its starboard engine which burst into flames. The crew immediately baled out and as they hung in their parachutes saw two aircraft falling in flames; the second ball of flame was the Mosquito which is assumed to have collided with the wreckage of the Ju188.

Combat Report

Night of 20/21 April 1944

No.264 (Madras Presidency) Squadron

Mosquito XIII A.I. Mk. VIII

2355 Hours

Off east coast in area B 65

Clear starlight with good visibility

One He177 destroyed

I took off from Church Fenton at 2156 to take part in a local Bullseye Exercise but after making 3 "kills" I was diverted at about 2300 hrs to patrol for hostiles approaching Hull.

While patrolling between Skegness and Humber mouth at 19,000 ft. I was told by the Patrington controller, F/Lt. Harvatt, that there was trade coming in from the east between 14/18,000 ft., I was then given a vector and "Punch" but without result. The Controller then said, "You are with them, continue orbitting" and a moment or two later my operator, F/O Bines, reported contact 4 1/2 miles to port and above on a target which showed no I.F.F. on interrogation. I turned to port and climbed and my operator told me that we were 3 miles behind and below the e/a which was dropping "Window", I continued to close at 220 A.S.I. my operator continuing to hold the e/a which was weaving gently and dropping "Window".

Having reached 20,000 ft. I got a visual of a large twin engined a/c but could not see any exhaust flames, I then closed in and from a position about 100 yds below definitely identified the e/a as a He. 177 by its very large wing span and long protruding nose and by its large square single fin as I pulled away to the side. The e/a was not burning resin lights.

I dropped back and fired a short burst from dead astern at 200 yds range whereupon the cockpit and fuselage immediately burst into flames and burning pieces of wreckage flew past my a/c, the Heinkel at once began to go down in a gentle dive and after circling round it I got in another short burst from which I saw strikes on the e/a wings which was then at 17,500 ft.

I and my operator then watched the Heinkel going down with flames spreading along the underside of the fuselage while I climbed to 18,000 ft. and gave "Murder" followed by "Canary".

The Controller then immediately gave me a vector west but on looking back we both noticed a large red glow well below us.

After returning to 5 miles south of the Humber G.D.A. 2 contacts were obtained but the first was lost due to our being brightly lit up by flares and the second on account of large quantities of "Window".

At 0030 hours a fourth contact was obtained showing no I.F.F. and no resins. I accordingly closed carefully and positively identified the a/c as a Halifax which then fired a long burst of tracer at us from the rear turret at about 200 yds range, the fire was accurate and I at once peeled off to port.

After several abortive vectors we returned to base and I landed safely at 0040. At 00.20 hours an international distress broadcast was picked up from a German Station to the effect that there was an airman down in the sea in area B 36.

I accordingly claim one He. 177 Destroyed.

Pilot F/O J.H. Corre

The aircraft engaged by F/O Corre was He177 6N+IK flown by Hptmn Herbert Dostlebe.

Luftwaffe Losses 20th-21st April 1944

Ju188E-1 3/KG2 U5+OP WNr 260338

Engaged by a night fighter on return from Hull.

Ogefr Franz Deiritz (Bf) (Inj), Uffz Theodor Piefke (Bs) (Inj), Gefr Walter Lange (Bs) (Inj). Two others safe.

Ju188E-1 4/KG2 U5+BN WNr 260336

Force landed with engine failure 18 km east of Handorf on return from Hull.

Uffz Johann Ringauf (Bf) (Inj), Gefr Adolf Seppel (Bs) (Inj), Ogefr Oskar Braun (Bs) (Injured), FF and Bo uninjured.

Ju188E-1 6/KG2 U5+RP WNr 260247

Shot down by a night fighter 10 km south-east of Handorf on return from Hull.

StFw Willi Hartwig (F) (safe), Uffz Baptist Paulus (Bf) (injured), Bo, Bm and Bs uninjured.

Ju188E-1 6/KG2 U5+PP WNr 260367

Possibly shot down by F/Lt Holland in a 605 Sqn Mosquito over Rheine on return from Hull.

Uffz Ulrich Bachmann (F) (Killed), Uffz Walter Hähne (B) (Killed), Uffz Gottfried Hartner (Bf) (Killed), Uffz Willi Laux (Bs) (Inj), Gefr Heinrich von Bünau (Bs) Killed.

Do217M-1 9/KG2 U5+AT WNr 6325

Damaged near Gilze-Rijen by F/O Walton in a 605 Sqn Mosquito on return from a sortie to Hull. Two baled out.

Gefr Herbert Leine (Bo) (Inj), Bernhard Schulzki (Bs) (Inj). Rest of crew stayed with aircraft uninjured.

Do217M-1 9/KG2 U5+CT WNr 6125

Failed to return from a sortie to Hull.

Ogefr Hermann Went (F) (Missing), Uffz Werner Fitjer (B) (Missing), Ogefr Friedrich Gehrke (Bf) (Missing), Gefr Alfred Reeh (Bs) (Missing).

Ju88 5/KG30 4D+KN WNr 140002

Failed to return from a sortie to Hull

Uffz Otto Heuer (F) (Missing), Uffz Klaus Schönstedt (B) (Missing), Ogefr Georg Krach (Bf) (Missing), Ogefr Franz Fuhrmann (Bs) (Missing).

Ju88A-4 2/KG54 B3+DK WNr 300224

Failed to return from a sortie to Hull.

Fw Heinz Fischer (F) (Missing), Ofw Kurt Wörmsdorf (B) (Missing), Uffz Max Kornetzky (Bf) (Missing), Gefr Rudolf Scharf (Bs) (Missing).

Ju88A-4 9/KG54 B3+ET

Failed to return from a sortie to Hull.

Lt Robert Klotz (F) (Mising), Ofw Hans Pfefferkorn (Bo) (Missing), Gefr Hans Blank (Bf) (Missing), Gefr Bruno Schmidt (Bs) (Missing).

Ju88A-4 9/KG54 B3+CT

Crashed near Stade on return from a sortie to Hull with Flak damage.

Uffz Erwin Bastian (F) (Inj), Ogefr Franz Ehm (Bo) (Inj), Uffz Karl Weigang (Bs) (Inj).

Ju88S-1 E-Staffel/KG66 Z6+HN WNr 300494

Failed to return from an operational sortie. Crashed at South Flevoland, Holland, where the wreck was discovered by the Dutch Air Force salvage team in the 1970s.

Uffz Ehrhardt Troitach (F) (Killed), Fw Hans Wien (B) (Killed), Uffz Walter Weber (Bf) (Killed).

He177A-3 2/KG100 6N+IK WNr 2357

Shot down during approach to Hull by F/O J. H. Corre in a 264 Squadron Mosquito 40 miles east of Spurn Head. 23.55 hrs.

The Mosquito crew had chased a target using Window at 20,000 ft from Skegness, identified aircraft as an He177 and closed to 200 yards. A short burst of fire set the cockpit and fuselage alight. Pieces of flaming wreckage flew past the attacking night fighter. The Heinkel then entered a gentle dive with flames spreading below the fuselage.

Hptmn Herbert Dostlebe (F) (Missing), Fw Hanse-Georg Vollandt (B) (was washed up at Ambland, Holland, 23/6/44) Ofw Anton Krebs (Bf) (Missing), Ofw Johann Konrad (Bw) (Missing), Uffz Gustav Neumann (Bs) (Killed), Ofw Hermann Koch (Bs) (Missing).

Ogefr. Hermann Went, pilot of Do217 U5+CT missing on this night.

Fighter Command Claims not attributable to a particular loss

A claim was made by F/Sgt Carter in a 25 Sqn Mosquito for a Ju188 shot down 25 miles east of Mablethorpe at 23.35 hrs. The aircraft was spotted at 17,000 ft and a three second burst delivered. The port engine and wing root burst into flames and the aircraft flipped over and went vertically down.

A claim was made by F/O H.E. White in a 141 Sqn Mosquito for a Do217 north of Paris at 00.00 hours.

A claim was made by P/O H.J. Collins in a 605 Sqn Mosquito for an enemy aircraft damaged near Juvincourt at 02.05 hours.

Luftwaffe Losses 20th to 22nd April

Ju88A-4 12/KG54 B3+BZ WNr 8589

20/4/44 Collided with B3+OY over Gardelegen.

Ofhr Helmut Kreiss (F) (Killed), Fw Heinrich Grenzebach (Bo) (Killed), Uffz Herbert Rettig (Bf) (Killed), Gefr Adolf Spiegel (Bs) Killed.

Ju88A-4 12/KG54 B3+OY WNr 141149

20/4/44 Collided with B3+BZ over Gardelegen.

Ofhr Manfred Hering (F) (Killed), Gefr Karl Dominatus (Bf) (Inj).

Me410 6/KG51 9K+BP WNr 420289

21/4/44 Crashed on take-off on operations at Soesterberg.

Hptm Dierk-Henning Vester (F) (Killed), Ofw Paul Horn (Bf) (Killed).

Me410 4/KG51 U5+DE WNr 420451

21/4/44 Crashed at Eindhoven on operations.

Uffz Franz Wachtler (F) (Inj).

Ju188F-1 1/(F)123 A6+PH WNr 280215

22/4/44 Shot down by F/O Weslyk and Sgt Thorne in 504 Sqn Spitfires east of the Orkneys.

Uffz Günther Poltrock (F) (Missing), Uffz Walter Przybyllek (Bo) (Mising), Ogefr Heinz Schwind (Bf) (Missing), Uffz Herbert Schönfeld (Bs) (Missing).

22nd-23rd April 1944

The 'Intruder' Menace

The involvement of KG51 in *'Steinbock'* was to prove somewhat marginal in terms of attacks on the British mainland. I/KG51 with its Me410s had only joined in from the $14^{th}/15^{th}$ March and then not on a regular basis. It had suffered several losses, most of which had been borne in the course of involvement with small-scale assaults on London along with the FW190s of SKG10. The twin-engine Me410 was relatively fast and manoeuvrable compared to the main force bombers and was generally proving to be difficult for the Mosquito night fighter crews to latch onto.

The concept of 'intruder' operations over Britain had been initiated as early as the autumn of 1940. Then, the few crews of I/NJG2 had created a disturbance factor among the airmen of RAF Bomber Command that was out of all proportion to the numbers of night fighters involved. Fortunately for the RAF, in October 1941 Hitler ordered all operations halted on the grounds that the German population would find it more of a morale-raiser to witness the demise of RAF bombers over Germany than any disruption or destruction that might be achieved over Britain; and therefore out of civilian sight!

During 1943 Luftwaffe thoughts on the value of 'intruder' operations had been revived, but not put into any large scale practice. This form of offensive action was one that the Me410 could play a real part in, given its heavy nose armament of cannon and machine gun-calibre weapons coupled with twin MG131s in flexible barbettes in the fuselage that provided a sound defensive armament. However, units such as II/ZG26 that began to convert to the Messerschmitt fighter in the autumn of 1943 were directed against the 8th USAAF heavy bombers. This was not an illogical action at the time, since the B-17s and B-24s were still bereft of escort cover over central Germany. It followed that the Bf110Gs and Me410s could strike home without risk of counter-attack, using not only their guns but also 210mm rockets in wing-mounted tubes.

The Messerschmitt Me410 was developed from the Me210 (pictured here) and proved to be a very fast and capable intruder aircraft.

V/KG2 had taken over the allocation of Me410s destined for 5/KG2 in mid-1943 and had commenced flying sorties over Britain in June 1943. In an action on 13th/14th July Flight Lieutenant Bunting of 85 Squadron downed the first of the unit's aircraft off the East Anglian coast. Over the ensuing months of 1943 ten more Me410s were taken down over south-east England or dispatched into the sea. Mosquitos proved to be the major destroyer, although AA batteries were credited with 1½. The 'half' victory credited to the AA guns occurred on 7th/8th October and was 'shared' with Leutenant Tarald Weisteen, a Norwegian pilot from 85 Squadron. Normally an even-tempered individual, his reaction when informed of the official decision to half the victory was to swear in his native tongue "Fahn" and add; "Those bloody guns! Which half did they shoot down, I'd like to know?" He and Flying Officer French were understandably upset because U5+KG flown by Feldwebel Slotczyg was already well alight and seconds away from smashing into the Channel off Dungeness before the gunners opened up.

V/KG2 had participated in *'Steinbock'* during January and February, but then dropped out of the campaign's operational ranks; this was a sound indication of a future change in role from pure bombing to an 'intruder' function. During March 1944 a change in title to II/KG51 was made and the unit moved to Soesterberg under command of Major Puttfarken, a Ritterkreuztrager (Knight's Cross holder). From here the crews began to range on solo runs over Britain and prior to 22nd April the crews submitted reports for around a dozen 'kills' or 'probables'. The 448th Bomb Group airfield of Seething was strafed and bombed on the 11th/12th April. The same night but well to the south, a 96th Bomb Group B-17G pathfinder bomber was circling Framlingham from where it would lead the 390th Bomb Group on the planned mission for the day. Suddenly a burst of gunfire set one wing on fire and the crippled machine was force-landed in a nearby park. Rescuers quickly on the scene dragged Lieutenant McGregor and eight of his crew clear before the bomber was torn apart by a huge explosion.

The Hamm Mission - 22nd-23rd April 1944

The afore-mentioned date was to loom large in 8th USAAF annuls, but in a sadly negative, and unusually expensive, manner. Up to now the B-17s and B-24s, although sometimes taking off in the early hours before dawn, had delivered their actual assaults and landed back in broad daylight or on occasions as the sun was setting; nocturnal operations were regarded as the province of RAF Bomber Command.

The Allied bomber fleets were engaged in what was known as the Transportation Plan. This was a concerted campaign to dislocate the Nazi road and rail systems stretching from

France and into Germany and thereby deny the Wehrmacht and SS units swift and effective access to the planned *'Overlord'* landings in Normandy when these were launched. The massive marshalling-yard complex at Hamm, north-east of the Rühr, was regarded as a vital target for destruction. As it was, the weather conditions over the target area on the 22nd were likely to preclude good visual sighting of the yards until 19.00 hours Double British Summer Time (DBST). It followed from this that if the American crews were sent out on what was officially titled Mission 311 their return to East Anglia would not be achieved until the last vestiges of daylight had disappeared. Blackout time on the ground was set for 21.38 hours.

On the other side of the North Sea German radio-monitoring stations were picking up the clear indication of a planned American aerial assault. Over 800 heavy bombers were to be provided with marginally under 1,000 USAAF and RAF fighters; the latter were not only to provide cover for the *'Big Friends'* but would also indulge in 'sweep' operations that would hopefully flush out or catch Luftwaffe fighters in the vulnerable stages of take-off or landing.

The B-17s of the 3rd Bomb Division would lead, with the other B-17-equipped Division (the 1st) in the middle and the B-24s of the 2nd Bomb Division taking up the rear position in the bomber-stream. Crossing-in south of Amsterdam, the formations then turned south-east and closed on their target. The majority of Groups bombed as briefed, but the lead 2nd Combat Bomb Wing of the 2nd Bomb Division encroached on the northern edge of the Rühr, thanks to a navigation error, before rectifying the situation.

Approximately three-quarters of the 1,948 tons of bombs and incendiaries was adjudged to have landed squarely on the primary aiming point, and although the subsequent PRU sortie was compromised by cloud and haze the USAAF hierarchy was satisfied that a good measure of destruction had been added to the rail facilities already sorely-tested by previous RAF incursions. However, railway systems were not easily knocked out of action and were regularly back in service within a day or so, as appears to have been the case here when German records were examined after WWII.

As the last flights of B-24s completed their bomb-runs and wheeled away to begin the homeward flight in an extended clockwise course that skirted the southern edge of the Rühr, the almost horizontal shadows cast on their fuselages by the steadily-sinking sun confirmed the likelihood of darkness shrouding their airfields prior to their arrival back....

Plan....

Meanwhile at Soesterberg, a small number of II/KG51 crews headed by Major Puttfarken were being transported to their Me410s after being briefed to infiltrate the ranks of the bombers as they approached the English coast or were in the process of entering the landing

The German plan was to infiltrate the vast formations of B-17s and B-24s as they headed home in the dark late evening skies.

patterns of their assigned airfields. The nocturnal shroud expected to be on hand at this point would ideally cloak the Luftwaffe 'intruders' from their lumbering and undoubtedly unwary prey - at least in Luftwaffe eyes. Take off commenced at two separate times (20.55 and 21.54 hours) according to an RAF Wireless Intelligence Service report. The first aircraft dispatched took up a south-westerly course towards Brussels; at a point west of that city the Me410s turned almost 90 degrees to starboard and began to close in upon the USAAF force. The 2nd Bomb Division was still at the rear of the bomber stream and it was its ranks that the Luftwaffe 'intruders' were soon to infiltrate. A fortuitous change in meteorological conditions had advanced the progress of the 1st and 3rd Bomb Division, so making their chances of interception by the Luftwaffe less likely compared to the not so favoured 2nd Division. Also, the tracks of the two B-17 Divisions from the Belgian coast onwards diverged to port in order to cross-in over Clacton, so placing their crews even further from the potential depredations of II/KG51. By contrast the outward track of the second KG51 section was recorded by the Wireless Intelligence Service as having been straight over the North Sea to cross the Norfolk coast north of Great Yarmouth, at which point it would add its weight to the anticipated mayhem.

....and counter-plan

Although the odds would be against the Americans in any attempt to evade lethal encounters, plans had been made within 8th Air Force circles to at least minimise the effect of such attacks. Several Group Commanding Officers such as Colonel Isbell (458th Bomb Group) had given thought to possible 'intruder' operations. Isbell had warned the gunners not to unload their weapons until on the ground; other precautions related to the need for pilots to switch to control tower frequency halfway across the North Sea and to limit the normal comprehensive identification lighting to the four blue, low-intensity, lights on the horizontal stabilisers and the red passing light mounted on the wing leading edge between Nos. 1 and 2 engines. Should 'intruders' strike or a radio 'alert' be issued the formation would disperse, with pilots taking up a pre-assigned heading and altitude towards the north for a set time-period. Finally, fuel loads had been increased to allow for an extra margin of around an hour; should the emergency arise and be over within this time, the provision would permit the crews to land back safely once the 'all clear' was announced. Now, as the bombers slipped steadily away from the Belgian coast and took up the final leg home, the Group personnel along with the other units so alerted were still 'dressed for battle' so to speak, but hoping that their apprehensions would not be realised. Little did they know what was soon to transpire in respect of such forebodings....

Final Approach to Chaos

Of the 277 2nd Division crews sent out to Hamm 265 had gone over either the Primary or 'Target of Opportunity' locations and 258 holding course for home. Navigation lights were in full evidence as the last vestiges of daylight rapidly gave way to total darkness. On the ground the civilian population living in the stretches of Suffolk and Norfolk to the east and south of Norwich slowly attuned their ears to the unusual and burgeoning song of hundreds of Pratt and Whitney motors coming from the south-east, with Orfordness and Aldeburgh as the bomber stream's epicentre.

Normally at this stage of any evening in 1944 the engine noises would have emanated from the Merlins and Hercules powering Lancasters and Halifaxes; furthermore, these RAF bombers would have been heading eastwards towards the Continent with the intention of handing out the latest battering to some German industrial city. It was little wonder that on this occasion thousands of individuals were already in the open or came outside, all craning their necks skyward to catch a glimpse of the USAAF formations in an action that was never to be repeated – and for good reason! By now the handful of Luftwaffe crews were well enmeshed within the stream and had already struck with deadly effect on at least one occasion while the Group was still tracking in over the North Sea....

A B-24 Liberator of the 453rd BG heads home on 21st February 1944, just two months before the 'night of the intruders'

First Strikes

The 453rd Bomb Group based at Old Buckenham was part of the 2nd Combat Wing that had encountered navigation problems during target approach. This in turn resulted in the Group formation fragmenting into three sections, two linking up with the 389th and 445th Bomb Groups to bomb Hamm, the third electing to retain its loads and only release over Koblenz on the return leg. No combat losses had been incurred during the mission.

On board H6: J/42-64492 – *Cee Gee II* - the tail gunner Staff Sergeant McClure remembered the advice of an RAF Lancaster contemporary and scanned downwards in an arc as the sea passed unseen below, hoping not to sight the outline of a 'bogey' but ready to react by firing first in an attempt to scare it away should the need arise. The close packed formation with all navigation lights exposed was another cause for concern since it was more likely to attract hostile attention.

Suddenly he caught a glimpse of a shadowy outline at the 8 o'clock low position and called on Staff Sergeant McKinney (the right waist gunner) to join in with his single machine gun. Scarcely had the .5 weapons thrown out their chains of heavy calibre bullets when a return hail of cannon and machine gun fire lanced into the fuselage and port wing to set No. 2 engine ablaze. Both gunners were knocked unconscious but McClure quickly recovered. After establishing that his fellow-gunner was at least alive, he scurried forward to inform Lieutenant Munsey (the pilot) of the fire.

Still some distance away from land, those crewmembers physically capable of baling out nevertheless resisted Lieutenant Munsey's call for them to do so. Meanwhile, the fire fed by the ruptured inner-port wing fuel tanks was steadily eating its way into the cockpit area but Munsey and Lieutenant Crall (co-pilot) still gallantly held to their task. The B-24 was describing an inexorable downward path as the vague outline of the Suffolk coastline slipped underneath. It was then that what McClure and Sergeant Brown (ball turret gunner) were certain were fuel tanks exploding, ejected them and the still-unconscious Sergeant McKinney out through the rear hatch and into space. Both pilots stood no chance as their charge apparently rolled over and bare seconds later smacked into entombing marsh land near Reydon. Three other crewmembers shared their fate. Although all three actually got out beforehand; one landed in the sea and drowned while the other two, one of which was McKinney, struck the ground with their parachute packs still intact.

Seething's Woes

A second suspected 'intruder' victim finding its last violent resting place in the sea belonged to the 448th Bomb Group, based at Seething; destined to be the hardest hit in terms of direct and indirect losses. One element of bombers led by Lieutenant Skaggs in 42-73497 - *Vadie Raye* (715th Bomb Squadron) was complying with the briefed night-landing procedure by completing a U-turn over the coast at Great Yarmouth and heading south-west on their final airfield approach. Not only were all lights displayed, but flares were fired as a further 'friendly' indicator to the AA defences, especially since some traces of gunfire could already be discerned. The gunners were surely responding to the first 'evidence' of the Me410s' presence, but nobody on board the three B-24s was yet even aware of the threat. Suddenly a vertical line of tracer bullets or shells entered the belly of Lieutenant Pitts' 42-52608 flying off Skaggs' right wing; the bomber erupted in flames and descended rapidly into the sea along with its ten-man crew, none of whom survived the incident. One member of Skaggs' crew was of the firm opinion that AA gunners had been the cause of the bomber's loss, especially given the angle of the gunfire; on the other hand the Me410 was fitted with weapons that could be deployed at a similar angle. As it was there were to be numerous reports of 'friendly fire' being responsible for the loss of, or damage to, bombers as the 'intruders' began to vent their spleen across the region. One replacement member on the Pitts crew had returned to combat flying only three days after being the sole survivor of his bomber's destruction by Flak over the sea. His fear that he would lose his nerve if not immediately restored to combat flying-status had tragically bought Tech Sergeant Robinson a bare 72 hours lease of life.

Vadie Raye, as well as the No. 3 in the element, had also been struck and set on fire, although it appears that the latter crew managed to get down in reasonable order. This was not to be the case for the Skaggs machine. First of all, fire seemed to take hold in the No. 2 engine's cowling as the bomber was headed in towards Seething's landing circuit; although the fire did not subside, neither did it increase. With landing gear safely down and locked the pilots were guiding their charge on the downwind circuit when a double row of tracers hit the lower fuselage; this time round there seemed little doubt the source was not 'friendly fire', further confirmation being established by at least one recorded strafing run across the airfield made by the attacker. Two crewmembers wasted no time in baling out despite the relatively low height; their parachutes deployed and they floated down within shouting distance of each other. The remaining eight airmen remained on board as the burning bomber, with fuel streaming out of the severed bomb-bay hoses, touched down. Several of the crew actually jumped off the aircraft as it skated down the tarmac before being eased off to one side to avoid a possible blockage of the runway. There were no fatalities as the machine burnt itself out, but Tech Sergeant Glevanik should not have been spared. Trapped in the bomb-bay by his flight clothing he was thrown forward, dragged along the runway surface – the doors having been opened – and further pinned down when the nose-wheel broke off. Fortunately an explosion temporarily raised the central fuselage and permitted him to struggle loose from the catwalk frame's lethal embrace under which he had been pinned and was in imminent danger of being incinerated!

Seething's troubles were doubled during the evening's lethal 'activities'. *First, Repulser* (41-28843/715th BS) flown by Lieutenant Pulcipher was crossing-in over Southwold when observers on the ground watched with a mix of frustration and horror as cannon and machine gun fire ignited the starboard wing-root. In a matter of seconds the B-24 rolled helplessly to one side and as it descended the entire wing detached; the truncated remains ended up strewn across the marshes near Kessingland, a bare mile from the sea.

All over East Anglia, B-24s were starting to fall to earth as the intruders took their grim toll.

The second crew, by contrast, were extremely fortunate in that they all survived. Once again witnesses watched what turned out to be Lieutenant Alspaugh's 42-94744 – *Peggy Jo,* (the fourth 715th Bomb Squadron bomber to be lethally attacked), absorbing punishment. The bomber was describing the 'U-turn' over the coast prior to making the landing approach when the Me410 struck to leave No. 3 engine wreathed in fire and the bomber in a steep dive. All ten airmen safely evacuated their doomed charge, which struck a railway embankment close to Worlingham, although none of the debris impeded train movements. The pilot was another individual who was convinced his bomber's demise was caused by 'friendly fire'.

Two further 448th Bomb Group aircraft would be 'written off' group records, although not thanks to the Luftwaffe. *Sky Queen,* flown by Captain Lamberton ran off the runway end and the B-24 became stranded after its huge main undercarriage wheels sank into the ground. Then, Lieutenant Williams touched down in *Ruth E K Allah Hassid* (41-29575/EI: K) and slithered to a similar mired-in halt almost a full wing-span away from *Sky Queen*. In the meantime Lieutenant Apple in *Ice Cold Katie* (41-28595/IG: D) had delayed his landing until the situation became more stabilised. Finally, after several circuits were completed but with the runway lights still extinguished, Apple used the reflected light from the burning hulk of *Vadie Raye* as a marker and managed to find the runway. It was only when he flicked on the landing lights that his horrified gaze took in the sight of the two other bombers perched at the far end. Realising that his bomber's forward momentum could never be halted in time to avoid a collision, he solved the potentially disastrous problem by guiding his charge into the space between the aircraft, although he excised both outer-wing sections in so doing. Scarcely had the B-24 come to a halt and the crew exited when another B-24 rolled into sight; this was *Tondelayo* (41-28240/IG: C) piloted by Lieutenant Barak. This time the errant B-24 smacked its right wing into *Ice Cold Katie* to shear off the tops of the fins and rudders as well as breaking its companion bomber's back just behind the wing-roots. Damage that proved irreparable was also inflicted on *Sky Queen*, which was slewed round to the left by the impact; next day it joined the truncated remnants of *Ice Cold Katie* on the 'Category E' list.

Seething's torment represented the total of the 20th Combat Wing's losses, whereas the 14th Combat Wing's force formed by the 44th Bomb Group and 392nd Bomb Group, and flying in the same right-hand column of the Division stream sailed blithely home to Shipdham and Wendling with no interference. On the other hand, the remaining two Combat Wing's sub-forces were to share in the punishment.

Hethel's Tithe

The 389th Bomb Group had provided pathfinder crews for the Division and had also led the 2nd Combat Wing, albeit with mixed navigational and bombing results. The village of Cantley lies approximately twelve miles north-east of Hethel and one of its youthful occupants who was a very knowledgeable aircraft-recognition enthusiast was enthralled by the ghostly aerial procession. Then, his keen eyes picked out the hostile shape of what he correctly identified as an Me410, which was manoeuvring below and ahead of one B-24. It was now that the *'Schrage Musik'* technique used by German night fighters against RAF Bomber Command was emulated by the Luftwaffe crew; in this case the side fuselage-mounted MG131 machine guns in their flexible barbettes were angled up and to the rear as the gunner sprayed his prey's underside with deadly effect. Fire caught hold as the bomber began to spiral in a deceptively gentle manner and parachute packs spewed forth their silken canopies before one wing detached, trapping those of the eleven-man crew still aboard. Lieutenant Wilkerson and four crewmembers survived the demise of 42-119915/EE: -Z, but others were discovered dead with unopened packs or in one case impaled on a tree. The crash site was alongside the Norwich-Great Yarmouth line, but once again this had no adverse effect upon rail traffic movements. It is possible that this was the aircraft credited to Bordfunker Feldwebel Delp, who would have been 'manning' the side-mounted guns.

The shattered starboard fin of Lieutenant Wilkerson's B-24.

Hethel was being visited by General Hodges (Commanding General, 2nd Bomb Division) and Ted Timberlake (Commanding Officer, 2nd Combat Wing), both officers having taken up station on the control tower roof. A collapsed nose-wheel on Lieutenant Rubich's bomber caused the main runway to be blocked by this B-24, but Flying Control moved swiftly and efficiently to put runway 17 into emergency operation – an act that was to unconsciously place the Generals' safety at risk within the next few minutes. Lieutenants Foley and Muir (co-pilot) were piloting 44-40085/HP:Z- on the downwind leg when their charge was similarly selected for instant destruction.

The No. 2 engine was set ablaze and, worse still, the damaged engine throttle linkage jammed the engines into the high RPM position, while the brakes were rendered inoperable. The latter deficiency would normally have left the pilots facing an over-shoot at the runway end. This was a risky enough option, but the problem was exacerbated for both crew and control tower personnel moments after the bomber settled down on the runway. The inexorable leftward drag caused by the deflated tyre forced the now errant aircraft onto a collision course with the tower structure. Fortunately the curved path traced by HP: Z- cleared the building by a safe, but still uncomfortable distance. However its momentum was still far from spent when it struck with the radar technician's workshop, demolishing it and taking the lives of the two occupants in the process.

HP-Z's starboard wing lies in the remains of the radar technician's workshop. The doomed B-24's tracks can clearly be seen in the turf, note the proximity of the control tower.

Two more views of HP-Z at Hethel.

Fire caught hold of the rear fuselage and it seemed there would be few if any survivors among the crew. Captain Driscoll (gunnery officer) led the way in gaining access to the forward fuselage where he dragged out several inert figures, as did other rescuers. Amazingly all ten airmen survived and the very next day Driscoll received the Airman's Medal from General Doolittle while standing by the remnants of the burnt-out B-24.

Bringing up the Rear

It was the 96th Combat Wing that had been the final force over Hamm. So far just one 458th Bomb Group crew had been lost from its ranks during the mission, but matters were now to take a decided turn for the worse both in respect of this Group and the 467th Bomb Group. Horsham St. Faith is located on the northern outskirts of Norwich and the Group was scant miles distant to the south-east when the 'intruders' struck twice in quick succession.

Lieutenant Harris piloting 42-52353/Z5:J noted how Lieutenant Stilson's bomber received punishment almost simultaneously with that handed out to his own aircraft, a situation suggesting two 'intruders' were present, although he later asserted that ground fire was also observed. He and Lieutenant Couch struggled to retain control of their bomber as it sagged out of the sky and finally crashed heavily at Lakenham. Harris was more fortunate than his co-pilot and five others since he was dragged out of the wreckage alive, albeit suffering a fractured spine that only healed after many months.

Lieutenant Stilson's 42-100357/Z5:D was in equally deep distress with Nos. 3 and 4 engines ablaze, while No. 2 finally went out of control as the Horsham runway was tantalizingly looming up. Its bid to remain airborne finally failing, the bomber was crash-landed into a field. The B-24's high wing configuration and weak bomb-bay centre-beam duly exposed its oft-repeated structural failure in such circumstances; the impact with the soil induced a double fuselage fracture just behind the cockpit and ahead of the waist gun positions, with the forward and rear segments canting off to one side. Among the civilian rescuers who hauled the eight survivors, including Stilson, out were a husband and wife who ironically were close friends of Lieutenant Couch, Lieutenant Harris's dead co-pilot. Two crewmembers were already dead and a third expired later in hospital.

Lieutenant Stilson considers his lucky escape surrounded by the remains of his crippled B-24 Liberator near Horsham.

The 467th Bomb Group had held the dubious honour of being the last Division unit to bomb and, by the time the Luftwaffe attacks were in full swing, the formation had separated into individual elements, each seeking out the directional signal from Splasher 5 at Mundesley on the coast and almost directly north of their base. Before this the Group had already lost one crew. While still some 20 miles to the south of Rackheath Lieutenant Roden's 42-52536/K that was leading one element had its tail section literally sawn off by cannon fire; it plunged into a wood at Withersdale, south-west of Beccles, where the blazing B-24 carcass formed a funeral pyre for all ten of its occupants.

Lieutenant S Reid was part of the 20th Combat Wing, but had returned within the ranks of the 466th Bomb Group. Once over land he guided 42-52445/D out of his 'adopted' Group and took up a course for Rackheath. His solo appearance over the airfield circuit resulted in him cutting across the landing approach being made by Lieutenant Newhouse, who cursed his fellow-pilot roundly. Almost immediately Newhouse was notified by one of his crew of the presence of a 'Messerschmitt' sidling in behind what he later asserted was Reid's 42-52445/4Z: D. The report turned out to be tragically accurate since tracers now reached out to grasp the B-24's left wing in a fiery embrace; four gunners in the rear of the doomed bomber managed to scramble out, but one suffered a failure of his parachute harness and fell to his death. In spite of the terminal damage suffered, the bomber must have staggered on for several minutes before finally succumbing, since its crash-site was at Barsham some 15 miles south-east of the airfield.

Blow for Blow….

II/KG51 did not emerge unscathed from their otherwise effective intervention this April evening. At least two B-24 crews, one each from the 389th Bomb Group and 467th Bomb Group, claimed to have shot down their assailant, but only one was to be confirmed. A waist gunner claimed to have engaged and fatally damaged an Me410 making its second pass that was then seen to crash somewhere 'south-east of Rackheath'. Another Me410 was seen by a civilian witness to close in upon a B-24; the fighter's gunfire was responded to by what was described as 'a waist gun position', whereupon the Luftwaffe machine burst into flames and dived into the ground at Ashby St. Mary, killing Leutnant Krüger and his fellow-airman.

The assault upon the 389th Bomb Group B-24 was observed as being from 'below and ahead' and was responded to by the nose turret and the right waist positions. However, the latter incident ended with witnesses asserting that the assailant, far from crashing, sped away seawards unscathed. Since the Krüger crash-site is 'south-east of Rackheath' and its loss attributed to a single flexible gunner's fire, the odds on the 467th Bomb Group being the victor appear to be stronger. Of course the witness in question was at least several thousand feet distant in vertical terms from the incident, so the fine detail of his statement, however sincere, could be deemed open to question. No matter who contributed to the Me410's demise, a small measure of revenge had been exacted for the Division's sufferings.

The Krüger crew's fate was firmly recorded, but II/KG51 suffered a second loss that must have shaken the Gruppe personnel. The last crew landed back at Soesterberg around 24.00 hours, but missing from among their number was no less a personality than the Kommandeur, Major Puttfarken. A Knight's Cross holder who had been awarded this prestigious decoration in October 1942, he had amassed a total of well over 250 sorties. Now he and his Bordfunker, Feldwebel Lux, were fated to join the thousands of Luftwaffe and Allied airmen whose assumed grave is the dark maw of the North Sea, since no trace of their 9K+MN was ever found.

An Over-view

The latent threat posed by the Luftwaffe operating in an 'intruder' capacity was rarely to be indulged in again before the end of WWII. On this occasion Allied radio intercepts had confirmed II/KG51's deployment with this type of operation in clear mind, but there was little that could be done to produce effective counter-measures. Warning the bomber crews of the impending infiltration within the Division stream might have mitigated the overall situation by their switching off all but the basic navigation lighting as advised, for example by Colonel Isbell, to his personnel. On the other hand the risk of mid-air collision would surely have been increased as a result, regardless of enemy intervention. Then the bombers had to be brought safely down, which in turn meant airfields had to be lit up. Also, normal fuel margins would not have sufficed for protracted orbiting to be indulged in during the estimated period of time the 'intruders' might spend over the 2nd Bomb Division zone.

Dispatching 256 aircraft to alternative USAAF or RAF airfields outside their geographic 'home' would not have been a secure alternative; The 1st and 3rd Bomb Division Bases would have been occupied with bringing in their own flocks, while RAF Bomber Command's dispatch of its own Main Force would have been even more restrictive in nature. One B-24 crew who did divert into an RAF bomber airfield was quietly rounded upon by the senior RAF staff, since their arrival had interrupted the take-off pattern! On this night nearly 840 'heavies' and Mosquitos were sent out to attack Düsseldorf and Brunswick. The aerial 'fox' was about to enter the USAAF 'hen-house' and the bald if uncomfortable truth was that the bomber crews would have to be left to their own devices, especially since an 'intruder' presence would most certainly have remained with the Division regardless of where it might finally attempt to disperse for landing.

When the feared assaults began to materialise a number of Mosquitos from 25 Squadron based at Coltishall were sent up, but their efforts came to naught; this was hardly surprising when given the huge number of aircraft in the air coupled with the problem of picking out either the visual image or the comparative speed of the Me410s in relation to their four-engine prey, the latter observation being established through the 'traces' on the night fighters radar screens.

A further issue that increased the chaos on 22nd April was the involvement of Allied AA batteries. The fact that strafing attacks were carried out over a number of the airfields did nothing to alley the doubts of the ground gunners about the fact of a hostile aerial presence. Whether or not the personnel concerned should have been more discriminating in picking out the lumbering forms of B-24s from the more agile and smaller airframes of the Me410s is a moot point. Aircraft recognition is an acquired art when practiced even in the relaxed atmosphere of peacetime, let alone in this dangerous and darkened WWII scenario. It is certain that a number of bombers were the unfortunate recipients of 'friendly fire', but whether the strikes proved fatal was never clearly established. What is certain is that at least twelve B-24s had either been shot down or ended up as 'Category E' wrecks.

The USAAF authorities had received a bruising, but far from fatal, rebuff courtesy of their Luftwaffe adversaries. For the remainder of the conflict the night skies would return to the almost universal charge of the airmen from RAF Bomber Command. For its part the Luftwaffe did continue to mount 'intruder' raids, but with real effect only on one more occasion.

On 3rd/4th March 1945 Operation 'Gisela' witnessed upwards of 150 Ju88G night fighter crews alerted to take off and interdict the RAF bomber stream on the final stage of its homeward course. Earlier some 436 Lancasters, Halifaxes with pathfinder Mosquito guidance had attacked Kamen and the Dortmund-Ems Canal. A further 312 other Command aircraft had indulged in diversion, RCM, mine-laying and 'intruder' duties, as well as striking at Berlin; the latter function was carried out by Mosquitos of the quaintly named but nevertheless effective 'Light Night Striking Force' from No. 8 (Pathfinder) Group.

The resultant operation proved to be a pyrrhic victory for the Germans. Although 20 RAF aircraft were shot down, seventeen Luftwaffe crews were either missing, lost in crashes over England, or forced to abandon their Ju88s on their return, while a further eleven night fighters crashed or were badly damaged while landing. Two further sorties on the 4th/5th and 20th/21st were mounted but these involved numbers of crews barely exceeding twenty and ten respectively who achieved little or nothing in the way of 'kills'. The Luftwaffe had shot its last bolt as regards 'intruder' activity over Britain.

Luftwaffe Losses 22nd-23rd April 1944

Me 410 A-1	6/KG 51	9K+HP	WNr 20458

Ashby Hall Farm, Ashby St Mary's, Norfolk. 22.10 hrs.

Following a formation of American B-24s back to base, the aircraft attacked a Liberator at a height of 3,000 ft, but return fire shot it down and it dived into the ground. It was noted that remains of crew were so few that they did not warrant burial.

Lt Klaus Krüger (F) (Missing). Fw Michael Reichardt (Bf) (Missing).

Me410A-1	5/KG51	9K+MN	WNr 420314

Failed to return from intruder mission to Cambridge.

Major Puttfarken was a Ritterkreuz holder with 250 war flights.

Major Dietrich Puttfarken (F) Missing), Ofw Willi Lux (Bf) (Missing).

Night Fighter Tactics

To date the bulk of the casualties suffered by the Luftwaffe bomber force over Britain had been at the hands of the RAF Mosquito and Beaufighters. On the face of it, their crews would appear to have an easier duty to undertake than the Ju88s, Bf110s and He219s ascending against RAF Bomber Command's incursions. Not only were the German bombers arriving in noticeably smaller numbers but the 'bomber stream' tactics adopted for *'Steinbock'* were apparently not resulting in a compact force arriving and departing; rather were the recorded numbers crossing-in well below the total number dispatched. In addition the scattered bombing results indicated a further dangerous loosening of the 'stream' pattern. Consequently the survival chances of individual bombers picked up by GCI Control and advised to the patrolling night fighters under such guidance (or alternatively being illuminated by searchlight batteries that provided a visual assist to the Mosquitos and Beaufighters) were marginal.

However, the Luftwaffe's Nachtjagd fighters, having been freed from close control under the 'Himmelbett' system from July 1943 onwards, were now being fed into their adversaries' ranks, whose large and relatively tight formations all too often provided the Bordfunkers with several 'traces' on their radar screens, after which the main problem for the pilots was which target to attack first. There were to be many occasions where a crew would land off an operation with multiple 'abschüsse' (victories) that could reach as high as eight or nine.

Another key advantage compared to the RAF lay in the advent from mid-1943 of the '*Schrage Musik*' (Jazz Music) armament layout on Luftwaffe night fighters. This consisted of two 20mm, or even 30 mm cannon, mounted on the spine of Ju88s or the rear cockpit of Bf110s and angled at 70 degrees. This in turn meant that the Luftwaffe crews could approach from underneath the Lancasters and Halifaxes which were almost entirely bereft of any underside defensive armament. Then, the gunfire could be concentrated not on the fuselage with its potentially volatile bomb load but on the wings that contained the fuel tanks. Once these had been fired the night fighter could ease away in search of its next victim in the almost certain knowledge that its current target was doomed.

Contrast this virtually un-challengeable position with the standard nose armament employed by the RAF throughout WWII. Although the RAF crews could close in on their target from the same relatively secure angle they were forced to come up into a level position with their target before firing, a course of action that contained several potential problems. First, the Luftwaffe crew might spot their attacker as he made his final approach and take evasive action, as well as rendering the latter liable to damage or even destruction from return fire. Even if surprise was achieved the bomber's narrow outline from directly behind meant it was none too easy to land an accurate strike other than on its fuselage. Should the bomb load still be on board then the cannon shells' impact could easily cause the target to explode with the attendant risk of the debris causing serious damage to the night fighter. The Mosquito with its oil-cooled Merlin engines and radiators set into the wing roots outboard of the cockpit was particularly vulnerable to damage from debris thrown back from the target. The wooden structure was equally vulnerable should the De Havilland design be forced to fly through the fireball created by an exploding bomber.

Of course, the RAF pilot could complete his approach from underneath and pull the nose sharply up to let the target fly through the path of his gunfire. However, should a decisive strike not be achieved, there was a chance of the bomber then gaining enough distance as the night fighter was brought back to level flight to at least present the latter with a tail chase in order to regain visual if not also radar contact.

The presence of the searchlight battery chain across the country was of prime importance in picking up enemy bombers, although there was sometimes a downside to this element of night fighting. On occasions requests from the night fighter to the batteries for the lights to be doused once radar and-or visual contact had been effected were not acted upon. The consequence was that the RAF crew would either have a problem in maintaining visual contact (although radar 'contact' was naturally not inhibited) or the Luftwaffe crew could see them, thanks to the searchlights having exposed their adversary, and then carry out evasive manoeuvres.

23rd-24th April 1944

As with Hull on 20th/21st, so a similar situation arose three nights later with Bristol as the return focus for attack. A marginally smaller force comprising 117 bombers was launched. II/KG30 sent all three Staffeln along with the Stabs Schwarm in transit from Zwischenahn to Orly. The normal Gruppe complement of 30 crews was being maintained, but approximately one-third of this figure comprised novice crews who were left behind since their level of operational preparedness was still regarded as not up to scratch. This situation was not uncommon among some of the other *'Steinbock'* units. The various IV Gruppen, whose basic brief was training, were still managing to at least turn out a steady, albeit not always fully adequate, flow of crews in the face of mounting technical difficulties.

The same pattern of routing to the target as displayed on 27th/28th March was briefed although for this Gruppe, and its companion III/KG30 at least, the return flight would be on a direct south-easterly course. *'Knickebein'* Stations 8, 10 and 11 were laid on, with the second one's bearing of 345.5T passing over the final turning point for the target; the other two beams were directed over the target as indicated on a captured map. The mixed red and white markers were to be released to form a square pattern just before 02.00 hours and the crews would track over the zone at 16,000 feet.

Fifteen to twenty II/KG30 bombers took off from Orly between 23.50 and 00.10 hours with one (4D+FM) tracking out via Caen and Guernsey to make landfall marginally further east at Weymouth, compared to the previously briefed location of Lyme Bay for the 24th/25th raid. On the other hand this landfall may well have been an error on the crew's part, especially given their ultimate position when fate intervened shortly after. Their Ju88A-4 was only fitted with the Fu.Bl 1 set, but this possessed a frequency compatible with *'Knickebein'* 10. In spite of this, the Beobachter was subsequently to state that he was using the D.R. method of navigation.

Whether or not Unteroffizier Detering would have succeeded in releasing his load over Bristol before running into Squadron Leader Barwell's 125 Squadron Mosquito is unclear. The night fighter's cannon fire hit the starboard engine and wing-root and a spinning action almost immediately ensued; in the scant seconds between the crew hearing the loud explosion and sighting the flames, three of them scrambled clear either through the entrance hatch or out over the fuselage after the canopy was jettisoned, leaving Unteroffizier Trauwald either dead or dying at his post. The burning aircraft spiralled to its doom at Manor Farm, Hill Deverill, near Warminster, Wiltshire. A study of a regional map shows that the aircraft was roughly 30 miles to the east of the briefed inward route at this point.

Victors and vanquished.
Above: the crew of 4D+FM Uffz Detering, Uffz Trauwald, Uffz Agten (with Uffz Rull).
Below: S/L Barwell DFC and his navigator Flt Lt Haigh.

Combat Report

125 Sqn. RAF Station, Hurn

Date. 23/24 April 1944
Squadron. 125 Squadron
A/C Type. Mosquito XVII/A.I. Mark X. A/C Letter "T".
Time Up. 0150 hrs. - Hurn.
Time of Combat. 0150 hrs.
Time Down. 0350 hrs. - Ford.
Place of Combat. Middle Wallop Fix at 0153 hrs. in Square U.37 (4 Miles South of Melksham).
Weather. Large amount of low stratus. Clear above.
Our Casualties A/C. Nil.
Our Casualties Personnel. Nil.
Enemy Casualties: 1 Ju.88 Destroyed.

General
S/Ldr. E. Barwell, D.F.C. (Pilot) F/Lt.D.Haigh (Navigator).
Call Sign: Goodwill 29.

Took off from Hurn at 0110, under Sopley G.C.I. Was on orbit "R" when many searchlights were seen in the distance, along the South coast, mainly Westwards. The light from several searchlights was seen through low stratus cloud. Gauntleted 1 o'clock but beam not penetrating cloud sufficiently to give intersection, but contact was soon obtained amid much window. Contact was obtained at 8 miles range, 16,000 ft. and target was slightly below to port, taking corkscrew evasive action, altering height by 5,000 ft. and dropping window. Speed of E/A varying from 140 to 260 m.p.h. Visual was first obtained at approximately 1,000 ft. range. Target 5 degs. above, at 12 o'clock but I could not identify it until at approximately 200 ft. range, when it turned out to be a Ju.88 and bombs were observed at the wing roots. At this range a short burst was given from almost dead astern and strikes were seen on starboard wing root and engine. E/A went down to starboard almost vertically and was then seen spinning, with starboard engine on fire and pieces, ablaze, falling from it. A glow was seen on the ground where A/C hit. Fix was given to Sopley. One inaccurate burst of return m.g. fire was observed. A further contact was obtained and followed until 1,500 ft. when resins were observed and at approximately the same time, navigator got a contact through mass of window on another A/C, close in front of what was assumed to be a friendly fighter, and pursuit was given up. Shortly afterwards, further contact was obtained on another A/C dropping window but as range was closed, weapon became bent and chase abandoned. Landed Ford 0350 hrs. E/A reported crashed near Warminster in Square U.39.

Intelligence Report

Place: Manor Farm, Hill Deverill, near Warminster, Wilts, (U.3161)
Date: 24th April, 1944
Time: 0200 hrs.

Type & Marks: Ju.88 A-4 4D+FM
Unit: 4/KG30

Start & Mission:
This aircraft was attacked by a nightfighter whilst on its way to the target. A loud explosion occurred in the cabin and the aircraft burst into flames, whereupon three members of the crew, though temporarily blinded, succeeded in baling out. The aircraft crashed and the body of the air-gunner was found amongst the wreckage.

The bomb load was still on board when the aircraft was shot down; it consisted of one A.B.1000 and ten 50 kg. incendiaries.

Morale:
The pilot and observer showed only medium morale but were security conscious. The W/T operator was very tough indeed. The whole crew had the E.K.1 and the bronze (20 war flights) badge.

What was to become clear as the raid progressed was that the debacle of the March raid was recurring in equally full measure, with no recorded incidents of bombs or incendiaries striking anywhere in, or even near, the city. In fact it was the Poole to Bournemouth stretch of the Channel coast within which a number of loads from the 35 aircraft noted on British radar plots descended!

Additionally, this time round, there was no indication as to whether any pathfinder flares had even been sighted, let alone correctly positioned. Although four claims by night fighter crews were submitted only Squadron Leader Barwell's was confirmed. The only other bomber falling over British territory was claimed by AA batteries based at Arne, just west of Poole, but even further to the east of the target-approach route. U5+GH was a Ju188A-1 that was engaged at 17,000 feet and descended in a steady dive before crashing into a small wood; all five of Leutnant Christoff's crew were later discovered dead in the wreckage by the investigators.

Intelligence Report No. 8/127 - Ju 188

This is the first of a new sub-series to be shot down over this country, and is of great interest being fitted with Jumo 213 A-1 liquid-cooled, in-line, 12-cylinder, inverted-V engines. The engine bears little resemblance to previous Junkers products, and has been sent to R.A.E., Farnborough for detailed examination.
This aircraft was engaged by anti-aircraft guns at a height of 17,000 ft., came down on a level keel and eventually crashed into a small wood at 0215 hrs. on the 24th April near Arne, Dorset, map ref. U.4008.
Except for the engines, which are reasonably intact, the aircraft was entirely disintegrated by impact with the trees.

Identification Markings:
U5+GH Works No. 5021

Camouflage:
Greeny-blue with black wavy lines on upper surfaces, spray painted black on lower surfaces.

Engines:
Jumo 213 A-1.
Port engine No. 1021520751. Maker jfr.
Starboard engine No. 1021520726. Maker jfr.

The following points were noted during a brief site examination:
(i) The supercharger is of entirely new design.
(ii) A master control unit (Kommando Gerät) is fitted. This has not previously been seen on Junkers engines.
(iii) The fuel injector pump is of a new type and it would appear that fuel is injected into the induction pipe instead of direct into the cylinders as previously.
(iv) The external over-all measurements approximate those of the DB603 engine.

Armament:

1 x mG 151 (20 mm. calibre) presumably from the nose position.

2 x MG 131 (13 mm. calibre) 1 from Wireless Operator's position and the other from the dorsal turret.

1 x twin MG 81 (7.9 mm. calibre) from the ventral position.

Two UX AB 1000 incendiary bomb containers were found in the wreckage.

10 x 50-kilo. Slips were carried in the rear fuselage bomb bay, but no small bombs were found.

Internal Equipment:

All the instruments were destroyed, but the following radio equipment was identified:

FuG 10 P. FuG 16, FuG 101 A, FuBl 2 and two PeGe 6 sets.

Special points noted were as follows:

Two recognition lights about 10" apart were situated on the underside of the fuselage about 4' forward of the tail wheel. The covers of these had been broken off, the colours therefore being unknown.

A new type of gun control switch box VSK 8a was found, and is being further investigated.

There were large cast iron ballast weights, estimated to weigh 1 ½ cwt. bolted to brackets situated on the floor of the fuselage just forward of the tailwheel assembly.

A new type of Revi gunsight was found, but was too badly damaged to ascertain its method of working.

A single-axis automatic pilot had been fitted.

BZA dive-bombing equipment was fitted.

Balloon cable-cutter was fitted in the leading-edge of the mainplane and round the nose of the fuselage.

De-icing of the main and tailplanes was by hot air.

The letters "A.T.G." were painted in red on the starboard rear main spar boom.

Luftwaffe Losses 23rd-24th April 1944

Ju188A-2 1/KG2 U5+LH WNr 180419

Failed to return from a sortie to Bristol.

Ofw George Rösler (F) (Missing), Uffz Friedrich Kreissl (B) (Missing), Uffz Rudolf Fietz (Bf) (Missing), Fw Günter Hosters (Bs) (Missing), Ogefr Emil Weissbrich (Bs) (Missing).

Ju188 A-2 1/KG 2 U5+GH WNr 80414

Salterns Wood, Arne, Dorset. 02.15 hrs.

Engaged by 3.7 inch guns from Holton Heath at 17,000 ft, came down on a level keel and eventually crashed into a small wood where it disintegrated.

Lt Wolfgang Christoff (F) (Killed Wareham, Dorset), Uffz Heinrich Schnuer (B) (Killed Wareham, Dorset), Ogefr Wolfgang Biegerl (Bf) (Killed Wareham, Dorset), Ogefr Theophil Joretzki (Bs) (Killed Wareham, Dorset), Fw Horst Huffsky (Bs) (Killed Wareham, Dorset).

Do217M-1 9/KG2 U5+IT WNr 6256

Crashed at Savigny, France, during a sortie to Bristol. 00.30 hrs.

Uffz Heinrich Rosemann (F) (Killed), Ogefr Kurt Deutrich (B) (Killed), Ogefr Franz Harnoth (Bf) (Killed), Uffz Willi Tettschlag (Bs) (Killed).

Ju88 5/KG6

Failed to return from a sortie to England.

Uffz Karl Geher (F) (Missing), Gefr Franz Hartmann (B) (Missing), Uffz Josef Getzinger (Bf) (Missing), Uffz Alfred Stenzel (Bs) (Missing).

Ju88 II/KG30

Shot down by a night fighter over Carentan, France.

Uffz Karl Wenzmann (F) (Killed). Rest of crew baled out safely.

Uffz Alwin Sclemm

Ju88 4/KG30 4D+OM WNr 142570

Failed to return from a sortie to Bristol.

Uffz Alwin Schlemm (F) (Missing), Gefr Gerhard Klingler (B) (Missing), Uffz Horst Steinmetz (Bf) (Missing), Uffz Franz Rametsteiner (Bs) (Missing).

Ju88 A-14 4/KG30 4D+FM WNr 144501

Manor Farm, Hill Deverill, Wiltshire. 02.10 hrs.

Shot down by S/Ldr E G Barwell DFC in a 125 Sqn Mosquito.

Took off from Paris / Orly at 23.50 hrs for Bristol. This aircraft was attacked by a night fighter at 20,000 ft whilst on its way to the target.

Markings: Call sign BH+PY. Upper surfaces mottled greenish grey, undersides spray painted black.

Uffz Rudolf Detering EKI (F) (PoW injured), Uffz Johann Agten EKI (B) (PoW injured), Uffz Walter Kempter EKI (Bf) (PoW), Uffz Helmut Trauwald EKI (Bs) (Killed Bath).

Above left: Uffz Albert Kempter. Above right: Johann Agten and Helmut Trauwald pose for a photo in the cockpit of their Ju88.

Ju88A-4 1/KG54 B3+KH WNr 800939

Failed to return from a sortie to Bristol.

Uffz Günter Fedler (F) (Missing), Uffz Walter Marke (B) (Missing), Uffz Heinz Reinecke (Bf) (Missing), Ogefr Franz Woznicki (Bs) (Missing).

Ju88A-4 3/KG54 B3+GL WNr 1221

Crashed in a forced landing approx 2 km south-west of Tour en Bessin, France, on return from Bristol.

Lt Gerhard Jandke (F) (Inj), Uffz Bernhard Frank (B) (Inj), Uffz Horst Seeck (Bf) (Inj), Uffz Karl Wolla (Bs) (Killed).

Ju88A-4 7/KG54 B3+HR

Failed to return from a sortie to Bristol.

Uffz Heinz Strobel (F) (Missing), Uffz Maximilian Brachtel (Bo) (Missing), Uffz Werner Holl (Bf) (Missing), Uffz Josef Götz (Bs) (Missing).

Ju88A-4 8/KG54 B3+FS

Failed to return from a sortie to Bristol.

Lt Stephan Pauli (F) (Missing), Uffz Werner Perlik (Bo) (Missing), Uffz Karl-Heinz Behling (Bf) (Missing), Uffz Walter Wickborn (Bs) (Missing).

Ju88A-4 9/KG54 B3+DT

Failed to return from a sortie to Bristol.

Lt Erhard Eubel (F) (Missing), Fw Josef Lichtl (Bo) (Missing), Uffz Erhard Granow (Bf) (Missing), Fw Hans Adam (Bs) (Missing).

Ju88 4/KGr101

Failed to return from a sortie to Bristol.

Uffz Hans Bauer (F) (Missing), Uffz Josef Krekeler (Bo) (Missing), Uffz Eugen Ritz (Bf) (Missing), Uffz Karl Bachus (Bs) (Missing).

Fighter Command Claims not attributable to a particular loss

A claim was made by F/Lt V P Key in a 125 Sqn Mosquito for a Ju188 shot down south of Lyme Regis, Dorset, at 02.00 hrs.

A claim was made by P/O W A Beadle in a 125 Sqn Mosquito for a Ju188 shot down near Swanage, Dorset, at 01.47 hrs.

A claim was made by S/Ldr L W Gill in a 125 Sqn Mosquito for a Ju88 damaged near Winterbourne Houghton, Dorset, at 02.05 hrs.

A claim was made by F/Lt R W Leggett in a 125 Sqn Mosquito for a Ju88 damaged near Blandford, Dorset, at 02.20 hrs.

A claim was made by P/O W A Pargeter in a 125 Sqn Mosquito for a Ju188 shot down 10-20 miles south of Berry Head, Devon, at 01.47 hrs. At 17,000 ft the starboard engine was set alight and the aircraft fell, burning, in a spiral dive.

A claim was made by W/Cdr K M Hampshire in a 456 Sqn Mosquito for a Ju88 shot down 5 miles south of St Albans Head, Dorset, at 02.10 hrs. The port side of the aircraft was hit and it spiraled down in flames before diving vertically into the sea; confirmed the Royal Observer Corps.

A claim was made by W/O G F MacEwen (RCAF) in a 406 Sqn Beaufighter for a Ju88 shot down off the south-west coast at 02.09 hrs. The starboard engine exploded and flames spread to the whole aircraft before it dived into the sea and continued to burn for a minute.

Final Target Switch

By this stage of 1944 preparations for Operation *'Overlord'* were well in hand. Troop and equipment build-up was occurring along the central and western zones of the Channel coast. To date, little or no Luftwaffe reconnaissance of these zones had been attempted, but this was none too surprising given the degree of Allied air supremacy reigning by day and, to a scarcely lesser degree, during the hours of darkness. Although the German High Command was still being successfully fed the duplicitous 'information' emanating from Operation 'Fortitude South' – namely the establishment of FUSAG (First U S Army Group) headed by General Patton and based in Kent, with a view to effecting landings in the Pas de Calais – there was always the doubt in the Allied Planners' minds that if aerial reconnaissance of the main build-up zones were ever achieved, this in turn could easily blow the deception plan apart.

Reconnaissance Limitations

The Luftwaffe reconnaissance unit 1(F)121 (F= Fern, or long-range in German) was now on hand with its Me410s, but had so far not attempted any sorties by day. Now, on the 25th /26th April one crew was briefed for a nocturnal run over Portsmouth, where the bombers were going to attack shipping and suspected concentrations of landing craft. Confirmation of the target had been made early in the morning by one of the unit's crews. The unit was one of two such specialist outfits currently subordinate to Aufklarungsgruppe 123 whose HQ was in Paris/Buc and whose brief was to fly night sorties with a view to confirming the strike and damage results (if any) accruing from bomber assaults. This was a distinct switch from its normal brief of strategic or even tactical reconnaissance operations.

For some time confirmation of the effect of attacks on British targets had proved almost impossible when employing twin-engine aircraft; even the use of fighters such as the FW190 with their higher speed and superior manoeuvrability had not yielded much in the way of results, so Luftflotte 3 demands for cover by Aufklarungsgruppe crews went unanswered. Indeed, so desperate was the situation that the use of captured airworthy Allied aircraft was seriously mooted. A natural recourse to night sorties had been made, but the results were disappointing to say the least – all the stranger since German camera technology, as with other products of that nation's industrial and commercial output, was regarded as world-class. German examination of film from a reconnaissance Mosquito downed in France impressed the investigators, who stated frankly that their adversary's photographic practice and the quality of the exposed film was far superior to their own!

Major Bomber Command Operations
24th to 30th April 1944

24-25 April	**Karlsruhe-118 killed**	**637 aircraft-19 lost**
24-25 April	**Munich-88 killed**	**360 aircraft-9 lost**
26-27 April	**Essen-313 killed**	**493 aircraft-7 lost**
26-27 April	**Schweinfurt-2 killed**	**247 aircraft-21 lost**
27-28 April	**Friedrichshafen-136 killed**	**323 aircraft-18 lost**

25th-26th April 1944

Another Fiasco

The first of four nightly raids on Portsmouth was duly launched on April 25th/26th but once again no real concentration of bombing occurred even along the coastal region surrounding the city, let alone in the city itself. At least four Gruppen were involved as part of the bombing force while 1(F)122 also provided photo reconnaissance. The efforts of I/KG66 to carry out its target marking brief had come to naught, but the reason for this was not obvious; the coastal location of Portsmouth should have made it easy to pick out.

Two of the Luftwaffe losses were from 1(F)122. The first aircraft was almost certainly the one involved in an interception noted in 85 Squadron records. Flight Lieutenant Rogers flying his Mosquito under Wartling Control was directed onto and engaged an Me410.

Strikes were noted, but the Luftwaffe pilot managed to pull away from the Mosquito during this and a second attacking run by his adversary, by which latter point the Mosquito was running short of fuel and turned back for West Malling. The crash of an Me410 off Le Havre around this time was recorded by the Luftwaffe, which seems to tie in as the culmination of the foregoing encounter. Feldwebel Kurt Stoll's specially adapted Me410 had been carrying a third crew member to operate the reconnaissance cameras and all three were killed in the crash.

In the early hours of the following morning Leutnant Hermann Kroll of 1(F)122 was flying his second photo-recce sortie to Portsmouth that night. His Me410 was roughly 50 miles away and closing from the east of Portsmouth around 05.00 hours. Fifteen miles further east was Flight Lieutenant Branse Burbridge's 85 Squadron Mosquito and he was informed by Wartling Control of the bandit's presence at an altitude of 23,000 feet.

Diving to pick up speed and directed by Wartling, Burbridge's radar operator, Flight Lieutenant Skelton, soon picked up a 'trace' at 3 ½ miles - dead ahead; however he advised his pilot that the radar scanner was 'sticking' in the upper position and that it was imperative the Mosquito match the target's altitude as closely as possible. Speed was maintained while the night fighter was in a climb by opening and closing the radiators, and eventually a dim silhouette at around 500 feet was discerned that was identified as an Me410. Burbridge noted in his report:

"I then drew astern and fired a long burst of about 7 seconds from 150 yards range: the time was 0507 hours. There were strikes and two very bright flashes in the starboard engine of the e/a, which burst into flames and continued to burn steadily. Oil which streamed back over our windscreen made observation difficult, but the e/a seemed to be flying on, weaving erratically and losing height gently in spite of the bonfire in its starboard engine. I positioned myself astern again and tried to fire a further burst, but the guns would not respond: this was probably due to overheating.

I flew alongside for a few moments, and observed that the top hatch was apparently open. The fuselage and tailplane were well illuminated by the increasing flames, so I drew away to starboard, and turned in to expose several feet of cine film independently of the guns.

I tested the guns again and they seemed to be all right; but further shooting was rendered unnecessary by the sudden steep dive to port of the e/a. It went straight down. I dived down after it through a layer of cloud, and F/Lt. Skelton and myself saw it hit the sea with a big explosion at 0509 hours. Orbitting the position, I gave 'Canary' to Wartling who told me I was about 5 miles off Selsey."

Of the two crewmembers, Oberleutnant Kroll (Staffelkapitän) went down with the aircraft, but Oberfähnrich Meyer was later picked up from his dinghy.

Intelligence Report A.D.I.(K) 190/1944

Place, Time and Date.
In sea off Portsmouth, 26th April 1944, about 05.00 hours.
Type and Marks.
Me.410
Unit:
1(F)/122
Start and Mission:
Place of start not yet established. Mission was to take photographs of Portsmouth after the raid earlier in the night. Six photographic flash bombs carried.

This crew flew two sorties on the night in question. In the first sortie they were to be over the target at about 0100 hours; they were accompanied by a second aircraft which failed to return to base.
On the second sortie the present aircraft operated alone. It was flying at about 26,000 feet when it was attacked by a night fighter, the first burst from which hit the cabin and the second the engines.
The intercom was put out of action and when the W/T operator saw the pilot open the cabin roof, he baled out without further ado from a height of 10,000 feet. He came down in the sea and was picked up and was brought into Portsmouth.
P/W gave his unit as 1(F)122. His pilot, who is presumably drowned, was the Staffelkapitän of the unit; his name had been known since 1940, when he was an Oberfeldwebel, and was awarded the Ritterkreuz as long ago as March 1942. The W/T operator claimed 169 operational flights and had been awarded the Deutsches Kreuz and the Ehrenpokal (Göring's Cup of Honour); he was about to receive his commission.

Morale:
Very high.
Crew:
Pilot Leutnant Hermann Kroll .... Missing, assumed drowned.
W/T: Oberfähnrich Werner Meyer 27 Jun. 21 (4 ½) .. unwounded.

Leutnant Schröder's had been one of four crews from 5/KG2 recently involved in supplementary target-marking operations. This would probably have been another sortie with this duty in mind, since his Ju188 U5+EN was carrying two AB1000 containers and what was listed by intelligence as 'some 50kg. bombs'. Having taken off from Holland (the unit was normally located at Soesterberg) the pilot was approaching from due south of Portsmouth when his course took him close to, or over, the south-east fringe of the Isle of Wight. AA batteries at Sandown homed in on the bomber and struck with lethal effect by knocking out both engines. Schröder jettisoned the bomb load before ordering a bale-out and followed the other four out into a black void that ended with his descending into the Channel. Good fortune attended his situation since he not only got into his dinghy, but was later picked up by a passing convoy to become the sole survivor of his crew, the others having presumably drowned.

The following morning the Australians of 456 Squadron based at Ford were in high spirits. Three of the Mosquito crews had brought down bombers. Flight Lieutenant Lewis had claimed a Ju188 at 23.57 hours, later Flying Officers Houston and Roediger both made claims at around 05.00 hours south of Portsmouth. Fellow pilot Flight Lieutenant Brooks had a ring-side seat and confirmed seeing both enemy aircraft going down in flames.

Luftwaffe Losses 25th-26th April 1944

FW190G-3 3/SKG10 WNr 160488

Crashed whilst on operations 500 metres south of Lion sur Mer, France.

Hpmn Georg Gawlina (Killed).

Ju188E-1 U5+EN 5/KG 2 WNr 260378

In the Solent between Portsmouth and Sandown, Isle of Wight. 00.05 hrs.

Started from a Dutch base to attack Portsmouth. When over the target the aircraft was hit by AA, as a result of which both engines cut, the bombs were jettisoned and orders were given to bale out. The bomb load was two AB 1000 incendiary containers plus some 50 kg bombs.

Lt Kurt Schröder (F) (PoW), Uffz Hans Wolff (B) (Missing), Uffz Helmuth Wefels (Bf) (Missing), Uffz JHans Tschenscher (Bm), (Missing) Gefr Anton Golias (Bs), (Killed buried at Gosport).

Do217M-1 7/KG2 U5+GR WNr 6047

Failed to return from a sortie to Portsmouth.

Uffz Richard Trollhagen (F) (Missing), Fw Hans-Joachim Hoth (B) (Missing), Uffz Fritz Bening (Bf) (Missing), Fw Heinrich Niewerth (Bs) (Missing).

Ju88S-1 1/KG66 Z6+DH WNr 140610

Failed to return from an operational sortie.

Oblt Alexander Pfeiffer (F) (Missing), Ofw Johann Engler (B) (Killed), Fw Roland Gabler (Bf) (Missing).

He177A-3 **3/KG100** **6N+FL** **WNr 2506**

Failed to return from a sortie to Portsmouth.

Fw Franz Pomper (F) (Missing), Lt Hermann Friedauer (Bs) (Killed), Fw Walter Peters (Bf) (Missing), Uffz Heinz Hoffmann (Bs) (Missing), Uffz Fritz Jakobi (Bs) (Missing), Fw Günther Kocem (Bm) (Missing).

Me 410 **1(F)121**

Failed to return from Photo-reconnaissance of Portsmouth.

At 01.00 hrs the crew signaled that one engine was damaged. Crashed at Le Havre, France. A third crew member was carried to operate the camera.

Fw Kurt Stoll (F) (Killed), Fw Herbert Kraupatz (Bf) (Killed), Uffz Beno Zingler (Bs) (Killed).

Me 410 **1(F)/121**

Sea - off Portsmouth. 05.07 hrs.

Shot down by F/Lt B A Burbridge in an 85 Sqn Mosquito.

Oblt Hermann Kroll RK (F) (Killed. Buried at sea off Portsmouth by RN), Oberfahn Werner Meyer (Bf) (PoW).

Groundcrew refuel a Junkers 88. As the Allied bombing campaign intensified in mid 1944, fuel supplies to the German bomber force were reduced to the point where it ceased to be an effective fighting unit.

Fighter Command Claims not attributable to a particular loss

A claim was made by F/Lt V P Key in a 125 Sqn Mosquito at 04.55 hrs for a Do217 destroyed 6 miles south of St Catherine's Point, Isle of Wight. The port engine was seen to catch fire and later a bright glow was seen on the sea.

A claim was made by F/O K A Roediger (RAAF) in a 456 Sqn Mosquito at 05.16 hrs for a Ju188 destroyed off Portsmouth at 18,000 ft. The starboard engine blew up and the aircraft fell in flames on its back.

A claim was made by F/O G R Houston (RAAF) in a 456 Sqn Mosquito at 04.57 hrs for a Ju88 destroyed off Portsmouth at 23,500 ft. The port engine and wing were in flames and the aircraft disintegrated at 20,000 ft.

A claim was made by F/Lt W R V Lewis (RAAF) in a 456 Sqn Mosquito at 23.57 hrs for a Ju188 destroyed 25 miles south-west of Portsmouth. The port engine exploded with a blinding flash and the Mosquito's windscreen was covered with oil.

26th-27th April 1944

The second Portsmouth raid (26th/27th April) repeated the failure of the previous night at a cost of six crews. British intelligence was little impressed, noting simply:

"On Wednesday/Thursday (26th/27th April) 50 aircraft came overland between the Needles and Worthing, the majority being active in the Portsmouth area."

The only aircraft to fall on land was not connected with the Portsmouth raid; an Me410 'intruder' from Stab/KG51. Leutnant Wolfgang Wenning's aircraft collided with his intended victim, an Airspeed Oxford, and both aircraft crashed in flames near Rugby.

Luftwaffe Losses 26th-27th April 1944

Do217M-1 7/KG2 U5+DR WNr 6253

Failed to return from a sortie to Portsmouth.

Hpmn Fritz Hauptmann (F) (Missing), Uffz Johann Hopf (B) (Missing), Fw Hans Deuerlein (Bf) (Missing), Uffz Gerhard Reichel (Bs) (Missing).

Ju88 8/KG6

Crashed at Cherbourg whilst on operations.

Uffz Rudolf Brunner (F) (Killed), Uffz Gerhard Friedel (B) (Killed), Ogefr Karl Konrad (Bf) (Killed), Gefr Hubert Titzrath (Bs) (Killed).

Ju88 5/KG30 4D+AC WNr 801333

Failed to return from a sortie to Portsmouth.

Uffz Herbert Simma (F) (Killed), Gefr Heinz Lensing (B) (Killed), Uffz Rudi Nitsche (Bf) (Killed), Ogefr Ernst Höfer (Bs) (Killed).

Me 410 A-1 Stab/KG51 9K+ZP WNr 420445

Manor Farm, Frankton, Warwickshire. 04.30 hrs.

During an intruder sortie collided with Airspeed Oxford LX196 flown by P/O Moore, who was killed.

Markings: Z in black outlined yellow. On the base of the tail fin 42 was painted in black and below this on the fuselage 750 in black on a white background. Blue grey on top surfaces, spray painted black on undersurfaces.

Armament: four MG 151/20 and two MG 17 in nose, two MG 131 mounted in barbettes. The two extra MG 151's were mounted in the bomb bay. Two 66 gallon external drop tanks were carried. They were carried on a special mountings fitted with explosive charge for shearing the single retaining bolt, this being the only method of releasing the tank.

Wolfgang Wenning is reputed to have been wearing full mess dress under his flying suit. The wireless operator held the Gold (110) War Flights Badge.

Lt Wolfgang Wenning (F) (Killed CC 3/78), Fw Gustav Delp EKI (Killed CC 3/79).

Ju88 2/KG54 B3+MK WNr 1109

Failed to return from a sortie to Portsmouth.

Fw Werner Reichardt (F) (Missing), Uffz Ulrich Embritz (B) (Missing), Gefr Heinz Richter (Bf) (Missing), Uffz Heinrich Prokscha (Bs) (Missing).

Ju88 2/KG54 B3+BK WNr 301548

Failed to return from a sortie to Portsmouth

Uffz Werner Kretzschmar (F) (Missing), Uffz Lothar Klotz (B) (Missing), Gefr Karl Schäfer (Bf) (Missing), Fhj-Fw Friedrich Leidolf (Bs) (Missing).

He177A-3 2/KG100 6N+HK WNr 2235

Crashed 8 km south-west of Cloys, France, returning from a sortie to Portsmouth.

Hptmn Gustav Heckewerth (St Kp (F) (Killed), Fw Adolf Fischer (B) (Killed), Uffz Alexander Leichenich (Bf) (Killed), Uffz Karl Petermann (Bm) (Killed), Uffz Alfred Reinsberger (Bs) (Inj), Gefr Joseph Steirer (Bs) (Inj).

Fighter Command Claims not attributable to a particular loss

A claim was made by W/Cdr J G Topham in a 125 Sqn Mosquito at 02.00 hrs for a Ju188 destroyed 10 miles south of St Catherine's Point, Isle of Wight.

A claim was made by W/O T S Ecclestone in a 515 Sqn (BC) Mosquito at 03.10 hrs for an enemy aircraft destroyed landing at Le Coulot.

A claim was made by W/O T S Ecclestone in a 515 Sqn (BC) Mosquito at 03.15 hrs for a Ju88 destroyed landing at Brussels-Evre.

28th-29th April 1944

WEEKLY APPRECIATION OF DAMAGE TO KEY POINTS AND PROGRESS OF REPAIRS.

Period from: 09.00 hours Wednesday 26th April
to: 09.00 hours Wednesday 3rd May 1944.

GENERAL.

No appreciable bombing attacks have been made on land targets during the week; most of the activity has had the appearance of reconnaissance and of tentative efforts to probe coastal points where concentrations of shipping were probably suspected. Altogether, about 100 aircraft crossed our coasts during the week, but relatively few of these were engaged in bombing attacks on land-targets. On Wednesday/Thursday (26th/27th April) 50 aircraft came overland between the Needles and Worthing, the majority being active in the Portsmouth area, and on Saturday / Sunday (29th/30th April) 20 aircraft flew over parts of Cornwall and Devon with a minor concentration on Plymouth.

In addition to this activity, hostile aircraft were overland without dropping bombs on Thursday/Friday (27th/28th April) mostly Isle of Wight/Portsmouth/Hayling Island, and on Friday (28th April) at Plymouth.

Civilian casualties for the week total 56 fatal and 45 serious. The G.A.F. is reported to have lost 9 aircraft.

Two Key-points were affected by enemy-action, and in addition there were 3 incidents involving railways and 1 airfield.

Old, Bold Pilots

Six crews from II and III/KG6 were assigned to carry out a variation in terms of *'Steinbock'* operations, namely the dropping of sea-mines in the Channel waters off the Isle of Wight. Each of the five Ju188s and the single Ju88 were loaded with two externally-slung BM1000 weapons. Hauptman Fuchinger (III/KG6 Kommandeur) informed the personnel that the mines were to be released from between 600 and 700 metres at around 00.45 hours over an area marked out by pathfinder aircraft. On no account were any mines to be dropped on land, while strict radio silence was to be maintained.

The Ju88 involved was 3E+DM of 4 Staffel, but it was being flown by Unteroffizier Kachant's 5 Staffel crew. Following take-off commencing 23.00 hours the outward route was flown at low level directly to a turning point near Cherbourg. In Kachant's case he was ahead of time at this stage so he elected to fly a left-hand circuit prior to setting a course of 9 degrees while maintaining a minimum altitude of just 50 metres. Arriving off the Isle of Wight the pilot again found himself ahead of schedule and this time flew a right-hand circuit before climbing to release altitude and successfully carrying out his duty.

The bomber now described a left-hand orbit before being eased down to just above the sea. So far the sortie had gone to plan, but as the sea surface sped past Feldwebel Schmitz, the Bordfunker with over 120 sorties to his credit, expressed his doubts about Kachant holding course at what he later stated was a dangerously low height. Scarcely had he uttered the advice when the bomber literally flew into the water. Amazingly, Schmitz was not only thrown clear, but survived with minor injuries, whereas his three fellow-airmen were killed.

Good fortune further shone upon him when he was subsequently fished out of the sea by an anonymous Naval or merchant vessel and delivered into captivity. No doubt the combination of the pilot's operational inexperience mingled with the heady sense of speed at full power had produced a deadly cocktail that had tragic consequences. The 'Old pilots and bold pilots – but no old, bold pilots' syndrome had found its latest lethal expression here!

Luftwaffe Loss 28th-29th April 1944

Ju88 **3E+DM** **4/KG 6**

In the sea 11½ miles south of Portland Bill. 01.00 hrs.

Left Le Culot in the afternoon and, after making a stop, took off for the purpose of laying mines in the Solent, carrying two BM 1000 mines, one under each wing. Having released the mines, and on the return flight, the pilot flew too low and touched the water. The aircraft sank almost immediately, but the wireless operator managed to get away in his one man dinghy. Fifteen minutes later he hailed a passing Naval vessel and was picked up.

The wireless operator held the Gold (110) War Flights Badge.

Uffz Hans Kachant (F) (Missing), Fw Ulrich Engelhardt (B) (Missing), Fw Heinrich Schmitz EKI (Bf) (PoW injured), Uffz Rudolf Köhler (Bs) (Missing).

29th-30th April 1944

The *'Fritz-X'* Factor

During WWII the Luftwaffe held the advantage in technical issues covering aircraft designs and weapons, at least in a potential, albeit thankfully not often fully realised, manner. Another field in which Germany was dangerously ahead of the Allies lay in guided weapons. The *Fritz-X* was a leading operational example; weighing-in at 1,500 kgs, this armour-piercing bomb developed by a Dr. Kramer from Ruhrstahl AG bore the official nomenclature of PC (Panzer-Cylindrische) 1400X. When released from the recommended altitude of nearly 20,000 feet the bomb was capable of piercing 5 ½ inch armour surfaces.

Plymouth was a key Royal Naval base in which German intelligence understood two Capital ships were currently berthed, one of which was believed to be a King George V-class battleship. III/KG100 with its Do217s was detached from Toulouse/Francazal to Orleans on the morning of 29th April. Such was the haste with which the action was taken that the Gruppe's Erste Warts (chief mechanics) flew in the bombers while the other support staff clambered into a commandeered French Leo 451 and followed on.

The King George V-class warship was briefed as the focus of assault and KG66 crews were to carry out the necessary illumination. This was to take the form of a cross of white flares released on the four cardinal compass-points, the centre of which would (hopefully) reveal the area in which the warships were berthed. In an interesting variation the KG100 crews were also briefed to ignore the red flares that were to be utilised by the other attacking Gruppen. By this stage of *'Steinbock'* any form of morale-raising statement was seemingly in vogue; on this occasion the figure of 400 aircraft was quoted during the briefing as forming the overall attack force! British intelligence sources later estimated the number of attackers as around 70. The crews were specifically ordered to make their target-approach along or at a very fine angle to the vessel's length; no release was to be made in the event of failure to locate the warship.

The outward route was from Orleans to *'Knickebein'* 11 (Morlaix) and using the *'Funkfeuer'* beacon at Rennes as a navigation check. The *'Knickebein'* was aligned over Plymouth. After attacking, the crews would take up a course back to Toulouse via Morlaix and Limoges. Cloud conditions were briefed as 2/10th in intensity but with otherwise clear visibility. The crews were to fly at around 22,000 feet over the Channel before dropping in a shallow glide to 20,000 feet for the attack approach. This rate of descent would be accelerated on the return leg so that the bombers would cross the French coast between 3,000 and 1,500 feet.

Although fifteen crews were now on hand at Orleans, three to five of these, thanks to human or technical failure with their bombers, failed to participate. The others lifted off at 30-second intervals. In view of the specific skill required to handle the launch and accurate aiming of *'Fritz-X'* it is surprising that some crews, including the Gruppenkommandeur, had little or no operational experience in this respect.

The raid failed in its primary purpose thanks to a combination of technical and natural limitations. The clear visibility that was forecast steadily surrendered to a developing haze over the Channel. Then, the marker flares did not burst out until four minutes after the briefed time of around 03.30 hours. This in itself should not have been an insuperable problem for those crews orbiting Plymouth; what did create a real bar to success was the existence of a smoke screen, an issue that had not been raised at the briefing.

Despite the focus on the shipping and the novel weaponry, the people of Plymouth suffered. At Oreston village four men, eleven women and three girls were killed when two shelters were hit by bombs. In Plymouth nine people were killed when the bus depot at Prince Rock received a direct hit.

A Dornier 217K-2 with extended wings capable of carrying the Fritz-X bombs

One bomber that had got through the defences was 6N+IT in Leutnant Palme's charge. He was over the target at 03.30 hours, but at 22,000 feet rather than the briefed altitude of 20,000 feet. Also, the mist conditions precluded the pilot from confirming where he really was although the existence of solid AA and searchlight concentrations provided a reasonable indication. He now carried out a wide turn to port in order to await the arrival of the target marking KG66.

The first flares were recorded at 03.34 hours, but only marked the east-to-west element of the 'cross'. Palme took the initiative of investigating the marked zone on a north-south course, but found that nothing below could be identified; this was as much ascribed to the steadily failing brilliance of the flares and their non-renewal as to the smoke screen. He nevertheless decided to make his bomb-run, but as he was doing so he lost control. AA fire had apparently caused damage to the ailerons, which failed to respond, and Palme promptly gave orders for the *'Fritz-X'* to be jettisoned. Searchlights were now blinding his vision and attempts at regaining control of the aircraft were proving fruitless, so Palme gave the order to bale out. In fact the Do-217 had become the first of Squadron Leader Williams' two victims that night. The bomber finally came down at Blackawton, Devon, along with Unteroffizier Katzenberger, the other three airmen having baled out.

Do217K-3 (6N+AD) from Stab.III/KG100 had the Gruppenkommandeur, Hauptmann Pfeffer aboard. Having been guided to the target by *'Knickebein',* the pilot took evasive action over the Channel. On reaching Plymouth he was forced to make no less than five orbits, during the last of which the Beobachter said he could discern nothing. At 04.05 hours the bomber descended into the waters off Plymouth harbour with its starboard wing ablaze, Squadron Leader Williams' second victim.

Once again the efforts of the *'Steinbock'* crews to even reach a target, let alone attain a measure of destruction upon it, had failed dismally. No vessels in Plymouth were in any way affected by the assault. This was at the cost of four crews, with a 5/KG6 Ju88 and an FW190 from 3/SKG10 also going missing. A further technical failure only arose in the light of the raid's investigation. Despite all that the crews had been told regarding the need to retain their *'Fritz-X'* weapons in the event of their not finding the target, two of the missiles were discovered buried in the ground, but still in a largely intact state. The explosive charges built into the radio control equipment mounted in the tail had served their purpose since little of value was established from this section of the weapons.

Combat Report

Date. April 29/30, 1944

Unit. 406 Squadron R.C.A.F.

Type. Mosquito XII-Mark VIII A.I.

Time of attack. 03.54 and 04.04 hrs.

Place of Attack. Y.26 and Y.15

Weather. Clear, moonlight, visibility good.

Enemy casualties A/Craft. 2 DO.217s destroyed.

General Report

Verdict 30, S/L. D.J. Williams DFC, and F/O. C.J. Kirkpatrick, both Canadian, was scrambled under Exminster control, (F/L. Gott), and sent to orbit beacon where no joy was obtained. A free lance chase to a well illuminated target due south was then made and A.I. contact was obtained at 5 mile range on a violently jinking target. Closing in at Angels 16/ this was identified as a DO. 217 and attack was made at minimum range while the enemy aircraft was still illuminated. Hits were seen on the starboard engine, causing immediate flames to spread and pieces were seen falling off the wing. The aircraft then spun straight in, landing on ground at Y.26 and control reported body found.

The fighter was held illuminated for several minutes and flak was heavy in spite of the pilot's every endeavour to call for douse. This was partly due to the subsequent discovery that Mark II IFF was not working.

During this time a second contact had been held at two miles range to starboard at Angels 11 which was then followed out to sea, jinking violently. This was also identified as a DO. 217 and attack was made at 100 yards with a short burst on the starboard side, the enemy aircraft bursting into flame, turning on its back and crashing into the sea at Y.15, also observed by Verdict 40. No return fire was experienced in either case.

Luftwaffe Losses 29th-30th April 1944

Leo 451 **1/KG2** **WNr 537**

Shot down by an enemy fighter at Chemirie-Charnie, nr Le Mans, France.

Uffz Leo Reith (Wart) (Killed), Uffz Bernard Hundopohl (Wart) Killed).

Ju88 **5/KG6**

Failed to return from a sortie to England.

Believed that claimed by Lt S. I. Kvam (US) in a 406 Sqn Mosquito at 03.10 hrs 40 miles south of Start Point.

Uffz Eberhard Bernsdorf (F) (Missing), Uffz Gerhard Pale (B) (Missing), Ogefr Helmut Groenke (Bf) (Missing), Gefr Hans Schöttler (Bs) (Missing).

Ju88A-4 **9/KG54** **B3+ER**

Failed to return from a sortie to Plymouth.

Uffz Hubert Bach (F) (Missing), Ogefr Rudolf Bohl (Bo) (Missing), Gefr Bernhard Niedurny (Bf) (Missing), Ogefr Erich Karos (Bs) (Missing).

Do217 K-3 **Stab III/KG 100** **6N+AD** **WNr 4701**

In the sea off Plymouth. 04.05 hrs. Shot down by S/Ldr D J Williams DFC.

Took off from Orleans to attack a King George V Class battleship in Plymouth. At the briefing for the attack the crew was told that their target was to be the battleship King George V as well as a 15,000 ton ship, probably a cruiser and other naval units lying in the harbour. Approaching the target the starboard engine burst into flames. The gunner and wireless operator baled out immediately, not waiting for orders from the pilot. The two survivors came ashore in a dinghy at Whitesands and the body of the observer was later washed ashore. Herbert Pfeffer was the Gruppenkommandeur of III/KG 100.

One PC 1400 FX bomb was carried.

Hptm Herbert Pfeffer (F) (Missing), Fw Heinrich Penz (B) (Killed CC 7/78), Uffz Wilhelm Friedrich (Bf) (PoW), Uffz Alfred Pietzsch (Bm) (PoW injured).

Do217 K-3 **9/KG 100** **6N+IT** **WNr 4716**

Pasture Farm, Blackawton, Devon. 03.54 hrs. Shot down by S/Ldr D J Williams DFC in a 406 Sqn Mosquito.

Took off from Orleans to attack a King George V Class battleship in Plymouth. While flying over the Plymouth area at a height of 18,000 ft. the ailerons ceased to function; at this moment the pilot was blinded by a searchlight so that he could not see his instruments and lost control. The aircraft went into a spin, so jettisoned the bomb load armed and the crew baled out. The pilot was certain that no night fighter attacked and assumes that he had been hit by AA fire, although no bursts were felt.

This was the first time a K-3 has been encountered, having a wing span of 80' 6", also carrying one PC 1400 FX bomb.

Markings: 6N+IT, I in yellow, T in black. Call sign RO+YD. The undersurfaces were sky blue and the fuselage and top surfaces a very light blue with light green wavy lines superimposed.

Armament: One PC 1400 FX (Fritz X Radio Controlled) bomb carried. Three twin MG 81, two lateral and one nose gun, single MG 81 position unknown, one MG 131 from dorsal turret, one MG 131 from ventral position. Internal bomb stowage normal but two external carriers ETC 2000/XII D-1 were fitted; these are for carrying FX bombs.

Equipment: Radio consists of FuG 10 P, FuG 16, FuG 101 A, Feilgerät 6, FuBl 2H.

The wireless operator held the Gold Deutches Kreuz and had completed 449 operational flights.

Lt Herbert Palme (F) (PoW), Uffz Erich Katzenberger (B) (Killed CC 7/77), Ofw Edmund Gopp (Bf) (PoW), Ogefr Hans Gerds (Bs) (PoW).

FW 190G-3	**3/SKG10**	**Yellow 6**	**WNr 160609**

Pilot baled out during a non-operational flight, but parachute failed. Crashed at St Brieue, France.

Ofw Hans Rudolf Lüders (Killed).

FW 190A5/U8	**3/SKG10**	**Yellow 2**	**WNr 184488**

Failed to return from a sortie to Plymouth.

Lt Herbert Möller (Missing).

'Fritz-X'

The 'Fritz-X' guided missile was one of two such weapons developed in WWII and used operationally by the Luftwaffe against shipping. The 'Fritz-X' was controlled by tail-mounted spoilers, a feature that was to be common to the entire X-series. Tests of the spoiler equipment were originally carried out by Dr. Kramer in 1938 at the Deutsches Versuchsanstalt für Luftfahrt (DVL) using SC250 bombs.

In 1940 the Reichsluftfahrtministerium (RLM = German Air Ministry) contacted Dr. Kramer and his Ruhrstahl Co. team and selected what it termed the PC1400X, but what the company labelled as X-1, as a candidate for use against shipping, particularly armoured warships

The missile's length of around 11 feet formed a gradually tapering pattern that became parallel-sided in its end section, and appeared in outline to be a scaled-down version of the RAF's late-war 'Tallboy' and 'Grand Slam' aerodynamic bombs. Four centrally-mounted plain cruciform fins placed on the forward section formed the aerodynamic pivotal points for control, while tail-mounted spoilers controlled the pitch and yaw factors, and a second

A Fritz-X bomb mounted underneath a Heinkel 177. One of the first ever guided missiles, it was just another example of how far ahead the Germans were in the field of military technology at the time.

set also in the tail roll-stabilized the missile automatically under the commands of a single gyroscope. The structure built round the four tail fins served as an air-brake ring with a view to limiting the weapon's final velocity. The thick-wall, armour-piercing warhead formed of either cast or forged steel was capable of penetrating up to 5 ½ inches of armour plating when released from 20,000 ft. Two fuses were fitted; the warhead was detonated by a Type AZ 38B electrical micro-delay unit, while a Type AZ80 was installed to destroy the control unit in the event of the missile's failure to explode.

The guidance electronics placed in the tail involved the Kehl/Strassburg system with the receiving antenna built into the tail shroud. A battery provided power for the gyroscope and receiver generators as well as directly supplying all other circuits. Wire-link control was also developed, being designated as Dueren/Detmold (FuG208/238). This took the form of a simple direct-current system, with twin wire transmission lines unwinding from tail-mounted bobbins with a five-mile capacity. This was one more example of just how far the Germans were ahead of the Allies in military technology.

An experimental series of missiles was built and tested in 1942, first in Germany but later at Erprobungsstelle Süd at Foggia in southern Italy where clearer weather conditions were realised. Problems arose particularly with jammed spoilers but subsequent wind-tunnel tests at the DVL solved the issue. Almost half the tested missiles landed directly on their test targets. A further series of tests to determine 'Fritz-X's' operational feasibility was then conducted at Garz/Usedom by a specially formed unit, the Erprobungs und Lehrkommando 21, and by July 1943 the first weapons were being issued to III/KG100 and its Do-217K-2 bombers based at Istres in southern France.

The Italian Naval bases of Genoa and La Spezia contained the bulk of that nation's warship strength at this time and both were well within range of the KG100 crews. Therefore, when on 9th September four Capital ships along with their cruiser and destroyer support steamed southward to surrender to the Allies, III/KG100 took to the air to block their progress. One of the four battleships was the Fleet Flagship *Roma* upon which Feldwebel Degens and his Beobachter focused their attention. The latter airman steered his 'Fritz-X' un-erringly to an impact point on the centre starboard beam of the huge warship. The second 'Fritz-X' was launched and another strike was achieved ahead of the bridge. The vessel slowed to a halt as fire began to rage internally. The flames reached the forward magazine and precipitated an enormous explosion that split the huge warship in two and consumed most of those on board in the process. A second strike was recorded upon *Italia,* but although seriously damaged it avoided the fate of its fellow capital ship and limped on.

Allied landings at Salerno had commenced the same day and the mass of shipping laying off the invasion beaches naturally attracted III/KG100's attention. Although only one Royal Navy destroyer and one cruiser were sunk, damage was inflicted on several other warships. HMS *Warspite* was so badly hit that she had to be towed back to Malta. Also affected to a lesser degree were the US Navy heavy cruisers *Savannah* and *Philadelphia.* The 'Fritz-X' was proving to be rather more than a weapon of nuisance value, but extended operations by day were steadily inhibited thanks to increasing Allied fighter presence. This threat was magnified by the bombers' need to close to minimum distance from the target thanks to the weapon having little or no gliding properties; in addition the crews had to maintain a steady course at a minimum speed with lowered flaps during the launch and delivery sequence in order that the Beobachter's line of sight not be lost, so making the aircraft an easy target if intercepted. 'Fritz-X's' moment of glory was at an end. Although over 1,300 were to be produced up to December 1944 - a total that in itself fell far short of the planned monthly output of 750 - it was never again used operationally in a wholesale manner, the Plymouth raid being an isolated attack.

WEEKLY APPRECIATION OF DAMAGE TO KEY POINTS AND PROGRESS OF REPAIRS.

Period from: 09.00 hours Wednesday 3rd May

to: 09.00 hours Wednesday 10th May 1944.

GENERAL.

During the past week enemy activity has been very slight and confined mainly to reconnaissances, which were flown overland on 6 days and 1 night.

On the night of 5/6th May, machine–gunning occurred at Edinburgh. The following night (6/7th May) two minor bombing incidents occurred in Dorset. During the night of 7/8th May bombs fell at two places in Dorset and at one point in Sussex.

Only 1 serious civilian casualty was caused. No enemy aircraft were destroyed.

Key Points were not affected during the week.

Luftwaffe Losses 3rd to 12th May 1944

Ju88A-4 12/KG54 B3+MZ WNr 141068

3/5/44 Crashed at Erfurt.

Ogefr Maximilian Egger (F) (Killed), Gefr Johann Kristler (Bo) (Killed), Ogefr Fridolin Krüger (Bf) (Killed), Gefr Franz Sturmhöfel (Bs) (Killed).

Ju88A-4 10/KG54 B3+BX WNr 1292

5/5/44 Crashed at Wernigen on a night flight.

Ofhr Heinrich Oto (F) (Killed), Gefr Rolf Lixenfeld (Bo) (Killed), Gefr Franz Träger (Bf) (Killed), Ogefr Erich Tomski (Bs) (Killed).

Ju88 IV/KGr101 WNr 14321

7-8/5/44 Failed to return from a sortie to the Dorset Coast.

RAF intelligence reported 5 hostiles approaching Dorset coast, with 3 making landfall near Kimmeridge. On the previous night anti-personnel bombs were dropped at a camp near Wareham causing service casualties, indicating that this unit used the Dorset coast as a training target.

The cause of this loss cannot be established, but the body of Rudolf Klemans was washed ashore on 11/5/44 and buried at Portland, Dorset.

Fw Karl Brobeil (F) (Missing), Gefr Rudolf Klemans (B) (Killed), Uffz Alfred Lebherz (Bf) (Missing), Uffz Günther Hellberg (Bs) (Missing).

He177A-3	1/KG100	6N+BH	WNr 2294

8/5/44 Crashed at Lechfeld whilst on a non-operational flight.

Lt Helmut Fritsch (F) (Killed), Uffz Eugen Strasser (B) (Killed), Uffz Ifred Backer (Bf) (Inj), Fw Herbert Menge (Bw) (Inj), Uffz Alois Dullinger (Bs) (Inj).

Me410A-1	5/KG51	9K+DN	WNr 420201

11-12/5/44 Shot down by an intruder 2 km north-east of Beauvais.

S/Ldr Harrison of 151 Sqn claimed an aircraft identified as a Ju88 near Beauvais at 01.50hrs which probably relates to this loss. Oblt Klaus Bieber (Killed), FJ Fw Heinz Closken (Killed).

Major Bomber Command Operations

1st to 14th May to 1944

3-4 May	**Mailly-le-Camp-218 killed**	**360 aircraft-42 lost**
10-11 May	**Railway targets*-48 killed**	**506 aircraft-13 lost**

***5 cities in France and Belgium**

14th-15th May 1944

WEEKLY APPRECIATION OF DAMAGE TO KEY POINTS AND PROGRESS OF REPAIRS.

Period from: 09.00 hours Wednesday 10th May

to: 09.00 hours Wednesday 17th May 1944.

GENERAL.

Enemy air-activity against this country shows little change from that during recent weeks; on two nights the number of aircraft overland was provisionally estimated at 80, but on neither was there any discernible effort at a concentrated attack on a land –target. Daylight reconnaissances have been flown at sea but none of these aircraft have made landfall.

On Sunday/ Monday (14th/15th May) 80 aircraft came overland and penetrated parts of Southern and South-Western England. The attack was scattered and ragged. On the following night the same number of aircraft were plotted overland, mostly in the Portsmouth/ Southampton area. On neither night was appreciable harm done.

Total civilian casualties for the week are 23 fatal and 26 serious. The G.A.F. is reported to have lost 21 aircraft (21%).

Destination Bristol

Operation *'Steinbock'* was for all practical purposes over by the end of April 1944. The numbers of bombers dispatched was meagre at best and the selected targets had either been marginally affected or, worse still, left totally unscathed. It was little wonder that the first two weeks of May passed by with no further sorties being launched, but this did not mean that General Pelze's personnel were finally done with attempting to assault southern Britain.

On 14th May the city of Bristol was placed on the briefing maps of the Gruppen assigned to make the latest sortie to that key, but so far untouched, target. As usual when operating from the western end of their operational zone, some units transferred from their normal airfields to more suitable locations. For example, during the previous night ten Ju188A-2s from 7/KG2 and four from 1/KG2 had been transferred from their new airfields at Achmer/Bramsche and Osnabrück/Voerden to Kerlin/Bastard (Lorient) on the French coast; only two crews from 1/KG2 actually completed the move however. The Geschwader's former airfields in Holland occupied by I and II Gruppen had been given up for home bases located within the Osnabrück/Münster region. 7/KG2 was all that was operationally available to III Gruppe, this depletion being due to a recent effective Allied bombing raid on Achmer/Bramsche; crews from the other two Staffeln had transferred to Hesepe where they were converting onto the Ju188. This was an ironic variation on the already intended switch by III/KG2 onto the Junkers design, since it had been accelerated thanks to Allied, rather than Luftwaffe, action!

An interesting aspect of operational procedure was outlined by Major Schönberner to the KG2 Bordfunker; they were advised to constantly 'listen-out' since he said it might be necessary to change the original briefing orders during the sortie. A seed change in the type of ordnance to be used also cropped up here. Incendiaries had formed a sizeable proportion of the overall tonnage in the past. Tonight there would be a total absence of these fire-raising weapons in favour of high explosives; furthermore the crews were told to disregard any fires, on the grounds that they were to be treated as decoys.

The crews of I/KG6 were informed that 150 aircraft would comprise the attacking force, with KG30, KG66 and KG100 further participants. The island of Guernsey was the briefed turning point that would be marked by a cone of four searchlights and reached between 01.00 and 01.15 hours. From there a direct course would be flown to Bristol, with bombing due to commence at 02.15 hours. The return flight would be a reciprocal as far as 50.8N – 02.35W at which point a compass course of 138 degrees would be taken up to bring the aircraft over the French coast at Cap la Hague. Then a new course of 117 degrees would bring the aircraft back to Bretigny.

***'Knickebein'* Stations were in operation as follows;**

Station	Direction	Time
No. 8 (Caen)	332.5T	x-25 to x+10
No. 10 (Cherbourg II)	345.5T	x-30 to x+40
No. 11 (Morlaix)	11.5T	x-30 to x+40

It seems that the perceived effectiveness of this original electronic aid was still regarded as valid by the German authorities, regardless of the scepticism that had been regularly expressed by PoWs under interrogation!

Beams 10 and 11 would intersect over the mouth of the river Wye with 8 and 10 aligned on the target. The former intersection's use to the KG2 crews would appear to have been superfluous since their bomb-runs were to be made directly from south of the target (marked out by red and white flares from I/KG66 bombers) after which the bombers would turn on an immediate reciprocal course, whereas the mouth of the river Wye was located some miles north of Bristol. The presence of *'Knickebein'* would prove completely irrelevant in the light of what transpired….

Gefr. Büttner's wartime grave

Some twenty-five I/KG6 crews were participating from their airfield at Bretigny; their tenure of occupancy at Chievres in Belgium had been ended following an Allied raid on 15th March, after which Melsbroek had been temporarily used until the last few days of that month. One of the crews taking off from Bretigny was Leutnant Wentz's in 3E+LK that lifted off the runway at 00.30 hours. This bomber would have to rely on the dispensing of *'Düppel'* to keep the RAF night fighter 'hounds' off its tail since it was not equipped with tail-warning radar. On crossing the English coast near Portland Bill the bomber was fastened onto by searchlights that proved impossible to shake off despite Wentz's very best efforts at evasive action. This 'moth in the candlelight' scenario proved the prefect guide for a Mosquito whose pilot delivered the first of two attacks from above, during which Unteroffizier Korf (Bordfunker) was mortally wounded. The bomb load was jettisoned and, after a second attack caused the already stricken machine to go into a dive, the four uninjured airmen baled out. Only three survived the descent as Gefreiter Büttner's parachute failed to deploy. One of the bombs jettisoned over Wincanton during the pursuit struck a bank, one of whose staff was killed by the blast.

Gefr. Büttner's aircraft, a Ju188 3E+LK which came down near Temple Combe, Somerset on 15th May 1944.

The wreckage of 3E+LK was found strewn over the Somerset soil at Temple Combe; it was one of three Ju188 A-2s that had been brought down over Britain. In this instance, although somewhat battered by the impact, the airframe was the most intact out of the three and provided investigators with the best detailed evidence of the Junker's variant. Of particular interest was the replacement of BMW801 radial engines by the Jumo213 in-line motor. A further technical amendment involved the dorsal turret; the original electro-hydraulical turret mounted an MG151/20 cannon-calibre weapon had given way to an electrically-powered DL131 unit fitted with an MG131 heavy machine-gun. Also unearthed was a Revi E2A gun-sight that could be adjusted to accommodate the varying ballistic characteristics of each ammunition class – explosive, armour-piercing, etc.

Bristol once again confirmed its 'bogey' reputation as regards Luftwaffe attempts to strike the city because it enjoyed complete immunity from assault. Barely one-third of the quoted number of participating crews (150) mentioned at I/KG6's briefing session had been tracked over England by the defences. The relatively few bombing incidents noted this night were in the region of Southampton and Portsmouth and therefore well off course for the briefed target's position on the Bristol Channel.

Eleven aircraft failed to return, four crashed on land. Two, including Leutnant Wentz's 3E+LK, were almost on track for Bristol, but the remaining pair fell some 30 and 70 miles east of the inward route! This quartet of unfortunate bombers and their crews were shot down inside a 25 minute spell according to the RAF combat reports.

Wentz's bomber had only just crashed when Do-217/U5+MR flown by Oberfähnrich Domschke was coming under attack from Flying Officers Jeffs and Spedding of 488 Squadron. Once again violent evasive action by the German pilot availed him naught as the port engine and wing bore the brunt of the punishment, followed by further strikes on the other wing. The last sight Jeffs reported of the Do217 was of its vertical and precipitate descent; the actual crash was reported by another 488 Squadron pilot just landed back at Zeals about ten miles to the north-east. Shortly before, Jeffs had engaged another bomber identified as a Ju188 according to his combat report. It was possibly Leutnant Wentz's aircraft - last seen descending in a vertical dive with the starboard engine blazing and one crewmember baling out. However, another 488 Squadron pilot, Flight Lieutenant Hall along with Flying Officer Cairns, was credited with this 'kill'.

Also getting in on the scoreboard was Flying Officer McEvoy of 456 Squadron. Having 'scrambled' from Ford at 01.00 hours, the night fighter was heading west-north-west of the Isle of Wight one hour later when GCI advised McEvoy and his navigator Flying Officer Austin of a 'bogey' tracking in from the south. Sure enough, a 'trace' appeared on the radar screen crossing from port to starboard at 18,000 feet and 5 ½ miles range. The aircraft was releasing a constant trail of 'Düppel' and flying a weaving course. U5+HH flown by Feldwebel Mühlberger was visually picked up, but then temporarily lost before being again sighted in a circling manoeuvre. The single burst of gunfire proved sufficient to seal its fate since the starboard engine and a large section of the starboard fuselage disintegrated, throwing a mass of debris in the Mosquito's path. The bomber's flaming remnants struck the ground near the Larkhill artillery range at Netheravon and debris was scattered over several acres; the sole survivor was the pilot.

The Beobachter's logbook from this Ju188 revealed that while training with IV/KG2 between 21st March and 17th April he had completed 83 day and 22 night flying sessions; however the average flight-duration was no more than ¾ hour - an illustration of the constraints now being placed upon Luftwaffe training schedules. A shortage of fuel was also a contributory factor, and this was the state of affairs even before the Allied bombing campaign against Germany's synthetic-production plants was put into operation in mid-May. A further constraint was due to the ever-increasing threat of Allied fighters. This crew for example had been detached to German airfields to practice in relative peace – USAAF fighters permitting! Another KG2 prisoner volunteered the fact that the flow of gunners and Beobachters from the specialist schools had been very slow; in the case of his fellow-specialists, this was in spite of the courses having been reduced from four months to six weeks.

Combat Report

Date: 14/15 May 1944.

Squadron: 488 (N.Z.) Squadron

Type & Mark: Mosquito XIII. Mark VIII. A.I.

Call Sign: Dorval 36.

A/C Letter: "W"

Time Up: 0113 hrs.

Time of Combats: 0148 hrs. and 0204 hrs.

Time Down: 0320 hrs.

Place of Combats: (i) Approximate fix by Operations U0827. (2) Very approximately 15 miles NNW of Orbit "C" U1022.

Weather: Cloudless with slight ground haze.

Enemy Casualties: 1 Ju.88 or 188 destroyed (changed to probably destroyed) 1 Do.217 probably destroyed (changed to destroyed).

General

After take off at 0113 hrs. we received various orders to go over to various controls. Finally I was told to contact Zeals Flying Control and while trying to do this I saw an illuminated target about 3,000 ft. above. We were at 13,000 ft. We climbed after Bandit who was illuminated throughout the chase, although he was taking violent evasive action. Contact was also held throughout. When range was reduced to 700 ft. I identified Bandit as a Ju.88 or 188. At this range I opened fire from dead astern with two bursts of 3 and 1 second respectively. Target was still illuminated. Strikes were observed on port wing and a large explosion seen at port wing root. The starboard engine burst into flames. The A/C appeared to go out of control, one member of the crew was seen to bale out and the machine was last seen going vertically downwards to port, with starboard engine burning. I experienced no return fire. Enemy aircraft reported crashed by R.O.C. at 0156 hrs. at U.0520. F/Sgt Mitchell (Dorval 20) reports …… "control gave a gauntlet of 310 degs. and a visual was obtained of a Ju.88 or 188. As we were closing in, after three or four minutes flying, at 210 or 220 m.p.h. I noticed another friendly A/C a little ahead and above us. We broke slightly away and I saw strikes on the Ju.88's starboard motor. The time was approximately 0146 hrs. The E/A's motor appeared to blow up and the A/C went down in smoke".

A minute after this combat I called Sector Control and gave Canary. The position, as given by them, is U.1022.

I was then told to go over to Longload G.C.I. and go to Orbit "C". Before reaching Orbit "C", I observed another illuminated A/C about 2/3,000 above me. I was at 13,000 ft. I closed target, being helped by my navigator as S/Ls several times momentarily lost target. Finally I closed to 900 ft. and identified the target as a Do.217. The target throughout this chase was taking violent evasive action. From this range I gave a three second burst from dead astern, observing strikes on port engine and wing. The Do.217 then did a violent starboard turn and I got in a short deflection burst, observing a few strikes on the starboard wing. The E/A then turned straight on to his port wing tip and was last seen going vertically down with smoke pouring from its port engine. One S/L from the cone was observed by me to be holding E/A as he went down, until lost to sight underneath me. One burst of return fire was experienced just after my burst, as our S/L's flicked over my A/C.

F/Sgt. Concannon N/R of 488 Squadron, who landed at Zeals at approximately 0148 hrs. observed, after leaving his A/C a few minutes later, an A/C with port engine streaming smoke, and held by one searchlight, hit the ground in a direction between W. and S.W. of Zeals A/D. This was also seen by other Squadron personnel on a visit to Longload G.C.I. Station.

In view of the foregoing, F/O R.G. Jeffs requests that his claim of 1 Do.217 probably destroyed be upgraded to a destroyed.

Information since received from 10 Group confirms that this Do.217 crashed at T.9844.

Pilot: F/O R.G. Jeffs.

Navigator: F/O E. Spedding

Mosquito Loss

Flight Lieutenant Ramsey DFC was piloting his Mosquito out of 264 Squadron's airfield at Hartford Bridge along with his navigator, Flying Officer Edgar DFC. At 02.05 hours he was directed towards a searchlight concentration in which he could discern the outline of a 'bogey' that developed into a Ju188. Four bursts of fire were delivered which prompted Oberleutnant Von Manowarda to jettison his load of 'incendiaries' - presumably the 1/KG6 Staffelkapitän was acting as a 'backer-up' to I/KG66. If so, his bomber was the furthest off-course of the four aircraft brought down, as he was positioned directly north of Portsmouth! Von Manowarda had flown operationally in the Battle of Britain and was later attacked by a night fighter on 24th/25th June 1942 when one of his crew had been killed. His aircraft was attacked again on 4th/5th January 1943 when one of his crew had been injured. This time his luck had run out. The Ju188 was set on fire around the cockpit and inner-starboard wing area, and shortly after the wing broke off. The aircraft tumbled to its fate near Alton, Hampshire, with Von Manowarda and his radio operator the only survivors. When it fell in and around Manor Farm burning rivers of fuel ran down the road and set fire to crops and bushes, lighting up the surrounding area.

No return fire had been seen by Ramsey during the combat but as he gained his final glimpse of his prey from directly above, the Mosquito lurched into what developed into an ever-steeper dive. With the gyro instruments tumbled by the night fighter's wild plunge it was only when Ramsey gained a sight of the ground against the flaming remnants of his victim that he realised just how terminal was the situation facing him and Edgar. He managed to slow his dive after ordering Edgar to bale out, but as the Mosquito was being levelled out 'something broke' and the aircraft went into a spin.

With Edgar appearing to have difficulty in clearing the cockpit via the lower hatch, and therefore blocking Ramsey's chance of exit in that direction, the pilot jettisoned the roof hatch and levered himself out. Despite striking the fin, he still managed to pull his ripcord and float safely to the ground scant seconds later. He released his canopy and ran over to the burning wreck of his Mosquito but saw no trace of Edgar. Sadly the navigator was later found dead, but whether in the aircraft or elsewhere was not confirmed. The entry hatch that also served as a principal means of evacuating the Mosquito in an emergency was small; this fact, coupled with the bulky chest-pack normally used by the crews, could have impeded Edgar's attempt at exiting.

Intelligence Report

Place, Date and Time:

Manor Farm, West Worldham, near Alton, Hants.

(Q.1756). 0215 hours, 15th May 1944.

Type and Marks: Ju.188 (Jumo 213 engines). 3E+MH.

Staffel colour: white.

Unit: 1/K.G.6.

Start and Mission:

According to British sources this aircraft flew over the Portsmouth area on a northerly course at about 15,000 feet and came under heavy A.A. fire. It was then picked up by searchlights and shot down by a night-fighter.

One of the survivors from the aircraft stated that the night-fighter was seen by the crew and the pilot took violent evasive action followed by a steep dive. In spite of this the night-fighter kept contact with its quarry and scored hits with the third burst of fire. The Ju.188 caught fire and broke up immediately; wreckage was scattered over a wide area.

The pilot and W/T operator baled out but both were suffering from burns. Two other members of the crew were found dead in the wreckage and the body of the third, with an unopened parachute, was found nearby.

Morale:

The pilot, Oberleutnant Von Manowarda has been the Staffelkapitän of 1/K.G.6 since late in 1943, when he was transferred from K.G.2. At the time it was reported that although of Viennese origin, he was "more Prussian that the Prussians".

In spite of his injuries he showed high morale and fanatical arrogance; he even gave his religion at "The Führer". The W/T operator, although not so fanatical, showed equally high morale.

Combat Report

Date Night of 14/15th May 1944

Unit 264 Squadron (Madras Presidency)

Type and Mark of Aircraft Mosquito MkXIII. A.I. Mk VIII.

Pilot F/Lt Ramsey DFC **R.O.** F/O Edgar DFC.

Time attack was delivered 02.08 hours

Place of attack Q1657

Weather Clear, starlight, no moon.

Our Casualties - Aircraft One Mosquito MkXIII - Cat 'E'.

Out Casualties - Personnel F/O Edgar DFC - Killed

Enemy Casualties in Air Combat One JU.188 Destroyed

Pilot's Report

I was scrambled from Hartford Bridge at 01.18 hours on the morning of May 15th. I was told to orbit searchlight beacon O at 18000 feet. Shortly after I was told to go to forward orbit 5 at 18000 feet. Whilst on orbit 5 I was gauntlet twice on cones to the S.E. but was told not for me. At 0205 I was asked if I could see candles S.W. 8 miles. I could see large intersection of beams and gauntleted in dive towards intersection, and when 2 miles away saw E/A taking violent evasive action in searchlight beams coming towards me on a N.E. course. I turned to starboard and then turning to port closed in behind; at one mile observer obtained contact. E/A commenced steep diving weave; as I closed in behind I recognised E/A as a JU.88 or 188 by general appearance.

At 300 yards range and at 14000 feet high I opened fire with 10 to 15 degrees angle off, half ring deflection, but no strikes seen. E/A then jettisoned incendiaries. Second burst given with more deflection but no strikes were seen. Third burst given with 2 to 3 rings deflection 30 degrees angle off, at 150 yards range on target still doing diving turns. E/A immediately caught fire in cockpit, wing roots and starboard engine. I tried to drop back without success, and I saw starboard wing of E/A break off at the engine just before I passed over him at 12000 feet approximately. No return fire was seen, possibly owing to target being illuminated. I was now in a very steep dive. The gyro instruments had toppled and the searchlights doused, so I tried to recover on the remaining instruments by easing the stick back. The altimeter continued to show a very rapid loss of height. I then saw the ground by the light of the burning E/A and I was diving vertically down. I gave the order to bale out. I increased the backward pressure on the control column and when about halfway out of the dive something broke. The 'G' stopped, the controls became slack and the R/T dead, the speed dropped off and the aircraft went into a spin. The observer jettisoned the door and appeared to be getting out. For some time he was near the door and I thought that he may have been having difficulty getting his parachute on. As I was very near the ground and there was nothing more I could do, I decided to try to get out of the top hatch which I accomplished successfully after a short struggle. As I left the aircraft I hit the tail. On pulling the ripcord the parachute opened immediately and at the same time I saw the aircraft hit the ground and burst into flames. I landed on the edge of a ploughed field and ran to the crash which was 400 yards away, but I could not see any sign of the observer.

A Mosquito MkXIII similar to the one flown by Ramsey and Edgar on their fateful patrol.

Luftwaffe Losses 14th-15th May 1944

Ju188 A-2 1/KG 2 U5+HH WNr 160089

Greenlands Artillery Range, Larkhill, Wiltshire. 02.00 hrs. Shot down by F/O A S McEvoy (RAAF) in a 456 Sqn Mosquito.

Took off Korlin / Bastard (Lorient) to bomb Bristol Docks and also jam radio transmissions. Attacked by a night fighter en-route to target and blew up, wreckage being scattered over 5 acres of the ranges. Four of the crew were killed, one by a bullet through the head.

Markings: The camouflaged upper surfaces were pale blue with wavy black lines superimposed, the underside was black. Spinners dark green.

Fw Heinz Mühlberger EKI (F) (PoW injured), Ogefr Willi Eberle (B) (Killed CC 2/228), Uffz Artur Krüger (Bf) (Killed CC 2/230), Fw Werner Heinzelmann (Bs) (Killed CC 2/229), Ogefr Ewald Steinbeck (Bs) (Killed CC 2/231).

Do217 K-1 7/KG 2 U5+MR WNr 4410

West Camel, Somerset. 02.30 hrs. Shot down by F/O R G Jeffs in a 488 Sqn Mosquito.

The crew started from Lorient at 00.40 hrs to attack Bristol Docks. It was their first operation. Soon after crossing the coast they were intercepted by a night fighter at 5,500 metres, but evaded. They were then picked up by searchlights and held for 10 minutes. They lost the searchlight by going into a diving turn, but the pilot lost control. Three of the crew baled out and aircraft crashed, being almost totally consumed by fire.

Markings: MR outlined in white. Upper surfaces light blue with wavy black lines superimposed; lower surfaces spray painted black.

Ofrich Hans Domsche (F) (Killed CC 8/48), Uffz Emil Chmielewski (B) (PoW injured), Uffz Waldemar Jungke (Bf) (PoW), Uffz Otto Schott injured (Bs) (PoW).

Do217K-1 7/KG2 U5+BR WNr 4421

Failed to return from a sortie to Bristol.

Uffz Helmut Dahm (F) (Missing), Ogefr Kurt Wepreck (B) (Missing), Ogefr Friedrich Fischer (Bf) (Missing), Ogefr Günther Schiewe (Bs) (Missing).

Do217M-1 7/KG2 U5+FR WNr 4454

Damaged by a night fighter 30 miles south of Torquay during a sortie to Bristol. Believed crashed on return. Possibly engaged by S/Ldr Mansfield in a 68 Sqn Beaufighter.

Uffz Franz Hildebrandt (Bs) (injured). Rest of crew safe.

Do217K-1 7/KG2 U5+DR WNr 6396

Failed to return from a sortie to Bristol.

Uffz Günter Zimmermann (F)(Missing), Ogefr Johann Grabner (B) (Missing), Uffz Heinz Steigemann (Bf) (Missing), Gefr Johannes Priebs (Bs) (Missing).

Ju188 A-2 1/KG 6 3E+MH WNr 180440

Manor Farm, West Worldham, Hampshire. 02.25 hrs. Shot down by F/Lt C M Ramsay DFC in a 264 Sqn Mosquito.

While flying over Portsmouth this aircraft was picked up by a searchlight. Soon after the crew spotted a night fighter and took evasive action including a steep dive, but the Mosquito kept contact and at 16,000 ft. attacked. The aircraft immediately blew up, the wreckage being scattered over a wide area. The Mosquito was in a vertical dive after the attack and the pilot ordered his radio operator to bale out; it then suffered structural failure and went into a spin. F/Lt Ramsay baled out, but his radio operator, F/O Edgar DFC was killed in the crash.

Markings: M outlined in grey, H in black. Call sign BS+TN. The works number 180440 was found on the top of the fin but the number 5050 was painted on the base. The complete aircraft was painted off white, mottled with a very pale grey, a type of camouflage not previously encountered.

Two 1,000 kg bombs were carried under the wing and were found unexploded in the neighbourhood.

Oblt Karl von Manowarda StKp (F) (PoW with burns), Fw Henrich Kaiser (B) (Killed Brookwood, Surrey), Ofw Ernst Fröhlich (Bf) (PoW with burns), Ofw Paul Schmaler (Bs) (Killed Brookwood, Surrey), Fw Horst Wolf (Bs) (Killed Brookwood, Surrey).

Ju188A-2 1/KG6 3E+DH WNr 180441

Failed to return from a sortie to Bristol.

Uffz Gottfried Biedermann (F) (Missing), Uffz Georg Malek (B) (Missing), Uffz Walter Ziener (Bf) (Missing), Fw Karl Hartmeier (Bs) (Missing), Gefr Franz Hense (Bs) (Missing).

Ju188 A-2 2/KG 6 3E+LK WNr 160069

Inwood House, Temple Combe, Somerset. 02.00 hrs. Officially credited to F/Lt J A S Hall, but it was more probably the aircraft claimed by fellow 488 Sqn Mosquito pilot F/O Jeffs.

Took off from Bretigny to bomb Bristol. Picked up by searchlights on crossing the coast at Portland Bill at 17,000 ft. Duppel was dropped in large quantities to confuse searchlights, to little effect. The pilot dropped to 5,500 ft when they were attacked by a night fighter from above. Gunfire killed the wireless operator who was shot through the head, and the pilot jettisoned the bomb load. After a second attack the aircraft went into a steep dive, the remaining crew baled out and the aircraft broke up in the air. The gunner, Gerhard Büttner, was found dead with an un-opened parachute.

One of 3E+LK's Jumo 213 engines lies in a field at Temple Combe. The 'off white with pale grey wavy lines' camouflage is visible on the cowling panels.

Markings: L outlined in red, K outlined in black. Call sign TA+PS. Camouflage, off white with pale grey wavy lines.

Engines: Jumo 213 A, port no. 1021520775, starboard no. 1021520892

Armament: one MG 151/20 turret, one MG 151/20 nose, one MG 131 rear dorsal, twin MG 81 ventral. Bomb stowage consisted of the usual ten 50 kg bomb slips in rear bomb bay and one ETC 1000 carrier under each wing.

Equipment: Kutonase cutter fitted.

Lt Gerhard Wentz EKI (F) (PoW), Uffz Karl Friedrich Fritsch EKII (B) (PoW), Uffz Hilmar Korf EKI (Bf) (Killed Bath, Somerset), Uffz Karl Hoyer EKI (Bs) (PoW), Gefr Gerhard Büttner (Bs) (Killed Bath, Somerset).

Ju188 2/KG6 3E+BK WNr 180436

Failed to return from a sortie to Bristol – possibly shot down.

Uffz Ernst Holst (F) (Missing), Ofw Walther Hielscher (B) (Missing), Uffz Emil Machwart (Bf) (Missing), Uffz Kurt Wienerl (Bs) (Missing), Gefr Siegmund Urban (Bs) (Missing).

Ju188A-2 3/KG6 3E+ML WNr 180411

St Helier, Jersey.

Experienced engine failure over the Channel coast. Apart from the two crew members below it is surmised that the remainder baled out safely.

Fw Hans Pax (F) (Killed), Uffz Heinz Schwöbel (Bf) (Killed).

Ju88 3/KG30 4D+AC WNr 301324

Failed to return from a sortie to Bristol.

Fw Walter Haller (F) (Missing), Gefr Guido Frauscher (B) (Missing), Uffz Hans Ueckermann (Bf) (Missing), Uffz Peter Ostler (Bs) (Missing).

Ju88 5/KG30 4D+BN WNr 550449

Failed to return from a sortie to Bristol.

Lt Walter Bierbrauer (F) (Missing), Oblt Rolf Sellmann (B) (Missing), Uffz Alois Krebs (Bf) (Missing), Uffz Helmut Bierle (Bs) (Missing).

Ju88 1/KG54 B3+NH WNr 0885860

Failed to return from a sortie to Bristol. The pilot, Uffz Drago Verhove, was Croatian. This same crew had landed at Dübendorf, Switzerland, when they ran out of fuel on 21st October 1943 and had been released by the Swiss authorities in March 1944.

Uffz Drago Verhove (F) (Missing), Uffz Heinrich Schümann (Bo) (Missing), Uffz Robert Schneider (Bf) (Missing), Ogefr Georg Fellner (Bs) (Missing).

Fighter Command Claims not attributable to a particular loss

Three claims were submitted by P/O W G Muschett (RCAF) and his operator P/O Hall in a 406 Sqn Beaufighter off Portland Bill:

01.48 hrs. Ju88 at 15,000 ft, starboard engine and fuselage burst into flames, it turned on its back and crashed in flames.

01.51 hrs. Ju88 coned by searchlights, starboard engine caught fire and spread to fuselage burst into flames, it turned on its back and went down in a spiral.

0153 hrs. Ju88 at 17,000 ft, starboard wing and engine hit. Fuselage burst into flames and it span down.

A claim was made by S/Ldr L W G Gill in a 125 Sqn Mosquito for a Ju88 destroyed north of Cherbourg at 02.15 hrs.

A claim was made by F/Lt R C White in a 125 Sqn Mosquito for an Me410 damaged 10 miles north of Portland Bill at 01.55 hrs.

A claim was made by F/Lt H D McNabb in a 406 Sqn Mosquito for a Ju88 probably destroyed 20 miles south-east of Guernsey at 01.20 hrs.

A claim was made by F/Lt H D McNabb in a 406 Sqn Mosquito for an enemy aircraft probably destroyed 20 miles south-east of Guernsey at 02.10 hrs.

A claim was made by W/Cdr R C Fumerton in a 406 Sqn Mosquito for a Ju88 destroyed 20 miles south of Portland Bill at 01.50 hrs.

A claim was made by P/O D J M McConnell in a 406 Sqn Mosquito for a Ju188 destroyed south of the Channel Islands at 03.23 hrs. The port wing and engine caught fire and lit up the sky before it broke up and fell into the sea. The Mosquito's starboard wing was scorched by the heat.

A claim was made by P/O D J M McConnell in a 406 Sqn Mosquito for an He177 probably destroyed south of the Channel Islands at 02.40 hrs.

A claim was made by S/Ldr R A Kipp in a 418 Sqn Mosquito for an He177 destroyed near Mont de Marsan airfield at 01.22 hrs.

A claim was made by F/O D W Arnold in a 456 Sqn Mosquito for a Ju88 destroyed near Medstead at 00.20 hrs.

A claim was made by F/Sgt R W Mitchell in a 488 Sqn Mosquito for a Ju188 damaged near Ilchester at 02.40 hrs.

A claim was made by F/O R M MacDonald in a 604 Sqn Mosquito for a Ju88 damaged north-east of Poole at 02.00 hrs.

A claim was made by F/Sgt J C Surman in a 604 Sqn Mosquito for a Do217 destroyed 20 miles south of the Needles at 02.50 hrs.

The Deserting Messerschmitt Pilot

Intelligence Report

15/5/44 18.57 hrs.

Me 109 G-12 1/Jagdfliegerschule 102 White 22 DG + NR

Herringfleet Hill, nr Lowestoft, Suffolk.

Started from Zerbat at 17.10 hrs with the intention of deserting. The pilot, an Austrian, flying solo circuits and bumps was ordered to make a flight of about one hour. The pilot made his way in cloud via Hanover and Zuider Zee crossing the sea at 30 - 40 ft. climbing to 300 ft. to cross the coast north of Lowestoft. Running short of fuel he attempted a belly landing, but the aircraft crashed into a ravine, hit a tree and broke up. The pilot suffered a broken leg and other injuries. The aircraft had been converted into a two-seater with dual control for blind flying training. One drop tank was carried.

Markings: On side of fuselage 22 DG + NR. Near the tail on the side of the fuselage in 1½" white letters was painted Zerbst T.E.F. 870/71. Duck egg blue underneath with mottled greenish grey upper surfaces. The engine cowlings, spinner and rudder were yellow, the rudder and elevator trimming tabs in red.

Equipment: Neither guns or armour plate was fitted, but the pilot had the normal bullet resistant screen. No radio equipment was carried, neither was there any balloon cable cutter or de-icing system. The petrol tank under the pilot's seat was of metal and not self sealing.

Ofw Karl Winberger (PoW injured).

ADI(k) noted of his interrogation:

"On the face of it, P/W's story that he deserted because of anti-Nazi convictions appears genuine, but it must be borne in mind that he had spent a long and safe period on target towing work and that the decision to desert did not come until his entry into operations as a fighter pilot was imminent. On the other hand desertion from a point so far inside Germany as Zerbst is a dangerous undertaking and would suggest a very firm resolve."

15th-16th May 1944

Fruitless finale

The Luftwaffe's attempts to attack Portsmouth during *'Steinbock'* had proved almost as fruitless as the forays against Hull and Bristol. In spite of this failed version of Robert the Bruce's 'try, try and try again' theory, the crews were again called to a briefing on the evening of the 15th whose focus was centred upon the naval port. As with the previous raid little or nothing in the way of success attended the attacking force. Only one of the aircraft that failed to return came down on English soil; at Medstead in Hampshire. Its loss was later ascribed to an anti-aircraft / night fighter combination. First the Portsmouth's gun batteries reportedly struck Unteroffizier Meyer's Ju88 which staggered on in a northerly direction - an illogical course - with all four men still aboard. Then Flying Officer Arnold with navigator / radar operator Flying Officer Stickley in their Mosquito added the latest 'kill' to 456 Squadron's record by dispatching the Luftwaffe aircraft along with all of the four-man crew.

Flying Officer Arnold later reported to the Intelligence Officer of 456 Squadron. *The target was weaving and peeling off mildly each side at 400 ft it was seen from 10 degrees below astern and slightly to port as a Ju88 or 188 – lower exhaust positions on both engines being noticed. Between 3-400 ft a long burst was given, 5 degrees to port on the same level as the e/a, and strikes were seen on the port engine, followed by an explosion. The e/a dived to port and then to starboard, and F/O Arnold following down, gave a long burst from the same range, seeing further strikes on the starboard engine and a flash. The e/a again dived, this time straight down, and the blip disappeared down off the tube.*

ROC reported and a/c seen in a dive at 0020 which later crashed and burnt out at approximately Q.15. A S/L site (T.G. 1036 at Q0953) reported contacting an e/a flying above cloud at 17,000 ft. When it broke cloud in a dive it was caught and held by several beams. It flattened out and circled and eventually dived steeply, crashing, after dropping its bombs, at Q.104570 (0040). Fragments of either a Ju88 or a Ju 188 covered a wide area.

Luftwaffe Losses 15th-16th May 1944

Ju188	**2/KG2**	**U5+CK**	**WNr 180403**

Failed to return from a sortie to Portsmouth.

Fw Kurt Freigang (F) (Missing), Gefr Wolfgang Jünger (B) (Missing), Uffz Heinrich Druss (Bf) (Missing), Fw Helmut Kraass (Bs) (Missing), Ogefr Bernhard Kaiser (Bs) (Missing).

Do217M-1 7/KG2 U5+LR WNr 6261

Failed to return from a sortie to Portsmouth.

Ofhr Siegfried Radler (F) (Missing), Uffz Rudi Paukstat (B) (Missing), Uffz Josef Klee (Bf) (Missing), Ogefr Otto Postl (Bs) (Missing).

Ju88A-4 7/KG54 B3+AR WNr 141068

Failed to return from a sortie to Portsmouth.

Uffz Bruno Lehrmann (F) (Missing), Gefr Helmut Stolte (Bo) (Missing), Ogefr Werner Plöger (Bf) (Missing), Fw Theo Maar (Bs) (Missing).

Ju88 A-4 9/KG 54 B3+DT WNr 550581

Medstead, Hampshire. 00.25 hrs. Shot down by F/O D W Arnold in a 456 Sqn Mosquito.

Held in searchlights whilst flying at a height of 10,000 ft. and appeared to be in difficulties, having been damaged by AA fire over Portsmouth. Also attacked by a night fighter, the bombs were jettisoned live. It crashed almost vertically into a field and was completely destroyed.

Markings: 'D' outlined in yellow. Some records suggest the individual code letter was 'B'.

Uffz Heinrich Meyer (F) (Killed Brookwood, Surrey), Uffz Karl Hansen (B) (Killed Brookwood, Surrey), Gefr Herbert Steinbrecher (Bf) (Killed Brookwood, Surrey), Ogefr Heinrich Zimmer (Bs) (Killed Brookwood, Surrey).

Fighter Command Claims not attributable to a particular loss

Two claims were made by S/Ldr M J Mansfield in a 68 Sqn Beaufighter for two Do217s destroyed 30 miles off Torquay at 01.24 and 02.14 hrs.

A claim was made by F/Sgt J H Peters in a 68 Sqn Beaufighter for an He111 destroyed over the Channel at 02.00 hrs.

A claim was made by F/O G Wild in a 68 Sqn Beaufighter for a Ju88 destroyed 25 miles south-west of Portland at 02.00 hrs.

A claim was made by S/Ldr P B Elwell in a 264 Sqn Mosquito for an Me410 destroyed 30 miles south of the Isle of Wight at 00.15 hrs.

A claim was made by W/Cdr Maxwell in a 604 Sqn Mosquito for a Ju188 destroyed south-west of the Isle of Wight at 00.25 hrs, confirmed by another crew.

A claim was made by P/O D J McConnell in a 406 Sqn Beaufighter for an He177 destroyed south of Bolt Head, Devon at 00.57 hrs. The port wing and engine were hit and burst into flames. It exploded and pieces hit the Beaufighter. A German dinghy was found in the area the next day.

Major Bomber Command Operations
15th to 31st May to 1944

21-22 May	**Duisburg-124 killed**	**522 aircraft-29 lost**
22-23 May	**Dortmund-360 killed**	**375 aircraft-18 lost**
22-23 May	**Brunswick-0 killed**	**235 aircraft-13 lost**
24-25 May	**Aachen-259 killed**	**442 aircraft-25 lost**
27-28 May	**Bourg-Léopold**	**331 aircraft-10 lost**
24-25 May	**Aachen-167 killed**	**162 aircraft-12 lost**

Non Operational Luftwaffe Losses 16th to 21st May 1944

Ju188E-1	**6/KG2**	**U5+AP**	**WNr 260242**

16/5/44 This aircraft crashed at Vannes whilst on a non-operational flight.

Uffz Kurt Mauser (F) (Inj), Uffz Dietrich Hinrichs (B) (Inj), Ogefr Alfred Wrobel (Bf) (Inj), Ogefr Bernhard Bierwald (Bs) (Inj), Ogefr Alfred Adler (Bs) (Inj).

Ju88 A-4	**5/KG2**	**P1+AP**	**WNr 2570**

21/5/44 Shot down whilst on a non-operationl flight by German AA fire and crashed near Beauvais, France.

Fw Eberhard Trougebrodt (F) (Killed), Uffz Herbert Hornschuch (B) (Killed), Uffz Paul Ranch (Bf) (Killed), Fw Karl Metzner (Bs) (Killed).

22nd-23rd May 1944

The '*Steinbock*' campaign dragged on during May. Portsmouth was again targeted on the 22nd/23rd but with no more success than on the previous sorties. Nine more crews were added to the loss-lists, including the Ju188 of Oberst Rath (Geschwader Kommodore of KG2). The combats all took place far into the Channel and none of the aircraft fell on land.

WEEKLY APPRECIATION OF DAMAGE TO KEY POINTS AND PROGRESS OF REPAIRS.

Period from: 09.00 hours Wednesday 17th May

to: 09.00 hours Wednesday 24th May 1944.

GENERAL.

Enemy air-activity during the last week has continued on the lines stated in recent Weekly Reports. On one night (22/23rd May) a force of about 75 aircraft was engaged in an attack on Portsmouth, but they accomplished almost nothing. The remainder of the activity has been on a small scale.

No aircraft have flown overland by daylight.

On Thursday / Friday (18th/19th May) four aircraft appeared off the North of Scotland. Two made landfall. One at Castletown (Caithness) and the other South East of Inverness. A third was plotted off the Isle of Lewis, and the fourth over Scapa Flow. No bombs were dropped.

On Friday / Saturday (19th/20th May) the Dover area was shelled without effect, both in the early morning and again after midnight.

On Saturday/ Sunday (20th/21st May) a single aircraft made brief landfall, and a minor incident occurred near Dover.

On Sunday/ Monday (21/22nd May) activity was conducted in three phases. Between 2250 and 2338 landfalls were made by single aircraft at Peterhead and Inverness: no bombs were dropped. At 0036 two more landfalls were plotted at Dungeness and a bomb was dropped on Air Ministry property at Kingsworth, causing some service casualties. Between 0300 and 0415 two or three intruders operated over Norfolk and Suffolk: cannon fire of no consequence occurred at Wisbech.

On Monday / Tuesday (22/23rd May) operations were again carried out in three phases. Between 2304 and 2325 single machines were plotted near Dundee and over Perth/ Angus. No bombs were dropped. Shortly before midnight about 75 aircraft flew from France to attack Portsmouth. 60 making landfall. They failed to accomplish anything of note. About 0300 six aircraft, doubtless intruders, appeared over Norfolk and Suffolk.

On Tuesday/Wednesday (23/24th May) enemy coastal batteries shelled the Kent Coast. Two people were killed at Folkestone.

Civilian casualties for the week total six fatal, three missing believed fatal, and two serious. The G.A.F. is known to have lost 6 aircraft (8%).

No Key-Points were affected by enemy action during the week, but 1 railway point and 3 airfields were affected.

Luftwaffe Losses 22nd-23rd May 1944

Ju188E-1 Stab /KG2 U5+AA

Failed to return from a sortie to Portsmouth.

Major Wilhelm Rath (Geschwader Kommodore) (F) (Missing), Lt Gerd Hofmann (B) (Missing), Uffz August Drechsler (Bf), (Missing), Ofw Josef Traut (Bs) (Missing), Uffz Hermann Witt (Bs) (Missing).

Ju88 5/KG6

Failed to return from a sortie to England.

Uffz Hermann Schlichte (F) (Missing), Uffz Bruno Witt (B) (Missing), Uffz Gerhard Baier (Bf) (Missing), Uffz Günther Moos (Bs) (Killed) Body located on 30/5/44 and buried at sea in the Channel by the Royal Navy.

Ju88 3/KG30 4D+EM WNr 300644

Failed to return from a sortie to Portsmouth.

Oblt Alois Klemp (F) (Missing), Uffz Philipp Heinrich (B) (Missing), Fw Helmut Disel (Bf) (Killed), Uffz Erwin Merz (Bs) (Killed).

Ju88 6/KG30 4D+LP WNr 301339

Failed to return from a sortie to Portsmouth.

Oberfahnr Alfred Freu (F) (Missing), Gefr Fritz Dörfel (B) (Missing), Uffz Otto Ullrich (Bf) (Missing), Uffz Robert Sindlinger (Bs) (Missing).

Ju88A-4 8/KG30 4D+AS WNr 550071

Crashed at Villaroche during take off for a sortie to Portsmouth.

Ofw Werner Kebe (F) (Killed), Uffz Werner Grein(B) (Killed), Uffz Karl Mechel (Bf) (Killed), Uffz Bruno Selke (Bs) (Killed).

Ju88A-4 8/KG30 4D+DR WNr 550078

Failed to return from a sortie to Portsmouth.

Uffz Robert Schneider (F) (Killed), Uffz Walter Ueker (B) (Killed), Uffz Rolf Lichtenfels (Bf) (Missing), Gefr Horst Loeffler (Bs) (Missing).

Ju88A-4 7/KG54 B3+BR

Failed to return from a minelaying sortie to Portsmouth.

Uffz Karl-Heinz Möckel (F) (Missing), Gefr Josef Stutenkemper (Bo) (Missing), Gefr Wilhelm Kipp ((Bf) (Missing), Ogefr Adolf Tost (Bs) (Missing).

Ju88A-4 **8/KG54** **B3+BS**

Failed to return from a minelaying sortie to Portsmouth.

Uffz Josef Kretchmer (F) (Missing), Uffz Werner Kottenhagen (Bo) (Missing), Ogefr Heinz Müller (Bf) (Missing), Ogefr Josef Mayer (Bs) (Missing).

Fw190G-3 **3/SKG10** **Yellow 4** **WNr 093**

Failed to return from a sortie to Portsmouth.

Fw Otto Heinrich (Missing).

Fighter Command Claims not attributable to a particular loss

A claim was made by F/O K O'Sullivan in a 125 Sqn Mosquito for a Ju188 destroyed 50 miles south of St Catherine's Point at 00.20 hrs.

A claim was made by F/Lt G F Simcock in a 125 Sqn Mosquito for a Ju88 destroyed 17 miles south of St Catherine's Point at 00.45 hrs.

A claim was made by F/O I W Sanderson (RAAF) in a 456 Sqn Mosquito for a Ju88 destroyed 45 miles south of the Isle of Wight at 00.24 hrs. Both engines were hit and the aircraft was seen to roll onto its back and go down vertically. A piece of the Ju88 was found in the radiator of the Mosquito the following day.

A claim was made by W/Cdr K M Hampshire in a 456 Sqn Mosquito for a Ju88 destroyed 30 miles south of the Isle of Wight at 00.23 hrs.

Luftwaffe Loss 26th May 1944

Ju290 **1/FAG** **9V+GK** **WNr 164**

26/5/44 17.30 hrs. In the Atlantic, 41°33'N, 18°28'W.

Started from Mont de Marsan about 11.00 hrs to shadow an Allied convoy; no bombs carried. Attacked by two Hurricanes at 400 metres, setting the port-inner engine on fire and the aircraft ditched. The large dinghy was holed, so survivors made use of one man dinghies. Later spotted by a biplane, they were picked up by a Naval unit.

1st Pilot: Lt Kurt Nonnenberg (F1) (PoW injured in attack), 2nd pilot: Ofw Hartig (F2) (Killed), Lt Hans Koitka (B) (PoW), Fw Wilhelm Meyer (Bf1) (PoW), Uffz Elies (Bf2) (Killed), Fw Budschelders (Bm) (Killed), Ofw Lohschelders (Bm) (Killed), Fw Herbert Kohler (Bs) (PoW injured), Uffz Hans Baur (Bs rear) (PoW), Uffz Demarteaun (Bs) (Killed).

An unusual loss on the 26th May was a Junkers 290 similar to this one, shot down over the Atlantic by two Hurricanes.

WEEKLY APPRECIATION OF DAMAGE TO KEY POINTS AND PROGRESS OF REPAIRS.

Period from: 09.00 hours Wednesday 24th May

to: 09.00 hours Wednesday 31st May 1944.

GENERAL.

Enemy air-operations against this country have again been directed at night, primarily at ports and coastal points generally, with little achieved in the way of results. Intruder operations have also continued.

On Wednesday/Thursday (24th/25th May) 10 aircraft operated over parts of East Anglia, and 14 off and over the South Coast between Sandwich and Beachy Head and between Selsey Bill and St. Catherines Point. The only incident occurred near Newmarket.

On Saturday/Sunday (27th/28th May) 45 aircraft operated off and over the Dorset coast, mostly in the neighbourhood of Weymouth which was bombed.

On Monday/Tuesday (29th/30th May) about 30 aircraft operated off the South Coast between Worthing and the Isle of Wight, none coming overland: 40/50 operated off the Cornish Coast, the majority perhaps laying mines and 10 attacking Falmouth: and in a third phase 15 aircraft operated off shore between the Needles and Beachy Head, making shallow penetrations. At Falmouth damage was done to Swanvale Oil Installation.

Total civilian casualties for the week are 22 fatal, 6 missing believed fatal, and 30 serious.
The G.A.F. is known to have lost four aircraft (2% of the total operating).
3 Key Points were affected by enemy-action: in addition there were 3 railway incidents and 6 incidents at airfields

28th-29th May 1944

Friend or Foe?

The force dispatched to Torquay lost one crew. At 01.30 hours flares were laid across the bay and another row was dropped over the town, but failed to release from the containers. 39 HE bombs and six SD2 anti-personnel bombs were dropped with mines in the bay. The Bay Court Hotel received a direct hit where several people were killed and injured. The total casualties in the town were 25 killed and 33 injured.

Flight Lieutenant Harvey DSO was airborne from Fairwood Common in a 68 Squadron Beaufighter, with Flight Lieutenant Wynell-Sutherland as his navigator / radar operator. They were vectored by their GCI station Hope Cove onto some 'trade' and closed to 100 yards, directly below their target. They reported, *"We decided the a/c was Ju.188 owing to large wing-span; long pointed wing-tips and also by long tapering tail-plane; length of wing very noticeable. We discussed size of four very large bright red exhausts each side of the engine nacelles (two to each engine). Fighter then dropped back to 250 yds. Astern and gave short burst from below. Target immediately exploded and fell away to starboard leaving a long trail of sparks, and was seen to hit the sea by N.R. We gave 'Murder' and were asked by Hope Cove the type of aircraft which we gave as Ju.188."*

The Beaufighter crew had interrogated the IFF and noted 'Window' being dropped by their prey, as well as making a visual identification. However, a Court of Inquiry concluded that they had brought down a Mosquito of 604 Squadron. The pilot, Flight Lieutenant Harris, baled out and was picked up from the sea by a naval motor launch, but the navigator / radar operator, Sergeant Hopkinson drowned. Post-war research reveals that a Ju188 was indeed lost this night.

On a particularly bad night for Fighter Command, Flying Officer Webbe and Warrant Officer Newman in a 488 Squadron Mosquito brought down two 'enemy aircraft' over Shaftesbury. It soon became clear, however, that they had brought down two Wellingtons from 82 Operational Training Unit returning from a 'Nickel' operation to Nantes; nine of the eleven Canadians aboard the aircraft were killed.

Luftwaffe Losses 28th-29th May 1944

Ju188	2/KG6	3E+BK	WNr 160084

Failed to return from a sortie to Torquay - believed shot down.

Hptmn Erwin Lissat (F) (Missing), Lt Paul Felkl (B) (Missing), Gefr Christian Stuckert (Bf) (Missing), Gefr Werner Kiesewetter (Bs) (Missing), Uffz Werner Rosenberg (Bs) (Missing).

Above left: Gefr Christian Stuckert who went missing in Ju188 3E+BK.
Above right: Wg Cdr Wight-Boycott a Mosquito pilot of 25 Squadron who claimed an Me410 off Cromer.

Me410A-1	6/KG51	9K+KP	WNr 420006

Failed to return from an intruder operation to Cambridgeshire.

Fw Ernst Dietrich (F) (Missing), Uffz Walter Schamnies (Bf) (Missing).

A claim by W/Cdr C. M. Wight-Boycott and F/Sgt Reid in a 25 Sqn Mosquito for an Me410 destroyed east of Cromer, Suffolk, at 03.36 hrs probably relates to this loss. The aircraft was chased at sea level and was hit in the port wing root. It then blew up with a blinding flash and was seen burning on the sea in two pieces.

Me410	5/KG51	9K+AN	WNr 420431

Collided with 9K+EN at Gilze-Rijen on a non-operational flight.

Oblt Helmut Niebler (StKp) (F) (Killed), Fw Otto Recknagel (Bf) (Killed).

Me410	**5/KG51**	**9K+EN**	**WNr 120008**

Collided with 9K+AN at Gilze-Rijen on a non-operational flight.

Uffz Arthur Döhler (F) (Inj), Uffz Hans Obere (Bf) (Inj).

29th-30th May 1944

Only nine of the ten Ju88s from 5/KG6 sent to Falmouth landed back on their airfield.

The small-scale attack struck lucky when a bomb scored a direct hit on tank holding 1,250,000 gallons of petrol and set it alight. Blazing fuel then followed the course of a small stream that threatened to pour a ribbon flame 70 feet high into the village of Swanvale below. After many hours of fighting the fire with water and foam two American soldiers volunteered to drive bulldozers through the flames to dam the stream and save the village. For their actions the soldiers received British Empire Medals. In all 28 pumps, 200 firemen and 500 American troops were involved and finally put out the flames 24 hours later. Bombs were scattered around Falmouth and many buildings damaged; three people were killed and seventeen injured.

Luftwaffe Loss 29th-30th May 1944

Ju88	**5/KG6**

Failed to return from a sortie to Falmouth. The body of Erich Schwarz was buried at sea, 12 miles south of the Isle of Wight by the Royal Navy on 14/7/44.

Lt Kurt Niemayer (F) (Missing), Uffz Arno Mai (B) (Missing), Uffz Josef Benesch (Bf) (Missing), Uffz Erich Schwarz (Bs) (Missing).

A claim was made by F/O B Kneath in a 151 Sqn Mosquito for an aircraft (identified as an He111) destroyed 10 miles south of Falmouth at 00.40 hrs. The port engine blew up and the aircraft dived steeply, emitting flames and debris. It hit the sea with a large explosion.

Luftwaffe Loss 30th May 1944

Ju188F-1	**(F)120**	**A6+RH**	**WNr 280216**

Shot down by F/O Parker and W/O Taylor on 118 Sqn Spitfires in the North Sea during a reconnaissance of Scapa Flow.

Oblt Rolf Wagner (F) (Missing), Hptm Friedrich Heidenreich (B) (Missing), Ofw Bernhard Reichle (Bf) (Missing), Ogefr Horst Weichert (Bf) (Missing), Uffz Alfred Lorberg (Bs) (Missing).

Reasons for failure

If the '*Steinbock*' campaign had been planned to exact any great revenge on Britain for the RAF and American bombing of Germany it must be seen as a failure. Although civilian casualties were caused in the early attacks, operations had little effect on war operations or preparations for the D-Day invasion.

The primary reason for this failure lay in the lack of accuracy of some raids. This can be put down to several factors:-

Inexperienced Crews

A lot of crews were new to combat flying and were over awed by the defences.

The full moon periods were avoided and attacks were started in moonless periods in January, not the best time to introduce new crews. From local reports in the Home Counties it would appear that some crews were dropping their bombs at the first sign of heavy AA and searchlights, or when they believed they were over, or near, London.

Navigation

The Luftwaffe's main force Beobachters (equivalent to RAF navigators) relied on dead reckoning supplemented by navigational aids. Several RAF intelligence reports noted that crews believed that navigational aids were frequently blocked by British counter measures. To rely on dead reckoning accurate winds had to be forecast. After take off the crews made for coastal beacons before setting off for England, if a crew made the coastal beacon correctly on the planned course they would likely accept the wind forecast and carry on as planned. Unless they could pick out exactly where they crossed the English coast, any change to the forecast winds would not be noticed, which could lead to major problems over the UK.

Weather Forecasts

The same wind forecasts would be used to drop the target indicator flares. If the wind was different to forecast the target flares would be laid in the wrong place or dispersed. RAF Bomber Command developed low level checking of target indicators with corrections passed to the Master Bomber. They also laid flares accurately from very low level, a thing not attempted by the Luftwaffe. The interrogation of crews captured after the disastrous London raid on 18th/19th April noted that the wind forecast used by the Luftwaffe was completely wrong.

Decoys

The use of dummy sites and decoys played its part in misleading crews. The Fishponds site near Bristol attracted a number of bombs during the first Bristol Raid.

Civilian Morale

In January 1944 the civilian population of Britain had just commenced its fifth year of full involvement with war and all its on-going and timeless hardships. The first nine months of the 'Phoney War' had provided little or nothing in the way of preparation for the 'Total War' atmosphere that first manifested itself in the latter months of 1940 when the 'Blitzing' of the nation's major cities commenced with almost unremitting ferocity. Inevitably, London became the focal point of the Luftwaffe campaign due to a number of factors. The first was its relative proximity to the Continent coupled with the clear navigational guide provided by the Thames estuary. Although the Capital was a prime industrial target in numerous technical respects, added to this 'legitimate' reason for its selection for assault was the perceived psychological kudos of striking at what was the British Capital; a factor not lost upon the Allied leaders later on in WWII when Berlin became a similar epicentre for attack. 'London can take it' became a propaganda counter-slogan that stood, not only for its embattled citizens, but by extension for all within Britain who were bearing the physical and mental pressures arising from aerial bombardment.

Although the 'Blitz' was finally stopped in mid-1941 there had already developed the insidious, but even more potentially fatal, pressure upon national survival induced by the U-Boat offensive. This time round the fate of the nation lay in the hands of its Naval defenders aided by the RAF and, even prior to Pearl Harbor, by the subtle interventions of the US Navy in establishing a restriction zone within the western Atlantic affecting any hostile act by the Kriegsmarine, regardless of the nationality of the vessels concerned.

Within Britain the ever-increasing rationing of food and clothing only added to the sense of continuing hardship with no sign of ultimate, or even temporary, improvement in sight. 'Dig for Victory', 'Go to It!' and 'Beat the Squander Bug' were typical slogans to be seen on posters and in newspaper advertisements that exhorted individuals to hold out with the promise of better things to come. The question was 'when?'.

The 'Hinge of Fate' as Churchill titled one of the chapters in his post-war memoirs, that encounters such as the Battle of Midway, El Alamein and Operation 'Torch' cast up for the Allied cause's reversing the tide of Fascist conquest was, in turn, the catalyst for hope on the Home Front. Although the U-Boat menace was still to suffer its irreversible decline from mid-1943 onward, the steady influx of US troops and equipment and the visible presence by day of USAAF bombers were further pointers to a future free from the soiling fingers of war.

However heartening the fore-going developments might have been for the British population, these could not disguise the stark fact that, regardless of the massive military build-up as 1944 commenced, the Western Allies were still firmly ensconced on the wrong side of the English Channel. Furthermore, there was no guarantee at all that the projected invasion force would succeed in gaining a foothold on the Continental shoreline, let alone expand into the enemy-controlled hinterland. The tragic fiasco of the 'Reconnaissance in Force' raid upon Dieppe in August 1942 must have concentrated minds wonderfully among Government and senior military circles.

With this key uncertainty constantly gnawing at the minds of the British civilian population, the onset of *'Steinbock'* must have been a nasty culture shock, for Londoners in particular, since it was their Capital that was destined to bear the brunt of the assault. In a statement that aptly summed up the average Londoner's mood of renewed depression between late January and April, a woman reportedly said; "The bombing has caught us at the wrong time – we are war-winter-world weary". It was probably just as well that she and the other Capital dwellers had no inkling of the V-1 offensive planned by the Nazis, otherwise the general state of depression would have been even more pronounced.

The Robot Age beckons

On May 16th General Wilhelm Keitel, Hitler's Chief-of-Staff for the Wehrmacht, issued his Führer's instructions for what was termed the 'long-range bombardment of England'. Although bombers from Luftflotte 3 were to be involved, the primary thrust of the assault would come from twin ground-based sources. The first and more conventional weapon involved the use of specialised long-range artillery, whose shells were confidently expected to be propelled as far as London; in the event these guns never came into service.

A greater threat to southern Britain would be posed by what was technically termed the Flugzeug (FZG) 76, but was to become known and rightly regarded with apprehension as the V-1 *'Flying Bomb'* or *'Doodlebug'*. The ever-resourceful German scientists in concert with the military had been in the forefront of rocket-propulsion experimentation from well before WWII. By now, and despite RAF Bomber Command's attempt to destroy the main experimental plant at Peenemunde on the Baltic in August 1943, the weapon that was about to usher in the age of the un-piloted or electronically-controlled missile was on hand in more than sufficient numbers for the Germans to launch a sustained campaign.

The Pas de Calais region in north-east France would provide the base for the launch-ramps. These efforts were to be supplemented by numbers of He111 bombers adapted to carry single V-1s with the intention of launching these across the North Sea and into the central, western and even extreme northern regions of Britain that could not otherwise be reached from the current ground bases.

Britain's ordeal at the hands of the conventional bomber was effectively over. What lay ahead, especially for the south-east of England, was a frightening but ultimately limited aerial assault delivered by the 'perverted lights' of Nazi Germany's scientists.

The First V1s

The War-time Diary of Miss J. M. Oakman - Chelsea

Tuesday 13th June 1944

03.50 sirens – First alert of the invasion. Odd pop or two from guns. One plane brought down on railway at Victoria Park E.

Thursday 15 June 1944

23.36 sirens. Rocket guns and planes over almost at once. Odd bursts of gunfire throughout the night at intervals – mostly S and NE directions. Cloudy and a drizzle.

Friday 16 June 1944

09.30 all clear. Last burst of gunfire at 9.15. A long raid over 9 hours. The whole raid seemed mysterious especially the plane flying low overhead – it seemed on fire and got caught in the searchlights (At about 3.30 in the morning Mr. Philipousky the pianist told me in a whisper "They are pilotless planes!")

12-13/6/44 04.20 hrs. V1. Pilotless aircraft.

Swanscombe, Kent. R032916.

Landed in an open field, producing a small crater and a wide blast effect.

Considerable quantity of wreckage was recovered, including the motor unit, the main spars and an altitude control, presumably calibrated in metres, reading from 550 to 1000. The remains of a barometric capsule were also found.

12-13/6/44 04.30 hrs. V1. Pilotless aircraft.

Railway bridge, over the junction of Grove Road and Burnside Road, Bethnal Green. L.794014.

The bridge was of steel girder construction and was very badly damaged by blast, two of the tracks being blown into the road below. Blast damage was considerable over a radius of 400 yards.

From the wreckage of this crash the fin and rudder were recovered in reasonable shape and also the sparking plug which is made by Bosch Model W.145 F.1.

12-13/6/44 04.30 hrs. V1. Pilotless aircraft.

Whitemans Green, nr Cuckfield, Sussex. Q.740450.

Crashed into a wheat field forming a very shallow crater, but wide area of blast effect. A farmhouse some 300 yards from the point of impact suffered superficial damage. The wreckage of this aircraft produced parts of the wire wound spheres believed to contain compressed air and also what might have been a clock to control the range.

12-13/6/44 05.07 hrs. V1. Pilotless aircraft.

Crouch, 6 miles east of Sevenoaks, Kent. R.060740.

This aircraft was seen approaching by an eye witness who stated that the sound of the propulsion unit became very irregular, and the aircraft shortly afterwards crashed into a strawberry field, forming a small crater, 4 ft. deep by 6 ft. in diameter, but the blast effect was very severe over a circle having a diameter of 80 yards. Cottages in the neighbourhood, which were protected by woods, were damaged up to a distance of 300 yards. The wreckage of this aircraft was completely disintegrated.

Appendix 1
Luftwaffe Losses in or around the UK
June 1944 to May 1945

2/6/44	**Me 410A-1**	**4/KG51**	**9K+MM**	**WNr 420448**

Shot down by night fighter and crashed at Nouilly, France. Lt Martin Kneis (Inj).

6/6/44	**Me410A-1**	**4/KG51**	**9K+AM**	**WNr 420428**

Shot down by night fighter when landing at St Andre sur L`Eure, France.

Ofw Hermann Bolten (Inj), Fw Wilhelm Lohe (Killed).

7/6/44	**Me410A-1**	**4/KG51**	**9K+IM**	**WNr 420200**

Failed to return from an intruder mission to Raum C.

Uffz Karl-Heinz Mond (Missing), Uffz Hugo Hagel (Missing).

7/6/44	**Me410A-1**	**4/KG51**	**9K+HM**	**WNr 420654**

Failed to return from an intruder mission to Raum C.

Hpmn Werner Dürr (Missing), Fw Walter Heinemann (Missing).

7/6/44	**Me410A-1**	**6/KG51**	**9K+DP**	**WNr 420018**

Failed to return from an intruder mission to Raum C.

Fw Hans Seemann (Missing), Uffz Karl-Heinz Sneffen (Missing).

7-8/6/44

A claim was made by S/Ldr Burke in a 219 Sqn Mosquito for a 'Ju188' destroyed 15 miles east-south-east of Harwich at 23.59 hrs. The aircraft hit the sea and exploded leaving burning wreckage on the surface; confirmed by naval staff at Harwich.

7-8/6/44

A claim was made by F/Lt Greaves DFC for an Me410 destroyed 60 miles off Happisburgh at 00.30 hrs. The port engine was seen to be on fire and another two second burst caused fire to break out in the fuselage. Me 410 then dived steeply and exploded on the sea.

12-13/6/44 Me 410 6/KG 51 9K+HP WNr 20027

03.42 hrs. Choats Manor Way, Barking Marshes, Essex.

Aircraft was flying up the Thames Estuary at 400 ft. when it was engaged by anti aircraft guns. It dived into the ground and burned out after the wireless operator attempted to bale out. It is thought that this crew was spotting the fall of V1s.

Markings: H in black outlined in yellow. The upper surfaces bluish grey, undersurfaces black.

Fw Siegfried Schönberger (F) (Killed CC 1/380), Uffz Kurt Quatfasel EKI (Bf) (Killed CC 1/381).

15/6/44 Me410A-1 5/KG51 9K+GN WNr 420417

Failed to return from an intruder mission to Cambridgeshire.

Uffz Heinrich Ramm (Missing), Uffz Karl Seeland (Missing).

21/6/44 Ju188 F-1 1(F)/120 A6+HH WNr 280608

01.15 hrs. Rothes, Morayshire.

Started Stravanger / Sola. While on a reconnaissance flight hit the top of a hill some 1,200 ft. high and was partially buried in a peat bog with wreckage being widely scattered.

Markings: Very dark green on upper surfaces, duck egg blue on lower. The outer 4 ft. of the under surface of the wings were painted white. Call sign VL+MZ.

Equipment: The standard cameras, one 50 x 30 cms and the other 30 x 30 cms, together with films were recovered. There was also a hand camera, size 12.5 cms in the wreckage.

Fw Friedrich Schanze (F) (Killed Lossiemouth, Morayshire), Oblt Joachim Winne (B) (Killed Lossiemouth, Morayshire), Uffz Werner Stallmann (Bf) (Killed Lossiemouth, Morayshire), Gefr Werner Sebisch (Bs) (Killed Lossiemouth, Morayshire).

23-24/6/44 Ju188 F-1 3(F)/122 F6+JL WNr 281620

00.23 hrs Padley Water, Chillesford, nr Woodbridge, Suffolk.

Started from Soesterberg at 21.00 hrs on a shipping reconnaissance. Shot down by a Mosquito night fighter at 5,000 metres. The wreckage was widely scattered and the front portion burnt out. This was the first German aircraft discovered fitted with night cameras.

Markings: Upper surfaces dark green, lower surfaces sprayed black over light blue.

Only internal bomb stowage was provided and believed that some photo-flash bombs had been jettisoned.

Equipment: FuG 10 P, FuG 16, FuBl 2F, FuG 25 A and FuG 216; rearward looking AI.

The new types of camera were 50 x 30 cms and labeled Nrb and carried works nos. 75 and 77.

The second gunner, Uffz Willi Scheel, was thrown out of aircraft and slightly injured; he had completed 58 operations.

Oblt Hans-Georg Kasper EKI (F) (Killed CC 5/211), Ofw Gunther Hupka EKI (B) (Killed CC 5/212). Uffz Bernhard Morweiser EKI (Bf) (Killed CC 5/210), Ogefr Peter Werkhausen (Bs) (Killed CC 5/209). Uffz Willi Scheel EKI (Bs) (PoW).

East Suffolk Police

Tunstall Station
27th day of June 1944
Superintendent Boreham. M.B.E.

Reference Daily Situation Report

I beg to report that during the alert period on night of 23/24th. June, 1944, at 0028 hours a German aircraft (Junkers 118) [sic] approached the mainland from East to West at approx 22,000 feet, when it was attacked from above by a Mosquito. The Mosquito fired 2 short bursts at the German aircraft when it suddenly lit up in the air. A terrific dive was heard and the plane was then well on fire. Before reaching the ground a brilliant flash was seen, since proved to be caused by flash bombs which the aircraft was carrying. The incident referred to was seen from this station, and 'Snap' report immediately telephoned to P.H.Q. from this station.

As a result of a report from S.c. Pratt of Chillesford later, a further 'Snap' report was telephoned and P.c. Howard accompanied by Dh/Sp. Palmer and S.c. Read visited the scene.

Upon arriving at Padley Waters, Chillesford at map reference M. 825705, a portion of the plane was found burning inside a 'Fir Tree plantation'. This was being dealt with by the Military and N.F.S. Two other minor fires caused through explosion of Flash bombs N.E. of the main fire was also being dealt with.

Upon reconnaissance of area, it was found that the plane had exploded in air and spread over a considerable area. From various parts examined then, it was found to be a German aircraft. Reports to this effect were sent to P.H.Q.

Having identified type of aircraft a search of the area was carried out for members of the crew.

The first body to be discovered was that of Hans Kasper, 20 yards north of the wreck. The police noted, that he had been hit by machine-gun fire, wore and 'Iron Cross' and was assumed to have been the pilot. 80 yards further on a second body was discovered wearing an unopened parachute, but his name could not be ascertained. The following morning Bernhard Morweiser's body was found, again with an unopened parachute.

At 06.00 hours on 24th June an NFS dispatch rider reported that a German airman was in Butley Street and P C Green was dispatched on a motorcycle to 'affect and arrest', after which P C Clark took 22 year old Willi Scheel to Ipswich hospital. Schneel volunteered that information that there had been five men in the aircraft, so the search continued. Two unexploded flash bombs were found and a guard mounted on the wreckage that was scattered from Butley Church for two miles. The tail unit was discovered with 281620 and F6+JL painted on it. Finally that day a used parachute was found at Capel St. Andrew.

The following day, Sunday 25th, the search continued. Three more flash bombs were found and a used parachute harness marked 'Ltn Kasper' at Butley. 300 yards away the canopy was found, folded under a tree. It had been badly torn, the work of a local who had taken some of the parachute silk; P.c. Clarke was told make his enquiries to 'detect the offender'.

Finally, on Monday 26th, Peter Werkhausen's body was found in dense woodland only 250 yards from the main wreckage.

53 years later, in 1997, Willi Scheel returned to the post office at Butley. Scheel had walked 500 yards with two broken ribs to the post office, where he met the postmaster's daughter, Joyce Hazlewood, who took him in and gave him cocoa before P C Green appeared to arrest him. He could speak almost no English and said simply, *"Mosquito – boom, boom, boom – bang, down."* Joyce and Willi were reunited and Joyce recalled, *" All I can remember is someone knocking on the door. My brother said, 'Oooh, there's a German'. I invited him into the kitchen and gave him a drink. He was just a young man who looked very shocked. Anyone would have done the same."*

13/7/44 Ju88 G-1 7/NJG 2 4R+UR WNr 712273

04.25 hrs. Woodbridge aerodrome, Suffolk.

Started from Volkel at 00.15 hrs on a night fighter patrol over a sector of the North Sea off the Dutch coast. Experiencing trouble with radio navigation equipment and wireless transmitter, continued patrol in 10/10ths cloud. After the pilot got lost and flew a reciprocal course and believed himself very near to Berlin, being very low on fuel, spotted an airfield and made a wheels-down landing. Captured by an RAF Sergeant.

The airframe is that of a Ju88 C or R, except that a Ju188 tail had been fitted.

Markings: Call sign GF+XO. The camouflage is duck egg blue on all surfaces with dark grey mottling superimposed on the top surfaces.

Engines: BMW 801 G-2 fitted with VDM, three bladed metal propellers. Port no. 326729, starboard no: 327293.

Armament: The forward firing armament comprised four fixed MG 151/20. These guns are mounted in a large blister, measuring 11' 3" long by 12" deep by 26" wide on the port underside of the fuselage. The breeches are in the forward bomb bay and above them are the ammunition tanks which are estimated to hold 250 rounds each. The rearward firing armament consists of one MG 131 in a manually operated dorsal ring, the ammunition tank designed for holding 500 rounds. There was no bombing equipment on this aircraft.

Equipment: Revi 6 D gunsight fitted for forward armament.

The German AI apparatus, Lichtenstein FuG 220 (model S.N.2.) is fitted. A new installation for homing onto Allied Radar, (eg Monica) is also installed, comprising a receiver and C/R tube indicator designated FuG 227. FuG 25A IFF is fitted.

Communications equipment consisted of FuG 10P with PeGe 6. The pilot's VHF R/T set was an entirely new designation FuG 16ZY. Blind landing equipment FuBl 2F fitted.

Only two of the crew were wearing a parachute and single seater dinghy.

Uffz Hans Mackle (F) (PoW), Ogefr Heinz Olze (Bf) (PoW), Ogefr Hans Mockl (Bs) (PoW).

Ju88G-1 4R+UR which landed in error at Woodbridge on 13th July 1944.

20-21/7/44 Me109 G-6/U-2 1/JG 301 16 + WNr 412951

02.40 hrs. Manston aerodrome, Kent.

After an uneventful Wilde Sau operation over Northern France, made a wheels down landing after pilot thought he was landing at a German airfield and was surprised to find he was in England.

Markings: 16 in white followed by a 2 ft. wide brown band. Call sign NS+FE. Maker mcu. The aircraft was painted grey all over with khaki and blue mottling on the upper surfaces. The spinner was painted alternate black and white spirals.

Engine: DB 605 A-1, works no. 007/07111, maker hsq.

Armament: one MG 151/20 firing through propeller hub, two MG 151/20 in under wing gondolas, two MG 131 over engine.

Equipment. Revi 16 B gunsight. FuG 16Z and FuG 25A wireless fitted. For the first time in a fighter ultra-violet cockpit lighting installed. A 66 gallon jettisonable fuel tank was carried on the fuselage bomb rack.

Pilot: Lt Horst Prenzel (PoW).

20-21/7/44 Me109 G-6 3/JG 301 8+ WNr 163240

02.45 hrs.Manston aerodrome, Kent.

Started from St Dizier at 00.45 hrs on a Wilde Sau operation over Northern France. With radio communications badly jammed and lost in poor visibility, pilot realised he was over England and low on fuel, carried out a wheels down landing but retracted the undercarriage soon after, damaging the propeller blades and underside fittings of the aircraft. The pilot had been awarded the EKII for shooting down a Lancaster on 8-9/7/44.

Markings: 8 in yellow, followed by a 2 ft wide brown band. Call sign RQ+BD. Manufacturer mep. The aircraft was painted grey all over with khaki and blue mottling on the upper surfaces. The spinner was painted alternate black and white spirals.

Engine DB 605 A-1, no. 27204 maker hss.

Pilot: Fw Manfred Gromill (PoW)

10-11/8/44 Mistel 2/KG 101 5T+CK

23.35 hrs. Slade Bottom Farm, Binley, Hampshire.

The lower component of a composite aircraft crashed and exploded. The explosion was so violent that the aircraft was entirely disintegrated, but it was established that the airframe was a Ju88 A-4.

Markings: C in black on yellow is the only marking. Dark green upper surfaces, light green on some lower surfaces. The whole of the undersurface of the mainplane appeared to be yellow.

Engines: Jumo 211 J, fitted with Schwartz wooden propellers.

Armament: Fragments of the warhead were recovered and these were made up of many laminations welded together. The warhead was constructed on the hollow charge principle and it is estimated that its weight was 8,000 lbs, of which 4,000 lbs. was explosive filling. ZC 50 bombs, which are 50 kg practice bombs, were carried in the fuselage bomb bays as ballast.

Equipment: The aircraft is controlled in flight, after it has left the parent machine by means of a three output Ward Leonard converter. A single output Ward Leonard converter was also found and it is possible that this supplies power to the servo operating the throttle lever. A normal Patin master compass and Kurszentrale were found but these are not thought to have been connected with the automatic pilot.

The 'Mistel' was a combination of a fighter and an unmanned bomber, in this case an FW190 on top of a Ju88. The fighter released the bomber, which was packed with explosives, to be guided down towards the intended target.

22-23/8/44 Do217 M 3/KG 2 U5+ WNr 3028

00.20 hrs.Covert Wood, nr Elham, Kent.

The aircraft had been plotted flying an extremely irregular course, continually crossing and re-crossing the English Channel, before it came within range of the Dover guns and was shot down by AA fire at 2,000 ft. The aircraft broke up completely on impact with trees and parts caught fire.

Markings: Mottled grey blue on upper surfaces, black undersurfaces.

Fw Lukas Joosz (F) (Killed Folkestone, Kent) ,Fw Herbert Grzybowski (B) Folkestone, Kent), Ogefr Alfred Korner (Bf) (Killed Folkestone, Kent), Uffz Ernst Schluter (Bs) (Killed Folkestone, Kent).

30/8/44 FW190 A-8 3/U.F.GrW 1 3 + WNr 171747

13.00 hrs. Monkton Road Farm, Birchington, Kent.

The pilot took off 11.30 hrs from Wiesbaden to deliver the aircraft to JG 26 at Brussels / Melsbroek. Due to bad weather the pilot decided instead to fly to England to desert. He flew at 50 ft. via Koblenz, Bonn, Aachen and thence to Brussels. He then made for Ostend and flew at low level across the Channel. The pilot decided to belly land rather than land with the undercarriage down at an airfield in case he was shot down. This was a brand-new aircraft being delivered to its first operational squadron.

Markings: 13 on the rudder in large white figures. Grey green upper surfaces, light blue undersurfaces. Spinner dark green with white spiral.

Engine: BMW 801 Q-2, works number: 332379 Maker jha.

Armament: two MG151/20 in wing roots, two MG131/13 over engine. Provision for fitting one MG151 in each outer wing. One ETC 501/X11A bomb carrier fitted under fuselage, on which drop tank had been carried. There were also switches labeled Gerät 21 for firing 21 cm rockets and jettisoning the tubes.

Equipment: FuG 16 ZY

Pilot: Johannes Kuhn (Dutch Ferry Pilot)*

**Kuhn had flown in the pre-war Dutch airforce and had been shot down on 10th May 1940 in his Douglas DB-8. His injuries prevented him from flying until October 1942, when he applied to join the Luftwaffe. By 1944 he had become a ferry pilot with III/Überführungsgruppe West responsible for delivering aircraft from factories to operational units. On 30th August 1944 he was tasked with delivering one of fourteen FW190 to JG26 at Brussels-Melsbroek; and decided to take the opportunity to desert.*

1-2/9/44 Ju88 Mistel III/KG 66

23.30 hrs. Warsop, Nottinghamshire.

Aircraft flew in very low on a north-north-westerly course and crashed from lack of fuel, landing in a potato field and causing no crater. The explosion, however, leveled off the furrows over a distance of 600 ft. About ¼ mile from point of impact pieces of laminated warhead were found in a corn field that had started to burn.

1/9/44 Ju88 Mistel III/KG 66

23.45 hrs. Hothfield, nr Ashford, Kent.

Aircraft came in low over Ashford with engines running irregularly and crashed on the edge of a potato field, causing a crater 40 ft. across and 12 ft. deep. Remains of ZC.50 cement practice bombs were found, which had been used as ballast.

5/10/44 He111 H-6 8/KG 3 - - + FS

19.30 hrs. In the sea - 50 miles off Great Yarmouth. 52° 55'N, 02° 48' E.

Took off Ahlhorn at 18.00 hrs to attack London with a V1 flying bomb. Flying at a height of 100 metres and at 19.30 hrs the port engine caught fire, so the flying bomb was jettisoned and then the aircraft ditched. The wireless operator was killed in the aircraft. The rest of the crew took to their one man dinghies, but the observer drifted away and was not seen again; the rest being picked up at 14.00 hrs on the 6th.

Uffz Klaus Schulte (F) (PoW), Uffz Toni Schlick (B) (Missing), Uffz Walter Kirchvogel (Bf) (Missing). Uffz Heinz Weber (Bm) (PoW), Ogefr. Heinz Muller (Bs) (PoW).

25/10/44 Ju52 floatplane 2/TG 20 - - + IK

Took off from Trondheim / Hammelvick at 12.30 hrs to desert. Being transferred north, the crew took the opportunity to try to fly to Iceland, but low on fuel and in poor weather they were forced to ditch. They were picked up by a fishing trawler far south of their planned route.

Ofw Heinz-Jakob Murk (F) (PoW), Ogefr Hans Maas (Bf) (PoW).

26/12/44 Me109 G-14 7/JG 77 WNr 463224

15.31 hrs. Dyce airfield, Aberdeenshire.

Eight Me109G-14s took off from Aalborg at about 13.50 hrs on a flight to Stravanger, Norway. This pilot had problems the starting engine and once airborne lost the rest of the formation, so took the opportunity to desert. Instead of following the formation the pilot flew west and at 1,000 metres he reported that the engine had caught fire and he was ditching. He then dropped to 25 metres and flew to Dyce. The pilot attempted a wheels-down landing, but bounced badly, hit a patch of rough boggy heather and overturned.

Markings: Yellow equilateral triangle, 2ft. along base. Sprayed mottled pale blue underneath while the upper surfaces were dull greyish blue. The spinner was painted black with superimposed white spiral.

Engine: DB605 A-1, works number 0206451.

Armament: one MG151/20 firing through propeller hub. Two MG131 fitted over engine, synchronized to fire between propeller blades. FuG 16 ZY, Fug 25-A. Revi 16 B gunsight.

Pilot: Uffz Willi Drude (PoW).

28/12/44 Ju188 D-1 1(F)/120 A6+FH WNr 230443

18.00 hrs.Little Loch Broom, nr Ullapool, Ross and Cromarty, Scotland.

Started from Stravanger / Sola to carry out a photo reconnaissance of Scapa Flow. The crew was lost and trying to get a fix, so the pilot flew up and down the coast, but the starboard engine overheated and caught fire. The port engine started to fail, so the crew baled out. The bordmechaniker, who had flown 75 operations, landed in 2 ft of water in Little Loch Broom.

Uffz Werner Grundmann (F) (Missing), Oblt Werner Neugebauer (B) (Killed CC 3/534), Uffz Heinz Kostner (Bf) (Missing), Uffz Heinz Josaf. (Bm) (PoW).

3-4/3/45	Ju88 G-6	5/NJG 4	3C+KN	WNr 621805

01.37 hrs.Perimeter of Metfield aerodrome, Suffolk.

While trying to shoot down an ATC Liberator, which was coming into land at 300 ft, by flying below on its starboard quarter and using upward firing guns; the pilot misjudged a turn and a wing tip hit the ground. Wreckage was scattered over several fields and burnt out.

Markings: Works number on fin and underneath in 4" high letters V DR.

Armament: four MG151/20 fixed, forward firing in belly fairing, two MG151/20 oblique, upward firing, one MG131 free in dorsal position.

Equipment: FuG 25 A, FuG 350 Zb (Naxos) and SN2 tail warning radar carried.

Ofw Leo Zimmermann (Killed CC 1/299), Ofw Paul Vey (Killed CC 1/296), Uffz Heinz Pitan (Killed CC 1/297), Uffz Hans Wende (Killed CC 1/298).

3-4/3/45.	Ju88 G-6	7/NJG 5	C9+RR	WNr 620397

01.45 hrs Welton, 2½ miles east of Scampton aerodrome, Lincolnshire.

Took off Lubeck / Blankensee. Attacked a car being driven by an Observer Corps official and while diving to attack, the aircraft struck telegraph wires and crashed on top of the car. Both aircraft and car were completely wrecked and wreckage scattered over a wide area.

Markings: Mottled pale blue all over.

Engines: Jumo 213 A-1 engines, nos: 1021521729 maker jfr & 521859.

Armament: four MG 151/20 fixed, forward firing in belly fairing, one MG 131 free in dorsal position.

Equipment: FuG 10 P, FuB1 2F, FuG 101 A, Fug 16 ZY, FuG 220 installed.

Uffz Alfred Altenkirch (Killed Scampton, Lincs), Lt Gaul (Missing), Ofw Werner Nollau (Killed Scampton, Lincs), Uffz Rudolf Scherer (Killed Scampton, Lincs).

3-4/3/45	Ju88 G-6	7/NJG 3	D5+AX	WNr 6215868

01.51 hrs. Elvington airfield, Yorkshire.

The crew had been strafing airfields and any other lights they could see, when the starboard wing of the aircraft hit a tree while attacking a car, continued through a line of trees and burnt out.

Markings: D5 (small) + AX (both black). Undersurface light blue, mottled with white, continuing up the sides of fuselage and fin. Upper surfaces dark blue mottled with grey and white.

Engines: Jumo 213 A-1 with VS 111 wooden propellers. Works number Port 1021523338, Starboard 1021521785 manufactured by jfr.

Armament: four MG 151/20 fixed, forward firing in belly fairing and two MG 151/20 oblique, upward firing fitted.

Equipment: FuG 25 A, FuG 350 Zb (Naxos) and SN2 tail warning radar carried. A type of Lux S flame float was found in the wreckage.

Hptm Johann Dreher RK (F) (Killed CC 8/68), Ofw Hugo Boker (Killed CC 8/72), Fw Gustav Schmitz DK (Bf) (Killed CC 8/67), Fw Martin Bechter (Killed CC 1/73).

2/5/45	Ju188 A-3	9/KG 26	1H+AT	WNr 190335

13.52 hrs. Fraserburgh, Scotland.

This aircraft was flown by a crew of deserters who carried out a wheels-down landing.

Markings: 1H in small black letters, the A and T being normal size painted black whilst the "A" outlined in yellow. Camouflage a greenish-grey on both upper and lower surfaces with white mottling.

Engines: Jumo 213 engines with wooden propellers.

Armament: Twin MG 81 in ventral position, one MG 151 in a hydro-electric dorsal turret and one MG 131 in a hand held dorsal position.

Equipment: FuG 10 P, FuG 16 ZY, Fug 25 A, FuG 200, FuG 101 A fitted.

Pilot: Oblt R Kunze and four passengers (PoW).

The wreckage of Ju88 G-6 C9+RR which hit a car near Scampton on 4th March 1945.

Appendix 2

A.D.I.(K) Report No. 150/1944

On 22nd March 1944 RAF crash investigators found the personal diary of a 2/KG6 Wireless Operator in the wreckage of a Ju188 shot down over London. The following is the official RAF 'K' report relating to this unusual find.

THE FOLLOWING INFORMATION HAS BEEN OBTAINED FROM P/W. AS THE STATEMENTS HAVE NOT YET BEEN VERIFIED, NO MENTION OF THEM SHOULD BE MADE IN INTELLIGENCE SUMMARIES OF COMMANDS OR LOWER FORMATIONS, NOR SHOULD THEY BE ACCEPTED AS FACTS UNTIL COMMENTED ON IN AIR MINISTRY INTELLIGENCE SUMMARIES OR SPECIAL COMMUNICATIONS.

RECENT ACTIVITIES OF 2/K.G.6

1. Amongst the aircraft shot down in the attack on London on the night of March 21/22nd was the Ju.188 3E+EK of 2/K.G.6. Three members of the crew were killed and the sole survivor, the Bordmechaniker, was seriously injured, but the documents recovered included a detailed diary belonging to the dead W/T operator.

2. This diary gives an excellent picture of the activities and movements of 2/K.G.6 since the present series of attacks on this country began, and it affords a classic example of the sort of document which should NOT be taken on an operational flight. A translation of the relevant extracts is given below.

January 21.
First sortie. Take off 19.40hrs from Chievres. Load 2 x AB 1000 and 10 x SD 70. Fw. STREBE failed to start.
Intercom. trouble turned back half-way over Channel. Landing 22.30 hrs at St Dizier. Recognition signal red. Hotel Deutsches Haus.

January 22.
Take off 13.05hrs. Returned to Chievres via Rheims and Laon.

January 24.
Take off at 03.03hrs for Ahlhorn with six aircraft. Landing at 09.40 hrs, fine airfield, quite new.

January 26.
(From the second operation in the early hours of Jan. 22 our Staffelkapitän Oberleut. HASCHKE did not return).

January 28.
As usual after lunch flew circuits with all aircraft, DIEPHOLZ - VECHTA - AHLHORN. Take off 15.35 hrs. Landing 16.00 hrs.

January 29.
At 16.30 hrs briefing for large scale operation against London. A repetition of January 21. Approach from Ahlhorn via beacon Nora marked with Flak star shells (Lichtspucker). Height of attack 6000 metres, over the English coast at 7000 metres; nose down and evasive action. Throw out Düppel a little before the coast and approach night fighters without firing. Twin engine - white - probably Whirlwind (sic).

Fairly considerable Flak from the coast onwards and searchlights under the 10/10ths cloud at 500/1500 metres. Gave no great trouble. Over London itself unbelievably heavy Flak and search lights. Light of fires clearly visible through cloud cover. Searchlights and lamps (sic) - green, red, yellow, and white. Good (target marker) lighting provided by us over the cloud.

No night fighters over London. Saw one aircraft shot down. Our bombs in the target area at 21.00 hrs. Returned flat out on the reciprocal course over the Thames Estuary, then South over Ostend direct home, making good landing (Chievres) as first aircraft home. Take off 19.08 hrs. Landing 21.55 hrs.Uffz. GAFFKE did not return. Our Ju 52 shot down over Aachen (Ofw. KREIDLER), Ofw. STUHR, Fw. ROTHENBERG, Uffz. JÄNISCH, Fw. BINNER, dead. OGefr. MÖLLER injured.

February 4.
Our "Schwarm" at readiness, nothing happened. Preparations for a sortie in the early hours of the morning.

February 4.
"First breakfast" at 00.30 hrs. Operational rations with real coffee. Our new Staffelführer (Leut.L not allowed to take part) he wishes us all good luck. At 01.00 hrs we dressed ourselves up in our Channel outfits, going off at 01.15 hrs for briefing. Oberlt. Von M. is our formation leader. Briefing as usual. Target "Seeschlange" (= London). Take off was to be at 03.55 hours but at 03.45 hrs we were still looking for our "Caesar". We finally found her and were the last to take off at 04.15 hrs in foul weather. Today a second A/G flew for the first time as fifth man.

Seemed fairly unintelligent to me but - thank Heavens - he is only helping out. Load 2 x AB 1000 and 10 Phosphorous H.E (Br.c.50). Ofw. B and Uffz. H fail to start. Ostende (Zange (directional searchlight) and Flak star shells) over sea. First turning point at 4000 metres. First attack by nightfighter noticed by RUDI; we finally curved away from the blighter. Arrived at the coast - Düppel. Over the target at 05.40 hrs. Bombs away at 05.43 hrs. An astonishing amount of Flak today and a number of searchlights coming through the 6-8/10ths clouds. Many fires and explosions. Once a fine bundle of Flak cloudbursts passed us by (damned close!). With all speed out of the muck. We thought we had already come too far and were to the right of the airfield. Then we got an astonishing q.d.m. of 120° and there we were. Everyone circling round the airfield. We wait around and make a smooth landing. The Flak still firing away at night fighters. Report to I.O. and home to bed.

February 5.
Got up at one o`clock with the 10.5cm Flak firing like mad at a single Boeing II flying solemnly at 1800 metres over the airfield. Five men baled out and she flew on. I never saw anything like it at that height before. The squadron scrambled to catch Ps/W and fighters must have finished her off.

February 6.
........Stag party for Major FROMM`s birthday with Hauptmann EICHLER, Hauptmann SCHAID and me. 8 bottles of white Bordeaux and Champagne and then about 40 liqueurs. Very tight, but all under control in the presence of the Gentlemen of the Artillery and their ladies. Played the piano. Just got the train. Then I felt worse than I ever did in my life. Into bed like a sack, snoring like a horse.

February 7.
Up with the most infernal hangover - but not too badly for a really good lunch.

February 9.
Woken at 05.00 hrs. At 6.45 hrs off to the airfield with luggage. Briefing. Moving to Ahlhorn. Take off 08.45 hrs. Landing at 10.00 hrs. As we were landing, two fighters appeared but thank Heavens they flew by. Landing in snow. In the old billet and a miserable lunch. At 02.00 hrs to the airfield and hear that we are to move straight off again. Lets hope it will be to Tours. We shall see how we enjoy flying in a snowstorm. Well! It turned out to be only taxi practice round the airfield but there was a crazy storm. White/ green at take off means "break off".

February 10.
Preparations for a social evening, dinner and afterwards. The dining room full, the whole Gruppe. Herr Major F. With wife and Frau Waldecker (a charming blonde). At first it was fairly solemn. Two Blitz-mädels sat at our table in civilian clothes. Two of the few that turned up. Our pilot came straight over to us also Siegfried. He brought another bottle to add to official ration of cognac. It was then a little more cheerful. Then Leut. KARGE came with his lady and a bottle of Armagnac. The atmosphere improved. Leut. HANZIG also honoured us and LAHL fetched another good bottle of Kerman We spent the rest of the evening drinking and were delighted with an excellent band. We took our ladies to the car about midnight, and went peaceably off to bed. It was quite a good party, but nothing great.

February 11.
Got up at 09.30 hrs. Breakfast. Moved by Staffeln in the afternoon to Chievres. The flight took us low over Brussels and we had great fun shooting up the rooftops.

February 13.
Medical inspection in the morning. Nothing in the afternoon. There is a balloon going up tonight. Leaving at 16.45 hrs. Briefing at 17.00 hrs. Operation Seeschlange with 2 x AB 1000 and 5 Brand C50. It is going to be a big thing again. A combined attack. We are flying. Had to break off twice as the rev counter showed only 2400 but then it reached 2700 and we were off, the last aircraft. In consequence we fly with 1.2 boost and a short cut to the target. Our compass out of order, we strayed returning home on emergency compass and landed at the third attempt. Two 217`s fell down onto the airfield - and then a night fighter came. The devil of a blaze and monster fire work display on the perimeter. Take off 19.30hrs. X (Target) 21.00 hrs. Landing 22.00 hrs.

February 14.
At 05.30 hrs wake up again after three hours sleep. Ready to move, but then again to bed.

February 15.
Lectures in the morning and a lecture in the afternoon on "Sea Rescue" - most interesting. It looks as if there were another balloon going up. We will see what comes of it. Weather seems 10/10ths and perhaps quite favourable. At dinner we are told that the show is called off.

February 18.
Lectures finished at 16.00 hrs followed by bed. Briefing at 18.00 hrs - London. 4 x SC500 - just the same as last time; again the revs drop to 2400 at the take off. Off to the hut by car. This sortie soon reached its undistinguished finish.

February 19.
The whole day at rest and peace. The Kommandeur made a belly-landing. WEBER and the (Staffel) Kapitän landed elsewhere. HOLST had an engine on fire and landed at Melsbroek.

February 20.
Slept in the morning. Lunch. Preparations in the afternoon for a fresh sortie. Lets hope we pull it off this time. We came early to take off and got off without incident at 19.18 hrs. Came to the first control point Rotterdam with searchlight cone and Flak star shells. Came correctly to the turning point - Nora. Then climbing. She is not too good at climbing this time and at 5000 metres she already begins to vibrate. And even at the target we were no higher than 5200 metres. There may have been some icing up or some trouble caused by the newly reduced r.p.m. setting. The devil`s own flak over the target. Heavy medium and light bursts and rocket guns. No night fighters seen. We were once in the searchlights but got out. Fairly considerable searchlight activity. Target marking somewhat late but good. Bombs soon out and away. We saw them explode and hope they took a corner off. Then petrol was short on the return home. Rudi had to pump or we would not have made it.

Coming through the snow clouds and snow we probably passed the airfield without seeing it. After firing off "reds" we came to an airfield "Vitry". A fine large airfield. After landing we went straight to battle H.Q. and were received by the C.O. and local Staffel Kapitän with Cognac. After making our report and drinking a few Cognacs we went off by bus to food - which was good. Broth, roast potatoes, roast meat and red cabbage, lemonade and we went straight to bed and slept well.

February 21.
Woke up at 08.30 hrs and after a good breakfast went off to the airfield. Take off at 12.00 hrs and made a good landing at home. No work in the afternoon.

February 22.
Today there is another balloon going up, but we shall not take part, worse luck. Our pilot has toothache and HOLST is taking our "Caesar". Lets hope he brings her back in one piece. We have the honour of serving dinner.

February 23
Gerd GUDER came to me at 07.00 hrs and asked me to come with him on a workshops test flight. From 09.25- 09.55 hrs in the Kommandeur's aircraft, the AB. The devil of an aircraft. Back at 11.00 hrs. Preparations in the afternoon for another sortie. We are not taking part. The chief is taking the "Caesar" himself. Lets hope it gets back. They rumbled off about 21.00 hrs.... They got back about 02.30 hrs, all crews back and no losses. The Spiess has just come and told me that our Staffel-Führer Leut. L. has been shot down over the airfield and our good old "Caesar" our ship of State, is finished. She is said to be quite burnt out. It`s a pity. We may soon get another. Fw. EDER and Uffz. BRABANT of the crew are in hospital.

February 24.
Orderly Corporal. At midday hear that a balloon is going up again this evening. Our good old "Caesar" was finished off yesterday. The Kommandeur, Uffz. HOLST and Uffz. BRINSCHMITZ scrubbed. SCHMALE already has 9 sorties. Food at 17.15 hrs. We are flying again today. Let`s see what the M.O. says to LAHL`s toothache. We got ready. The M.O. says LAHL can't go so we stay.

February 25.
We wanted to go to Ath this morning but as usual, when we would like to go - Hell / Terrorists have blown up the line again.

February 29.
Woke up at 06.00 hrs. Off at 09.10 hrs. Moving. Take off at 10.20 hrs and land at 11.10 hrs at Dreux. Then lunch. It was the devil`s own hedge hopping with Ofw. SPRINGER and Uffz. WEISELSTEIN. Rest in the afternoon. Shave and wash. The evening meal at 17.00 hrs. A balloon is said to be going up..? It can`t be bad if its against some other dungheap and not against London. Briefing by the "Pippin" who told us of the loss of the Kommandeur Major FURHOP and of Uffz. MEIER. Attack on Plymouth. As he is giving landing and take off instructions, a telephone call comes through from BOHNAU "operation called off".

March 1.
Got up at 08.30 hrs. Washed, breakfast and then for a little morning walk to Dreux. Lunch. Hptmn THÜRNER (Staffelkapitän of 6/K.G.6) arrived as our new Kommandeur. Not allowed out of camp. Something happening in the second half of the night. Off at 22.40 hrs. Briefing.
At 23.00hrs, "new target" beginning with "L". We again as the only ones with 4 x 500 SC and 10 x 50 BC last to take off with the tired GK. We try to start, 1,........2,..........10, nothing - Hell - the dog just will not come. One engine starts up, there is not a sound from the other. In the end the others have all

gone - 10 of them - and we are still there. At last we taxi to the take off, get a red in front and stay put. We are not allowed off. It might have been done but Tommy is already flying over us, so we miss another good sortie. We go home, sleep for three hours and get up at six again.

March 2.
Up and away at the crack of dawn. Take off 07.30 hrs, a good landing at Chievres at 08.20 hrs. GUDER comes after us from Melsbroek and SCHMALE from Le Culot. We are told in the afternoon that there is a sortie this evening. We are flying with LOMMEL`S LK. Briefing at 01.30 hrs. It was to be a coastal target, and there we are, all keen types when "185" comes through. It is a long while since I have been so angry about anything.

March 3.
Tight again this evening and that after a couple of bottles of Anice Martini - that gets you down. Ghastly......It was a party with the "Houschrecken" and Uffz WEBER who are posted to 1/ K.G.66 w.e.f. today as Beleuchter.

March 5.
Today the funeral of our old Kommandeur and of Uffz MEIER`S crew. Certainly one of the worst losses our Gruppe has had. Once again Orderly Corporal with RUDI; we shall survive the night. I see that the C.O. has had a mail inspection. My letter to Father was opened.

March 10.
A cheerful evening with our "Long" LAHL. Played Skat till 2 in the morning, drinking champagne, Kirschwasser, Turks Blood, and red wine. A really good evening. In spite of all good intentions quite satisfactorily drunk.

March 11.
Up at 09.00 hrs for briefing, with the Devil`s own head after four hours sleep. The Gruppe was to go to Ahlhorn, but nothing came of it and we only had a lecture about it - from the Kommandeur. In the evening JURTZ came with his guitar and WITICH came as guest. We emptied a good old bottle of Liqueur.....noticed that the whole Schloss was drunk (SCHMALE, LOMMEL etc). Farewells and arrivals of Technical personnel.

March 13.
...........at 17.30hrs the evening meal, away at 18.00 hrs. There was to be a sortie against London with a "new target" Today we were to fly for the first time with the "Marie".
The Kommandeur Hpt. THURNER arrived from Geschwader H.Q. - "185". We returned home for a pleasant evening. LAHL came to us and played Skat.

March 14.
Rest ordered for today, it looks as if something were happening again. 17.15 hrs dinner. 18.00 hrs leave for briefing conference at 18.30 hrs. At last it has worked. Take off 60 minutes late at 21.15 hrs for the first time with the MK. She is not too bad. The engines good. Then came the crazy approach first out to sea on the Norwich-Rotterdam level; from there in the direction of Cambridge; then turning point to London. From there to Calais - Le Havre and home. Bomb load 2 x AB 1000 and 10 B.r.C.50. Approach height 6500 metres, over target 5000 metres. One night fighter between Cambridge and London. Amazingly powerful searchlights and ground marking for night fighters in the Northern area of the approach i.e. Cambridge - Ipswich - Norwich. Colossal rocket flak over the target. Some heavy flak; on the return flight more rockets and search lights.

Approach - clear 3/10ths. Target and return flight 8/10ths, 10/10ths. q.b.b. 300-1500 metres. On coming through the clouds we see an airfield and land. In spite of failure of the approach lighting and artificial horizons. We taxi to the lights and see that we are in Abbeville on our course, half an hour from our own airfield. Two Ju.88 crews of K.G.30 from Germany arrive and one Dornier 217 makes a crash landing. Report to I.O., then to the Mess a good meal, and bed.

March 15.
Wake up at 06.00 hrs. Breakfast. Take off at 08.00 hrs. For a long time starboard engine wouldn’t start. In spite of MYO (warning) landed ½ hour later. No fighters. Flak hits from last night in fuselage and propeller. We drive home and the Alert sounds just as we are about to eat. Our friends make a fair mess of the airfield. Hell`s own carpet. In the Mess they say that the Repair Shops have had it, and the aircraft RK. There is no trace of our ship the MK, for she is standing in the middle of the mess and the burning wood behind the Chateau de Bauffe.

March 16.
This morning we are said to be moving - where?

March 17.
Start packing up at midday. We fly the BK.

March 18.
We got away in the morning..........to Melsbroek, off to a good lunch. The whole afternoon standing by our aircraft and luggage about the airfield. A real mess up. We wait to see the aircraft loaded up and for the briefing at 18.00 hrs. All is ready when the show is called off. We got to our new home as it was getting dark.

March 19.
At last all the luggage comes. I shall not unpack much. There`s an operation in the evening. 18.00 hrs briefing. Drove there in a bus. 13 crews with Kommandeur and all the Staffelkapitäne. Today we go to Hull. Nora. Son turning point - Hull. Take off at 19.48 hrs. Attack between 22.00 and 22.12 hrs. Approach at low level over Holland and then quite low over the sea to the climbing point. Climbing then with 1.2 boost over the turning point (well marked but too far to the left) about 4000 metres. Knickebein was further to the right. In this way we got to the coast too early, south of Hull somewhat North of the Wash. Here we stooged around, searched for by a thousand searchlights, using up valuable fuel until at 10 minutes after zero hour the lighting was laid over Hull. We see it far away to the right and fly off to 33 (sic) for the bombing run. We were the last to drop our load into the town which was burning at every corner. Out of 2900 litres of fuel we have now only 800 litres left and must make for home. Direct to Nora and through flying at most economical speed still had 500-600 litres. Made a good landing at home at 23.47 hrs.

March 20.
Got up at 10.00 hrs. Lunch at 12.00 hrs. Packing up for the move in the evening.

March 21.
Slept until 09.00 hrs.......then loaded up....packed hand luggage and bedding for possible operation. Prepare for another night in the monastery in Zawernden (?). The others go off by train. We care to go to Couvron by aircraft after one more sortie (our sixth).

Losses
3. The following losses were listed at various places in the diary; some of them appear in the text reproduced above, but none has been given in a previous A.D.I. (K) report

January 21/22 (second sortie)	Pt	Oberleutnant HASCHKE	MIA
	Obs.	Unteroffizier CHOBOT	"
	W/T	Unteroffizier KOCH	"
	A/G	Feldwebel FÜRCH	"
January 29/30		Unteroffizier GAFFKE	MIA
		Unteroffizier DAMASCHKE	"
		Gefreiter DIETRICH	"
		Gefreiter BERGER	"

February 3/4	Feldwebel WINTER ? EHRHARDT ? DYLANDER ? OTTENJAMS	MIA " " "
February 3/4	Leutnant OSTENDORF ? GÖTTE	MIA "
February 23/24	B3+CK shot down over Chievres Leutnant L...........(Staffelführer) Feldwebel EDER (wounded) Feldwebel BRABANT (wounded) A.N. other	
February 29 (move to Dreux)	Major FURHOP (Gruppenkommandeur) SCHUBERT EICHSCHMID RENFELD Unteroffizier MEIER BRAUTIGAM ZIMMER	

4. It seems clear from the diary that these two losses on February 29th occurred during the flight from Chievres to Dreux, which took place between 10.20 and 11.10 hrs. On that morning Typhoons claimed two Ju. 88`s destroyed west of Cambrai.

(on test flight?) Oberleutnant HEILBRONNER (Technical Officer)
2 Mechanics

S.D Felkin

Wing Commander

Appendix 3

RAF Intelligence summary of bombing

21st January 1944

Between 20.40 hours and 22.09 hours an attack was made by 57 aircraft which flew in over the east coast and operated mainly in south-east England, Essex and Greater London, 13 penetrated to Greater London.

Between 04.13 and 05.45 hours an attack by 40 enemy aircraft flew over the same area. Eleven aircraft penetrated to Greater London.

Casualties; 11 killed, 163 seriously injured.

Damage Reports:

Berkshire:

Maidenhead – IB.

Pinkneys - Green 2 IBENs.

Buckinghamshire:

Beaconsfield – AA.

Iver – UXB.

Cambridgeshire:

Soham – HE.

Stow Fen - 8 HE.

Essex:

Dagenham – HE, slight damage to the Union Cable Co. UXB, Factory evacuated.

Gt Warley – HE and IB.

Kelvedon – 2 UXB.

Little Camfield – HE road blocked.

North Ockenden – 3 HE. 2 HE severely damaged a Hall, church, rectory, public house, 2 shops and 40 houses.

Purfleet - HE in river, SD to Thames Mills Ltd. 1 seriously injured

Tilbury - IB London Dock Co, Tilbury Works. UXB road blocked.
Romford – IB, serious fire in brewery, 1 killed, 1 seriously injured.
South Hornchurch – HE, 200 homes damaged. Casualties 2 seriously injured, 20 injured.
Rainham – IB Junior school gutted. 5 seriously injured 5 injured.
Waltham Holy Cross – HE.

Greater London:
Total casualties in Greater London area: 4 killed, 74 seriously injured, 73 injured.
Battersea – AA shells Nine Elms goods yard. SD to trucks.
Barking – HE and IB.
Beckenham – IB. 2 UXB on railway property. Traffic suspended between Shortlands and Beckenham Junction.
Bexley – IB and AA shells. Communications between Bexley control and depot interrupted. Rest centre opened. Damage to houses. 3 casualties.
Camberwell – AA shells, 1 casualty.
Chelsea – UXB.
Crayford – HE, damage to gas main by UXB. Rest centre opened.
Ealing – HE, 3 UXB.
Enfield – UXB, goodsline interrupted.

Greenwich – 2 HE, serious damage to houses. Casualties, some trapped. Railway line damaged.
Heston – UXB, fractured water main, 10 houses evacuated.
Hendon – HE.
Ilford – HE and IB, water main damaged.
Lambeth – IB County Hall and Westminster Bridge. Slight fire St Thomas's Hospital. 1 casualty.
Lewisham – IB.
Penge – 1 casualty by AA shell. IB and IBENs. Gas main and electricity cables damaged.
Poplar – IB Fire at PLA canteen. 2 UXB in coal wharf. LMS line blocked. High Street closed by UXB.
Rottenden – 6 UXB.
Sidcup – 7 HE and IB, gas main damaged.
Wandsworth IB.

Wembley – Machine-gun fire, 1 casualty. IBENs, 2 UXB, 8 seriously injured.
Westminster – NFS station damaged, 2 casualties.
West Ham – HE, LNER track damaged. 2 seriously injured and 2 injured by AA shells. 6 UXB.
Woolwich – 2 HE and IB, 1 casualty. Gas main on fire.

Hants:
Alton – 3 HE.
Bordon – 2 HE.
Isle of Wight – 2 UXB.
Lymington – Damage by AA shells.

Hertfordshire:
Potters Bar – 350 IB on LNER cutting at Stony Hill.

Kent:
Appledore – HE and IB.
Ash – 10 HE.
Bromley – HE and IB.
Canterbury – 2 houses, a fruit warehouse, a garage destroyed. St Dunstan's Church damaged.
Challock – 4 HE, 500 IB.
Chart Sutton – IB, no damage.
Chiddingstone – IB.
Chilham – HE and IB.
Cranbrook – IB.
Cudham – 2 HE.
Darenth - 15 HE.
Dartford – HE and IB. 1 HE on Bexley Mental Hospital – direct hit on ward – 13 killed, 3 seriously injured, 10 injured.
Dover – 4 HE. 2 UXB. IB. 19 houses destroyed, 2 killed, 2 seriously injured.
Erith – 2 HE, Fire Station destroyed. Wing of town hall destroyed. 1 seriously injured, 6 injured.
Eyneford – IB.
Farningham – IB.
Faversham – HE.
Framfield – IB.

Goudhurst HE, 1 UXB.

Gravesend – IB. 13 HE, 1 UXB. 1 seriously injured.

Gillingham – AA shells.

Halstead HE, IB.

Hawkinge – 1 HE.

Hoo – 2 HE.

Horton Kingley – 1 HE.

Hythe – 3 HE.

Igtham – IB.

Kingsdown – 3 HE.

Littleholm Dallington 3 HE, IB.

Longfield – IB.

Lympne - 3 HE, water main damaged.

Meopham - IB.

Northfleet – HE.

Old Romney – 3 UXB.

Orpington – 3 UXB.

Pembury – 3 HE.

Rochester – 2 seriously injured by AA shells and IB.

Saltwood – IB.

Sevenoaks – IB.

Southfleet – IB.

Sheerness – IB.

Shoreham – HE. 3 killed.

Suttome at Home – 3 HE road blocked, gas main damaged.

Stone – 4 HE electrical cables damaged.

Tunbridge Wells IB.

Upchurch – 4 UXB, 33 evacuated.

Wateringbury – IB

Willington HE and IB.

Surrey:

Banstead – Gas main damaged.

Caterham – IB.

Coulsdon – 2 HE and IB.

Effingham – HE and IB.

Esher – AA shells, casualties.

Haslemere – Enemy aircraft crashed and caused fires.

Godstone – HE, UX IBENs. 1 killed.

Leatherhead – IB.

Limpsfield – IB.

Tandridge – HE.

Thursley – HE.

Sussex:

Balcombe – UXB.

Bexhill – UXB on railway line.

Burlcombe – IB.

Biddingham – 4 HE, 3 casualties.

Cotsfield – IB.

Crowhurst – IB.

Dallington – HE and IB.

Crowhurst – IB.

East Grinsted – HE.

East Hoathley – 1 killed.

Forest Row – HE.

Frinton – IB.

Glynde – 2 HE. UXB on railway – traffic on down line suspended.

Guestling – HE and IB.

Lewis – 2 HE.

Lower Beeding – 1 HE, 3 UXB.

Appendix 5
Fighter Command night fighter casualties
January to May 1944

3 January	**Mosquito VI**	**LR268**	**148 Sqn.**

Lost on an intruder sortie to Diepholz.
F/O JE McGrath (P) (Killed), F/O D C Bissell (N) (Killed).

10 January	**Mosquito VI**	**HJ784**	**605 Sqn.**

Lost on an intruder sortie to Schipol.
F/Sgt R G Aldworth (P) (Killed), P/O K J Malcair (N) (Killed).

13 January	**Beaufighter VI**	**MM918**	**409 Sqn.**

Crashed near Wisbech.
F/O West (P) (Safe), F/O H J Kirton (N) (Killed).

28 January	**Mosquito NFXII**	**HK122**	**85 Sqn.**

Abandoned off Dungeness after engine caught fire.
S/Lt J A T Parker RNVR (P) (Killed), S/Lt T H Blundell RNVR (N) (Killed).

28 January	**Mosquito VI**	**HJ722**	**418 Sqn.**

Lost on an intruder sortie to Vechta.
F/Lt T E Dubroy (P) (Killed), F/O F W D Haynes (N) (Killed).

8 February	**Mosquito NFXIII**	**HK374**	**85 Sqn.**

Collided with Wellington LN185 off Beachy Head.
F/Lt A Woods (P) (Killed), Lt J O R Bugge (N) (Killed).

10 February	**Mosquito VI**	**HJ715**	**418 Sqn.**

Crashed shortly after take off near Ford, Sussex.
F/Lt A L Sanagan (P) (Killed), P/O P Aiggle (N) (Killed).

13 February	**Mosquito NFXIII**	**HK429**	**410 Sqn.**

Damaged after combat with a Ju88 off Clacton, Essex.
F/O R D Schultz (P) (Safe), F/Lt V Williams (N) (Safe).

21 February	**Mosquito NFXIII**	**HK367**	**488 Sqn.**

Crashed near Bradwell Bay, Essex.
P/O T R Riwai (P) (Killed), F/Sgt I Clark (N) (Killed).

21 February	**Mosquito VI**	**HX968**	**605 Sqn.**

Lost on an intruder sortie to Dinard and crashed near Cherbourg.
F/Lt R C Pickering (P) (Killed), F/O E J Edwards (N) (Killed).

22 February	**Mosquito NFXIII**	**HK371**	**29 Sqn.**

Lost on a patrol over the Channel.
W/Cdr R E X Mack (P) (Killed), F/Lt B C Townsin (N) (Killed).

2 March	**Mosquito NFXIII**	**HK377**	**151 Sqn.**

Damaged by pieces from an He177 that had been shot down.
W/Cdr G H Goodman (P) (Safe), F/O W F E Thomas (N) (Inj).

9 March	**Mosquito VI**	**LR270**	**418 Sqn.**

Lost on an intruder sortie to Avranches.
W/Cdr R J Bennell (P) (Killed), F/O F Shield (N) (Killed).

19 March	**Mosquito NFXII**	**HK255**	**25 Sqn.**

Damaged in combat with Ju88s off Cromer, Norfolk and crashed on landing.
F/Lt J Singleton (P) (Safe), F/O W G Haslam (N) (Safe).

22 March	**Mosquito VI**	**HX812**	**418 Sqn.**

Lost on an intruder sortie to Stuttgart.
F/Lt C A Walker (P) (Evaded capture), F/O T J Roberts (N) (PoW).

23 March **Mosquito VI** **HX823** **605 Sqn.**

Lost on an intruder sortie to Lagen Garde.
F/Lt J R Beckett (P) (Killed), F/O F D Topping (N) (Killed).

24 March **Mosquito NFXVII** **85 Sqn.**

Damaged in combat with a Ju188 near Hastings.
F/O E R Hedgecoe (P) (Safe), F/O N E Bamford (N) (Safe).

24-25 March **Mosquito NFXII** **HK222** **488 Sqn.**

Lost off North Foreland, Kent, during a combat with a German bomber.
F/O C M Wilson (P) (Killed), F/O A W Wilson (N) (Killed).

27-28 March **Mosquito NFXVIII** **HK286** **456 Sqn.**

Damaged in combat with a Ju88 off the Devon coast.
W/Cdr K M Hampshire (P) (Safe), F/O T Condon (N) (Safe).

6-7 April **Mosquito VI** **NS875** **605 Sqn.**

Lost on an intruder sortie to Baltringen.
S/Ldr M Negus (P) (Killed), F/O A J Gapper (N) (Killed).

11-12 April **Mosquito NFXII** **HK132** **307 Sqn.**

Lost 50 miles off Spurn Head, Lincs, during an interception.
W/O J Wisthal (P) (Killed), W/O J Wozny (N) (Killed).

20-21 April **Mosquito VI** **NS928** **605 Sqn.**

Lost on an intruder sortie to Rheine.
F/Lt G A Holland (P) (Killed), F/O W H Wilkinson (N) (Killed).

28-29 April **Mosquito NFXVII** **HK321** **456 Sqn.**

Lost over the Chanel during an interception.
F/O R M J Pahlow (P) (Killed), F/O F M Silva (N) (Killed).

8-9 May **Mosquito VI** **MM421** **418 Sqn.**

Lost on an intruder sortie over Germany.
F/Lt J M Connell F/O (P) (Killed), D W J Carr (N) (Killed).

10-11 May **Mosquito VI** **NT117** **418 Sqn.**

Crashed in the Channel on return from a sortie to France – the crewmen were rescued.
W/Cdr A Barker (P) (Safe), F/Lt R G Frederick (N) (Safe).

10-11 May **Mosquito VI** **NS945** **605 Sqn.**

Crashed near Dover on return from Venlo with damage.
F/Lt T L M Woods (P) (Killed), F/O K H Ray (N) (Killed).

15 May **Mosquito NFXIII** **HK501** **264 Sqn.**

Damaged during combat with a Ju188 and crashed near Alton, Hants.
F/Lt C M Ramsey (P) (Safe), F/O J A Edgar (N) (Killed).

20-21 May **Mosquito NFXIII** **HK414** **96 Sqn.**

Crashed on landing at West Malling.
P/O J C O Allen (P) (Safe), F/Sgt Patterson (N) (Safe).

25-26 May **Mosquito VI** **NS942** **605 Sqn.**

Lost on an intruder sortie to Venlo.
F/Lt J Fotheringham-Parker (P) (Killed), F/Sgt R A Bond (N) (Killed).

29 May **Mosquito NFXIII** **MM503** **604 Sqn.**

Shot down by a Beaufighter over Lyme Bay, Dorset.
F/Lt C L Harris (P) (Rescued), Sgt E B Hopkinson (N) (Drowned).

The last resting place for many of the young men who took part in Operation Steinbock.